POLICY DEVELOPMENT IN SPORT MANAGEMENT

HAROLD J. VANDERZWAAG, Ph.D.
University of Massachusetts
Amherst, MA

Benchmark Press, Inc.
Indianapolis, Indiana

Dedication

This book is dedicated
to
all past and present students
in
the Sport Management Program at the University of Massachusetts/Amherst
for
the most satisfying experience in my professional career

Library of Congress Cataloging in Publication Data:

VANDERZWAAG, HAROLD 1929-
POLICY DEVELOPMENT IN SPORT MANAGEMENT

Cover Design: Gary Schmitt

Library of Congress Catalog Card number: 86-71385

ISBN: 0-936157-09-7

Printed in the United States of America
10 9 8 7 6 5 4 3 2 1

Preface

Academic preparation for work in sport management has now moved beyond the genesis stage. Although a few programs of this type have been in existence for some 20 years, the development has accelerated significantly in recent years. This development is manifested both in the number of such programs and the kind of course work considered most applicable or appropriate for students in this field.

The latter aspect generated the idea for writing this book. Beginning programs tend to be in physical education departments where students take a core of the more traditional physical education courses and then are "farmed out" to schools or departments of business administration for preparation in the business aspects of administering a sport program. There is a general need for a more specific curriculum which is designed for sport management per se.

A policy course is among the possibilities for inclusion in a sport management curriculum. There would appear to be little doubt that the success or effectiveness of a sport organization will be largely determined by the kind of policies which are developed and the degree to which those policies are carried out. Students should have an understanding of the nature of policies generally and the kind of policies needed in the sport enterprise specifically. They should also understand the various issues and problems which confront administrators and coaches when faced with the need to formulate policies for the management of a sport program.

The various policy topics were selected somewhat arbitrarily. They by no means cover all of the potential for policy development in sport management. The one common denominator among these topics is that each represents an area wherein significant issues and/or problems can be identified. That is not to say that each issue or problem is of equal magnitude or that the need for policies is self-evident in all cases. Much of the focus is on personnel policies regarding athletes, particularly at the collegiate level. A quick scan of newspaper and magazine accounts would indicate that there is some justification for establishing that emphasis.

Many of the ideas for this book also come from the experience of working with undergraduate and graduate students in the Sport Management Program at the University of Massachusetts/Amherst. In particular, one class of the latter group did much of the research for various topics. Their specific contributions are acknowledged on a separate page. As a group, they rank among the best of a continuing flow of top quality graduate students I have had the privilege of working with during the past several years.

I also wish to give special thanks to those who provided the secretarial assistance: Donna Carew, for typing a major part of the total manuscript; for the contributions of Kate Cote and Tammy Hodge; and to Susan McBride, for completion of the project. Also, the publisher, I.L. (Butch) Cooper of Benchmark Press, deserves thanks for his faith in the project and encouragement along the way. Finally, I recognize that this as well as other professional work would not be completed if it were not for the encouragement, support, and understanding of my wife, Jane, and the other members of my family.

Harold J. VanderZwaag

Amherst, Massachusetts
November 1, 1987

Acknowledgements

I wish to give special recognition and thanks to a group of former graduate students in the Department of Sport Studies at the University of Massachusetts/Amherst. These students (with one exception) were among those enrolled in a graduate policy class during the spring semester 1985. Their research contributed most significantly to several chapters in this book.

Chapter 1 — Robert Barry (The related literature on the topic and particularly the case study involving the Springfield, Mass. high schools)

Chapter 2 — Michael Ward (The University of Florida case study)

Chapter 3 — Neil Rosa (The case illustrations)

Chapter 4 — Christine Sailer (The bulk of the research for the chapter)

Chapter 5 — Neil Macready (The "Mark Hall" case study)

Chapter 6 — Lauren Plasha (Some of the background information on drug education)

Chapter 7 — Troy Engle (Virtually all of the information contained in the chapter)

Chapter 8 — Glenn McNett (The National Hockey League case study)

Chapter 9 — Gregory Cluff (The Burlington Vermont High School case study)

Chapter 10 — Brian Austin (The case study and other related literature)

Chapter 11 — Lisa Marlow (The case study and other selected ideas)

Chapter 12 — Michael Heslin (The bulk of the research for the chapter)

Chapter 13 — Stephen McKelvey (The bulk of the research for the chapter)

Chapter 14 — Lisa Hackett Morse (The case studies and other selected information)

Chapter 16 — Christopher Baumann (The University of Connecticut case study and other selected information)

Chapter 18 — Jack Grassetti (The Springfield College case study)

Chapter 19 — Barnaby Hinkle (The bulk of the research for this chapter)

I also wish to acknowledge the contributions of three other graduate students who did additional research for this book during the academic year 1986-87: Scott Devine, Timothy Hassett, and Anita Kubicka.

Selected material from the 1987-88 *NCAA Manual* is reprinted by permission of the National Collegiate Athletic Association. This material is subject to annual review and change.

Contents

PART II   PROGRAM

Introduction: The Perspective

What is covered under the title "policy development in sport management"? There is good reason to suspect that the various components of the title may well convey different messages to various people. Consequently, it seems desirable to begin by setting forth a perspective, the frame of reference from which this book was written. Key questions require answers before proceeding. What is sport? What is management? What is policy development? Answers to those questions still yield a fairly broad territory. What areas will we consider in discussing some of the need for policy development in sport management?

SPORT

Most of what we know about sport as a generic activity comes from a recognition of the specific activities that contribute to the whole enterprise. We are able to identify sports — baseball, golf, tennis, football, and bowling — the kinds of activities one reads about in the newspaper or in a weekly periodical such as *Sports Illustrated*. They also are covered by radio and television. Thus, even though we may not have given much thought to the parameters of sport as a collective enterprise, we have little difficulty identifying most of the parts.

When one examines the parts (the sports) more carefully, certain common denominators emerge. First and foremost, every sport is **physical** in nature. That is not to say that it is exclusively physical. One must think to physically act in a controlled context. One of the principal challenges in sport is to effect the necessary union between the mind and the body. Physical demands also vary considerably from sport to sport. Football is not the same as golf or bowling in terms of the physical abilities that are required for the effective performance. If one had to identify a single physical performance attribute pervasive among sports it would probably be coordination. The bottom line is that each sport tests the physical abilities of the participants in one way or another.

1

Another prime characteristic of sport is that it is **competitive**, at least in the more typical or developed form. The reason for the qualification is that there are certain basic sport skills which can also be considered as a part of the total sport domain. Examples would be running, kicking, throwing, hitting, skating, skiing, swimming, and surfing. By and large these activities lead up to full-fledged participation in sport. In the more fully developed form, sport is competitive because it involves a contest. This may be a struggle between two or more individuals or two or more teams for supremacy or victory. Thus we end up with the common notion of winners and losers in sport.

Certain other concepts have also been widely associated with the idea of sport. Perhaps foremost among these are **play**, **games**, and **athletics**. Volumes have been written in an effort to sort out the relationship among these concepts. It hardly seems necessary here to rehash the various analyses. However, a few thoughts may be worthy of attention.

Play is a much broader concept than that of sport. There are many forms of play that are not sport. By the same token, sport may or may not be play for the participant. Games are a form of play, but again play is the broader activity or idea. At the same time, we note physical contests (sports) that are not games (e.g., gymnastics and swimming races). In the United States, the tendency has been to use the term athletics more or less interchangeably with sport. The one distinction may be that inter-scholastic or intercollegiate sport is commonly referred to as athletics.

A couple other characteristics of sport are worthy of attention. One of these is that a sport tends to have unique **dependence on specialized equipment and facilities**. The equipment and facilities for golf are unique to golf. The same can be said about tennis, baseball, football, and most other sports. There is no magic behind the recognition that modern sport has developed through the medium of the sporting goods business. The implications of this for those in sport management positions are extensive. In most cases a sport program is only as good as the quality of the facilities and equipment that can be made available. The relative importance of a high-quality facilities is particularly evident in the realm of highly organized, commercial sport, specifically aimed at attracting spectators.

Each sport also has its particular and unique **dimensions of time and space**. Game time is very different from the local standard time. In some sports the game clock is a most determining factor. There are certain special dimensions of time. This may be the last two minutes in the half of a football game or the last four minutes of a basketball game. The "shot clock" has also emerged as a key element in basketball. On the other hand, sports such as baseball, tennis, and golf are not governed by special time considerations. The unique space characteristics are even more evident in all sports. This ties in with the high importance of facilities in the sport realm. Whether it is a football field, baseball diamond, a golf course, or a swimming pool, there is no exact counterpart outside the environment of the sport. Again, the implications here for policy development in sport management are considerable.

At least one other distinguishing characteristic of sport should be mentioned. This is the relative importance of **records** in sport. The records are essentially of two types: those that indicate current standing in relationship to other teams or participants or those that indicate the highest level of achievement in a given activity. This is the feature of sport which provides much of the content for the news media.

Other characteristics of sport could also be noted. During the past 20 years numerous authors of books or articles on sport theory have advanced theses about the nature of sport. However, with the foregoing characteristics we have some of the key elements to present a definition to use in understanding what is meant by sport in the context of this text.

Sport is a competitive physical activity, utilizing specialized equipment and facilities, with unique dimensions of time and space, in which the quest for records is of high significance. (Note: This definition assumes that there are various lead-up activities to the full-fledged sport participation as outlined in the definition.)

Scope of The Sport Enterprise

Having examined the general nature of sport, we should now be somewhat more specific about identifying the scope of the sport enterprise. This is the realm wherein managers will have to develop policies for the conduct of sport activities. Where do we find programs that sponsor or promote this activity of sport as it has been delineated? At least 16 sources can be identified.

1. *School and College Sport Programs:* This is one of the prime sources for sport sponsorship in the United States. From a quantitative standpoint, high school sport programs are the single most significant dimension in the entire sport enterprise. Generally speaking, there are three components of the total sport program in the schools and colleges: interscholastic or intercollegiate sport, intramural sport, and sport instruction through physical education classes.
2. *Professional Sport:* Here we include the commonly recognized professional teams and individual sports such as golf and tennis in which the promoters and participants are closely involved in a commercial activity aimed at making a profit through a large audience. This is not the place to debate the obvious overlap with a segment of college sport and so-called amateur competition in international sport.

3. *Amateur Sport Organizations:* This category includes sport organizations established to facilitate national and international competition outside the realm of collegiate sport. The various sport federations and Olympic Committees are prime examples. Again, whether or not these are truly amateur organizations can be debated and will be a topic for consideration under the issues and problems discussed in this text. Here it is only necessary to identify these organizations as another component of the sport enterprise.
4. *Private Club Sport:* Prime examples in this category are tennis, golf, swimming, gymnastics, and racquetball clubs found throughout the United States and other parts of the world. The trend toward the multi-use facility, particularly involving various forms of weight equipment, should also be noted. In this component one finds an extension beyond sport per se, but the dimension of sport is still at the forefront.
5. *Other Commercialized Sport Establishments:* In addition to private club sport, there are other forms of commercial sport aimed at mass participation in lieu of spectatorship. Bowling alleys, ski resorts, and public golf courses are some of the prime examples in this segment of the sport enterprise.
6. *Arenas — Coliseums — Civic Centers — Stadia:* In this area of large facility management, the overlap outside the sport enterprise is most evident. Nevertheless, many of these facilities have been built primarily for the purpose of offering one or more sports, and some are used almost exclusively for that purpose. Here we also note some overlap with the professional sport component of the total sport enterprise. In some cases, the facilities are owned by professional sport teams. In others, the facilities are made available to sport teams on a lease basis.
7. *Sport Programs Under Community Recreation:* The very title indicates that sport is only one aspect of this broader category. However, numerous sport programs are most visible in this realm. The array of youth sport programs outside school are prime examples. Beyond that, community recreation programs also sponsor many sport opportunities for adults.
8. *Industrial Sport Programs:* Large industries typically offer various sport programs for employees. In some cases a corporation sponsors a sport team for competition outside the company. However, in general this is another one of the large segments of participant sport. The parallel with community recreation programs is evident in that sport is but a part of the total recreational opportunities for employees.
9. *Sport Programs In Social Agencies:* This category again includes a host of possibilities wherein sports are offered as part of a larger recreational program. Some prime sources are the YMCA, YWCA, Jewish Community Centers, CYO, Boy Scouts, Girl Scouts, and Boys' Clubs.

10. *Military Sport Programs:* Every relatively large military establishment offers a diversified sport program extending from highly organized, competitive teams to participant sport on a recreational basis for military personnel. The existence of specialty military positions in sport testifies to the significance of sport programs in this sector.

11. *Sport Marketing and Consulting Firms:* These companies exist outside sport organizations as such and offer promotional and placement services. Some examples are the International Management Group, Athletic and Sports Consulting Service, Louis Zahn Data, Service Corporation, and Charles J. Brotman and Associates. This aspect of the total sport industry has experienced rapid growth in recent years.

12. *Developmental Programs For Sport:* Here again is another broad and somewhat elusive category. Nevertheless, it has to be taken into account when assessing the scope of the total sport enterprise. These organizations serve to develop existing sport programs in several ways. Many of these programs work from an educational context. Examples are the United States Sport Academy, the Athlete Institute, The Womens' Sports Foundation, the American Sports Education Institute, the President's Council on Physical Fitness and Sport, the National Golf Foundation, and the Tennis Foundation of North America.

13. *Corporate Advertising Through Sport Tournaments:* Some sports, particularly tennis, are promoted by outside corporations through the sponsorship of tournaments. Avon Tennis, Virginia Slims Tennis, and the Volvo International Tennis tournament are principle examples.

14. *The Sporting Goods Industry:* In one sense, this broad area is peripheral to the sport enterprise as such. Yet, in another sense the production and distribution of sporting goods is the key to all sport development. In many cases the relative success and popularity of a sport can be directly traced to the design and production of its equipment. The relationship between the sport of skiing and ski equipment is a clear example.

15. *Sports News Media:* Here we are including newspaper, magazine, radio, and television coverage of sport. The situation is roughly analogous to that noted with regard to the sporting goods industry. The difference is found in the news media's almost exclusive impact on spectator sport. In that regard there is a mutual support relationship between the news media and the heart of the sport enterprise.

16. *Academic Programs In Sport Management:* This is another of the more recent developments. Basically, these are academic programs, at the bachelor's and/or master's degree levels, to prepare students for positions in most of the 15 components of the sport enterprise noted above. The relative success and future for these programs is at least twofold. The extensive scope of the sport enterprise

offers an extensive market for management positions, and the overall popularity of sport stimulates an abundant supply of students.

One can be assured that these 16 sources of sport sponsorship do not cover the entire scope of the sport enterprise. There are so many facets and loose ends in the enterprise that it is almost impossible to account for all of the diverse dimensions. It may also be true that these categories are not the most representative of the total structure. Nevertheless, we trust that they are sufficient to provide the parameters for the territory involved when assessing the potential for sport management.

MANAGEMENT

In many respects the problems with defining management are not unlike those noted in regard to sport. Management is more easily identified as an activity than understood. We hear about, read about, see, and sometimes work for or with people who are considered to be effective managers. Ineffective managers are also readily identified. Often overlooked are those characteristics that determine the quality of management. Before examining some of these characteristics, it might be helpful to distinguish among the terms management, administration, leadership, and supervision.

The distinction between management and administration is quite significant. Management is the much broader of the two concepts. All administrators are managers, but not all managers are administrators. Administration is that part of the management process which is institutionalized. Be they full-time or part-time, administrators are appointed with distinct managerial responsibilities, often involving budgetary control. Personnel with other primary roles report to an administrator. In many cases, these other personnel are also managers, but they are not administrators. For example, teachers and coaches (particularly head coaches) are managers. They are not administrators unless they have been also assigned to that role as one of their major responsibilities. The fact that teachers and coaches are managers will be clearer when we consider the characteristics of management.

The distinction between management and leadership is also significant. Leadership is a component of management. Once again, management is a much more inclusive concept. Leadership is actually an ability which is particularly evident in carrying out the directing function of management. Essentially a leader is one who provides the external motivation for carrying out assigned tasks. The effective manager must provide leadership. However, one can be a fine leader and yet fall short in terms of other managerial responsibilities.

Like leadership, supervision is another aspect of management which is clearly linked to the directing function. Supervisors carry out certain functions under the managerial domain, but they are not involved with all the functions of management. To supervise is to oversee the direction of at least one component of the program.

We have noted that management is related to administration, leadership, and supervision. In one way or another, management is more inclusive than the related concepts. What, then, are the characteristics that enable one to identify the parameters of management? In considering these characteristics, it should be noted that the basic characteristics of effective management are being identified. Needless to say, there are many management situations which somehow fall short in meeting the criteria of being completely effective.

First and foremost, management is goal-oriented. Management works within the context of a purposeful organization. Those who manage within such an organization must agree on clearly defined, realistic goals and direct the activities of the group toward the realization of those goals. Goals, objectives, aims, and similar ideas are all used interchangeably in this context. Everything else in the management process is likely to fall short of expectations if management cannot agree on and successfully communicate the objectives to those who work for the organization. Such objectives or goals are both institutional and individual. Managers are careful to distinguish between the two sets of goals and are interested in maintaining the proper balance between the two.

Management also involves the selection of appropriate strategies to meet objectives. Managers consider alternative strategies and choose those most promising strategies. First of all there must be agreement on priorities. Personnel strategies and physical resource strategies are two general categories from which more specific strategies are developed. The former includes the means for the attainment of staff and the subsequent assignment of staff members. The latter includes the efficient utilization of facilities as well as strategies for all forms of financial procurement, expenditure, and control.

The most direct manifestation of management is found in actions taken to carry out the strategies. This involves the issuance of orders and instructions. It is at this point that we particularly observe the leadership and supervisory components of management.

Finally, management also involves the responsibility for objectively judging the progress and results of the work. At this point the direct consideration of objectives again comes to the forefront. Evaluation should be carried out only in relationship to the objectives established as part of the planning process. A complete evaluation will also make provision for arriving at new goals or adjusting previous ones. Management is a continuous process; it does not cease when one concludes the assessment phase.

After considering these characteristics of management, five distinct managerial functions can be identified, although there is obviously overlap among all these functions:

Planning — determining a course of action
Organizing — providing a structure for the work of the organization
Staffing — selecting and assigning personnel to carry out the work
Directing — making provision for the actual conduct of the work
Controlling — evaluating the progress of the work and taking steps to change or modify the future plans and actions.

Management is a goal-oriented social process involving selection of appropriate strategies, provisions for directing the work of the enterprise, and the control of performance in an effort to meet the objectives of the organization.

POLICY DEVELOPMENT

If sport and management are both somewhat elusive in their meaning, this is even more true of policy. There is a tendency to use the term "policy" in a variety of senses, some of which do little to explain how policy fits into the total managerial spectrum. Policy is often confused with philosophy, objectives, strategy, and procedures.

Various characteristics of policies can be noted. To begin with, policies have wide ramifications. They are related to the total system or organization. A policy is not established to guide the work of only an individual or part of a group. This feature distinguishes a policy from a procedure. Policies also tend to have external as well as internal implications. Even though they are developed to guide activities within the organization, they are often directed at affairs with external import.

Policies are also extended from a time perspective. Essentially they involve standing decisions on important, recurring matters. They are designed to have an effect over an extended period of time. This is why it is appropriate to think in terms of policy development. The idea of development also has an extended time connotation. Basically, development represents change in a continuous direction. Such is the basic design of policy formation. The import of policies indicates that they should evolve. Although we may begin with certain initial policy decisions, it is safe to say that sound policy has to stand the test of time.

Policies are also aimed at those activities in the organization which involve the critial resources, classified as either human or financial. Thus we typically find a whole array of personnel policies involving matters such as recruitment, selection, retention, advancement, discipline, and various forms of reward. Public relation policies also reflect the crucial human resource. The critical nature of the financial resource is reflected in policies guiding financial acquisition and financial control, as well as the entire domain of facilities and equipment.

Significant decision making is at the heart of the policy development process. The real basis for decision making is to be found in the existence of numerous alternatives and the selection from among those alternatives. If an alternative does not exist, there really is no need to have a policy as such. This is where issues and problems come into the picture. It is also why issues and problems have been selected as the pillars for policy development in sport management. Suffice to say that the decision-making aspect of policy development is either directed to taking a stand on an issue or solving a problem. The footnote would be that this might also be an anticipated issue or problem.

A final characteristic of policy development is that it is directed toward a dynamic social process in a changing environment. In some respects this characteristic is closely related to the extended time perspective and the fact that policies evolve. Even though policies involve standing decisions, this does not mean that they lack the flexibility to meet changes involving the critical human and material resources.

Policy development is the continuous process of making significant decisions on recurring matters resulting from issues or problems involving the use of critical resources from the standpoint of a long-term perspective.

Sequential Program Development

Thus far we have noted at least five principal characteristics of policy development. Further insight regarding the nature of policies may be gained by considering how they fit into total, sequential program development and the total managerial picture.

1. *Basic mission:* This is the raison d'etre of the program. For what basic purpose does the program exist? In the broadest sense, a statement of mission specifies the scope of operations. Usually, this is expressed either in terms of product and market or service and client.
2. *Objectives:* As noted earlier, other terms could be used in place of objectives. These might be goals, aims, targets, or desired results. Whatever the particular label, the intent of this step in program development is the same: what does the organization hope to accomplish toward meeting the mission? These objectives or goals may be fairly general or relatively specific. In either case they are a refinement or breakdown of the mission.

3. *Policies:* Here is the precise place when policies fit into the total scheme of things. Summarizing what was said earlier, policies are broad guidelines for the achievement of objectives. They naturally have to be developed after the objectives are established, and they provide the parameters for the specifics which are to follow.

4. *Strategies:* These are the specific major actions or patterns of action for reaching objectives and carrying out policies. One of the real tests for coherence in a program is whether the strategies are consistent with the objectives and policies.

5. *Program or Structure:* This is the composite of generalized procedures for the actual conduct of affairs. The program or structure is the direct answer to the question: What is offered? If it is not consistent with the mission, a disparity is most evident. This is the point at which policies may be revealed as the key link. If the organization lacks sound policies, difficulty may be encountered in offering a program that is consistent with the mission.

6. *Roles:* These are the particular behavior patterns of the individuals that are necessary to carry out the program. Each role must be clarified in relationship to the objectives, policies, and strategies that have been developed for the organization. The role of an individual player on a sport team is a vivid example of how role definition is the culminating component in sequential program development.

The following examples (Exhibits I-A and I-B) from the field of sport management illustrate the nature of sequential program development and how policy fits into the total structures. High school sports programs and professional sport programs offer interesting comparisons.

The Policy Domain

Thus far we have briefly considered the nature of policy development, including how policy fits into the total picture of sequential program development. Before making further application to the sport enterprise, it might be advantageous to further specify the territory of policy. What is the basis for the development of policies? Or, why are policies really needed? Could we not move directly from objectives to strategies for carrying out those objectives? The answer to any one of these questions is found in two related and yet quite different concepts: issues and problems. Essentially a policy is required either to take a stand on an issue or to provide direction toward the solution of a problem. Consequently, the policy domain largely revolves around issues and problems. These will be used as the guidelines for the policy development in sport management as set forth in this text.

EXHIBIT I-A. Professional Football Team

1. Basic mission: To make a profit through the entertainment business for football spectators.
2. Objectives:
    a. To win the NFL championship.
    b. To develop individual player excellence.
3. Policies:
    a. A sound public relation program will be established.
    b. Efforts will be directed toward gradually building the program through player development.
    c. An attractive, comfortable, and safe facility will be maintained.
    d. The front office and field operations will be closely coordinated.
    e. The club will work closely with the NFL office to maintain the integrity of the game.
4. Strategies:
    a. The club will work to strengthen the various relations with the news media.
    b. The draft will be used to develop younger players in lieu of obtaining veterans through trades.
    c. The stadium will be well maintained and clean at all times.
    d. Facility staff members will be well trained in effective crowd management procedures.
    e. Crowd management techniques will be periodically reviewed for effectiveness.
    f. Organizational relationships will be carefully delineated.
    g. Considerable attention will be given to the legal orientation for all employees.
    h. There will be a set procedure for determination of salaries and the renegotiation of existing contracts.
5. Program: A competitive but developing team.
6. Roles:
    a. General Manager — success in signing young players.
    b. Head Coach — leadership ability in developing young players.
    c. Public Relations Director — success in carrying out marketing techniques.
    d. Players — willingness to work on development.

EXHIBIT I-B. High School Sports Program
1. Basic Mission: To provide a sport program which will contribute to the education of the student body and serve as a means of developing interest in and support for the school.
2. Objectives:
    a. To be competitive in all sports in the interscholastic league competition
    b. To provide a means of recreation for the student body
    c. To contribute to the social development of students
    d. To develop skills in various forms of sports participation
    e. To enhance the image of the school through the sport program
3. Policies:
    a. An integrated sport program will be offered involving interscholastic competition, intramural sport, and instruction.
    b. A diversified program will be offered for both boys and girls.
    c. Academic standards for interscholastic participants will receive high priority.
    d. Continued effort will be made to affiliate with a conference that offers balanced competition.
    e. The physical conditioning of participants will receive high priority.
4. Strategies:
    a. The focus will be on interscholastic sport and intramural sport for those students who do not qualify for the former.
    b. Sport instruction will be offered only in sports that are new to the students involved.
    c. Approximately the same number of sports for girls as for boys will be offered.
    d. Booster club support will contribute to the total budget for the sport program.
    e. A nucleus of a full-time sport staff will be maintained.
    f. Additional coaches will be employed as part-time coaches with major responsibility as classroom teachers.
    g. Two full-time trainers will be employed.
    h. There will be a director for the intramural sport program.
5. Program: Diversified sport offerings with balanced competition in all sports.
6. Roles:
    a. Athletic Director — success in developing and maintaining an integrated and well-balanced sport program that is consistent with the educational objectives of the school.
    b. Coaches — success in developing the participants as students and athletes.
    c. Trainers — success in contributing to the total physical conditioning of all participants.
    d. Intramural Sport Director — success in developing a viable attractive program which meets the needs and interests of all students.

An issue is an idea or activity about which there is debate. The parties involved tend to hold contrasting positions either in their understanding of the idea or with regard to the conduct of the activity. Furthermore, there are legitimate grounds for each position. A policy is needed to decide the approach that will be taken by the group. This may result from either mutual consensus or compromise. Regardless of the means taken to arrive at the policy, the need was dictated by the contrast in positions. The issues leading to policies are major. It was noted earlier that policy development is the process of making significant decisions on recurring matters. There will always be varying opinions on a host of minor issues. Such is not the basis for policy development.

Issues frequently lead to problems but the differentiation between the two is significant. Essentially a problem is an obstacle to be overcome. When an organization has a problem, something stands in the way of the ability to achieve an objective or at least some aspect of that objective. Thus problem solving is aimed at eliminating the obstacle. A problem may also be expressed in terms of deep-seated dissatisfaction with one or more particulars of the current situation. As noted below, the difference between the current situation and the desired situation is the extent or size of the problem.

Facts = Current Situation
Goal = Desired Situation
Problem = Difference between The Two

The primary difference between a problem and an issue is that a problem does not necessarily reflect a difference of opinion about the way things should be or the goal which is sought. There may be considerable differences of opinion about how the problem can be solved. However, such differences involve the means and not the desired results.

Whether it be to resolve an issue or solve a problem, policy development is the key stage in the attempt to reach the objectives of the program. Policy regarding either an issue or a problem can be developed by using the basic techniques of case method analysis.

Case Method Analysis

1. *Situational Analysis:* This begins by recognizing the existence of either an issue or a problem. Are there legitimate grounds for debate, or does something stand in the way of mutual interests in reaching a goal? Why did the issue or problem arise? Who is concerned? How critical is the situation?
2. *Analysis and Use of Evidence:*
   a. Quantitative Data — What kind and amount of data are available? What is the applicability of the data to the problem or issue at hand? How appropriate is the data in terms of precision or estimation?

b. Other Evidence —
      1. Is there an adequate accumulation of other evidence to support the idea that there is a legitimate issue or that a real problem exists? These must be definite instances, not just generalizations.
      2. What is the balance in terms of the evidence? Considerable support from both sides indicates that there is a real issue.
      3. How valid is the evidence? This is determined by weighing facts against opinions.
      4. What is the effect of such evidence on the problem or issue which is at hand?
      5. How objective is the evidence? This is aimed at the attempt to avoid bias or prejudice.
      6. What is the thoroughness of reasoning? How important or controversial is a particular point?
3. *Identification and Evaluation of Action Alternatives:*
   Basically the identification step consists of providing an answer to either one of these questions.
   a. What are the possible solutions to the problem?
   b. What are the alternatives of action for resolving an issue? Evaluation of action alternatives is accomplished by considering such factors as feasibility, time involved, and the possible contribution in either solving the problem or resolving the issue.
4. *Conclusions and/or Recommendations:*
   a. Must show a relationship to the analysis.
   b. Detail of development should be set forth.
   c. What is the action decision? (Note: This is essentially the policy.)

SELECTED TOPICS

Thus far we have considered the scope of the potential territory for policy development in sport management. The question now is where does one begin? What kind of policies are needed within the framework? Since issues and problems more or less point to the policy domain, one could begin by selecting issues and problems that are relatively pervasive or critical in the sport enterprise. Here the news media can be of some assistance. Many of the larger issues and problems are regularly presented by the news media.

Further direction is provided by considering the unique quadrangular dimension of sport, that involving the roles of the athlete, coach, official, and spectator. This points to the need for certain kinds of personnel policies. Furthermore, among the major personnel components, the athlete is the bottom line. When searching for an initial basis for policy development in sport management, the athlete is a logical place to begin. It is not too much of an exaggeration to suggest that when things are right with the athlete, the program is all right. The reverse is also true. Consequently, the selected areas are heavily aimed at policies regarding athletes.

Next to the athletes, the coaches represent a primary consideration. Of course, policy regarding athletes and coaches represents a mutually dependent relationship. Quality athletes are the key factor in the success of a coach. On the other hand, a good coach is just as key in obtaining and developing the right kind of athlete.

Actually, the entire quadrangular dimension of sport is a good example of a mutually dependent relationship. Therefore, Part I, covering selected personnel policies, will conclude with some attention to policies regarding officials and spectators.

The selected areas included in Part II have been designated as program policies. Essentially they represent policy considerations which more or less affect the entire program and yet fall outside the realm of personnel policies as such. In addition to the heavy emphasis on personnel policies, a few other factors are instrumental in the selection of certain issues and problems as a preliminary basis for policy development in sport management. One of these is that college sport seems to have more than its share of issues and problems. Consequently, the bulk of the policy area is in collegiate sport. Beyond that, it is easy to recognize that finances, facilities, public relations, and promotion are principal concerns in the sport enterprise generally. Some of these concerns are addressed under the program policies in Part II.

1

Athletes: High School Eligibility

In April of 1983 the National Commission on Excellence in Education submitted a report to the Secretary of Education titled "A Nation at Risk." It spoke of the low level of achievement in our secondary schools, noting that SAT (Scholastic Aptitude Test) scores were at an all-time low, having dropped significantly during the past 20 years. Average verbal scores fell more than 50 points, and average mathematics scores were nearly 40 points lower. Among the additional findings of the Commission were the following:

1. 23 million American adults are functionally illiterate by the simplest tests of everyday reading, writing, and composition.
2. About 13 percent of all 17-year-olds in the U.S. can be considered functionally illiterate.
3. Nearly 40 percent of 17-year-olds cannot draw inferences from written material; only one-fifth can write a persuasive essay; and only one-third can solve a mathematics problem requiring several steps ("A Nation at Risk," *American Education*, April 1983, p. 6).

The conclusion was that an increasing number of young people come out of high school ready for neither college nor work, at a time when there is a rapidly accelerating demand for highly skilled workers.

Further evidence of the academic problem in the schools is found in the fact that 300 of the nation's largest companies now offer remedial courses in basic mathematics and English for entry line workers. John Naisbitt (1984) provides a succinct description of the current situation with regard to high school education: "The generation graduating from

17

high school today is the first generation in American history to graduate less skilled than its parents." (p. 25)

The report of the Commission also included several recommendations for improving the quality of education in our high schools. One of the more significant recommendations was to increase the requirements for graduation. By 1985, 43 states had increased their requirements, while five others were considering changes. Some improvement in scores was noted. The average composite SAT score in 1984 was 10 points higher than the 1981 average. However, in reference to the Commission's report, President Reagan still concluded in an address to the National Association of Independent Schools: "If an unfriendly foreign power had attempted to impose on America the mediocre educational performance that exists today, we might well have viewed it as an act of war." (*The Boston Globe*, March 10, 1985, p. B30).

THE ISSUE

The problem is clear: the United States is faced with the challenge of improving the quality of education in the schools. This problem transcends any considerations involving academic standards for athletes. However, we get to the particulars of the athletic situation through another recommendation of the Commission — to reduce time lost in the classroom by controlling extracurricular activities. This points to the issue and why there is need for policy regarding the eligibility of high school athletes.

The issue involves a twofold consideration. Should there be an eligibility requirement for participation in interscholastic athletics? If so, what should be the nature of the requirement? The first question ultimately results in a second consideration as to whether participation in interscholastic athletics is a right or a privilege for any student attending high school. If it is a right, there seems to be no basis for any requirement. On the other hand, if such participation is a privilege, the establishment of an academic requirement seems like a reasonable approach in terms of policy.

As with many issues today, the legal factor also has to be taken into account. Does a school district actually have a right to set a scholastic standard for participation in sports? Weistart (1979) answered in the affirmative. "It (grade requirement) will be authorized because the fostering of scholastic, not athletic, achievement is the primary objective of the academic institution." (p. 68) However, the relationship that does or should exist between athletics and education is not clearly resolved. Some recent court decisions present the conclusion that athletic participation is an integral part of the student's education. Thus, the right to participate in extracurricular activites goes along with the right to attend school. On the other hand, most court cases have assessed athletics as "simply physical diversion." (Weistart, p. 22) Their conclusion is that participation in interscholastic athletics is not a right guaranteed by the Constitution of the United States. At any rate, there is a lack of legal consensus at this time, and the issue remains unresolved.

Lurking beneath the surface is the controversy about what an athlete may gain through participation in an interscholastic program. Is participation in athletics basically a means for enjoyment or recreation, an opportunity to have fun within the school environment? Some would argue that athletic participation is educational in itself. If so, is it education in the same way as other components of the total educational program? Definitive answers to these questions are missing; speculation abounds. Nevertheless, the responses will largely determine the stance that is taken with regard to athletic eligibility.

The motivational potential of athletic involvement is another factor which might influence the policy decision. For certain students, athletics could be the single source of positive association with the school. Even though the athlete may not be up-to-standard academically, what will happen without athletic involvement? This argument is advanced by some coaches, parents, and administrators who oppose a more rigid eligibility policy. It can also be argued that there would be no motivation for any scholastic achievement in some cases if the eligibility requirement did not exist.

In spite of this basic debate, the idea that there should be some kind of scholastic eligibility requirement for high school athletes has been more or less established. The other part of the issue, which centers on the specific nature of the requirement, causes the most controversy and difficulty for school administrators in arriving at appropriate policy decisions. One of the considerations here is whether a high school eligibility requirement should be aimed at college admission and/or college athletic participation. Not all high school athletes plan to enter college. Fewer still will qualify for a college athletic team. The specific debate centers largely on the kind of courses to be required and the specific grade point average to be maintained.

A related aspect of the larger issue should also be noted. This involves the comparison or association of athletics with other extracurricular activities. By and large, existing policies are designed to cover all extracurricular activities, not just athletics. Yet, most of the publicity and controversy center on athletics — for the same reason that citizens of the community get upset when the school board threatens to drop sports from the school program. The news media focuses much more attention on athletics than on any other extracurricular or curricular activity. That recognition only raises other questions which have to be considered in policy development. Is there something about athletics which sets it aside as a special kind of extracurricular activity? If so, should there be a separate policy to govern athletic eligibility? Those who respond in the affirmative would likely support a statement made by Mickey Michaux, state representative in North Carolina. While voting in 1975 against an

EXHIBIT 1-1. Study of Grade Point Averages, Absenteeism, and Excused
Absences of Students Who Participate in
MSHSL Sponsored Activities

Participants in the extracurricular activity programs sponsored by the Minnesota State High School League (MSHSL) earn better grades and are absent from school less days than those who do not participate in extracurricular activities. This information is based on a 1983 survey completed by the MSHSL among its 500 member schools.

The survey was conducted by the MSHSL with the support of the Minnesota Secondary School Principals Association. It was the first study by any statewide organization to consider such a broad base of data.

Sixty-one percent or 305 of the 500 member schools responded to the survey. All data was based on information for the 1982-83 school year.

The member schools of the MSHSL sponsor a total number of activities in excess of 7,100 or an average 14.3 activities per school. This number includes 26 athletic activities, plus speech, one-act plays, debate, band, orchestra, and choir. The activities include 146,672 participants in boys' and girls' athletics and 62,599 in the fine arts programs.

GRADE POINT AVERAGES AND ATTENDANCE

The grade point average of the composite student body averages of the 305 reporting schools was 2.68. The average days absent for this group was 8.76 days per year.

STUDENT ATHLETES GPA ABOVE THE AVERAGE

Student athletes for whom GPAs were compiled had a 2.84 or about a "B–" average. The survey proved the attendance patterns also were better than the student body average, with the boy and girl student athletes only being absent 7.44 days for the school year.

In 73 percent of the schools who returned surveys, the GPAs of students involved in athletics and fine arts activities were higher than those of the general student population. In 18 percent of the schools, the GPAs of participating students was within .1 of the general student population.

In the majority of schools, 10th grade students received the lowest GPAs and 12th graders received the highest.

FINE ARTS STUDENTS AVERAGES HIGHEST

The grade point average of the students who participate in speech, drama, debate, and music was 2.98 or "B." Their absences averaged only 6.94 days per year.

The GPAs and days absent data as established in the tables below are based on information reported by each of the 305 individual high schools that participated in the survey. There is no standardization for grade point averages from high school to high school, so care must be taken to understand that this data is merely the compilation of data from each member school. The GPAs are based on a scale of 4=A, 3=B, 2=C, 1=D, and 0=fail.

EXHIBIT 1-1. *(con't.)*

GPAs and days absent.

Average GPA	All Students	Athletic Participants	Fine Arts Participants
Grade 10	2.55	2.77	2.91
Grade 11	2.71	2.81	2.98
Grade 12	2.79	2.97	3.05
All Grades	2.68	2.84	2.98

Average Days Absent.

	All Students	Student-Athletes	Fine Arts Participants
Grade 10	8.09	6.78	6.02
Grade 11	8.74	7.14	6.77
Grade 12	9.46	8.40	8.03
Total	8.76	7.44	6.94

imposed 700 SAT minimum for entrance into North Carolina state colleges and and universities, she said: "God made some folks smart and God made some folks athletes and I think both ought to be given a chance." (*Chronicle of Higher Education,* April 3, 1985, p. 29)

Opponents of a stiffer eligibility requirement for high school athletes are quick to refer to data pointing in the opposite direction. A study in the state of Washington revealed that less than 2 percent of the athletes drop out of high school. The athletic department of the Seattle Public Schools reported that the average of grade point averages (GPAs) of athletes was above the average for the total student population (2.74 vs. 2.57). Only 15.6 percent of all the athletes had GPAs below 2.0. Further support is found in a 1983 study by the Minnesota State High School league (Exhibit 1-1). The 500 member schools were surveyed to determine attendance patterns and grade point averages. The conclusion was that the student-athlete is not only absent less than the non-athlete, but the athlete's GPA is higher than that of the general student.

Nevertheless, the controversy continues over the larger issue involving the relationship between athletics and education as well as the various sub-issues related to academic standards for athletes. The controversy is not likely to abate. Policy decisions have to be made. What efforts can be found to date?

VARIOUS POLICIES

Most states have a minimum standard, which is recommended by The National Federation of State High School Associations. That requires passing work in three subjects, with full credit toward graduation, in 15 periods per week. This minimum standard is obviously aimed at maximizing the number of participants. It is based on the assumption that a general standard should not deprive a large number of students from participating in athletics or any other extracurricular activity.

Beyond the minimum standard, one finds considerable variance in policies that are ultimately set at the local level. Some states set higher standards, which must be met by the local school districts. As of 1985, 25 states were following the minimum recommendation of the National Federation, while the other 25 states had either established tougher requirements or had no state standards. Within the five states in the latter category, the policy decision is made completely at the local or league level. The higher state requirement typically increases the number of passing grades to four subjects.

In terms of local policy, the Los Angeles, California, Unified School District was one of the first to set a more rigid policy in response to the 1983 report of the National Commission. The eligibility policy established in 1984 required a "C" average overall and no failure in any course. The immediate effect was felt throughout the district. Hollywood High School lost 20 percent of its athletes through scholastic ineligibility. Nine percent did not maintain a "C" average, 9 percent failed one course, and 2 percent failed 2 courses. There were not enough eligible athletes to field a junior varsity baseball team, and the school lost 10 musicians and three of its 10 cheerleaders. A year later, the number of ineligible athletes had dropped to 16 percent, but the school was still without a junior varsity baseball team.

The Los Angeles example was followed by a similar policy in the state of Texas. House Bill 72, passed in 1984, required all students to maintain a passing grade (70) in every subject to be eligible to participate in extracurricular activities. It was adopted for all public schools in Texas. The results were much like those in Los Angeles. For example, more than 39 percent of the students in Northside School District, San Antonio, lost eligibility by failing at least one class. Other schools and districts experienced similar problems. However, in February 1985, Nicholas Deluca of the University of Texas at San Antonio reported that, on the whole, the 12 school districts of Bexar County (San Antonio) were making substantial progress with implementation of the policy. He said it was too early to effectively evaluate the results but that for the most part House Bill 72 was having the desired effect of raising the academic performance level. Nevertheless, the opposition to the bill was extensive. Six lawsuits were filed in Houston.

Washington is an example of a state which has varying policies among school districts. Exhibit 1-2 shows the 1984 policies for Seattle, Tacoma, and Yakima. One notes contrasts in the scope of the policies, GPA requirement, courses required, and other procedures governing eligibility.

EXHIBIT 1-2. Examples of Academic Eligibility Requirements
Adopted by Local School Boards

SEATTLE
Policy summary:
* 2.0 GPA in all subjects the previous quarter
* Enrolled in courses to insure normal progress toward graduation
* Earn the number of credits for advancement toward a diploma (7.5 credits per semester; five classes)
* Applied to all extracurricular activities and is defined as any activity that has a fixed roster of participants.
* Policy becomes effective the fall of 1984: Must earn 2.0 GPA the second semester of 1983-84

Appeal procedure is provided.

Support system recommended.

Simulated 15.6 percent would be ineligible if policy were in effect now.

TACOMA
Policy summary:
* 2.0 GPA previous semester or quarter (for JH's)
* May not fail more than one subject
* Must earn minimum of four full-time credits

Remediation:
If ineligible, may regain eligibility after five weeks probationary period.

No second "probation period" allowed until end of semester.

If eligible at beginning of semester, OK for full semester. "Warning" is issued at mid-term.

Applies to all activities, including music. However, if participation in an activity performance has a bearing on a grade, student is allowed to participate.

Tacoma uses + and − in calculating GPA; thus a student with all C's and one C– would be ruled ineligible.

Policy in effect second semester 1983-84; adopted spring 1983.

YAKIMA
Policy summary:
* Passing in five subjects
* If passing only four; two-week make-up is allowed to be passing in five, while still eligible. Otherwise, ineligible until passing in five.
* Eligibility check six (6) times a school year (each mid-trimester and end of each trimester).
* Allowed is one "F" if student has an accumulative 2.0 GPA.

Applies to athletic eligibility.

In general, the various policies reflect the issues involved whenever a school district attempts to set a standard for athletic eligibility. Subsequent problems are reflected in the results and reactions whenever a school district raises the requirement. What happened in the Springfield, Massachusetts Public Schools in 1985 is a classic case in point.

Case Study

Ida Flynn, president of the Springfield chapter of the National Association for the Advancement of Colored People (NAACP) became very concerned when she received reports from employees that some city public high school graduates were applying for jobs and could not even spell the names of the streets on which they lived. She also noted the increased number of high school dropouts and extensive unemployment among the youth in her area.

In the fall of 1983 Mrs. Flynn went to the Springfield School Committee with a proposal to raise the academic requirement for participation in interscholastic athletics or any other extracurricular activity. At the time, the four public high schools (Classical, Technical, High School of Commerce, and Putnam Vocational Technical) followed the policy set by the Massachusetts Interscholastic Athletic Association (MIAA) for athletic participation, which required a *minimum* 15 credits of passing grades to maintain eligibility. The minimum passing grade was a "D," and 332 seniors in the four public high schools of Springfield graduated with "D" averages in June 1984.

Mrs. Flynn proposed that a student must receive a "C" or higher in each "major" subject, with no failures in any subject, to be eligible to participate in any extracurricular activity. Eligibility for participation would be determined at the end of each marking period. The Springfield School Committee agreed with Mrs. Flynn that an increased requirement was necessary and approved her policy recommendation in April 1984, to be effective in January 1985.

After the decision was announced, Mrs. Flynn and members of the school committee were flooded with letters protesting the change in policy. Coaches and parents believed that the new policy would severely harm the athletic programs and possibly eliminate some sports. This is in fact, exactly what happened when grades came out in January 1985. A decrease in the number of eligible participants left some sports without sufficient players to field a team. Technical High School and the High School of Commerce were forced to cancel girls' basketball games, and serious problems were created for wrestling, swimming, and hockey programs.

The attempt to define a "major" subject also posed a problem. The decision of the school committee was that each high school could determine the major subjects for that school. The reasoning was that a technical, commercial, and college prep high school would each emphasize different areas of study and would thus have different major subjects. However, this only added to the controversy surrounding the decision.

Based on the complaints and number of ineligible students, the school committee decided to collect data and review the new policy. The data revealed that the policy had created a real problem for the athletic programs at all the high schools. Classical High School reported that 40 percent of its athletes were declared ineligible, while Technical High School had 33 percent ineligible. The High School of Commerce was hit hardest with 45 percent of its athletes losing their eligibility. Putnam was the least hurt by the revised policy with only 14 percent ineligible.

The data also showed that almost every other extracurricular activity was adversely affected by the policy. There were significant cutbacks in participation across the board. However, the publicity and concern were mainly about athletics. The newspapers reported each event that was affected by the reduction in participants, and sports writers generally criticized the policy. (It is interesting to note that none of the newspaper articles questioned the reasons for the low levels of academic achievement. The concern was almost exclusively on the fact that the schools were now having difficulty fielding representative teams in certain sports.)

The results clearly demonstrated that the policy had created certain problems. However, prior to considering any modification, the school committee needed additional information on alternatives and projected results. To that end, the director of physical education of the Springfield schools requested policies concerning participation from various school districts throughout the United States. These were evaluated as possible alternatives to the existing policy in Springfield. Some of the possibilities were:

1. Raising the number of credits required to be eligible to participate in extracurricular activities. (It was also noted that MIAA had indicated that it would increase the required number of passing credits from 15 to 20 in 1986.)
2. Setting a score of 70 for a passing grade. (This is precisely the step taken in Texas.) The reasoning is that 70 is generally considered to be "C−" average, and a "D" average is not a satisfactory grade even if it is generally considered to be passing.
3. Allow no more than one failure to maintain eligibility. (The student would be required to maintain a satisfactory overall average, but the exception would be permitted in one major course.)
4. Create a probationary period that would allow the students a certain amount of time to bring up their grades.
5. Lower the minimum grade requirement for each of the major subjects from the present "C" to a "C−".
6. Requiring a "C" *average* in all major subjects in lieu of the present "C" in each major subject.

After tentatively deciding on alternative 6, the school committee collected further data to project the effects of the proposed change. Tables 1-1 to 1-4 provide the following categories of information for the four Springfield high schools as of February 1985.

1. The number of participants in each extracurricular activity in each of the high schools.
2. The number and percentage of students who would be ineligible under the minimum requirement of the MIAA (passing three major subjects).
3. The number and percentage of ineligible students under the existing policy (a "C" average *in all* major subjects).
4. The number and percentage of students who would be ineligible under the proposed policy (a "C" average *of all* major subjects).

The data clearly shows that a change to the proposed policy would result in a significant increase in the number of eligible students. Under the policy put into effect in January 1985 there were 285 ineligible students; under the proposed modification there would be "only" 104. Among the athletes, the number ineligible would drop from 104 to 37. Consequently, on February 7, 1985 the school committee revised the policy for athletic eligibility to read as follows:

> Eligibility for participation in extracurricular activities will be determined at the end of each marking period. In order to be eligible to participate in extracurricular activities, a student must receive marks in all major subjects, which together, average a "C" or higher, with no failures in any subject. (Courtesy of the Director of Physical Education, Springfield, Massachusetts Public Schools)

POLICY GUIDELINES

The experience in Springfield, as well as in other cities and states, indicates that a number of factors should be taken into consideration in developing a policy for athletic eligibility in the high school. The following are offered as guidelines. As with many policies, specifics can only be determined by situation or locale due to the diverse nature of public education in the United States.

1. Participation in interscholastic athletics may well be a privilege, but it is a privilege that should be reasonably accessible to the majority of the student body. In that regard, it is no different than any other extracurricular activity. On the other hand, any policy should reflect the fact that all extracurricular activities,

TABLE 1-1. Requirements for Eligibility for Extracurricular Activities

ROGER L. PUTNAM VOCATIONAL TECHNICAL HIGH SCHOOL

Activity	Participants	(Past) MIAA (Pass 3 Majors)	Ineligible (Current) C/Ave. In All Majors	(Proposed) C/Ave. Of All Majors
JV Boys' Basketball	15	0	0	0
JV Boys' Basketball	12	0	3	0
Girls' Basketball	16	0	2	0
Wrestling	40	3	6	3
Hockey	13	1	2	1
Student Council	23	4	7	4
Senior Class Officers	6	0	0	0
Newspaper	4	0	1	0
Cheerleaders	11	0	1	0
Total	140	8	22	8
Putnam Athletics	96	4 (4%)	13 (14%)	4 (4%)
Putnam Non-Athletics	44	4 (9%)	9 (20%)	4 (9%)
Putnam Overall	140	8 (6%)	22 (16%)	8 (6%)

TABLE 1-2. Requirements for Eligibility for Extracurricular Activities

TECHNICAL HIGH SCHOOL

Activity	Participants	(Past) MIAA (Pass 3 Majors)	Ineligible (Current) C/Ave. In All Majors	(Proposed) C/Ave. Of All Majors
Basketball Boys'	20	0	3	2
Basketball Girls'	8	0	8	3
Wrestling	21	0	5	2
Cheerleaders	8	0	5	1
Male Drill ROTC	11	0	6	1
Female Drill ROTC	10	0	5	0
National Honor Society	8	0	0	0
Drama Club	10	4	8	6
Drum Corps	13	0	2	3
Student Council	23	0	4	3
Mathletes	3	0	1	0
Total	135	4	47	21
Technical Athletics	49	0 (0%)	16 (33%)	7 (14%)
Technical Non-Athletics	86	4 (5%)	31 (36%)	14 (16%)
Technical Overall	135	4 (3%)	47 (35%)	21 (16%)

TABLE 1-3. Requirements for Eligibility for Extracurricular Activities

HIGH SCHOOL OF COMMERCE

Activity	Participants	(Past) MIAA (Pass 3 Majors)	Ineligible (Current) C/Ave. In All Majors	(Proposed) C/Ave. Of All Majors
JV Girls' Basketball	6	0	4	0
V Girls' Basketball	5	0	3	0
JV Boys' Basketball	10	1	5	1
V Boys' Basketball	12	0	3	0
Cheerleaders	9	0	3	0
Drama Club	16	0	8	0
Total	58	1	26	1
Commerce Athletics	33	1 (3%)	15 (45%)	1 (3%)
Commerce Non-Athletics	25	0 (0%)	11 (44%)	0 (0%)
Commerce Overall	58	1 (2%)	26 (45%)	1 (2%)

TABLE 1.4. Requirements for Eligibility for Extracurricular Activities

CLASSICAL HIGH SCHOOL

Activity	Participants	MIAA (Past) (Pass 3 Majors)	Ineligible (Current) C/Ave. In All Majors	(Proposed) C/Ave. Of All Majors
JV Basketball	11	1	3	1
V Basketball	11	0	2	0
JV & V Girls' Basketball	22	0	7	4
Cheerleaders	7	0	5	4
Hockey	19	1	6	5
Swimming Boys	23	0	5	1
Swimming Girls	20	0	10	0
Wrestling	31	3	20	10
Afro-American Club	9	2	6	4
AVA	13	6	9	2
Blue & White Business	23	2	7	4
Chess Club	5	0	2	1
Debate	9	0	4	2
Library Aides	18	3	14	7
Mathletes	14	2	3	2
National Honor Society	15	0	1	0
School Store	4	0	4	0
Student Government	26	1	7	4
Student Patrol Boys	29	2	17	10
Student Patrol Girls	25	3	10	5
Ski Club	23	5	21	8
Total	357	32	163	74
Classical Athletics	144	5 (3%)	58 (40%)	25 (17%)
Classical Non-Athletics	213	27 (13%)	105 (49%)	49 (23%)
Classical Overall	357	32 (9%)	163 (46%)	74 (21%)

including athletics, are secondary to the principal academic function of the schools.

2. To be eligible, the student should be required to take a sufficient number of courses to reflect the emphasis on scholastic endeavor. This can be manifested by requiring the student to be in class for more than 50 percent of the school day. For instance, if a school has an eight-period day and classes meet each day in a course, the student would be required to take a minimum of five courses. Various scheduling arrangements among school districts would require different specific policies to meet the overall requirements.

3. In addition to requiring a minimum number of courses, there should be some form of minimum grade point average requirement which is higher than a passing grade. Depending on the specific grading system, that might be a "C-," "C," 70, or 75. In any case, it should not be a "D" or the lowest passing grade because that is not satisfactory work for eligibility or for graduation. In setting the requirement for a minimum grade point, it seems much more reasonable to go with the overall average for a given marking period in lieu of a required grade for each course. The latter seems to unduly penalize a student who might have occasional difficulty with a particular course.

4. There should be some kind of core course requirement for eligibility purposes as well as for graduation. It is not sufficient to have a policy that requires a certain average in major subjects. As noted earlier, there is always room for debate as to what constitutes a "major" subject. A core requirement would cut across various curricular tracks at a variety of high schools. In formulating policy, there will also likely be debate about the nature of the core requirement. However, at least a consideration of English and mathematics is a logical place to begin. Standardized tests point in that direction. Beyond that, one might consider "Proposal 48," proposed by the National Collegiate Athletic Association (NCAA) in January, 1983, requiring 11 core high school courses, including three years of English, two years of math, two years of social science, and two years of natural or physical science. It also seems desirable to require a certain minimum grade point average for the core courses even though that might be set at a slightly lower level than the overall GPA.

5. The policy should not discourage students from taking advanced courses. It would defeat the purpose of the policy if students stayed away from advanced placement and honors courses because they feared ineligibility. As one possibility, a "C" in one of these courses might be awarded a 3.0 (in lieu of a 2.0) for purposes of eligibility determination only.

6. One of the real keys to sound policy development is provision for a comprehensive tutorial program. The lowest number of ineligible students can typically be found in schools that have such programs. As part of the tutorial assistance, some form of weekly, academic checklist could be required of all students in danger of losing their eligibility as well as those who have been previously ineligible. (See Exhibit 1-3 for an example.) Having the checklist helps to maintain communication on the academic standing of the athlete.

7. The extended tutorial program can also provide an incentive for regaining eligibility. For example, the policy might include a provision for regaining eligibility at the midpoint of the next grading period. Students could participate in extracurricular activities at mid-quarter or mid-semester by demonstrating satisfactory work and presenting documentations of improved grades to the athletic director (See Exhibit 1-4.)

8. Any policy in this area of eligibility must be easily understood or interpreted. At the same time, there must be sufficient flexibility to meet the variance in curricula and grading structures in different types of public schools. This is particularly true of statewide policies, but it is also a significant consideration in large school districts.

CONCLUSION

The central issue involving athletic eligibility in the high schools is likely to remain. There is always room for debate as to whether participation in extracurricular activities is a right or a privilege. The primary function of the schools is scholastic or academic in nature. Interscholastic athletics will continue to be a significant factor in American society. With that in mind, it is absolutely necessary to have a carefully conceived and well-established policy to assist students, parents, and coaches in putting athletics in right perspective. If all concerned will help students improve their levels of academic achievement, we can also preserve the benefits of interscholastic athletic participation.

Note: Additional updated information on high school eligibility can be found in Chapter 20 on pages 323 to 325.

REFERENCES

Naisbitt, John. *Megatrends: Ten New Directions Transforming Our Lives.* New York: Warner Books, Inc. 1984.

National Commission on Excellence in Education. "A Nation at Risk: The Imperative For Educational Reform." *American Education*, Vol. 19, No. 5, June 1983, pp. 2-17.

Reagan, R. "Reagan on Education." *The Boston Globe*, March 10, 1985, p. B30.

"Sidelines." *The Chronicle of Higher Education*, Vol. 30, No. 5, April 3, 1985, p. 29.

Weistart, J. and Lowell, C. *The Law of Sports.* Indianapolis: The Bobbs Merrill Company, 1979.

EXHIBIT 1-3. Weekly Report

HR Teacher: _____
Homeroom: _____

Student _____ Grade _____ Week _____

ENGLISH   A. All homework completed. YES ___ NO ___   On time? YES ___ NO ___
B. Grade for the week is C– or better.   YES ___ NO ___

QUIZZES: _____ TESTS: _____ OTHER: _____
COMMENTS:

_____
TEACHER'S SIGNATURE

MATH   A. All homework completed. YES ___ NO ___   On time? YES ___ NO ___
B. Grade for the week is C– or better.   YES ___ NO ___

QUIZZES: _____ TESTS: _____ OTHER: _____
COMMENTS:

_____
TEACHER'S SIGNATURE

SCIENCE   A. All homework completed. YES ___ NO ___   On time? YES ___ NO ___
B. Grade for the week is C– or better.   YES ___ NO ___

QUIZZES: _____ TESTS: _____ OTHER: _____
COMMENTS:

_____
TEACHER'S SIGNATURE

HISTORY   A. All homework completed. YES ___ NO ___   On time? YES ___ NO ___
B. Grade for the week is C– or better.   YES ___ NO ___

QUIZZES: _____ TESTS: _____ OTHER: _____
COMMENTS:

_____
TEACHER'S SIGNATURE

LANGUAGE   A. All homework completed. YES ___ NO ___   On time? YES ___ NO ___
B. Grade for the week is C or better.   YES NO

QUIZZES: _____ TESTS: _____ OTHER: _____
COMMENTS:

_____
TEACHER'S SIGNATURE

ART/MU   A. All homework completed. YES ___ NO ___   On time? YES ___ NO ___
GU/RE   B. Grade for the week is C– or better.   YES ___ NO ___
(please
circle)   QUIZZES: _____ TESTS: _____ OTHER: _____
COMMENTS:

_____
TEACHER'S SIGNATURE

PARENT'S COMMENTS: PHONE _____

PARENT'S SIGNATURE _____ DATE _____

EXHIBIT 1-4. Student-Athlete Interim Reports

Student Name: _____   Teacher: _____
Sport: _____   Class: _____
Coach: _____   Last Quarter Grade: _____
TODAY'S DATE: _____
Present Quarter Grade: _____

Please rate or comment on the student's progress in the following areas:

CLASSWORK:

HOMEWORK:

TEST SCORES:

ATTENDANCE:

If you were to grade this student today, he/she would receive (circle one):

A   B   C   D   F

COMMENTS:

Teacher Signature: _____

Thank you for your cooperation and help. Please return this form to your advisor's mailbox by _____ .

2

Athletes: College Recruiting Violations

The problem of recruiting violations in college athletes is far from being a recent development. It is generally well known that these viola-· tions have occurred ever since the *National Collegiate Athletic Association Manual* was first published. The immediate concern is that this problem only becomes more serious both in the number and severity of reported cases. It is also evident that the leaders in college athletics have become more and more frustrated in their efforts to solve the problem. In September 1984, Walter Byers, then executive director of the NCAA, for the first time publicly admitted that the association was having difficulty coping with the problem.

Violations of rules on recruiting and financial aid to athletes are so rampant in big-time college sports that the National Collegiate Athletic Association is having a difficult time tracking down the cheaters, according to Walter Byers, executive director of the association.

"I believe there is a growing acceptance of the belief that the conditions of intercollegiate athletics are such that you have to cut corners, you have to circumvent the rules," Mr. Byers said in a recent interview with the Associated Press.

"There seems to be a growing number of coaches and administrators who look upon NCAA penalties as the price of doing business: If you get punished, that's unfortunate, but that's part of the cost of getting along." . . .

It was the first time in Mr. Byers' 34 years with the NCAA that he publicly questioned whether the Association's enforcement division could keep pace with more refined types of cheating. "There are numerous successful programs that do not cheat," he said. "And I think the people on our enforcement staff and those who serve on the committee on infractions do a remarkable job of keeping the lid on as well as they do. But we are not keeping up." (*The Chronicle of Higher Education*, Sept. 5, 1984, p. 29)

Some specific points made by Byers at the same time point to the severity of the problem and raise some serious questions about the right approach in future efforts to solve the problem.

As many as 30 percent of the larger NCAA schools are cheating. "Ten to 15 percent are chronic violators, and 10 to 15 percent are dragged along because they give ground to stay apace."

Many college athletes are receiving thousands of dollars and automobiles in under-the-table payments. "Is that morally wrong, or is it wrong because we say it's wrong?"

Stiffer penalties are needed for violators, including punishment for the individuals involved. "I think intercollegiate athletics is out of control. . . ."

Maybe it is time to create an open division in the NCAA and pay student-athletes above the table.

A greater degree of involvement by the CEO's of member institutions is a necessity because some university presidents have already lost control of their own schools' programs. (*The Sporting News*, June 24, 1985, p. 12)

The magnitude of the problem is further demonstrated by the fact that 26 institutions were placed on NCAA probation for "major" rule-breaking between September 1980 and May 1985. It is important to keep in mind that the probation list would be considerably expanded by inclusion of those found guilty of "minor" infractions. In chronological order, those on the "major" list were as follows:

University of New Mexico — November 1980
University of Colorado — December 1980
California State Polytechnic at Pomona — February 1981
Southern Methodist University — June 1981
University of Miami — November 1981
University of Oregon — December 1981
Witchita State University — December 1981
University of Southern California — April 1982
Saint Louis University — March 1982
Western State College — September 1982
Clemson University — November 1982
University of San Diego — December 1982
University of Arizona — May 1983
California State University at Fresno — August 1983

University of Kansas — November 1983
University of Wisconsin at Madison — November 1983
San Diego State University — January 1984
University of Alaska at Anchorage — May 1984
University of Illinois — July 1984
University of Akron — September 1984
Arizona State University — December 1984
University of Florida — January 1985
University of Georgia — January 1985
University of Southern Mississippi — February 1985
Tennessee State University — February 1985
Alabama State University — May 1985

Perhaps even more significantly, the listing does not include those institutions that have not been caught with their violations. If Walter Byers was correct in his (probably conservative) estimate that 30 percent of the larger schools are cheating, the list could be much longer.

CASE STUDY

In an attempt to further explore the nature of the problem, the University of Florida was selected for a case study because it is a relatively recent case that received considerable publicity. When the university was placed on probation in 1985, it was described as the most serious case of infractions ever processed by the NCAA. What were the circumstances involved?

In 1979, Charlie Pell became the head coach of the University of Florida football program. He inherited a losing program, reflected in his first year record of 0-10-1. Then, from 1980 through 1984, Pell's teams combined a record of 41-16-2, including four consecutive post season bowl appearances, national rankings, and a Southeast Conference Championship. Behind that record is the story of what was done to bring about the major turnaround.

On November 4, 1982, the NCAA received a report from a confidential source of possible recruiting violations by several members of Florida's football coaching staff. Four days later, a prospective football player was interviewed routinely as part of the NCAA's Operation Intercept Program, and he also reported recruitment violations by the university.

These reports appeared to have substance. Consequently, on December 1, 1982, the NCAA notified the chief executive officer of the University of Florida of preliminary inquiries by the NCAA enforcement staff into the athletic policies and practices of the university. In May of 1983 the university received notice that the NCAA's preliminary inquiries were continuing.

Subsequently, the university's legal counsel met with NCAA enforcement staff members to discuss information obtained from the investigation to that point in time. On October 24, 1983, the legal counsel submitted to the chair of the NCAA's Committee on Infractions a request for permission for the university to appear before the committee in December 1983 to present its position. However, the request was denied, and the inquiry continued.

On July 31, 1984, the university's legal counsel again met with enforcement staff members and received notice of apparent violations in the Florida football program. In August the enforcement staff informed the Committee on Infractions that the university was prepared to acknowledge much of the information developed by the NCAA. The university also reported that it intended to take disciplinary action against three members of the football coaching staff who appeared to have been involved in the violations. Further, the university expressed a desire to develop a stipulated list of violations that would be acceptable to the institution and the NCAA.

Joint interviews of coaching staff members and student-athletes were conducted on August 28, 1984, and on September 11, 1984, a letter of official inquiry was hand-delivered to the chief executive officer of the University of Florida. The inquiry included 108 infractions.

Pell was terminated from his coaching position at Florida on September 16, 1984, and the following day the university's stipulated response to the letter of official inquiry was received by the NCAA. Subsequently, university representatives appeared before the Committee on Infractions to consider the stipulated response. Through a letter dated November 21, 1984, the university initiated an appeal of certain findings in accordance with official procedures governing the NCAA Enforcement Program.

In the final analysis, it was clear to the Committee on Infractions that some of the violations were intended to obtain a competitive advantage over other institutions and that these violations did, in fact, play a significant role in the university's recent success in football. It was noted that approximately 20 student-athletes involved in this case participated on the Florida football team in one or more seasons. Furthermore, several of these players were substantial contributors to the success of the university's football team during that time.

The conclusion was that the University of Florida infractions case involved approximately 58 violations of various NCAA regulations. Among the violations were cash inducements to prospects, cash and other benefits to enrolled student-athletes, complimentary tickets for the players, outside funds maintained by Pell and an assistant, the arrangement of cost-free room and board for "unaided" student-athletes, the secret scouting of opponents, the conduct of out-of-season practices, and the use of an excessive number of coaches in recruiting. The Committee on Infractions felt that the violations went beyond technical violations of NCAA rules or inadvertent actions. Rather, the violations reflected a deliberate and calculated effort by the coaching staff to do whatever was necessary to achieve a superior football record by disregarding the restraints imposed by NCAA rules.

On January 13, 1985, John L. Toner, president of the NCAA, announced that the University of Florida had been placed on probation for a three-year period for violations occurring from 1979 to 1983 in the conduct of its intercollegiate football program. Toner's announcement followed the NCAA Council's consideration of the university's appeal of certain findings and penalties proposed by the NCAA Committee on Infractions.

The penalties prohibited postseason football competition and "live" television appearances for at least two years. It was understood that the third year of probation and sanctions regarding postseason events and television appearances would be suspended if the university met prescribed monitoring conditions requiring written reports and periodic on-site reviews of the athletic program. If the university was successful in gaining a suspension of the final year of penalties, the university's football team would be prohibited from appearing on live telecasts during the 1985 and 1986 football seasons, and the NCAA's ban regarding postseason football competition would be applied to the 1984-85 and 1985-86 academic years. This possibility for reduction in penalties was included because of the prompt corrective and disciplinary action taken by the University of Florida as well as the university's demonstrated commitment to develop full information in this case.

Additional sanctions stipulated that no more than 20 new student-athletes in the sport of football would be permitted to receive athletically related financial aid during the 1985-86 and 1986-87 academic years, and the university would be limited to a total of 85 football team members who could receive athletically related aid in the 1985-86 academic year and a total of 75 in the 1986-87 academic year.

Several additional actions were taken by the university during processing of the case, including: 1) terminating employment of the head football coach and two assistant football coaches; 2) restructuring the athletic department to make the head football coach directly responsible to the athletic director; 3) adopting a more stringent complimentary ticket policy than that required by the NCAA; 4) prohibiting seven outside representatives from engaging in any recruiting activities on behalf of the university during the probationary period; and 5) admonishing 10 additional representatives to take precautions to avoid future violations of NCAA rules.

Following the official notice of probations, President Marshall Criser of Florida issued a statement in which he expressed regret that the NCAA chose not to modify its earlier decision on the penalties to be imposed. At the same time he resolved to maintain complete compliance with NCAA and Southeastern Conference (SEC) regulations in the future.

The University of Florida Case is a classic example of what can happen when there is lack of internal control in an athletic program. It also exemplifies the steps many large collegiate programs take to gain a competitive edge.

THE ISSUE

Thus, the problem is clearly before us, as it has been for many years: recruiting violations are the name of the game in "big time" college sport. This raises the issue: what can be done to resolve the problem? There appears to be only two real choices, and both are difficult. The first is to take further steps to control the recruiting efforts. The second is to establish a new, open division in college sport wherein some teams are recognized as having professional or semi-professional status at the collegiate level. A third choice might be to eliminate major college football and basketball programs, but that is hardly viable in light of the significance of these programs in American society. Edwin Cady, the Andrew W. Mellon Professor in the Humanities at Duke University, (1978) makes that point very clearly.

> But the American Big Game, repeated annually and often simultaneously on dozens of fields and floors, is a college game. . . .
> Nevertheless, the Collegiate Big Game is different. Nothing elsewhere resembles it. Nothing in professional sport captures, for all the flattery money can buy, the same glamour or intensity of significance. . . . The difference arises from the unique involvement of major institutions of higher education and learning. It locks in symbolic combat the peoples of "sovereign states": Texas-Oklahoma; Tennessee-Kentucky; Wisconsin-Minnesota. It confronts massive regional and cultural differences: Notre Dame-UCLA; Penn State-Alabama; Virginia-DePaul. It pits life styles and social convictions: Stanford-USC; Duke-Carolina; Rice-Arkansas. It is symbolically fratricidal: Grambling-Florida A.M.; Yale-Harvard; Providence-Marquette. Whole spectra of the national life clash fraternally in the Big Game. (pp. 3-4)

So, we are faced with the realization that the "Big Game" (major college football and basketball) is here to stay. This leaves higher education with the first two choices. What are the arguments for each? More important, what kind of policies can be developed to carry out a decision in either direction?

Control

Perhaps the strongest argument for the control thesis is found in the idea that college administrators really have no choice. If further efforts are not made to control college sport, there will only be chaos, and the college game will eventually destroy itself and the institutions it represents. This is essentially the position taken by Cady. It is also the position manifested in the historical and current actions taken by the NCAA. The only difference is that Cady has some doubts about the NCAA legislation. (More about that will be noted shortly.)

The concept of control is the central theme of Cady's work. He discusses "internal control" and "external control," but he clearly believes any key to real success is found in the former. The burden of responsibility for controlling college athletics falls on the shoulders of college presidents, who must hire trustworthy people capable of exercising the necessary controls to keep college athletics in the necessary academic perspective. Cady introduces the last section of his book with a warning: "The president who does not steadily face the realities of his intercollegiate athletics situation puts himself in jeopardy where they play the Big Game. If he does not keep it under control, if he tries to ignore its realities, it will come and get him." (p. 143)

In terms of external control, Cady makes a specific suggestion: "A committee of one hundred presidents ought now to prepare to put the process of constitutional renewal in motion." (p. 224) With that suggestion, he revealed remarkable foresight, in light of the fact that his book was published in 1978 and the NCAA's Presidents' Commission was established in January 1984. (More about the Commission will also be said later.)

Under the heading of "Noble Experiments," Cady presents four suggestions that might serve as guidelines for policy development if one chooses to pursue the control thesis for intercollegiate athletics:

"1. We have to clarify our intentions to ourselves." (p. 223) (Essentially, the point here is that the NCAA and the major college conferences have to rethink their structures and rules in light of the realities of the late 20th century.)

"2. We have to find talent and free it to work." (p. 223) (Colleges and conferences should seek and train additional qualified people to administer intercollegiate athletic programs.)

"3. I would start by sending all the books of rules for the conduct of intercollegiate athletics, including the NCAA's, to archives and begin again." (p. 223) (The current legislation governing college athletics is too cumbersome and "picky." We need a few simple, clear, rules, aimed at a bona-fide student-athlete.)

"4. I do not mean that I would destroy or even disable the present structures of people and operations through which the NCAA, for instance, provides indispensable services to the Big Game and all the lesser games." (p. 224) (In spite of their difficulties with legislation and enforcement, the NCAA and conferences offer many valuable services to the colleges. Those functions should be preserved.)

The Presidents' Commission established in January 1984 is perhaps the best example of recent steps to put more teeth into the external control of intercollegiate athletics. How did the Commission come into existence, and what are the developments to date?

In August 1983, The American Council on Education's (ACE) Committee on Division I Athletics (consisting of 28 college presidents) proposed a "board of presidents" that would have had greater autonomy over college sport by having authority to veto or modify NCAA rules, as well as being able to impose new rules of its own design. The NCAA Council opposed the proposal and submitted an alternate proposal which would create a Presidents' Commission with much more limited authority than that proposed by the American Council's committee. Basically, the Commission would serve only in an advisory role to the NCAA Council.

The ACE committee slightly modified its proposal and submitted it to the NCAA convention in January 1984. However, the proposal was soundly defeated, and, in place, the convention approved the establishment of the Presidents' Commission, along the lines of the NCAA Council proposal.

As established, the Presidents' Commission has the power to review any NCAA activity; to place any topic on the agenda for a council meeting or a convention; to commission studies; to sponsor changes in rules at conventions; to demand a roll-call vote on any issue it deems important enough, thus putting members votes on record; and to call special conventions. The proposal also stipulated that Commission members were to be chosen by a mail ballot of all NCAA members' presidents.

In April of 1984, 44 presidents were elected to the Commission and John W. Ryan, then president of Indiana University, was selected to be the first chair. One of the first actions by the Commission was to conduct a confidential survey on issues dealing with the integrity and finances of college sport. The results of the survey were reported in April 1985 and showed that a majority of presidents desired stricter rules and tougher penalties for violations by coaches, players, and institutions. The Commission called a special convention for June and prepared proposed changes in the rules, based on the results of the survey.

Policy For External Control: A total of 198 presidents were among the 840 delegates who attended the special convention in New Orleans in June 1985. They passed 12 proposals by unanimous or near-unanimous votes. Collectively, these probably represent the best effort to date to develop policies aimed at external control. Following is a summary of the policy decisions that relate either directly or indirectly to recruiting violations:

1. Each member institution is required to conduct self-study of its

intercollegiate athletic program at least once every five years as a condition and obligation of membership in the NCAA.

2. To be eligible for NCAA championships, a Division I institution is required to report annually to the NCAA, providing information on the academic status of entering freshmen, compliance with continuing eligibility requirements, and graduation rates for recruited athletes compared with other students.

3. Violations of NCAA rules are divided between "major" and "secondary" classifications. Penalties are specified and strengthened. A team that was penalized for a previous major infraction within the previous five years will be barred from all intercollegiate competition for up to two years for a second, more recent infraction.

4. All coaches in that sport are prohibited from coaching during the same period, even if they move to another institution.

5. Each member institution's athletic budget is to be controlled by the institution. It is to be subject to the institution's normal budgeting procedures and approved by the chancellor, president, or a designee.

6. There will be an annual audit of all expenditures for each member institution's athletic program by an individual from outside the institution, selected by the institution's chancellor or president.

The delegates also passed two resolutions aimed at the need for policies to provide external control over the conduct of intercollegiate athletic programs. The essence of these resolutions was as follows:

1. Student athletes should be held accountable for their involvement in serious rules violations and should be declared ineligible for intercollegiate competition.

2. A one-term affidavit program should be established. This would require every head coach and scholarship athlete to sign a statement attesting to current compliance with specifically identified rules.

Following the special convention there were mixed reactions regarding the potential significance of the actions taken at New Orleans. One's perspective obviously made quite a difference.

NCAA president Jack Davis surveyed the audience of 840 college presidents, chancellors, and other assorted delegates at the organization's special convention last week in New Orleans. . . . "This is a momentous occasion," Davis said. He urged the delegates to applaud themselves, and they did so earnestly.

But Davis and his colleagues may have been a bit overzealous. Passage of the proposals drafted by the NCAA's 44-member Presidents' Commission was a welcome first step toward a reform of college athletics, but more steps obviously are needed. . . .

The convention's actions were mostly symbolic. Davis admitted that if a school's entire athletic budget were jeopardized by the suspension of a big-money sport as the result of the two-major violations rule, "the infractions committee would probably make an exception the first time for football — that's the reality of it." He also allowed that the new legislation didn't really get at the evils of over-commercialization. But he promised that with the presidents now playing a more active role, the NCAA will no longer shrink from tackling the tougher issues. "We'll reduce pressure on coaches," he said, "and allow them to operate on a higher level of trust." . . .

Ryan said his commission was on the "threshold of action" on these issues. He promised that more legislation would be introduced at next January's regular NCAA Convention. Never has a pledge carried more potential consequence for intercollegiate sport. If significant reform is not addressed at that time, the high-minded rhetoric of New Orleans will ring hollow. (*Sports Illustrated,* July 1, 1985, p. 9)

Policy For Internal Control: If there is to be any significant degree of success in efforts at external control, there must be consistent policies at the institutional level. Internal control is the key to solving the problem of recruiting violations through control. Only the individual institution can develop specific policies that reflect its structure and functions. However, the following ideas are suggested as policy guidelines for the internal control of college athletics.

1. The president or chancellor should appoint an athletic advisor to his or her staff. This advisor will not be a member of the athletic department but will work in conjunction with the athletic director in securing institutional control through overseeing all recruitment activities.
2. All business transactions for the express purpose of recruitment should be monitored by the president's or chancellor's athletic advisor and staff.
3. A strong and effective faculty athletic council or committee should be established. This committee should maintain close liaison with the athletic advisor, and the committee should receive regular reports on the status of recruitment practices and expenditures.
4. The chair of the athletic committee or other representatives of that committee should have an active role in conference and NCAA affairs.

5. There should be regularly scheduled meetings including individuals in the following positions to discuss the total athletic recruitment situation at the institution:

President or Chancellor
Athletic Advisor
Athletic Director
Chair of Faculty Athletic Committee
Director of Freshmen Admissions
Head Coaches of Football and Basketball
Booster Club President
Athletic Business Manager

In the final analysis the real key to internal control lies in the appointment of responsible people along with the built-in provision for continuing communication regarding the recruiting activities. Specific policies developed by the president or chancellor should reduce the gaps between the information available at the top level and the activities of the athletic department.

Professionalize College Athletics

As noted earlier, there are some who argue that the solution to the problem of recruiting violations is not to be found in further efforts at control. Their argument proceeds by pointing out that the NCAA has more or less worked at control over the past 80 years, and there is little evidence of success. Why continue to fight a losing cause?

The other possible solution to the problem would be to recognize and grant professional, or at least semi-professional, status to college football and basketball powers that are at the heart of the problem. Within the past few years, several proponents of this idea have emerged, including Howard R. Swearer, president of Brown University. In February 1982, *The New York Times* published the speech he delivered to the midwestern meeting of the Brown Corporation, the university's governing body. Excerpts point to the essence of Swearer's stance:

May not the time have arrived when it would be desirable to recognize openly this symbiotic relationship between the big athletic powers and professional sports, and make the necessary structural changes?

The fictions are wearing thin. I, for one, see no harm in associating a professional or semi-professional team with a university; and I do see a number of benefits. It would help clarify what is now a very murky picture. Athletes should, of course, have the opportunity to take courses and pursue a degree, if they wish; but they would be regarded as athletes first and should be paid accordingly. By so doing the regulatory and enforcement burden and the temptations for illegal and unethical practices would be dramatically eased. The clear separation between the academic and athletic purposes of the university would be beneficial to both. . . .

If the big powers were to choose this course, I think it would benefit all intercolleagiate athletics. High school seniors would be given a more clearly defined choice among different kinds of post-secondary athletic experience. The general public could recognize more clearly the nature of athletic competition in different leagues. The pressures toward professionalism on those institutions that chose a different course might be lessened.

The possibility I have sketched out is not a choice that I believe Ivy League and similar institutions should or would take. However, I hope that the Ivy League will also take a positive and active role in the long-term restructuring of intercollegiate sports. (*The New York Times*, Sunday, February 21, 1982, p. 52. Copyright © 1982 by The New York Times Company. Reprinted by permission.)

Although Swearer was not the first to advocate the professionalization of a segment of college athletics, his statement prompted considerable debate because of his position. Many people consider it unrealistic to have professional sport in the college context. They contend that such action will only lead to further abuses and that college athletics would eventually be destroyed. Their answer is to work hard at further efforts to control the situation. The reaction of Bill Atchley, president of Clemson University, more or less typifies this counter point of view:

Brown University's president, Howard R. Swearer, proposed some time ago that big college athletic programs be turned into professional or semiprofessional farm teams. . . . The idea has been batted around over the years, but not until recently has it been taken seriously. When you stop to think about the actual mechanics of professional athletic teams coexisting with a university and competing under the school's colors, the idea becomes unrealistic. . . .

Despite growing athletic budgets and lucrative television contracts, students and alumni see college athletics as amateur competition. It may not be amateur competition in the fullest sense, but that is how it is perceived. How else could the rural campus and town of Clemson, with fewer than 20,000 inhabitants, attract more than 70,000 paying fans for a Saturday afternoon of football? I can think of no professional team that has succeeded so well in such an unlikely market. A professional team representing Clemson University would eventually be overshadowed by teams from metropolitan markets like Atlanta. (*The New York Times*, Sunday, July 4, 1982. Copyright © 1982 by The New York Times Company. Reprinted by permission.)

The debate continued. On April 25, 1984, *USA TODAY* devoted an entire page to the debate on the central issue involving the professionalization of college athletics. Excerpts from that source reflect the opposing views.

Howard R. Swearer — "Why not pay athletes who play at colleges? — When a university football program grosses $15 million a year, as some do, it is no longer a sport. It is a business. . . . A semi-pro situation would force people to see the system for what it is. That could ease the tension that exists between the demands of academics and the demands of athletics. Coaches and athletes would be paid. Athletes could take courses, but no one would have to pretend that they were students first and athletes second. We must try to make regulation effective. But if it fails, semi-pro status may be the best way to protect academic integrity and to recognize the role of sports for what it has become."

Editorial Opinion — "Colleges will lose by paying athletes — Last week Louisiana State Chancellor James Wharton said colleges may soon be hiring athletes as entertainers — they might not have to hit the books at all. Some say that's just facing the truth: College sports is already big business, so why not just start paying athletes? But turning college teams into pro teams is no way to end the abuses. Colleges would launch bidding wars for stars. Hardened pro athletes with no interest in education would be hanging around campuses. School spirit, which is the heart of student and alumni support, would die. Only 2 percent of college athletes can make a living in pro sports. Our colleges and universities owe the 98 percent who can't make it an education, not exploitation."

Frank E. Vandiver, president, Texas A&M University — "Sports no threat to education — Universities with big-time athletic programs are often accused of using athletes to enhance their image — at the expense of academics. That may be true at some schools, but it is not the case at Texas A&M. . . . Having 'big-time' athletics doesn't prevent us from having big-time academics. In fact, the two enhance each other. We don't have to choose between academic or athletic All-Americans. We have both." (*USA TODAY*, Wednesday, April 25, 1984, p. 8A. Copyright 1984, *USA TODAY*. Excerpted with permission.)

Another Suggested Policy

Before concluding our consideration of this problem of recruiting violations, a policy proposed by well-known sportswriter Leonard Koppett is worthy of consideration. Perhaps the most unusual feature about Koppett's proposal is that he would have a professional college athlete pursuing a normal college education. In fact earlier in his book, *Sports*

Illusion, Sports Reality, he bluntly makes the point that amateurism should be abolished altogether as a category for major commercial events, including college athletic and international competition. Later, in "Under Reform the NCAA" he presents his policy suggestion regarding student status:

> There is, however, a simple and practical way to get the NCAA out of the policing business without weakening its other powers. Junk all the detailing restrictions concerning recruiting methods, high school grades, scholarship limits, and the rest, and zero in on the basic idea and basic problem. Call it graduation. The relevant standard for a college athlete should be his bona-fide status as a student working toward a degree. He is being presented to the public as that, not as an achiever of certain grades, or a person with a certain income, or one who spoke with his prospective coach only three times. A student. And the measure of a student's success, as a student, is graduation. He gets his degree.
>
> My proposal, then, would work this way. First, determine the 'normal' percentage of graduates at any particular college. Then require every athletic squad to meet (or exceed, if you want to be stricter) that figure.
>
> Any year in which the percentage isn't met, that school would go on probation (in that sport) the following year, and stay on probation until it gets back to the required percentage.
>
> That's all. That's the whole rule. It would be self-policing. It would be effective and it would be to the point. All the NCAA would have to do would be to process the graduation records submitted by the college presidents. It would collate and enforce, not judge. (Koppett, 1981, pp. 290-291).

CONCLUSION

From an ideal standpoint, I am inclined to support the attempt at control. I hope that the Presidents' Commission will be successful in its efforts to provide the necessary control. However, the reality of the situation forces me to support Howard Swearer's position that it will be necessary to recognize professional or semi-professional status for a segment of college athletics.

In terms of the professional route, there are some attractive features to the proposal presented by Leonard Koppett. Again, ideally, one would like to see a situation in which most college athletes at the higher level of competition could receive their degree. However, in my opinion, Koppett's proposal also lacks realism. Further problems would be created. There is too much variance in the quality of degrees from institution to institution and even within a given institution. The graduation percentage rate is only a part of the total picture. Under Koppett's plan, institutions with lower academic standards would have a distinct advantage. Coaches would work even harder at pushing athletes into "soft" majors to meet degree requirements. Unfortunately, in some cases one would even have to question the validity of information coming from the institutions regarding the graduation percentage rates for athletes and other students.

As I see it, this leaves the Swearer proposal as the best choice, even though one might not favor the professionalization of college athletics from an ideal perspective. If the NCAA pursued that proposal, what kind of policies might be developed?

1. There would be two basic divisions within the NCAA — one for institutions offering sport programs that are major commercial events (football, basketball, and probably ice hockey) and the other for all other institutions. It is assumed that the first division would include current Division I institutions that choose to pursue the professional route. The second division, to be called Division II, would include the current Division IAA, II, and III membership, plus current Division I schools that wish to change the direction of their programs.

2. Division I institutions (those offering major commercial sport events) would have dual membership in Division II for matters involving all other sports.

3. For Division I sports, there would be no restrictions on recruiting or financial aid for athletes in those sports. Essentially, it would be an open, competitive market. An institution would offer a prospective professional college athlete what it could afford to pay. This might prove to be financially destructive for the institutions involved. In that case, it might be necessary to establish a draft system for Division I athletes.

4. Many Division I athletes would clearly be recognized as athlete-students. In otherwords, they are first and foremost in college for athletic purposes. Were it not for their athletic ability, they would not be college students. They would be required to take at least one course per semester or term. However, this could be a remedial course in English, mathematics, or public speaking. At the same time a sound advising system would be maintained to permit the academically qualified athletes to pursue degree work at the appropriate pace. Division I athletes with first rate academic qualifications might be able to receive degrees in four years.

5. Something must be done to maintain standards regarding recruitment and academic progress for the proposed Division II athletes (by far, the bulk of the college athletes). The answer is

not to be found in retention of the present *NCAA Manual*. In view of that, I would recommend that Koppett's proposal be adopted as the policy for Division II athletes.

Note: *Additional updated information on college recruiting violations can be found in Chapter 20 on pages 315-317.*

REFERENCES

Atchley, B. L. "Keep the Pros Out of Colleges." *The New York Times*, Sunday, July 4, 1982, p. 2S.
Cady, E. H. *The Big Game: College Sports and American Life*. Knoxville: The University of Tennessee Press, 1978.
Koppett, L. *Sports Illusion, Sports Reality*. Boston: Houghton Mifflin Company, 1981.
Nightingale, D. "Calling For Change In the NCAA." *The Sporting News*, June 24, 1985.
"Scorecard." *Sports Illustrated*, July 1, 1985, p. 9.
Swearer, H. R. "An Ivy League President Looks at College Sports." *The New York Times*, Sunday, February 21, 1982, p. 2S.
The Chronicle of Higher Education, September 5, 1984, p. 29.
USA TODAY, April 25, 1984, p. 8A.

3

Athletes:
College Admissions

Superficially, it might appear that the topic of college admissions is a repeat or extension of the previous chapter. Is there not a close connection between recruiting violations and the admission of college athletes? To a certain extent the link is there, but more careful consideration will reveal that recruiting violations are not really in the area of admissions. By and large, major recruiting violations involve excessive financial offers to prospective athletes. Contrasted with the legislation restricting financial aid, the National Collegiate Athletic Association (NCAA) rule governing admissions is general and vague. Under the section "Principle of Sound Academic Standards," the organization's manual merely states the following in regard to the admission standard:

> A student-athlete shall not represent an institution in intercollegiate athletics competition unless the student-athlete: (1) Has been admitted as a regularly matriculated, degree-seeking student in accordance with the regular, published entrance requirements of that institution; . . . (*1987-88 Manual of the National Collegiate Athletic Association*, Article 3, Section 3, p. 19) Reprinted by permission of the National Collegiate Athletic Association. This material is subject to annual review and change.

Basically, this means that admission standards are left as an institutional responsibility. It allows special consideration for the selection of candidates with different qualifications as long as both athletes and non-athletes compete and qualify under similar conditions.

THE PROBLEM

This points to the problem, which is simple but, very severe and extensive. The essence of this problem is the shortage of student-athlete talent in the truest sense. There is a shortage of individuals who qualify as both real students and real athletes. There is no doubt that every institu-

51

tion and coach would desire to admit only those athletes who are also first-rate students. However, the reality is that there are not enough true scholar-athletes to meet the needs of the vast array of college sport programs.

The result is that it is frequently necessary to lower the academic standard to admit athletes. Beyond that it is a question of how low an institution will go in reducing the standard. Once again, the formula appears to be quite simple, but this only compounds the problem. In general, a college or university admits athletes who will enable the institution to be competitive at its level of participation. The higher the level of competition, the more difficult it becomes to find the appropriate athletes who also fully qualify from an academic perspective. The total available pool is reduced proportionately to the level of competition. It is no mystery why we hear and read about so many Division I football and basketball "blue-chippers" who have academic qualifications far below those of the typical college student.

Of course, the problem really unfolds after the athlete is admitted and is expected to pursue a normal course of study and to compete with students selected according to a higher academic standard. Here again, it is no mystery why many Division I football and basketball players fail to receive college degrees. They were admitted with deficient academic credentials. To that, one adds the extensive time involvement and emotional demands of competing at the highest level of college athletic competition. The more surprising fact is that many of these athletes receive degrees, as evident in the data.

THE ISSUE

The issue is a direct outgrowth of the problem. There is a shortage of student-athlete talent, particularly at the higher levels of competition. The issue, then, revolves around the extent to which athletes should be treated as special admissions cases.

One finds strong opinions on both sides of the ledger. On September 30, 1985, *Sports Illustrated* presented a 10-point special report titled "A Plan For Cleaning Up College Sports." The magazine stated that the first nine points were within the NCAA's jurisdiction. This was the number one proposal on the list:

> SHARPLY LIMIT THE NUMBER OF ATHLETES ACCEPTED AS SPECIAL CASES. One of the biggest scandals in college sports is the number of 'exceptions' that admissions directors make for athletes who don't meet normal entrance requirements. Some of these exceptions occur in affirmative action-type programs under which students from disadvantaged backgrounds can be admitted because of special talents or latent academic promise. At some schools 60% or more of all special admissions are jocks. Our proposal is to tie the

number of 'exceptions' for athletes to the percentage of athletes in the student body as a whole. A one-to-two ratio should do the trick: that is, if athletes make up, say, 3% of a school's enrollment, they should account for no more than 6% of special admissions and other exceptions. This would be preferable to controversial Proposal 48, which was enacted by the NCAA in 1983 and is scheduled to take effect next August. Proposal 48 holds that entering college athletes must achieve a specified minimum score on standardized national tests, thus imposing the same absolute admission standards on lesser schools as on Harvard, an obvious absurdity. Limiting special admissions would help assure that athletes are treated the same as nonathletes entering the same institution. (p. 36)

One would have to say that this is a fairly strong stance on the issue, particularly in that the proposal comes from the editors of a prominent national sport magazine. Shortly after the appearance of the *Sports Illustrated* plan, an editorial in *The Wall Street Journal* set forth an even stronger proposal:

A cry has gone up to tie the number of athletic scholarships a school can award to the number of recruited jocks it graduates. That's a bad idea. A school that will admit anyone will graduate anyone. Playing with athlete-graduation rates already is a popular campus sport. Ask some athletic departments about the proportion of jocks they graduate and they'll give you figures for seniors or lettermen, or they'll lump basketball players with golfers.

College sports need to be scaled down and placed in an educational context, and athletes' rights need to be protected. At the risk of being unoriginal and repetitious, here are some proposals: Colleges should stop admitting athletes in higher proportion than other students to programs that have lower-than-normal entrance requirements. (*The Wall Street Journal*, Oct. 16, 1985, p. 28)

One cannot help but note that this proposal stands in sharp contrast to Leonard Koppett's proposal, which was presented in the preceding chapter. Koppett would junk all restrictions concerning recruiting methods and high school grades and zero in only on graduation. He clearly views the athlete as being a legitimate special admissions case.

Well-known lay theologian and political writer Michael Novak would go even further in recognizing the special status of the college athlete. Note this if you are looking for the most extreme position on the issue! Apparently, he would offer degrees in football and basketball. At least he feels that a university could legitimately be a training ground for professional sport.

But should the universities allow themselves to be used as training grounds for the professionals? Well, there are schools of journalism and television, political science, and agriculture, chemistry and engineering, law and medicine, business and accounting, teaching and nursing. Is sports the only profession that ought to be excluded? It is not the least spiritual profession, nor the least mythic; nor the least central to a culture. The athletic programs of certain schools are likely to make as great a contribution to the life, vitality, imagination, and moral unity of a given region as any other school programs. It will pain professors in other fields to admit it. (Novak, 1976, p. 282)

Support for the special admissions of athletes also comes from Edwin Cady of Duke University, whose position is far different from Novak's. Cady advocates careful control of athletes in the normal academic structure, but nevertheless, he maintains that the athlete is a special kind of college student and should be treated accordingly.

Though some academic folk would prefer not to trouble themselves with thinking about it, the student athlete has become a specialized product of contemporary culture, and the facts make a difference which has to be taken into consideration. He, and now increasingly she, starts as a special sort of American person . . . (p. 144).

The truth is that the athlete's special situation skews his academic experience from his emergence in junior high school throughout his secondary and undergraduate years and perhaps afterwards. From his contemporaries and the community he may feel sharp pressure to conform to the jock stereotype; many an athlete has felt forced to keep the emergent life of his mind a secret. Unless he is lucky in his family, he may find the same pressure at home. At school his relations to what intellectual life exists may be complicated. Some teachers will scornfully put him down for a qualified idiot and penalize him. Others, equally unfair, may pet and patronize him, awarding automatically inflated, meaningless grades, making it clear that nothing is expected of him in class. (Cady, 1978, p. 153)

The treatment of college athletes as special admissions cases is an issue all college admissions officials must face, particularly those at institutions that compete at the Division I level. The issue is of direct concern to different people for a variety of reasons.

From a coach's perspective it is paramount to have an admissions policy that is compatible with the level of competition on which the team competes. In essence, the policy must be as strict or as lenient as those of the competitors. The coach's livelihood is on the line. Any skeptic on this point has only to note the series of firings or forced resignations following the completion of each collegiate football or basketball season. Termination of a coach's employment is usually related to a losing record. Some coaching failures can be traced back to the degree of success in admitting athletes who can compete at a given level.

Athletes, parents, and coaches are most directly affected by any admissions policy. But, beyond that, admissions is a general institutional concern due to the overall image factor associated with athletics.

Some universities use football and basketball programs as a primary means of gaining support through alumni contributions and the general publicity. The bottom line is that special admissions for athletes could well mean increased financial support for the university. Administrators at the "big game" schools cannot overlook the importance of the football and basketball programs, even if they might prefer to do so. It might be argued that administrators at most colleges have to give some kind of special attention to the relative success of their intercollegiate football and basketball programs. However, this very quickly becomes a two-edged sword in terms of admissions. The question largely becomes this: how far does an institution go in making exceptions to admit athletes without receiving the attendant, negative publicity associated with low academic standards? Faculty become concerned about a school's academic reputation, and other students and parents have vested interests in the academic profile. Thus, there is always a fine balance in the publicity that flows from athletic success.

CASE ILLUSTRATIONS

Policies for the admission of athletes as special cases have existed almost as long as intercollegiate sport teams have competed in the United States. Nevertheless, it is true that during the past decade the amount of negative publicity about extreme cases of special admissions for athletes has increased significantly. An examination of selected cases might serve to reinforce the significant nature of both the problem and the issue. This is done with the full recognition that these are only some of the cases which have been brought to public attention. It is difficult to estimate how many of these accounts would also be applicable to other institutions.

The University of Southern California (USC) Case

On October 12, 1980, the president of USC issued "A Report to the USC Community," based on the findings and recommendations of three advisory committees formed in the spring of 1980 to examine the circumstances that led to athletic sanctions imposed on USC by the Pacific 10 Conference. Excerpts from that report follow. (Material has been reorganized for this case illustration.)

The Past

1. For several years, the University, while adhering to NCAA admission standards for athletic eligibility, admitted some athletes who fell below normal USC standards of admission. (This practice also was applied to some non-athlete student applicants.) Between 1970 and 1980, these exceptions averaged 33 student-athletes per year (in all sports).
2. Academically marginal athletes have been admitted to USC in the past based chiefly on athletic prowess as judged by the Athletic Department, and without normal Admissions Office review.
3. Although the retention and graduation rate of USC student-athletes during the past decade has been approximately the same as for the undergraduate student body as a whole, only a small number of athletes admitted as exceptions have ever graduated from the University.
4. The program devised by the athletic department to meet the needs of special action students, while successful in certain respects, has suffered from being too closely identified with the Intercollegiate Sports program and has lacked sufficient controls.
5. Almost all student athletes enrolled in three Speech Communications courses during Fall 1979 were registered for the courses by the athletic department's academic coordinator.
6. Most students registered for the courses expected passing grades even though little or no academic work was anticipated.
7. Most student-athletes enrolled in Speech 380 did not attempt to meet a teacher, attend a class, or receive an assignment until midway through the semester when the University discovered the non-functioning course.
8. The 41 students (32 athletes) discovered to have registered in courses with the intent of receiving credit where little or no academic work was anticipated or performed, have been placed on disciplinary probation for the remainder of their careers at USC, without loss of designated privileges.

The Future-Reforms-After 1980

1. Responsibility for the admission of all students (including athletes) shall rest solely with the Office of Admissions acting in accordance with established University policies and procedures governing appeals and referrals.
2. The Admissions Policy of the University of Southern California is to identify students who can both contribute to, and benefit from, its special ambience by their individual excellence and intellectual promise. Admission to USC is not determined by a rigid formula. University-wide admissions standards are presently under discussion within the University Admissions Com-

mittee. A proposed policy governing regular admissions has been forwarded to the President's Advisory Council. The Admissions Committee will consider policies governing special action admissions later this Fall.

In the interim, the Office of Admission has been directed by the President to adhere to the following criteria for special action. Applicants falling below a minimum high school grade point standard of 2.7 on a 4.0 scale and combined Scholastic Test scores of 800 *normally* shall not be admitted to the University. (The average Freshman today enters USC with a 3.4 high school grade point average and combined SAT scores of 1040.)

However, applicants falling below these minimums may, in certain cases be admitted by special action to regular standing providing such students are able to demonstrate, through admissions credentials, potential for academic success at USC. Applicants subject to special action consideration shall be closely evaluated, in addition to grades and SAT (or equivalent ACT) scores, on the basis of trends in past academic performance, writing samples, personal interviews, cultural factors, class rank, extracurricular involvement, intenseness of secondary school training, and statements of teachers and counselors regarding academic potential.

Circumstances justifying special action review will vary, but may include special talent, i.e., musical, dramatic, athletic, and scientific. All students admitted by special action are required to enter an appropriately designated support program designed to encourage academic success.

The Creighton Case

The story of Kevin Ross brought national attention and embarrassment to Creighton University in the early 1980s when it was discovered that he enrolled at a preparatory school in Chicago to improve his reading skills reported to be at a second-grade level.

Ross was recruited by a former basketball coach and admitted to Creighton under "special permission" to follow a curriculum which included the theory of ceramics among other courses of that type. His high school grade point average was a 2.0, but his American College Testing scores were far below the Creighton minimum standard.

After reports of the Chicago preparatory school admittance, Ross defended his earlier admission to Creighton on the grounds that it brings in about 500 "special" students from underprivileged areas each year. Officials at Creighton also indicated that only about 10 percent of the 500 are athletes, and many of the special students graduate with solid academic backgrounds.

The efforts to guide Ross's academic development did not succeed. After two years it was evident that he would not make it as a student at Creighton. He was encouraged to transfer but requested another chance. This was granted, but the third year was the last for Kevin Ross at Creighton.

The Creighton situation is noteworthy because it is a case where a single admission brought considerable adverse publicity to the institution. Ross enrolled in the Chicago preparatory school in 1982. On May 19, 1985, *The New York Times* documented the subsequent effects on Creighton in an article titled "How Creighton's Dreams of Basketball Glory Came Apart." The "paranoia" following the disclosure of the Ross case was described as being both "internal" and "external." Within, there was reluctance to admit future "borderline" students. Externally, the quality of education for athletes at Creighton was viewed with deep suspicion.

The Chris Washburn Case

Information contained in two issues of *Sports Illustrated* tells the story about the Chris Washburn case and its implications for the special admission of selected college athletes. Specific points from each issue follow.

November 26, 1984 (From "Dear Chris" by Bill Brubaker — pp. 120-136)
1. In 1980, when Chris Washburn was 15 years old and in the ninth grade at Hickory (North Carolina) High School, he received letters from Dean Smith, the head basketball coach at the University of North Carolina, and Denny Crum, head basketball coach at the University of Louisville. Washburn was a 6'9" center with promise as a basketball player. Before he finished ninth grade he had also received letters from Clemson, Duke, Cornell, Wake Forest, and several other schools.
2. By his senior year Washburn was 6'11" and weighed 250 pounds. He played his senior year at Laurenburg Institute in North Carolina following a junior year stint at Fork Union Military Academy in Virginia. Both are prep schools for basketball players. Brubaker describes Washburn during his senior year as being "the most sought-after high school basketball player in the Western World." (p. 123) He received more than 1,000 letters from at least 150 colleges.
3. Tom Abatemarco, assistant coach at North Carolina (N.C.) State, contacted Washburn more often than anyone else. Over a period of 31 months, Washburn received 278 messages from N.C. State, including 209 from Abatemarco.

4. Next to N.C. State, Maryland and Virginia Tech also contacted Washburn frequently. The choice was eventually narrowed to those three institutions, and apparently Washburn had been accepted for admission by all three.
5. When signing a letter of intent with N.C. State in November 1983, Washburn noted that the letters "showed me how much N.C. State really cared about me." (p. 123)

Feb. 18, 1985 (From "Scorecard" — p. 9)

1. Washburn was dropped from the N.C. State basketball team after being arrested on Dec. 21, 1984, for theft of an $800 stereo from the room of another student. On February 4, 1985, he pleaded guilty to the misdemeanor charges.
2. Court documents brought forth the situation surrounding the special admission of Washburn to N.C. State. He had a combined SAT score of 470, with an absolute minimum score of 200 on the verbal portion and a 270 on the mathematics section.
3. Although there is no minimum SAT requirement at N.C. State, as a special admission case, Washburn's score is compared with a 1,030 average for his freshman class. Some other random examples of average freshman, combined SAT scores are 910 at Idaho and 983 at Pepperdine. Mississippi has a minimum of 680 for in-state students.
4. Until 1972 the minimum for admission to N.C. State was governed by the Atlantic Coast Conference, which first required a 750 and later an 800 for all its scholarship athletes. That was declared unconstitutional following a suit by athletes.
5. "N.C. State officials hasten to point out that Washburn passed all four of his courses during the fall semester: composition and rhetoric, history of American sport, sociology of the family and public speaking. But one would have to be exceedingly naive to imagine that the school admitted him because it saw in him some hidden glimmer of academic promise rather than because of his basketball skills," said *Sports Illustrated.*

The Tulane Case

In March 1985, John (Hot Rod) Williams was one of five Tulane basketball players accused of involvement in a point-shaving scandal. He was also accused of accepting payments in violation of NCAA rules. Considerable adverse publicity followed, and the situation involving special admission of athletes was in the spotlight.

On Aug. 26, 1981 Williams took the Scholastic Aptitude Tests, which are used by many universities as one of several criteria for admission. "I couldn't even read the English part," he told a Tulane assistant coach. "Congratulations, you passed." *SI*'s sources indicated that Williams scored close to the 200 minimum on the verbal

(English) portion and approximately 270, 20 points above the minimum, on the math. Anything below 250 verbal ranks in the bottom 4% of the one million high school students who take the test annually; anything below 300 math is in the lowest 6%. The national average SAT score last year was 426 verbal and 471 math; at Tulane, the average student entering the College of Arts and Sciences scored 538 verbal, 583 math. (*Sports Illustrated*, April 22, 1985, p. 37)

Williams's academic record at Tulane reflected his status as a special admissions case. Among many course failures, he flunked the same psychology course three times and also failed beginning golf. His curriculum was replete with courses such as volleyball, weight training, archery, first aid, and driver education. With that, the cumulative grade point average was below 2.0.

Subsequent events, reactions, and revelations at Tulane are a vivid example of what can happen when an institution fails to maintain control of the athletic situations, including the admission of bona fide students. The head basketball coach and his two assistants were forced to resign. The athletic director also resigned. The faculty were indignant and voted to eliminate all sports from the university. The president countered with the decision to drop the basketball program.

Faculty were particularly disenchanted with "University College," one of 11 colleges and schools that make up the university. University College students included physical education majors, and approximately 80 percent of the football and basketball players were enrolled in that college. They had SAT scores about 200 points below the university average. Typical faculty reactions were: "Students in University College are both academically and socially alienated, misfits in their own institution." (p. 43) "The university got itself into a nightmare with intercollegiate athletics." (p. 38)

The Georgia Case

On May 6, 1985, *Sports Illustrated* also reported on the academic status of athletes at the University of Georgia. The report was based on an investigation by Sportswriter Jackie Crosby, who won a Pulitzer Prize for his work which appeared in the *Macon Telegraph and News* in September 1984.

Crosby's findings certainly bear out the fact that special admissions for athletes must be rampant at Georgia. For example, 75 percent of the university's athletes take remedial course work (compared to 1 percent of the student body as a whole). Graduation rates over the past 10 years were 61 percent for non-athletes, 4 percent for black basketball players, and 17 percent for black football players. However, it is interesting to note that the corresponding figures for white athletes were 63 percent for basketball and 50 percent for football. Apparently, special admissions were particularly a factor in admitting black athletes. (p. 9)

SAMPLE POLICY

Before proceeding with some of my own ideas concerning policies for the admission of college athletes, it seems appropriate to examine a sample policy. Exhibit 3-1 was submitted to the president of The Florida State University by the President's Committee on The Student Athlete on April 17, 1984.

Exhibit 3-1. Sample Policy

Admissions

Recommendation 2.1

The admissions policy for athletes at Florida State should permit twenty-five automatic exceptions per year. An exception is defined as a student who scores below the Florida Board of Regents' minimum of an 840 SAT score and a 2.0 high school grade point average (GPA). Fifteen exceptions will be for men, slightly fewer than in recent years, and ten exceptions for women, the average over the past four years. The greater number for men reflects the larger number of athletes recruited by the football program. Those twenty-five exceptions are considered necessary if Florida State is to continue to compete at Division I-A level in the 1980's. With these exceptions announced in advance, coaches can recruit knowing exactly how many exceptions they will have every year and will also know that when that number is exhausted they will have no more.

These twenty-five exceptions will be granted automatically and will not be subject to review by any University body. Twenty-five should be the maximum number, and we urge the administration not to grant any further athletic exceptions. More than twenty-five annual exceptions (125 over a five-year period) would strain the University's advising and academic support resources beyond capacity. Indeed the 125 will necessitate an increase and improvement in resources presently available.

The twenty-five annual exceptions will be awarded to the respective sports by the Athletic Department. The only directive to the department will be that fifteen exceptions must go to men and ten to women. The Athletic Department should prepare a yearly report of test scores and high school GPA's of newly-enrolled athletes to be sent to the vice president for academic affairs and to the Athletic Board.

Recommendation 2.2

Every athlete admitted to Florida State as an exception (below 840/2.0) should be mandated to participate in an enrichment program administered by the Office of the Dean of Undergraduate Studies. There will be no exceptions to this rule.

In addition to involving academic exceptions in an enrichment program, the Athletic Department and the University are urged to provide greater counseling and academic support for these young men and women. Finally, the department Board on the academic progress toward a degree of each athlete who was admitted as an exception.

("Student Athletes At Florida State University," Presented By The President's Committee on The Student Athlete, April 17, 1984, pp. 10-11).

CONCLUSION

Whether or not one agrees with the foregoing policy, it serves as a splendid example of what is meant by policy. In the introduction to this book, I set forth various characteristics of policies. All of these have been met in the Florida State recommendations: 1) they have wide ramifications, external as well as internal; 2) they are extended from a time perspective; 3) they are aimed at critical resources within the university; 4) they involve significant decision making; 5) and they are directed toward a dynamic social process in a changing environment.

While I fully understand the position taken at Florida State, this is not what I would recommend in terms of future policy development to guide the admissions of college athletes. The Florida State committee was forced to work within the structure of the way things are now in Division I-A athletic programs. Consequently, there is good reason to believe that the 125 "on-board" exceptions will not really meet the criteria for student-athletes in spite of any efforts at the enrichment program, as set forth in the second recommendation. One need only to review the case illustrations found earlier in this chapter to find support for that assumption.

The following are proposed as policy guidelines for future decisions regarding the admission of college athletes. Once again, I would stress that these are only guidelines. Definite policies will have to be formulated to meet the exigencies and structure of the given institution.

1. Any policy regarding the admission of college athletes should be aimed first and foremost at an honest, straightforward attempt to spell out the difference between a student-athlete and athlete-student. Please note the discussion of that distinction in the previous chapter. Policies for recruiting and admissions should be consistent on this point.

2. Those admitted as student-athletes would be admitted in accordance with the general requirements for admission to the institution. Some marginal cases might be admitted as special admissions, but there should be an attempt to delineate the marginal limits. In any case, there would not be any automatic exceptions for student-athletes. All special admissions would be determined only by the admissions office.

3. It is assumed that the bulk of the "exceptions" or special admissions cases will fall in the category of being an athlete-student. Such athletes would be admitted under the assumption and open recognition that most of their academic work is likely to be remedial. They would not be placed in the disadvantageous position of having to compete with fully qualified students in standard curricula. The nature of the remedial or "enrichment" pro-

gram needs to be carefully spelled out. Counseling and tutorial service are not sufficient for the special admissions cases.

4. Some athlete-students (exceptions) might reach the point where they qualify for regular curricular pursuits. It would be necessary to establish a definite policy to guide the qualification and transition and a reasonable time period for completion of degree work (likely more than five years after the date of admission).

5. Following the proposed structure of two NCAA divisions (see previous chapter conclusion), it is assumed that athletes-students would be restricted to Division I institutions. Of course, these programs would also have some student-athletes who meet the academic requirements. Any policy to establish a ratio between student-athletes and athlete-students would be an institutional determination.

6. As an NCAA policy, there would be a requirement for each institution to maintain and present complete academic profiles on all athletes. The profile would be primarily aimed at showing distinctions between the two categories of college athletes. At the same time, the data can be used to show progress within both groups.

Note: Additional updated information on athletics and higher education can be found in Chapter 20 on pages 313-315.

REFERENCES

"A Plan For Cleaning Up College Sports," "Special Report," *Sports Illustrated*, September 30, 1985, pp. 36-37.
Berkow, I. "How Creighton's Dreams Came Apart." *The New York Times*, Sunday, May 19, 1985, Section 5, pp. 1, 6.
Brubaker, B. "Dear Chris." *Sports Illustrated*, November 26, 1984, pp. 120-136.
Cady, E. *The Big Game: College Sports and American Life*. Knoxville: The University of Tennessee Press, 1978.
Klein, F. C. "Designated Villains." *The Wall Street Journal*, Wednesday, October 16, 1985, p. 28.
Looney, D. "All I Want Is To Be Happy." *Sports Illustrated*, April 22, 1985, pp. 36-43.
Manual of the National Collegiate Athletic Association, 1987-88. Article 3, Section 3, p. 17.
Novak, M. *The Joy of Sports*. New York: Basic Books, 1976.
"Scorecard." *Sports Illustrated*, February 18, 1985, p. 9.
"Scorecard." *Sports Illustrated*, May 6, 1985, p. 9.
"Student Athletes at Florida State University." Presented by the President's Committee on The Student Athlete. Unpublished report, April 17, 1984, pp. 10-11.

4

Athletes: Academic Standards For Freshman Eligibility

Prior to 1986, freshman eligibility to participate in intercollegiate athletics was determined by the simple provision: at the time of graduation from high school a student must have "presented an accumulative six, seven, or eight semesters' minimum grade-point average of 2.000 (based on a maximum of 4.000) as certified on the high school transcript or by official correspondence." (1985-86 *NCAA Manual*, Bylaw 5-1-(j), p. 92)*

There were no provisions for a high school core curriculum or an entrance examination standard as requirements for freshman eligibility. Some college administrators suggested that it was too easy for students to meet the standard, particularly if their college athletics aspirations were known to the high school faculty. Also, high schools vary considerably in their grading practices. An average of 2.0 at one school cannot necessarily be equated with a 2.0 at another school. Furthermore, there was speculation that some high school athletes avoided rigorous courses and took carefully selected courses to obtain the necessary overall GPA of 2.0.

PROPOSAL 48

Consequently, on January 11, 1983, delegates to the NCAA Convention in San Diego passed Proposal 48, an amendment to Bylaw 5-1-(j). The proposal was slated to take effect on August 1, 1986. Two additional requirements for freshman eligibility were added:

1. The accumulative, minimum grade-point average of 2.0 must be

*Reprinted from the 1985-86 NCAA Manual by permission of the National Collegiate Athletic Association. This material is subject to annual review and change.

in a core curriculum of at least 11 academic courses, including at least three years in English, two years in mathematics, two years in social science, and two years in natural or physical science (including at least one laboratory class, if offered by the high school).

2. The athlete must have a combined score of at least 700 on the SAT verbal and math sections or a 15 composite score on the ACT. If a freshman failed to meet both requirements, he or she would be ineligible for competition and practice at a Division I institution during the freshman year. If the student demonstrated satisfactory progress toward a degree during the freshman year, he or she would be eligible for competition in the sophomore year. However, if the ineligible freshman accepted an athletic grant-in-aid for the freshman year, he or she would lose one year of collegiate athletic eligibility.

Academic standards outlined in Proposal 48 (also called Rule 48 and Proposition 48) attempted to address the limitations inherent in the existing policy. The core curriculum requirement would provide an athlete's exposure to a solid base of academic work. The test score requirement would guarantee some uniformity in standards and allow institutions to better distinguish among students who report similar GPAs from different high schools. Superficially at least, it hardly seemed unreasonable to require athletes to achieve test scores that were well below the national average. However, subsequent debate would show that not everyone agreed on that point.

Proposal 48 was initiated by an ad hoc committee of the American Council on Education (ACE) and passed by the NCAA for several reasons. It was a signal to the high schools that athletes with college Division I potential should pay close attention to their academic preparation if they anticipated having maximum eligibility while in college. It was designed to give these athletes a better chance of obtaining college degrees and to end the exploitation of talented athletes (primarily blacks) that had been commonplace at many Division I institutions.

Bartell et al. (1984) reported on a study of athletes who enrolled in Division I institutions in 1977. Among approximately 1,400 black males, only 14 percent graduated after four years in college and only 31 percent after six years of matriculation. By contrast, the corresponding figures for some 4,000 white males were 27 percent and 53 percent. Such data certainly supports the need for Proposal 48 or similar requirements.

Although Proposal 48 was adopted as a partial solution to a legitimate problem, it was the focus of extensive controversy before and after its approval. At the San Diego convention, Pennsylvania State University Football Coach Joe Paterno was one of the more vocal advocates of the proposal: "We have to challenge the athlete in the classroom as well as the field. We have raped the Black athlete, as I have said, and it is time to give him everything we have to offer in college. By upgrading high school requirements, we prepare him a bit better for our challenge in the college classroom." (*The New York Times*, Jan. 16, 1983, p. 45)

Opponents objected not only to the test score standard but also to the manner in which the proposal was drafted and the negative effects it would have on certain minority groups. The most vehement opposition was spearheaded by the presidents of predominantly black institutions, who believed that the proposal was inherently discriminatory. Jesse Stone, Jr., president of Southern University, described the proposal as "patently racist."

There was outrage over the glaring lack of black representation on the ACE ad hoc committee that initiated the proposal for presentation at the 1983 NCAA Convention. After vehement objection by presidents of predominantly black colleges, a black was finally appointed. However, the appointment of Luona I. Mishoe, president of Delaware State College, to the ad hoc committee of the ACE came only one week prior to the start of the 1983 NCAA convention. Black educators viewed the appointment as "cosmetic."

Proposal 48 also generated some debate regarding the specific standards or cut-off points for eligibility. For example, how did the committee arrive at the figures 700, 15, and 11? Could not the minimum test score requirement just as well be 650 or 800? Why not require 10 or 12 core courses? The standards seemed to be fairly arbitrary. Studies to determine the effect of such standards on athletic eligibility were not conducted until after the proposal was adopted by the NCAA.

Perhaps the most severe point of criticism was that Proposal 48 failed to take into account the vast differences among colleges and universities across the nation. Even within NCAA's Division I, these differences are readily apparent. Institutions range from relatively small universities with open admissions to large comprehensive research universities with highly selective admissions. In between, various combinations and deviations can be noted. Differences can also be identified with respect to goals or objectives, clientele, the geographic service area, and variety of programs. Critics questioned how such differences could reasonably be aggregated in a generalized standard or formula for determining freshman eligibility for athletic participation. Beyond that, Frederick Humphries, president of Tennessee State University, identified the real source of opposition: "Proposal 48 would have minimum impact on those institutions who generated it to clean up athletics and who have produced academic credibility problems, and maximum impact on those institutions in Division I, especially the historically Black colleges, who have a distinguished record of educating marginal students in higher education." (*The New York Times*, Jan. 16, 1983, p. 25)

Following the adoption of Proposal 48, 16 largely black colleges, all members of Division I, threatened to remove themselves from both the NCAA and the ACE if the new requirements were put into effect.

In response to the opposition to Proposal 48, the NCAA's Special Committee on Academic Research commissioned a study which was conducted by Advanced Technology, Inc., of Reston, Virginia. Results released on August 30, 1984, supported what the dissenters had been saying: the use of standardized test scores to determine athletic eligibility would have a disproportionate and quite negative impact on the eligibility status of black athletes. The study involved 206 Division I institutions (75 percent of the membership) and covered 16,000 male and female athletes who enrolled in 1977 and 1982 with full or partial grants-in-aid. Analysis showed that the application of the test score criterion alone would have disqualified a large percentage of black student-athletes who eventually graduated. For example, if the test score criterion had been applied to the 1977 freshmen student athletes, only 31 percent of black males and 41 percent of black females would have been eligible for intercollegiate athletics, compared to 86 percent of all white athletes (Table 4-1).

The Advanced Technology study also found that Proposal 48 would have had a significant impact on the eligibility of the 1977 freshmen scholarship athletes, based only on the core curriculum requirements. Only 35 percent of black males and 38 percent of black females met the core curriculum standards outlined in the proposal, contrasted with 62 percent of white males and 66 percent of white females. Yet, there was little opposition to the core curriculum component. It was not viewed as discriminatory; in fact, it was seen by black and white educators alike as a means to enhance the athletes' academic preparedness for college. Furthermore, the high schools would have had three years to meet the new curricular standards for prospective college athletes.

Other findings in the study are also worthy of note. 1) There was some improvement on standardized test scores of black student-athletes between 1977 and 1982. 2) Division 1-A graduation rates were slightly lower than those in Divisions I-AA and I-AAA. 3) Percentages of students who left an institution in bad standing between 1977 and 1982 were relatively similar for white males, white females, and black females, but the percentage for black males was much higher. 4) Although there was a discrepancy between the performance of white females and black females, it was a much smaller gap than that between white males and black males. 5) The sample of Division II student-athletes, while not representing a large enough group in some categories to be meaningful, resulted in figures comparable to those in Division I. 6) Those who took a core curriculum were much more likely to achieve the minimum test score, but the discrepancy between black and white males continued — 94 percent of white males with the core experience achieved the minimum test score, while 36 percent of black males did so.

Table 4-2 provides documentation of the basis for concern among the black presidents. The figures cited are based on information com-

TABLE 4-1. Effects of Applying the Test Score Criterion (SAT=700 OR ACT=15) to 1977 Freshman Student-Athletes

Race	Sex	N	(1) Percentage who did qualify	(2) Percentage of qualifiers who graduated or were continuing	(3) Prediction ratio graduated or continuing	(4) Percentage who did not qualify	(5) Percentage of non-qualifiers who left in bad standing	(6) Prediction ratio leaving in bad standing	(7) Percentage of graduated or continuing students who were non-qualifiers
Black	Male	1070	31	51	1.46	69	41	1.13	54
	Female	94	41	77	1.22	59	24	1.70	49
White	Male	3633	86	58	1.07	14	33	2.04	8
	Female	1103	86	67	1.06	14	18	2.32	9

TABLE 4-2. Effects of Applying Various Eligibility Standards to 1977 Freshman Grant-in-Aid Student-Athletes Attending Historically Black Colleges and Universities

Sex	Eligibility standard	(1) Percentage who did qualify	(2) Percentage of qualifiers who graduated or were continuing	(3) Prediction ratio graduated or continuing	(4) Percentage who did not qualify	(5) Percentage of non-qualifiers who left in bad standing	(6) Prediction ratio leaving in bad standing	(7) Percentage of graduated or continuing students who were non-qualifiers
Male	SAT=700 or ACT=15	20	50	1.44	80	31	1.06	71
	Core Curriculum	32	45	1.42	68	39	1.07	55
	Bylaw 5-1-(j)	12	64	1.79	88	37	1.10	79
	Core or 700/15	43	52	1.48	57	38	1.13	36
	Core, Test if needed	33	52	1.45	67	34	1.02	52
Female	SAT=700 or ACT=15	10	50	0.95	90	21	1.10	91
	Core Curriculum	24	75	1.42	76	31	1.31	67
	Bylaw 5-1-(j)	0	-	-	100	33	1.00	100
	Core or 700/15	22	100	2.25	78	43	1.28	50
	Core, Test if needed	22	100	2.25	78	43	1.28	50

piled by Advanced Technology in its study. Eight of the 15 historically black institutions were included in the study. One notes that if the Proposal 48 standards were in effect in 1977, only 12 percent of the male student-athletes and 0% of the female student-athletes would be eligible for athletic competition in their freshman year. Perhaps even more significantly, among the non-qualifiers, 79 percent of the males and 100 percent of the females either graduated or were continuing students. One has to wonder whether the academic standards in Proposal 48 would be valid predictors of success at an historically black institution.

Note: Additional updated information on Proposal 48 and related topics can be found in Chapter 20 on pages 319 to 321.

Case Study

Grambling State University is a state-supported institution which grants two-year associate's and four-year bachelor's degrees to its undergraduates. Founded in 1901, the university is located in Grambling, Louisiana, a town of about 5,000. The undergraduate student body at Grambling numbers slightly above 4,000. Of these, 99 percent are black, 79 percent are residents of Louisiana, and 98 percent receive some form of financial aid.

Grambling is well-known for its athletic program. A member of the Southwestern Athletic Conference, the NAIA, and the NCAA (Division I), Grambling offers nine sports for men (football, basketball, track, baseball, tennis, golf, swimming, cross country, and bowling) and five for women (basketball, track, cross country, softball, and volleyball).

Like most other Division I institutions, Grambling awards athletic grants-in-aid to gifted athletes. However, unlike many other Division I institutions, Grambling does not need to admit athletes as "special action cases." With its policy of open admissions, Grambling does not have to identify exceptions for athletes or other students. In fact, the academic credentials of freshmen student-athletes on scholarship are typical of the academic profile of the freshman class as a whole:

Mean Academic Credentials of 1984-85 Freshmen at Grambling

	All Freshman	Scholarship Athletes (n=38)
High School GPA	2.53	2.50
Composite ACT	10.00	9.60

Like most of the predominantly black schools, Grambling has historically offered opportunities to socially and economically disadvantaged students. The policy of open admissions for state residents is consistent with that stance. The only requirement for in-state applicants is graduation from an accredited high school prior to enrolling in the university. There are no provisions for a minimum high school grade point average, core curriculum, or ACT score. Although incoming freshmen are required to take the ACT test, scores are used only as an aid for placement and counseling.

As a result of Grambling's mission to educate students from disadvantaged backgrounds, it is not surprising that its students, on the whole, are less well prepared than the "average" college student. This is confirmed by the *Profile Research Service Report* of freshmen entering Grambling in the fall of 1984:

Comparison of Mean ACT Scores for Freshmen, 1984-85

	English	Math	Soc. St.	Nat. Sci.	Composite
National Mean	18.1	17.3	17.7	21.1	18.7
Grambling Mean	10.6	8.1	8.3	12.5	10.0

Comparison of Mean High School Grades for Freshmen, 1984-85

	English	Math	Soc. St.	Nat. Sci.	Composite
National Mean	3.02	2.77	3.12	2.95	2.96
Grambling Mean	2.56	2.40	2.10	2.58	2.53

Recognizing the wide variety in educational backgrounds and academic needs resulting from open admissions, Grambling developed an institutional remedial program known as Developmental Education. Supported by $500,000 in state funds per year, Developmental Education is offered as a formal program through the College of Basic Studies and Services. The purpose of this program is to provide underprepared students with the basic skills necessary for academic success at Grambling through a combination of small classes, individualized attention, special counseling, and tutoring. A student's placement in basic courses is determined by a review of both his or her ACT scores and high school grades. An estimated 80 to 90 percent of all Grambling students are required to take some form of Developmental Education, although many take only one or two courses.

This institution is quite unlike a majority of Division I institutions in terms of its basic mission, objectives, student body, and program service mix. Relatively few well known Division I schools have a policy of open admissions and a program of remedial education. However, Grambling has been very successful in its mission of educating the disadvantaged and underprepared student, as well as the scholar.

In light of this situation, it is not surprising that Grambling was one of the leaders in voicing opposition to Proposal 48. Even before the proposal was adopted, Grambling President Joseph Johnson presented objections shared by the predominantly black colleges. However, the target for criticism was the test score requirement. President Johnson supported the core curriculum provision. Johnson worked with a special NCAA committee charged with readdressing Proposal 48 to review suggested modifications and suggest a viable course of action.

After Proposal 48 was approved by the 1983 NCAA convention, Grambling continued to represent the interests of the black colleges in further study by the NCAA. Harold J. Lundy, executive director of planning and institutional research at Grambling, commissioned studies and presented findings that revealed the impact that the new eligibility rules would have on freshman athletes at Grambling. Lundy made presentations to representatives of both the NCAA and the National Organization for Equal Opportunity in Education (NAFEO), an organization composed of 114 predominantly black colleges and universities. He was seeking possible modifications to Proposal 48 that would better serve the interests and needs of the black colleges.

Data presented by Lundy confirmed that freshmen student-athletes at Grambling would be severely affected, should Proposal 48 be implemented in its original form. The vast majority of athletes would be declared ineligible to practice or compete in intercollegiate athletics during their freshman year. Tables 4-3 to 4-5 provide frequency distributions of thirty-eight 1984-85 freshmen on athletic scholarship at Grambling by high school grade point average, ACT scores, and number of core courses completed. Table 4-6 reveals the number of 1984-85 freshmen scholarship athletes at Grambling who would have been ineligible under the academic requirements outlined in Proposal 48.

With the high school grade point average in 11 core courses as the sole requirement for eligibility, 13.3 percent of the 38 students would be ineligible. By applying only the test score standard of 15 on the ACT, the percentage declared ineligible would rise sharply to 83.4 percent. When both elements are combined (Proposal 48), 90 percent of the 38 freshman athletes would be ineligible to practice or compete. Furthermore, since freshman student-athletes on athletic scholarship at Grambling are representative of the freshman class as a whole, it is reasonable to assume that 90 percent of all freshmen at Grambling would be ineligible for freshman year participation in intercollegiate athletics. The impact on the athletic program would be significant in terms of team depth and development of talent. Survey of 1984-85 freshmen at Grambling indicated that 15 percent hoped to play varsity athletics in their freshman year. That leads to a projection of about 150 potential, freshman athletes, 90 percent of whom might be ineligible under Proposal 48.

Quantitative evidence in the Grambling case is both valid and objective. National ACT averages were reported by the ACT service. High school grades, core courses, and ACT scores of Grambling students were verified by official high school transcripts.

Taken as a whole, the evidence points to an undeniable and pressing problem. Eligibility standards set forth in Proposal 48 would eliminate nearly all freshman participation in intercollegiate athletics at Grambling

TABLE 4-3. Frequency Distribution of Freshmen on Athletic Scholarship by High School Grade Point Average

GPA	f	Percentages
2.00 or below	1	2.63
2.01 – 2.50	16	42.10
2.51 – 3.00	13	34.21
3.01 – 3.50	5	13.16
3.51 – 4.00	3	7.90

TABLE 4-4. Frequency Distribution of Scholarship Athletes by ACT Score

ACT Score	f	Percentages
5 – 7	4	26.67
8 – 10	6	40.00
11 – 13	2	13.33
14 – 16	3	20.00

TABLE 4-5. Frequency Distribution of Scholarship Athletes by Number of Core Courses Taken

Number of Courses	f	Percentages
8 – 10	1	2.63
11 – 13	8	21.05
14 – 16	21	55.26
17 – 19	7	18.42
20 – 22	1	2.63

TABLE 4-6. Application of Proposal 48 to the 1984–85 Freshmen on Athletic Scholarship at Grambling

Component	% Eligible	% Ineligible
core courses only	86.67	13.33
test score only	16.67	83.37
Proposal 48	10.00	90.00

Tables 4-3 to 4-6 are taken from: Lundy, Harold J., *Verification of Actual vs. Self-Reported Data Pertaining To GSU's Freshmen on Athletic Scholarship.*

despite the fact that Grambling athletes have academic credentials similar to their non-athlete peers. Clearly, Proposal 48 created national academic standards for athletic eligibility that failed to take into account the diverse objectives and clientele of all Division I institutions. Furthermore, the test score requirement appears to be a measure of academic ability that is culturally and racially biased against blacks and other minorities.

What could be done about this situation? What alternatives were available to Grambling and similar institutions? In a presentation at the Ninth National Conference on Blacks in Higher Education, Lundy (1984) outlined three possibilities. 1) Black colleges could reconsider the exemption to the rule, as originally offered by the NCAA. This offer had been immediately rejected by the black college presidents as being "unnecessary, condescending and racist" and implying "that black schools were inferior institutions with lower academic standards." (p. 3) However, Lundy pointed out that the exemption might be reconsidered if the NCAA refused to modify the standards of Proposal 48. 2) Grambling could initiate an equal protection lawsuit against the NCAA on behalf of Grambling's black athletes. However, this option would involve significant cost, and the ensuing legal battle would presumably drag on for a number of years. In addition, Lundy noted that given the way the "Burger Court has handled recent court cases dealing with equal protection and purposeful racial discrimination . . . it will be no easy task to prove that Rule 48 has invidious discriminatory purpose." (p. 3) 3) Grambling could continue to work in cooperation with the NCAA and present alternative modifications to Proposal 48 to alleviate the discriminatory and disproportionate impact on black athletes. This course of action was eventually followed.

A fourth option might be to withdraw membership from the NCAA if the proposal was put into effect as stated. This possibility first surfaced when Proposal 48 was adopted at the 1983 NCAA Convention. However, due to the heavy costs associated with this plan of action (decreased athletic competition, loss of prestige, etc.), this option should be used only as a last resort.

Further Consideration

When the results of the Advanced Technology study were released, the NCAA announced that alternatives to Proposal 48 (Bylaw 5-1-(j)) were suggested by the Special Committee on Academic Research:

> First, the legislation might be altered to permit a student-athlete to gain eligibility as a freshman if either of the criteria were met successfully by the student. Labeled the 'or' concept, its primary deficiency is that it would permit an individual to gain eligibility without taking the core curriculum.
>
> Another alternative is to require all students to pass the core curriculum, and those individuals who do not establish a 2.000 grade

point then could qualify for freshman eligibility by achieving the minimum test score.

An index score also could be developed that would weigh the core curriculum and the test score separately before adding them together to establish a minimum qualifying standard for eligibility. (*The NCAA News*, Aug. 29, 1984, p. 16)

These alternatives were considered by the NCAA Council. At an October 1984, meeting, the Council voted to support a delay in the application of the test score requirement of Proposal 48. According to the Council's proposal, the core curriculum requirement would remain, but the standardized test score requirement would be delayed until 1988. During the two-year delay, those freshmen who did not maintain a 2.0 high school GPA in the core curriculum would still be eligible to compete if they met the standardized test score requirement.

Ted C. Tow, the NCAA's assistant executive director, announced that this proposal would be submitted for consideration by the Presidents' Commission of the NCAA. At the same time the Commission had developed its own proposed modification of Proposal 48: an "index score," which would allow athletes to balance poor performance in one category with a better performance in the other.

Other possible modifications of Proposal 48 were discussed by ACE's committee on Division I athletics. These included use of the core curriculum requirement only, and allowing combinations of grades and test scores. It is clear that there was a lack of complete consensus at that point. However, there was general agreement that the core curriculum requirement should not be changed and was much more significant than test scores in determining preparedness for college work. In October 1984, NCAA officials expressed hope that consensus could be reached among the various organizations and committees in time for a vote on a modified legislation proposal at the 1985 NCAA annual convention in January.

However, in November the NCAA announced that Proposal 48 would not be changed at the annual convention. Rather, the NCAA Council and the NCAA Presidents' Commission would cosponsor a resolution at the convention to conduct a cooperative study of possible modifications in Proposal 48. Plans called for a revised proposal to be announced to the NCAA membership no later than October 15, 1985, and to be presented at the January 1986 NCAA convention. November 1 was the deadline for submitting proposed legislation. Both the Council and the Commission agreed that more time was needed for further cooperative study. The delay also had the support of other key organizations.

Robert H. Atwell, acting president of the American Council on Education, which was instrumental in developing Proposition 48, said last week that delaying a decision on the rules 'is a very good and promising outcome. I'd be very hopeful that in the next year the groups that are concerned will be able to work out a solution that would combine grades and test scores into some kind of a predictor and meet some of the objections to Proposition 48 as it is now written.'

One of those groups that has voiced concern over the rule is the National Association for Equal Opportunity in Higher Education, an organization of 114 historically black colleges and universities.

Samuel L. Myers, president of the association, said last week that he concurred with the proposal to delay action on Proposition 48. 'We are pleased, first of all, with the various groups that have been sensitive to the broad impact of Proposition 48 on minorities,' he said. 'We are pleased they now want to study, in a deliberate way, the impact of a whole series of things before adopting something. This is the way to meet the objectives all of us have, to protect the athletes and assure that the chances of their getting an education are enhanced." (*The Chronicle of Higher Education*, Nov. 14, 1984, pp. 1, 31)

The resolution was presented as Proposal 25 and approved at the 1985 convention in Nashville. As a result of the passage, the Special NCAA Academic Standards Committee began its study in April 1985. The recommendation of that committee eventually resulted in Proposal 16.

PROPOSAL 16

Proposal 16 was presented by the NCAA Council and the NCAA Presidents' Commission and passed by Division I delegates to the 80th NCAA Convention in New Orleans on January 13, 1986, by a roll-call vote of 207-94, with four abstentions. Essentially, the legislation provided for a modification of Bylaw 5-1-(j) (Proposal 48) to permit indexing of grade-point averages for initial eligibility over the first two years after implementation:

For those freshmen entering subsequent to August 1, 1986, and prior to August 1, 1987:

GPA	SAT	ACT
2.200 - above	660	13
2.100 - 2.199	680	14
2.000 - 2.099	700	15
1.900 - 1.999	720	16
1.800 - 1.899	740	17

Fo those freshmen entering subsequent to August 1, 1987, and prior to August 1, 1988:

GPA	SAT	ACT
2.100 - above	680	14
2.000 - 2.099	700	15
1.900 - 1.999	720	16

Proposal 48's original standards would apply to a freshman who enters the college or university after August 1, 1988. Thus, the policy as originally adopted in 1983 would go into full effect for 1988-89.

Although Proposal 16 was eventually passed by a convincing margin, controversy surrounding Bylaw 5-1-(j) continued before, during, and after the convention. The consensus seemed to be that there were three basic positions within the Division I NCAA membership; one that would prefer not to have either 48 or 16, or at least not the test score provision; one that would have put 48 in effect on August 1, 1986; and one that supported Proposal 16.

Once again, President Johnson of Grambling State University led the opposition to the NCAA proposal. Statements by Johnson on the eve of the convention reflect the feelings of black educators who made one more effort to eliminate the test score requirement.

. . . "It's a misuse, and abuse of testing by the members of the NCAA," said Johnson, who will argue for two alternate amendments that would eliminate college board tests as a predictor of academic success altogether. . . .

Johnson said he believes the academic legislation is "being used by a lot of phony academicians at this particular time to come up with a quick fix to something they should've been doing for the last 10 years." . . .

"That's the heart of a sound educational background," Johnson said of the core curriculum. "We also believe in the 2.0 grade point average, but the tests themselves should be to find out where these kids' weaknesses are, and (allow the institutions to) channel them into areas of tutorial programs (where they belong). If they (major schools) had done this before, we wouldn't even have to have a Proposition 48. That's the solution to the problem." (*The Times-Picayune*, Sunday, Jan. 12, 1986, p. E-3)

Johnson and other members of the Southwestern Athletic Conference presented two other amendments, which were considered before Proposal 16. Proposal 14 would eliminate the minimum SAT or ACT score requirement for freshman eligibility at a Division I member institution. It was defeated 248 to 47. Proposal 15 would have approved the use of standardized tests only for diagnostic or institutional placements purposes. It was defeated 233-66. After the rejection of "14" and "15" and the passage of "16," Johnson and other black educators continued to voice their strong disapproval over the actions taken by the NCAA.

"Misguided and misdirected members of this organization," said Dr. Joseph B. Johnson, president of Grambling State University, "embarrassed by revelations of academic problems, are reverting back to slave days," after controversial Proposal 16 passed overwhelmingly on the opening day of the NCAA's 80th Convention.

"They built their programs on the backs of black athletes," said Johnson, "and now say, 'We don't need them anymore. There are too many blacks on our campuses.'" . . .

Nelson Townsend, athletic director at Delaware State, hotly stated after the vote, "one cannot legislate integrity, nor morality. That does not come from SAT scores. That's been the argument, but we're (predominantly black schools) not the ones whose integrity's been questioned. We don't get the Marcus Duprees (the superstar prospects) anyway."

The black college bloc may consider either leaving Division I-AA for a lower division where the test issue is not an academic criteria, or it may leave the NCAA altogether. (*The Times-Picayune*, Tuesday, Jan. 14, 1986, pp. B 1-2)

Johnson was also chairman of the athletics committee of the National Association for Equal Opportunity in Higher Education. In an interview after the passage of Proposal 16, he stated that his group would be looking toward some kind of legal challenge before August (the implementation date), perhaps some kind of injunction. He also indicated that the black colleges would be mounting some form of national campaign against the new academic standards by enlisting the aid of prominent civil rights leaders.

In the meantime, the NCAA presented research findings which indicate that the changes under Proposal 16 would assist student-athletes in attaining athletic eligibility, as contrasted with the original provisions of Proposal 48. The findings were based on the populations designated for the major research project in 1983-84, involving freshmen in 1977 and 1982. "Black male student-athletes (in 1977 and in 1982) show a gain of seven to 10 percent, and black female athletes could register a five to 12 percent increase with the amended requirements. White males show an improvement of *four* to *seven* percent, and white females show an improvement of *two* to *seven* percent." (*The NCAA News,* Jan. 29, 1986, p. 1) Tables 4-7 and 4-8 show details of projected changes under the revised legislation.

The administrative committee of the NCAA also issued a compilation of interpretations related to the applications of Bylaw 5-1-(j), after the

January 1986 revision, to assist Division I member institutions and high schools in following the guidelines for any prospective student-athlete entering a Division I institution in the fall of 1986. The interpretations (Exhibit 4-1) are included to demonstrate the detail in determining athletic eligibility.

TABLE 4-7. Percent of student-athletes* who would have been eligible under Bylaw 5-1-(j) as originally proposed and as amended in 1986

	Percent qualifying			
Population	B 5-1(j) 1977	(original) 1982	B 5-1(j) 1977	(original) 1982
SAT				
Black males	43	51	52	59
Black females	58	61	63	67
White males	89	89	94	93
White females	94	94	98	96
ACT				
Black males	21	28	27	38
Black females	47	37	59	46
White males	69	74	75	81
White females	69	82	76	89

*All student-athletes passed minimum of 11 courses in core curriculum and met other criteria for GPA and test score as specified in the regulations.

TABLE 4-8. Comparison of rates of graduation/persistence of student-athletes*, freshman class of 1977, under Bylaw 5-1-(j) and as proposed in Amendment No. 16

Black Males				
Percent eligible	43	52	21	27
Percent of those eligible who graduated/persisted	53	52	56	59
Percent ineligible	57	48	79	73
Percent of those ineligible who graduated/persisted	34	32	32	29
White Males				
Percent eligible	89	94	69	75
Percent of those eligible who graduated/persisted	64	63	56	53
Percent ineligible	11	06	31	25
Percent of those ineligible who graduated/persisted	31	25	34	36

*All student-athletes passed minimum of 11 courses in core curriculum and met other criteria for GPA and test score as specified in the regulations.

EXHIBIT 4-1. Bylaw 5-1-(j) Interpretations

The provisions of Bylaw 5-1-(j), as amended at the 1986 NCAA Convention, become effective August 1, 1986, and will be applicable to the 1986 high school graduating class. This column will provide member institutions a compilation of NCAA Council and Administrative Committee interpretations regarding the administration of the rule to assist in the recruitment of prospective student-athletes for enrollment in the fall of 1986. [Note: These interpretations are more extensive than, but do not contradict, those set forth in the Legislative Assistance column published in the September 23, 1985, edition of the News.]

Any entering freshman whose initial full-time attendance in a regular term occurs subsequent to August 1, 1986, must meet the core-curriculum and test-score provisions of Bylaw 5-1-(j), as amended to include the index table set forth in 1986 Convention Proposal No. 16. It should be noted that attendance in an institution's summer school will not be considered attendance prior to August 1, 1986.

The NCAA Council has approved a standardized reporting form to be completed by the high school principal that must be used in administering Bylaw 5-1-(j). Copies of this form were mailed to the principals of high schools throughout the United States, as well as to Division I member institutions, in October 1985. An additional mailing to high school principals will be made this month to emphasize the directions for completing the form appropriately. The primary stipulation in this regard is to utilize the form only for purposes of indicating the student's best grades in the 11 units necessary to meet the distribution requirements of the core curriculum. It is not necessary to list other core-curriculum courses on the form because only 11 units will be utilized to calculate the core-curriculum grade-point average.

The NCAA Administrative Committee asks each member institution to note that in accordance with the provisions of Case No. 173 (page 305 of the 1985-86 NCAA Manual), it is the responsibility of the member institution to determine whether a high school transcript is valid for purposes of applying appropriate NCAA legislation to the eligibility of the student-athlete. A member institution is obligated to administer its athletics program in accordance with the Association's constitution and bylaws, and this would include determining whether the information on which the administration of this legislation is based is valid.

In administering the provisions of Bylaw 5-1-(j), the following interpretations have been approved by the NCAA Council or Administrative Committee and serve as official interpretations of Bylaw 5-1-(j):

Definition of core course

For the purposes of meeting the core-curriculum requirement, a "core course" is defined as a recognized academic course designed to prepare a student for college-level work (as opposed to a vocational or personal-services course).

Courses that are taught at a level below the high school's regular academic instruction level (e.g., remedial, special education or compensatory) shall not be considered as core courses regardless of course content.

English

Core courses in English shall include instructional elements in the following areas: grammar, vocabulary development, composition, literature, analytical reading or oral communication.

EXHIBIT 4-1 *(con't.)*

Mathematics

Core courses in mathematics shall include instructional elements in algebra, geometry, trigonometry, statistics or calculus.

Social sciences

Core courses in social sciences shall include instructional elements in history, social studies, economics, geography, psychology, sociology, government, political science or anthropology.

Natural or physical science

Core courses in natural or physical science shall include instructional elements in biology, chemistry, physics, environmental science, physical science or earth science. In addition, students must complete at least one laboratory class, if offered by the high school.

Additional core courses

The two remaining years of additional academic credit must be from courses attempted in English, mathematics, social science, natural or physical science, foreign language, computer science, philosophy, nondoctrinal religion (e.g., comparative religion).

Computation of grade-point average

Each grade earned in a core course must be converted to a 4.000 scale (A-4, B-3, C-2, D-1, F-0). Pluses or minuses within a grade level shall not receive greater or lesser quality points. A school's normal practice of weighing honors or advanced courses may be used to compute the quality points awarded in those courses and the accumulative grade-point average.

Core-curriculum interpretations

A. The decision as to whether a particular course qualifies as a core course will be made by the principal of a high school from which a student graduated and must be properly verified by the member institution in accordance with Case No. 173 (page 305, 1985-86 NCAA Manual).

B. To encourage a student to take as many academic courses as possible, the core-curriculum grade-point average will be calculated using the student's 11 best grades from courses that meet the distribution requirements of the core curriculum.

C. A "unit" should represent approximately 180 classroom instructional hours.

D. Only courses completed in grades 9-12 may be considered core courses.

E. All core courses used to establish a student's grade-point average must be completed within the student's first eight semesters of high school (grades 9-12) in accordance with Case No. 343 (page 355, 1985-86 NCAA Manual).

F. A student may count a repeated course only once and must present 11 different (nonrepeated) courses in meeting the core-curriculum requirement. Further, the student may use the best grade in the repeated course in calculation of the grade-point average in the core curriculum.

G. Foreign student-athletes who meet the guidelines set forth in the NCAA Guide to International Academic Standards for Athletics Eligibility will satisfy the core-curriculum requirement.

EXHIBIT 4-1 *(con't.)*

H. Independent-study courses or correspondence courses may not be used to satisfy core-curriculum requirements. A college course may be utilized for this purpose if accepted by the high school and placed on the student's high school transcript prior to completion of the student's first eight semesters of high school (grades 9-12).

I. A one-year course that is spread over two years (e.g., elementary algebra) shall be considered as one course.

Test-score interpretations

A. The SAT or ACT used to establish eligibility must be taken by the student prior to initial enrollment in a collegiate institution; must be taken under normal testing conditions on a national testing date [i.e., no residual (campus) testing], and, while the test may be taken on any number of occasions, only the best scores from any single testing date may be utilized.

B. All students, foreign and domestic, must take a required test.

C. The GED test may be used for high school graduation but may not be substituted for the SAT or ACT. Further, the GED students must satisfactorily complete the core curriculum and the use of the GED must be in accordance with Case No. 337 (pages 353-354, 1985-86 NCAA Manual).

D. The Academic Requirements Committee may approve exceptions for SAT or ACT scores from special untimed tests administered for legally defined handicapped students.

Practice activities

A student-athlete who is only a partial qualifier under this legislation (i.e., one who earns an overall grade-point average of 2.000 in high school and graduates but does not meet the core-curriculum grade-point average or test-score requirement) may receive athletically related financial aid, but not practice or participate, during the first year of residency at the certifying member institution. Under such circumstances, the student-athlete may not participate in any manner (e.g., as a team manager) in any sports-related team practice activity during the first year of residency and loses one year of eligibility.

This material was provided by the NCAA legislative services department as an aid to member institutions. If an institution has a question that it would like to have answered in this column, the question should be directed to William B. Hunt, assistant executive director, at the NCAA national office. (From *The NCAA News*, Feb. 1986, Volume 24, Number 8, p. 16.)

Immediate Effect

There is no doubt about the fact that the effect of the legislation was felt immediately. During the last week of July 1986, *The New York Times* conducted a telephone survey with the athletic departments at 276 of the 286 NCAA institutions who compete in Division I football and/or basketball. The report showed that 205 football and basketball players failed to qualify according to the new academic standards. The group included some of the more highly recruited high school athletes in the United States. All of the athletes were offered scholarships to compete in 1986-87, but now alternate plans had to be made.

The colleges and athletes chose from a wide variety of options. In some cases, the college withdrew the scholarship offer because the athlete failed to get the minimum grade point average. However, in most cases the ineligibility resulted from the test scores and not the grade point average. Some of these athletes accepted the scholarship offer, and by sitting out their freshman year would be eligible for the three years of competition instead of four. Others chose to attend a junior college for one or two years. Still others agreed to pay their own way the first year, leaving them with four years of competition and a scholarship thereafter. Table 4-9 summarizes the immediate effect in Division 1 football and basketball.

CONCLUSION: THOUGHTS ABOUT POLICY IN THIS AREA

Whether Proposals 48 and 16 represent steps in the right direction remains to be seen. Nevertheless, there seems to be little doubt about merit in the intent of the legislation. That intent is understood to be setting standards that will meet the objective of obtaining a more qualified pool of freshman student-athletes with better chances for academic success in college.

In terms of a policy aimed at achieving that objective, there is also little room for debate about the desirability of a standard requiring a minimum grade point average in a core curriculum. It is not surprising that there was little controversy about that component in the discussions about Proposals 48 and 16. As a matter of fact, the core curriculum feature seems to represent the most positive action in this area to date.

The test score provision is another matter. It seems reasonable to assume that any policy should be fair and should not unduly affect any one group in a negative manner. Can anyone arrive at a minimum test score that would be equally applicable to the diversity of institutions of higher education in the United States? The Grambling case study indicates that the answer is no. The $300,000 study commissioned by the NCAA indicated that test scores were not predictors of academic success, particularly among black males.

The score of 700 may actually be far too low for many institutions. At

TABLE 4-9. Conference Report Card

The number of recruits, by conference, who were ineligible to compete for Division I colleges in the two major sports in the 1986-87 season because of the new NCAA eligibility rules.

Conference	Football	Basketball
Atlantic Coast	5	1
Big East	N.A.	1
Big Eight	5	2
Big Sky	2	1
Big Ten	5	6
Mid-American	10	7
Mid-Continent	N.A.	2
Mid-Eastern Athletic	2	2
Missouri Valley	4	3
Ohio Valley	10	5
Pacific Coast	6	2
Pacific 10	4	0
Southeastern	17	9
Southern	3	2
Southland	5	2
Southwest	10	1
Southwestern Athletic	26	1
Western Athletic	5	2
Gateway Athletic	2	N.A.
Independent	32	3

Figures obtained in a New York Times telephone survey of NCAA Division I athletic departments July 25-31. They include athletes who have had scholarships withdrawn and those continuing on scholarship without eligibility, and represent a minimum number of ineligible players. (*The New York Times*, Sunday, August 3, 1986, Section 5, p. 1. Copyright © 1986 by The New York Times Company. Reprinted by permission.

the time of the New Orleans NCAA Convention, Tom Butters, athletic director at Duke University, was quoted as saying: "I am intrigued by those who say that requiring a minimum 700 SAT score to be eligible for intercollegiate athletics as a freshman is unreasonable, unfair, and discriminatory. Such reasoning is beyond my comprehension." (*The Times-Picayune*, Sunday, Jan. 12, 1986, p. E-3)

One can certainly understand why he might react that way from his perspective at Duke. On the other hand, can we reasonably compare Duke with Grambling in terms of test score requirements? Although done with the right intent, it seems that the NCAA may have established a policy which is fraught with pitfalls.

REFERENCES

Bartell, T., Keesling, J., LeBlanc, L. and Tombaugh, R. *Study of Freshman Eligibility Standards - Executive Summary.* Reston, VA: Advanced Technology, 1984.

———— . *Study of Freshman Eligibility Standards - Technical Report.* Reston, VA: Advanced Technology, 1984.

Grambling State University Office of Planning and Analysis. "1984 ACT Class Profile Research Service Report: A Graphic Interpretation of the Freshman Class Entering Fall 1984."

Grambling State University. *General Catalog,* 1983-84; 1984-85.

Lundy, H. J. "Making Rule 48 More Palatable to Predominantly Black Colleges and Universities." Presented at NAFEO Meeting in Washington, D. C., April 10, 1984.

———— . "The Trend Toward Increasing Academic Standards and Rule 48." Presented at the Ninth National Conference on Blacks in Higher Education for NAFEO, Washington, D. C., March 19-April 1, 1984.

———— . "Verification of Actual vs. Self-Reported Data Pertaining to GSU's Freshmen on Athletic Scholarship: 84-85 Freshman Survey."

Mule, M. "NCAA Eases Academic Guidelines for Freshmen." *The Times- Picayne/The States-Item,* January 12, 1986, p. E3.

National Collegiate Athletic Association. *1985-86 Manual.*

National Collegiate Athletic Association. *1986 Convention Program.*

"NCAA Puts Off Move to Revise Proposition 48." *The Chronicle of Higher Education,* Vol. 29, No. 12, November 14, 1984, pp. 1, 31.

"Research Forecasts Effects of No. 48." *The NCAA News,* Vol. 21, No. 30, August 29, 1984, pp. 1, 16.

The NCAA News, Vol. 23, No. 5, January 29, 1986, p. 1.

White, G. S. "NCAA's High Aims Turn into Rights Controversy." *The New York Times,* January 16, 1983, p. 45.

5

Athletes: Satisfactory Degree Progress

The failure of many college athletes to make satisfactory progress toward an academic degree has been one of the most apparent inadequacies of intercollegiate athletics during the last decade. This problem must be addressed at the university, as well as the NCAA level.

The essence of the problem is that a large number of athletes have not earned enough credits to graduate when their athletic eligibility is completed. The loss of incentives to play on college teams, as well as scholarships to supply the finances necessary to complete their educations, causes many athletes to leave college without degrees. A 1984 *Boston Globe* article on the education of scholarship athletes reported that most athletes who leave school without degrees are approximately 20 credits short of graduation.

The typical case publicized by the news media is one in which a male athlete is attending a major university and participating in a revenue-producing sport. His success on the playing field has made headlines, and his failure in the classroom also receives public attention. "Majoring in eligibility" has become a popular theme. The problem is particularly acute among NCAA Division I athletes participating in football and basketball. In June 1985, *USA TODAY* reported a graduation rate of 26 percent for basketball players in a nationwide survey of 196 Division I institutions (Aschburner, 1986). Actually, the problem transcends specific sport barriers and also affects different levels of intercollegiate competition. Data presented for basketball players merely dramatizes the nature of the problem.

The NCAA has taken steps in the right direction in an attempt to alleviate the problem. Effective August l, 1985, the following rules apply. (These are abstracted from the *1985-86 NCAA Manual* by permission of the National Collegiate Athletic Association. This material is subject to annual review and change.

1. A student-athlete must satisfactorily complete 24 semester or 36 quarter hours of academic credit since the beginning of his or her last season of competition to be eligible for regular-season competition.
   or
   Satisfactorily complete an average of at least 12 semester or quarter hours for all terms that occurred during those academic years in which the student-athlete was enrolled as a full-time student in any regular term during an academic year.
2. Any student-athlete must be enrolled in 12 credit hours of approved course work to be eligible during any regular academic term. This constitutes full-time student status.
3. By the beginning of the third year of enrollment (fifth semester or seventh quarter), the student-athlete must designate in writing a declared major (a program of studies leading toward a specific baccalaureate degree at the certifying institution). This also applies to a transfer student from a four-year or a two-year collegiate institution who is entering his or her third year of collegiate enrollment, even if the student has not yet completed an academic year in residence or utilized a season of eligibility in a sport at the certifying institution.
4. Once in a declared major, satisfactory progress shall be based on the satisfactory completion of courses in that program, as well as the students' overall academic record at the institution. Satisfactory progress will be verified in writing by an academic official (academic dean, department head, or academic advisor) within the major program of study and must be affirmed annually.

ISSUES

In the attempt to solve the overall problem, a number of issues emerge. The first of these revolves around the very notion of satisfactory degree progress. What is meant by that concept? Superficially, satisfactory progress can be defined as the process of working toward a degree in a specific major within a specific time frame. But, what lies beneath the surface? When an institution certifies that an athlete is making satisfactory progress toward a degree, what is really known about the quality of the completed coursework? Is this merely "playing the numbers game?" Can one be assured that the athlete is actually pursuing coursework that will result in a meaningful, legitimate degree?

The issue involving possible hypocrisy in intercollegiate athletics also surfaces again. Are rules on degree progress really necessary? Do they merely support the pretense that college athletes are really students? There is a general trend of acceptance of these rules among those people most directly involved with college athletics. The consensus among college presidents, athletic administrators, and coaches seems to be that rules on degree progress are for the good of the athlete and for the overall welfare of college athletics. As evidence, there was relatively little resistance to the legislation which was passed in 1985.

There is also the issue of whether the NCAA can control and enforce the rules on degree progress. Some argue that it is too late for reformation. They contend that various attempts such as Proposal 16, the satisfactory progress rule, and declaration of major are futile. The American emphasis on collegiate football and basketball precludes the possibility that many student-athletes will pursue rigorous academic programs. In essence, we cannot turn back the clock.

Others suggest that the NCAA can do the job, if significant changes are made. The present NCAA manual may have to be scrapped and a new one devised. A clearer definition where the NCAA stands as a national governing body is essential. If things remain as they are, true control will be difficult. If the NCAA redefines its position and its rule book, there may be the opportunity to achieve control and to provide direction as a national governing body.

Still another position is that the only real solution is quality control at the institutional level. L. Jay Oliva, chancellor of New York University presents the case for accreditation review.

> My proposal for beginning the control of corruption in college athletics is applicable not only to Division III schools like my own, but to the most visible of the Division I powers: Follow the prescription we utilize in the rest of the academic enterprise and bring athletics under accreditation review.

> We do not expect a national agency like the National Collegiate Athletic Association to review the ethics and quality of our academic life with tons of regulations and a handful of overworked "policemen." Instead, we regularly expose our academic programs to the view of visiting accreditation committees, whom we ourselves invite, composed of experienced and tough-minded peers from other institutions. These committees report to an elected board of our colleagues and tell us when we are sailing smoothly and when we are missing the boat. . . .

> How and when was athletics divorced from this institutional quality control? Why should we not utilize peer review in athletics, which is mentioned in accrediting guidelines along with all other aspects of university activity? Why should we not invite groups of academic and public leaders with a knowledge of athletics to join the accrediting process and visit individual athletic programs as a major part of that process?

> Such groups would carefully examine the athletic enterprise, developing a confidential report as part of the general accreditation report to the president and board of trustees. . . .

Athletics will not be reformed nationally until it is reformed campus by campus. The NCAA cannot be blamed for failing to deliver what individual presidents and boards are reluctant or unable to enforce at their own institutions. Our American colleges and universities have built a respected and accepted system of accreditation for academic activities. The machinery is already in place. We have but to extend it over the entire institution. (*The New York Times*, Sunday, March 30, 1986, p. 25. Copyright © 1986 by The New York Times Company. Reprinted by permission.)

The idea set forth by Oliva seems to have considerable merit, at least on paper. However, I suspect skeptics would be quick to react by suggesting that accreditation review is not likely to materialize under present conditions. There is no real evidence to date that the college presidents are about to give up on the NCAA as a governing body. Also, with the possibility of losing significant revenue from college football and basketball, what reason is there to believe that most of the Division I powers would agree to the accreditation review?

CASE ILLUSTRATIONS

There are numerous case illustrations of athletes failing to make satisfactory progress toward degrees. As noted earlier, the news media keeps us well informed of any noteworthy deficiencies in the academic standings of selected athletes and programs. What is not generally known is the extent to which any given institution is making a real effort to guide athletes toward satisfactory degree progress. The following case illustrations show some of the extremes — evidence of real problems as well as solid efforts to adequately guide degree work among athletes.

Mark Hall v. The University of Minnesota

In the spring of 1981, Mark Hall, a star basketball player at the University of Minnesota, was in his junior year in a non-baccalaureate degree program within the General College. He had been heavily recruited by Coach Jim Dutcher in spite of a low academic profile. During Hall's freshman and sophomore years, Coach Dutcher received several memos from Hall's academic advisor outlining the athlete's poor academic performance. Yet, nothing was done to change the situation. No remedial work was assigned, and academic supervision was minimal, at best.

Through his junior year, Hall had completed only 48 percent of the courses he attempted during the regular school year. He was forced to attend summer school to acquire enough credits to maintain his athletic eligibility. During the summer of 1981, he enrolled in 30 credits of classes and completed 26 credits. This put him beyond the 90-credit mark, which was the limit for the non-degree program. In August 1981 and October of 1981 Hall applied for admission to the University Without Walls (UWW) degree program. Both times, the UWW admissions committee determined, solely on his application, that he should be admitted to the UWW introductory program. However, also both times, the director of the program intervened and, in essence, directed the admissions committee to reject his application.

Subsequently, Mark Hall was declared ineligible for basketball competition his senior year even though he met the NCAA and Big Ten eligibility requirements with regard to grade point average and credit accumulation. Hall was declared ineligible for not being in a degree program. At that time, the NCAA "major declaration" rule was not in effect, but according to Rule I, Section IA, Part Two, of the *Big Ten Handbook*: "A student-athlete must be a candidate for a degree to be eligible to participate in intercollegiate competition."

After being declared ineligible, Mark Hall sought a court injunction in December 1981 to regain his athletic eligibility, based on the fact that the university would not allow him to enroll in an academic program leading to a degree. In a widely publicized decision, U.S. District Judge Miles W. Lord on January 2, 1982, issued a temporary injunction requiring the University of Minnesota to admit Mark Hall into a degree program and to declare him eligible to compete in intercollegiate varsity basketball competition. The university actually lost the case due to the lack of due process afforded Hall. However, in elaborating on his decision, Judge Lord noted that Hall had been recruited to come to the University of Minnesota as a basketball player, not as a scholar. He added: "It may well be true that a good academic program for the athlete is made virtually impossible by the demands of their sport at the college level. If this situation causes harm to the University, it is because they have fostered it, and the institution, rather than the individual should suffer the consequences." (Hall v. University of Minnesota, 530 F. Supp. 104, Minn. 1982)

After obtaining his eligibility for the 1981-1982 season, Mark Hall rejoined the basketball team. Overweight and out of shape, Hall finished the season as a reserve player. As an incidental to the case, the timing of the court decision is also worthy of note. To be of benefit to Hall as a basketball player, a decision on the injunction had to be reached by January 4, 1982, the beginning of the winter term. Otherwise, he would have remained ineligible for the entire basketball season.

The court transcript reveals where the university erred in the admissions process. Prior to rejecting Hall's application for admission, UWW had distributed a pamphlet describing the policies and procedures used for admission to its program. The pamphlet contained the following material.

1. The information you present in your application will determine whether you are admitted to UWW.
2. Admissions decisions are based on your responses to the application form which appears at the back of the booklet.

3. Your application will be reviewed by an admissions committee made up of UWW advisors. You will be notified in writing of the committee's decision. If you are not accepted, the reasons for the decision will be explained.
4. The admissions committee will determine which applicants will be admitted for the introductory period.

Before intervening in the admissions process, one of the UWW directors had contacted Dean Jean Lupton of the General College regarding the Mark Hall case. The director then issued a confidential memorandum to the other directors of UWW summarizing the information received from Dean Lupton. The memorandum noted that the following facts weighed heavily on Hall's application:

1. The "political aspects" of admitting Hall;
2. Hall's "substantial" travel record (actually only one weekend trip to Chicago in the fall of 1981);
3. Hall had earned the grade of "A" in several courses he was not eligible to be in;
4. The General College had found it necessary to monitor his academic work . . .;
5. He had improperly turned in school work on Regents' letter-head stationery;
6. He turned in work done by others as his;
7. Every "W" (withdrawal on his transcript was originally an "N" (equivalent to an "F");
8. Within four weeks after the beginning of classes, he had typically earned a grade of "N";
9. He had put through fake approval forms on more than one occasion.

In addition to these facts, the memorandum also stated that Dean Lupton would reject Hall's application to the General College if he reapplied to that school. Hall was never made aware of the facts that weighed against him, and he was never given the reasons for denial of his application.

In filing the suit, Hall claimed that he had been denied his right to due process of law. In cases of expulsion, public education can be considered a property right. Therefore, his scholarship to the University of Minnesota could be considered his property, subject to rights of due process. Also at issue was the likelihood of Hall obtaining a professional contract, a right protected by due process. Even though Hall admitted he was using college only as a means of entry into the NBA, he claimed he would suffer a substantial financial loss if his career objectives were impaired by the UWW decision. At the end of Hall's junior year, most NBA scouts agreed that he needed a good senior year of college basketball to become a high, second round draft choice and possibly obtain a first year "no cut" contract. The decision to reject his application to the UWW had, in effect, expelled him from the university. Unable to play his senior year, Hall would most likely become a sixth round draft choice, at best. His chances of making an NBA team would be severely limited.

Policy violation and rights of due process were the crucial elements in this case. Mark Hall provided evidence which showed that the university had singled out his application to the UWW. He was successful in proving that the University of Minnesota violated its own policies regarding admission to the UWW. In the court's opinion, the directors of the UWW had acted in an erroneous and capricious manner.

The University of Minnesota did prove that Hall was a very poor student who had no intention of obtaining a degree. The court understood that Mark Hall was only in college to obtain a professional contract. He was majoring in eligibility, and the university had every reason to be concerned that its academic reputation was being compromised. But, the violation of policy was the overriding factor in this case. One has to wonder about the lack of policies to guide satisfactory degree progress or the failure to enforce such policies. It certainly would appear that the unfortunate circumstances at the University of Minnesota in 1981-82 could have been avoided if sound policies had been in place and carried out effectively.

> The primary factor against Halls' entering either the UWW or GC was his grade point average. David L. Giese, Coordinator for the GC baccalaureate (degree-bearing) programs, listed in his affidavit to the court eligibility criteria that included "the student must have a 'C' (6 on the UM grade scale) average, or there must be evidence from the student's recent performance that the person has a good probability of completing a four-year degree."
>
> Giese attested that Hall's application, which listed a 'C' average, had been computed incorrectly (not by Hall, but through a university grading error), and, that he was in a 'D' (4.67) range. "Moreover," Giese attested, "I did not find his application to contain evidence that his recent performance demonstrated a good probability of completing the four year program." . . .
>
> David L. Ekstrand, education skills counselor whose position includes advising U-Minnesota athletes on educational requirements, told the court in his affidavit that he had contacted Hall several times about eligibility requirements and received little response.
>
> In the memorandum to basketball coach Jim Dutcher dated June 18, 1981, Ekstrand attested, "I summarize Mark's overall record and advise Coach Dutcher that I had never seen an athlete with that poor of a record get into the Baccalaureate Degree . . . in my 12 years as Educational Skills Advisor, I have worked closely with hundreds of

student-athletes at the University of Minnesota. Mr. Hall has been the most frustrating student-athlete, from an academic point of view, with whom I have worked . . . " (*The Morning Union*, Tues. Feb. 16, 1982, pp. 18, 21)

Repercussions from the Mark Hall case were still being felt some five years later. In May 1986 the "Task Force on Intercollegiate Athletics" issued a 51-page report to President Kenneth H. Keller, urging extensive reforms in the athletic department. (Keller actually named the task force after a scandal in January 1986 involving rape charges against three basketball players.) However, the scandal also focused attention once again on the low graduation rate among basketball players at Minnesota. The essence of the report was that the university should make sure that student-athletes are first students, then athletes. Among the recommendations more directly relating to satisfactory degree progress were the following:

That freshman be ineligible to play football, men's basketball, and possibly ice hockey, but have four years eligibility to play in subsequent years. . . .

That Minnesota consider raising the grades required for continued sports eligibility above the Big 10's 1.7 grade-point average. The panel recommended that the university urge the Big 10 and the N.C.A.A. to follow suit.

That there be a special summer orientation program for athletes before the Fall quarter begins.

That the university recruit and keep only athletes with a "reasonable probability of graduating." . . .

The committee urged President Keller to persuade other Big Ten presidents to limit the length of season and travel schedules . . . coaches should avoid scheduling practices that conflict with classes. It suggested that academic counselors accompany the men's basketball team on the road . . . (*The Chronicle of Higher Education*, May 21, 1986, pp. 33-36)

Jan Kemp v. The University of Georgia

A widely publicized trial took place in the U. S. District Court in Atlanta, Georgia, during January and February 1986. The case involved a civil suit brought against two administrators at the University of Georgia: Virginia Trotter, vice president for academic affairs, and Leroy Ervin, assistant vice president in charge of the developmental studies program. The lawsuit was brought by Jan Kemp, a former English instructor in developmental studies, who claimed she was fired in 1982 for speaking out against the preferential treatment given to some athletes at Georgia.

Although she was suing for reinstatement and for more than $100,000 in damages, she was initially awarded $2.58 million on February 12, 1986, when the jury supported her claim. In April, U. S. District Judge Horace Ward reduced the award to $679,681, but gave Kemp the right to seek a new trial. However, on May 5 an out-of-court settlement was reached wherein Kemp received $1.08 million and was reinstated to the faculty at Georgia as co-coordinator of the English program in the division of developmental studies.

Some of the facts that came out during the trial are summarized below.

1. From 1974 to 1983 Georgia graduated only 17 percent of its black scholarship football players and 4 percent of its black scholarship basketball players. (These figures were initially reported in *The Macon Telegraph and News*, September 9, 1984, p. 7.) During the period of the trial, *Sports Illustrated* reported: "Since the color line was broken for athletes at the University of Georgia in 1969, approximately 200 blacks have worn Bulldog uniforms in one sport or another. And how many of them have graduated? Perhaps as few as 30." ("Scorecard," January 27, 1986, p. 13)

2. Responding to the claim that these athletes were being exploited, Georgia President Fred C. Davison said: "If they leave us being able to read, write, communicate better, we simply have not done them any damage." (*Sports Illustrated*, February 24, 1986, p. 42)

3. Developmental studies was created by the Georgia Board of Regents in 1976 because many students coming out of high school were not qualified to do college level work. Rather than admit that a student was not qualified, the developmental studies program was implemented to correct a flaw in the Georgia educational system that began at the elementary level and extended to the junior high and high school levels. Students enrolled in developmental studies were required to take placement tests to determine their proficiency in English, mathematics and reading. They were then placed in the appropriate level courses and had four quarters to either complete the courses and pass an exit exam or face dismissal from the university. This meant that a football player could take remedial courses for two playing seasons without having to take a legitimate, college level course. Students in remedial courses did not receive credit toward their degrees. The developmental studies program had 60 slots reserved for athletes.

4. Kemp testified that in 1981, after she had refused Ervin's request that she ask a developmental studies instructor to change the failing grades of five scholarship athletes to incompletes, Ervin

told her, "Who do you think you are? Who do you think is more important at this university, you or a very prominent basketball player?" When the athletic department's chief academic counselor, Dick Copas, took the stand, he seemed to have trouble clearly describing academic guidelines followed in developmental studies, a program through which a large number of scholarship athletes in revenue-producing sports at Georgia pass. (*Sports Illustrated*, January 27, 1986, p. 13)

5. Former and current faculty members testified that athletes with little hope of graduating from Georgia were kept eligible in developmental studies, where they would not have to face true college-level courses. A number of athletes were said to have received more than the specified four chances to pass developmental studies courses, and school records showed that several had been curiously "exited" into the regular university curriculum despite sub — 2.0 GPA's, one had a 0.29, roughly an F plus. (*Sports Illustrated*, January 27, 1986, p. 13)

6. The conflict came to a head in December 1981 when Trotter, a former assistant secretary for education in the U. S. Department of Health, Education, and Welfare, allowed nine football players to "exit" from the remedial learning program to the university curriculum, despite the fact that they had all failed their fourth and final quarter in English. The players went on to play in the 1982 Sugar Bowl, but in a position paper the athletic department said there was no wrong-doing. Trotter, a former home economics professor, admitted in court that athletes received preferential treatment at the university, but defended her action on promoting the nine students. "I felt they deserved an opportunity because of the work they had done," Trotter testified. "I felt they had made great progress." (*Sports Illustrated*, February 24, 1986, p. 41)

Following the trial, Chancellor H. Dean Propst of the University System of Georgia's Board of Regents called for audits of the remedial programs at all of Georgia's colleges. The first report was on the University of Georgia. It confirmed information brought out in the trial. Since 1981, athletes in the university were kept eligible through actions by various officials in the university. The report also cited pressure on developmental studies instructors by representatives of the University of Georgia Athletic Association. President Davison issued a 157-page response, which differed widely from the report of the auditors. However, the confrontation between the president and the state regents was established. Davison resigned on March 13, ending his 19-year presidency, saying he was insulted by the board's decision to delay a vote on his reappointment. The controversy continued to the next month after both the regents' audit and

Davison's response were made public. However, Davison confirmed that his resignation was firm, and the regents accepted it unanimously. The case was more or less closed, and the University of Georgia proceeded to do what it could be mend a tattered image.

The real significance of the case is found in the revelations about the academic status of scholarship athletes at Georgia. Beyond Georgia, the message was extended to others responsible for major college athletic programs. After the settlement, Kemp stated: "I hope this speaks to college administrators and athletic directors nationwide, that they've got to stop exploiting athletes. . . . It's a plantation system, and I think its a crying shame." (*USA TODAY*, Tuesday, May 6, 1986, p. 1C)

Georgia Tech

An interesting case comparison can be made between the situation at the University of Georgia and that of arch rival Georgia Tech. On Sunday, February 23, 1986, *The Atlanta Journal and Constitution* carried a special report titled "Athletics and Academics: How Tech Makes It Work." Following are selected excerpts from that report, which reveal quite a bit about the academic framework for athletes at Georgia Tech:

1. Within an athletic building, Tech built a $300,000 academic center that includes 44 individual study stations and seven personal computers. There, individual tutoring is available during the day, and group tutoring is offered during the evening.
2. Tech's tutoring budget is thought to be one of the highest in the country. In 1985-86, the athletic department spent at least $55,000 on tutors, most of whom were graduate students paid $10 per hour.
3. The athletic department's academic coordinator is Scott Zolke, a 32-year-old attorney who joined the department in 1982. He was described by a former assistant athletic director at Tech as "the most important and underpaid person in that athletic program." Since the addition of Zolke to the staff, only four Tech athletes have been dismissed from the school for academic reasons, compared to five football players in 1981 alone. Only six of 25 (24 percent) football signees graduated from the 1976 recruiting class. By contrast, while winning more games, 35 of 51 (68 percent) football players graduated from the '79 and '80 recruiting classes.
4. The athletic department now has three full-time academic employees.
5. "Within the academic center, numerous steps are taken to facilitate the mingling of academics and athletics. All freshmen athletes are required to attend study halls. Seminars are conducted on how to take notes, how to listen, how to minimize test anx-

iety, how to manage time, how to study. Zolke advises athletes on scheduling — for example, "we like to schedule calculus at 2 p.m. even if the athlete finishes his other classes at 11 a.m. That gives him a chance for a couple hours of tutoring going into class."

6. The football team practices at night on Mondays to avoid conflicts with Monday afternoon labs and to give players "an academic reinstatement," as termed by Zolke.

7. From time to time, memos are sent to coaches stating that a player will miss practice because he must spend the time studying.

8. Athletes are required to sign in at breakfast, with the idea that they are less likely to skip classes if they are out of bed anyway.

9. Zolke's approval is required before a member of Tech's coaching staff can visit a prospect. The decision is based on the high school transcript and standardized test scores. However, Tech does not offer the pretense of only bringing in top scholars to participate in athletics. Table 5-1 shows the relative profile.

TABLE 5-1. SAT Scores: Tech football vs. student body

	Verbal	Math	Total
1985 freshman football players	410	475	885
Management majors, football team	410	428	829
Engineering majors, football team	535	651	1,186
Overall Tech student body, fall '85	522	626	1,148
Freshman national average, fall '85	431	475	906
Freshman average in state, fall '85	399	438	837

10. Tech does admit a certain number of athletes as special admissions cases. These decisions are made on the basis of offsetting features on the high school record. Zolke explained it this way: "The biggest factor in determining whether we are justified in taking a risk student is conscience, having to live with him on a day-to-day basis and not exploiting him. We're not going to take someone's life and destroy it for the sake of winning football games."

11. Industrial management is the favorite major for athletes at Georgia Tech. Approximately 25 percent of the industrial

management majors are athletes. In 1986, the breakdown of majors among athletes was as follows:

Industrial Management   - 69%
Engineering   - 13%
Computer Science   - 8%
Biology   - 6%
Undecided   - 4%

12. There is agreement among coaches and professors that athletes do not seek or receive preferential treatment from professors at Georgia Tech. Chemistry professor Dan Berkowitz stated: "I'm in my second year here, and I've never spoken with a coach. I wouldn't know an athlete in my class from any other student unless he introduces himself as such, and, I think that says something for the fact that they're all students here. Athletes are not babied here, and I don't think they want to be. They know they have to do the work, and they do it." ("Athletics and Academics: How Tech Makes It Work," *The Atlanta Journal and Constitution*, Sunday, February 23, 1986, pp. 8-9D)

The Athletic Association of the University of Illinois at Urbana-Champaign

It is quite clear that any effective policies concerning satisfactory degree progress have to be in the form of institutionally derived guidelines. The NCAA legislation represents a step in the right direction. Beyond that, as long as college athletes are to be considered true student-athletes, the individual institution must develop appropriate policies for its situation. The Athletic Association of the University of Illinois at Urbana-Champaign offers a splendid example of what can be done in the way of policy development for college athletics generally. Selections from its *Policy and Procedure Manual (1984)* (Exhibit 5-1) relate to satisfactory degree progress for athletes:

EXHIBIT 5-1. University of Illinois — Policy and Procedures.

The Director of Academic Services (part of the Athletic Association) and his office staff shall serve as liaison between the Athletic Association and all faculty, staff, and University personnel. Any contact made with Admissions and Records, faculty, deans, or other related University personnel regarding academic matters shall be transacted by the Director of Academic Services. Coaches are explicitly prohibited from making contact with faculty and University administrative and academic personnel regarding any academic matters.

All services provided by the Academic Services Office shall be in total compliance with our institutional responsibility as it related to Conference rules, regulations, agreements, precedents and published interpretations of Big Ten Conference and NCAA rules. The principle of faculty control as defined by the Big Ten Conference shall at all times be coordinated with the Board of Control of the Athletic Association. All Conference and NCAA eligibility rules shall apply to all student athletes participating at the University of Illinois. . . .

EXHIBIT 5-1 *(con't.)*

The purpose of the Grants-In-Aid program at the University of Illinois is to insure that all financial assistance to student athletes is consonant with the regulations of the NCAA, Big Ten Conference, and the primary educational values of the University. To receive financial assistance from the Athletic Association is a privilege which student athletes must earn by participating to the best of their ability, not only on the playing field but in the classroom as well. Indeed, the scholarship aid is awarded to make this dual commitment possible. Its basic assumption is that students who are willing to devote long hours on the practice field may, through a regulated program of assistance, be relieved of the obligation to work part-time to subsidize their collegiate education. The primary purpose is to encourage academic success. To be sure, Grants-In-Aid are awarded only to those individuals who in addition to their academic qualifications show exceptional athletic promise. The justification of the program must ultimately reside in its capacity to permit students to meet the University's academic expectations while encouraging participation in an intercollegiate sport. . . .

Fifth Year Aid

The Athletic Association is committed to the educational pursuits of all athletes and will assist selected athletes in completing degree requirements in the fifth year under the following guidelines:

1. It should first be understood that athletes are expected to complete degree requirements within the normal four-year period.

2. Eligibility for Grant-In-Aid during the fifth 12-month period following the date of a student's matriculation in an institution of college grade will be provided only according to NCAA and Big Ten regulations governing the awarding of such aid.

3. In order to be eligible for fifth year aid the student athlete must have a minimum of 105 semester hours which count toward the student's degree requirements with a 2.95 grade point average at the start of the fifth year.

4. Fifth year aid will be provided only in cases where extenuating circumstances prevent the athlete from completing degree requirements within a four year period. Fifth year aid will be awarded on a semester-by-semester basis according to individual needs. . . .

Intersession and Summer School Aid

The Athletic Association is committed to facilitating and supporting each student athlete's active pursuit of a college degree and will provide financial aid to a student athlete to attend summer school in order to accommodate that goal. Intersession courses are not recommended for student athletes because of the intense nature of the work load unless there are extenuating circumstances which preclude the student athlete attending summer school. The Athletic Association will provide aid for summer school and/or intersession according to the following guidelines:

1. Aid will be provided only for those students who need to attend summer school in order to meet eligibility requirements or for those students who need additional credit hours to meet graduation requirements.

2. Aid will be provided only to those students who have been enrolled for a minimum of 12 academic hours throughout the previous two semesters.

3. Aid will be provided only to those students who have made a conscientious effort to pursue degree requirements and have given their full cooperation to

EXHIBIT 5-1 *(con't.)*

college, departmental, and Athletic Association personnel in all matters of an academic nature.

4. Students are expected to enroll in a minimum of three credit hours which apply to their degree objectives. Exceptions must be approved by the Director of Academic Services. . . .

Correspondence Courses

The University of Illinois has established basic policies and procedures for correspondence courses. It should be recognized by all student athletes that correspondence courses are not recommended for the purpose of improving grade point average or meeting additional hours required for eligibility for competition. Therefore, a deficiency of GPA or required hours for competition should be satisfied by attending summer school as opposed to taking a correspondence course.

The University of Illinois has established the following basic policies in regards to correspondence courses.

1. Students may not complete more than three lessons per week.

2. Lessons must be graded and returned before further lessons may be submitted.

3. A student must be enrolled in the course a minimum of six weeks before a final exam can be scheduled.

4. Final exams are not scheduled until all graded lessons have been returned to the student for review.

5. Correspondence courses do not count as enrolled hours and are only recorded upon completion of the final exams.

The Athletic Association does not believe the above conditions are conducive to a student athlete's successful completion of requirements which may be necessary to obtain eligibility. Student athletes are strongly discouraged from attempting correspondence courses as a solution for correcting an eligibility deficiency. . . .

Academic Standards

Every student athlete who participates in intercollegiate athletics becomes a member of a team. By accepting this privilege of team membership, student athletes accept the following responsibilities in addition to their regular responsibilities as students.

The major purpose of the Athletic Association is to have each student athlete pursue and obtain an academic degree. Student athletes have the responsibility of attending class on a regular basis, of completing all classroom assignments, and of conducting themselves in all academic matters in ways that are consistent with acceptable class-room performance. The student athlete is required to meet all University and college academic requirements as well as the eligibility rules of the University, NCAA, and Big Ten Conference. Although academic progress and eligibility are monitored by the Athletic Association, it is the responsibility of the student athlete to insure that applicable requirements are being met. If students have questions regarding eligibility requirements, they should consult with the Director of Academic Services. Important academic requirements include the following items:

a. To be eligible to practice or compete, all student athletes must be registered for a minimum of 12 semester hours.

EXHIBIT 5-1 *(con't.)*

b. Freshmen must maintain a minimum GPA of 2.70 their first semester of residence in order to be eligible for competition the second semester.

c. In order to be eligible for competition and Grants-In-Aid student athletes must meet additional requirements.

    (1) A minimum of 24 semester hours which count toward the student's degree requirements with a 2.70 grade point average at the start of the sophomore year.

    (2) A minimum of 51 semester hours which count toward the student's degree requirements with a 2.80 grade point average at the start of the junior year.

    (3) A minimum of 78 semester hours which count toward the student's degree requirements with a 2.0 grade point average at the start of the senior year.

    (4) A minimum of 105 semester hours which count toward the student's degree requirements with a 3.0 grade point average at the start of the fifth year.

d. Student athletes enrolled prior to August l, 1983, meet the academic requirements as follows:

    (1) A minimum of 24 semester hours which count toward the student's degree requirements with a 2.65 grade point average at the start of the sophomore year.

    (2) A minimum of 51 semester hours which count toward the student's degree requirements with a 2.75 grade point average at the start of the junior year

    (3) A minimum of 78 semester hours which count toward the student's degree requirements with a 2.85 grade point average at the start of the senior year

    (4) A minimum of 105 semester hours which count toward the student's degree requirements with a 2.95 grade point average at the start of the fifth year.

Eligibility

Every student athlete who competes in a varsity sport must be making normal progress toward his/her chosen degree This progress is closely monitored by the Academic Services Office, the Faculty Representative and the college Deans.

Those athletes who are freshmen or transfer students have their high school grade point average verified by a responsible representative from their high school. This verification must be secured by the Academic Services Office to certify eligibility for financial aid and competition. Eligibility lists are prepared and sent to the registrar to evaluate cumulative hours and grade point averages. Another list is prepared and sent to the college Deans for examination of progress toward degree requirements. Once the student has been cleared for eligibility, this list is signed by the Registrar, Faculty Representative, and the Director of Athletics and sent to the Conference Office. It is the responsibility of the Academic Services Office to see that this is done in an accurate and timely manner.

When a student athlete has been declared ineligible because of the application of any Conference rule, he/she may petition for reinstatement of eligibility.

Academic Counseling

Academic assistance is provided to any student who requires it. After evaluation by a college advisor, students are counseled by the Academic Services

Office on how best to schedule their classes and still keep their commitment to their particular sport.

During the counseling sessions and throughout each semester the Academic Services Office discusses the need for tutoring and provides it when required.

A study hall program is provided for those students who need additional tutorial assistance.

(Policy and Procedure Manual, Athletic Association of the University of Illinois, 1984, pp. II, 1-13)

Critique and Implications For Future Policy Development

The policies set forth at the University of Illinois offer a good example of what can be done to provide an effective framework for guiding the satisfactory degree progress by athletes. To be successful in carrying out these policies is another matter. Nevertheless, the efforts by Illinois represent a step in the right direction. What are the salient features of these policies? What might be improved? What are the implications for policy development at other institutions? The following points of critique are set forth as guidelines for policy development in this area:

1. **Academic services unit:** There seems to be considerable merit in having a distinct academic services unit responsible for coordinating and controlling all academic functions involving athletes. The idea that coaches are removed from academic contacts is a particularly strong feature. There might be some question as to whether the academic services unit should be under the jurisdiction of the athletic department, but, it can also be argued that athletic staff members are more aware of the special needs of athletes.

2. **Principle of faculty control:** This is a positive feature of Illinois policy, specifically, and Big Ten Conference policy, generally. All institutions should make the academic services unit accountable to the faculty in some formal way.

3. **Grants-in-aid-program:** The award of a grant-in-aid at any institution should be based on demonstrated academic achievement as well as athletic ability. The University of Illinois has set forth the type of policy needed in this regard.

4. **Fifth year aid:** The probability of degree completion by athletes increases significantly if there is a provision for fifth year aid, when earned by the athlete through academic achievement during the first four years. The Illinois policy is sound in expecting a normal, four-year completion for athletes while offering the fifth year as a possibility.

5. **Summer school aid:** The Illinois policy obviously encourages summer school attendance by athletes. Due to the heavy time demands on athletes while participating in intercollegiate athletics during the regular academic year, there is good reason to believe that summer school attendance will facilitate satisfactory degree progress for athletes at many institutions. Although intersession courses are not encouraged in the Illinois policy, the situation at some institutions may also enable the intersession courses to be a viable means of working toward satisfactory degree progress.

6. **Correspondence courses:** Although the Illinois policy does not prohibit athletes from taking correspondence courses, it is clear that correspondence courses are not recommended for satisfactory degree work. This is another strong feature of the Illinois policy. Academic problems at various institutions have centered around work in correspondence courses.

7. **Specific academic standards:** Any policy regarding specific academic standards for eligibility has to be defined within the context of standards for the institution as a whole. The real merit in the Illinois policy is found in the progression in required semester hours and grade point average from freshman year to fifth year. The exact grade point requirements have to be based on overall records of students in the college or university. The standards could be further strengthened by requiring a certain percentage of courses in the student-athlete's major during the junior and senior years.

8. **Academic counseling:** The Illinois policy is relatively weak in terms of spelling out the provisions for academic counseling. There is good reason to believe that there should be mandatory tutoring in core courses for freshman and sophomore athletes if they are admitted to the institution with academic records that are deficient in terms of high school grade point average or standardized test scores. Tutors should also be assigned whenever academic deficiencies are noted. Overall, there must be some form of careful monitoring of the academic progress.

CONCLUSION

Chapter 2 concluded with the thought that there probably should be only two NCAA divisions — one that truly had student-athletes and another with athlete-students, in essence, professional college athletes. Quite obviously, there is no particular need to be concerned about satisfactory degree progress if the latter approach was adopted. However, as long as college sport continues to promote the concept of student-athletes in any context, steps must be taken to guide these athletes toward satisfactory progress in obtaining degrees.

This is much more of a journey than a destination. Alleviating the problem of unsatisfactory degree progress by many college athletes will take untiring efforts by all concerned. The real key is the recruitment process. Coaches must recruit the right kind of people, and college administrators must maintain the control to insure that such recruitment takes place. The athletes need not be first-rate scholars, but they must demonstrate the potential to work at academic endeavors. Beyond that, the solution to the problem will largely be found in a well-planned system of advising and tutoring. The Georgia Tech case study demonstrates that it can be done.

(Note: Additional updated information on athletics and higher education can be found in Chapter 20 on pages 313 to 315.

REFERENCES

Aschburner, S. "Graduation Rate Embellishes Rich Basketball Tradition." *The NCAA News*, Vol. 23, No. 10, March 5, 1986, pp. 2-3.
Athletic Association of the University of Illinois. *Policy and Procedure Manual*, 1984.
Conkey, D. "The Mark Hall Case: An Attack on Academia." *The Morning Union*, Springfield, MA, February 16, 1982, pp. 18-21.
Davidson, D. "Athletics and Academics: How Tech Makes It Work." The Atlanta Journal and Constitution, February 23, 1986, pp. 8-9D.
Court Transcript, Mark D. Hall v. The University of Minnesota et al., United States District Court, District of Minnesota, Jan. 2, 1982.
Mayfield, M. "Kemp Settles for $1.08M, Her Old Job." *USA TODAY*, May 6, 1986, p. 1C.
Nack, W. "This Case Was One For the Books." *Sports Illustrated*, Vol. 64, No. 8, February 24, 1986, pp. 34-42.
National Collegiate Athletic Association. *1985-86 Manual.*
Oliva, L. J. "Put Athletic Programs Under Academic Scrutiny." *The New York Times*, March 30, 1986, p. 2S.
Wehrwein, A. C. "Stiff Academic Rules, Ban on Freshmen Urged by U. of Minnesota Reform Panel." *The Chronicle of Higher Education*, May 21, 1986, pp. 33, 36.

6
Athletes:
Drug Usage

If there was ever any doubt about the seriousness of drug usage by college and professional athletes, the summer of 1986 removed all uncertainty. On June 19, 1986, Len Bias, the former Maryland basketball star, died from cardiorespiratory arrest brought on by the use of cocaine. Eight days later, Don Rogers, a Cleveland Browns defensive back, collapsed in Sacramento, California and died as suddenly. Once again, cocaine was found in the body. There were striking similarities in the cocaine-related deaths of these athletes. At the time, toxicologists stated that the amounts of cocaine were no greater than those taken by many "weekend users." However, they also pointed out that tolerance levels to cocaine can vary widely.

The nature and extent of the problem was succinctly stated by Dr. Armond Nicholi Jr., a team physician with the New England Patriots as well as a faculty member with the Harvard Medical School and a staff member of the Massachusetts General Hospital:

> "The recent deaths of Len Bias and Don Rogers not only underscore the seriousness of drug use among professional athletes but also bring into bold relief the drug crisis sweeping the nation. The use of psycho-active drugs has spread rapidly into an epidemic of extraordinary scope.
>
> The professional athlete is particularly vulnerable. His time to spare between seasons and his ample financial resources make him a tempting target for drug dealers. In the National Football League, the death of Rogers adds one more name to the steady attrition of athletes during the past 20 years — the aborted careers, the broken homes, the imprisonments and the premature deaths. This continues year after year because no one in either management or the players union has yet demonstrated the courage or the conviction to insist on an effective drug program. For these reasons, many wait expectantly for the new National Football League drug policy soon to be announced by Commissioner Pete Rozelle.

How widespread is drug use in the N.F.L.? No one knows. We hear only the names of those who die suddenly — or slowly — from drugs. If we, however, take the most recent findings of highly reliable national studies released by the National Institute on Drug Abuse, we note that among the 18- to 25-year-olds — the age group comprising the bulk of N.F.L. players — the most conservative figures indicate that about 65 percent have used or are using drugs. If we extrapolate this percentage to the approximately 1,560 players that were members of the N.F.L. at the end of last season, including those on injured reserve, one could speculate that close to 1,000 players or an average of 35 a team use or have used drugs to some degree and in one form or another. If these figures prove to be only half that accurate, they nonetheless give some idea of the magnitude of the problem. One cannot help but wonder if an awareness of the magnitude may be the reason for past resistance to an effective drug policy indifference among players who fear exposure and among owners and officials who fear damaging the image." (*The New York Times*, Sunday, July 6, 1986, p. 2. Copyright © 1986 by The New York Times Company. Reprinted by permission.)

Basically what we note here is an extensive problem which is a reflection of a much larger, societal problem. Athletes are particularly vulnerable. While the problem is clear-cut, the solutions are not that clear. Various issues have come to the foreground.

DRAWING THE LINE

There are three principal types of drugs: 1) *restorative drugs*, including painkillers, anti-inflammants, tranquilizers, and others that work to restore the body to its optimal condition; 2) *additive drugs*, including stimulants that tend to increase performance beyond natural limits; and 3) *recreational drugs*, including cocaine, marijuana, and others that are basically used for enjoyment.

One of the issues involves the matter of where to draw the line in terms of permissible drug usage. Quite obviously, the overall problem has focused on the use of recreational drugs. However, there is some difference of opinion regarding the extent to which efforts should be made to restrict the use of restorative and additive drugs. For example, some doctors endorse the use of anabolic steroids, as an additive drug. The argument is that if anabolic steroids are legal and do not involve serious health risks, there is nothing wrong with using them to improve athletic performance. However, the majority in the medical profession are greatly concerned about the health risks involved. There is also the question about whether the use of such drugs is morally and ethically wrong. Overall, one question permeates the entire sport enterprise: to what extent should an institution or organization restrict or control drug usage in various forms?

THE LEGAL ISSUE

The legal issue centers largely on the use of drug testing. For the most part the question is not *whether* to implement a drug testing program but *how*. Attorneys have raised questions about the legality of mandatory drug testing programs. Is mandatory drug testing a violation of the Fourth Amendment regarding freedom from search and seizure? Would waiver forms signed by athletes stand up in court? What can be done to insulate an organization from litigation in the case of a testing error or a breach of confidentiality? Some lawyers contend that drug testing does not violate an individual's rights, since there is justifiable concern about how that drug use by some players may affect the safety of others.

College and university lawyers have suggested that these institutions may be on shaky legal ground if they test for use of recreational drugs. (Most testing programs test only for those drugs.) Testing for performance-enhancing drugs is based on the premise that these drugs have a direct connection to the welfare of students as college athletes. The justification for including recreational drugs may not be as strong, particularly during the off-season. However, other lawyers suggest that health considerations dictate that colleges test for all drugs. Proposed drug-testing guidelines set forth by the American Council of Education (ACE) in May 1986 included the following features:

> Testing should be scheduled so as to detect drug use likely to affect athletic performance, not merely the use of drugs at any time.
>
> Athletes should be afforded every opportunity "to complain about circumstances in which they are encouraged or induced to use performance — enhancing drugs." Such a policy protects coaches and staff members "against untrue allegations of complicity made after a student has tested positive on a drug test," the council said.
>
> A set of written rules should be followed closely as "any deviation would subject a school (and individuals) to possible liability for failing to uphold the safeguards protecting student participants."
>
> Athletes must provide "informed consent" to testing. The council recommended that information be given to athletes during the recruiting process, so that a form of contract exists.
>
> Athletes must be provided with "reasonable notice and an opportunity to be heard before sanctions are imposed." (*The Chronicle of Higher Education*, May 7, 1986, p. 31)

In responding to the guidelines, college lawyers expressed concern regarding the privacy of student records and the need for colleges to release drug testing results to the police when illegal activities are discovered. Another problematic area is whether athletes who test positive should be allowed to continue to participate until due process is satisfied. Overall, the various legal issues associated with drug testing must be carefully considered before a program is implemented.

THE MANAGEMENT ISSUE

There is debate regarding who should take the responsibility for drug testing and what kind of penalties should be imposed when athletes test positive. Collectively, this is a management issue. It has emerged at both the professional and collegiate levels.

On July 7, 1986, NFL Commissioner Pete Rozelle announced extensive changes in the NFL's drug program, including two unscheduled urine tests during the regular season and tougher penalties for positive results. Players who tested positive would either be hospitalized or treated as outpatients for 30 days. The random tests would be for cocaine, marijuana, heroin, amphetamines, and alcohol. Gene Upshaw, executive director of the NFL Players Association, immediately challenged the changes on the grounds that the existing collective bargaining agreement did not allow random testing. Rozelle cited a bylaw of the NFL constitution that empowers the commissioner to preserve public confidence in the league.

At the college level, the management issue was largely manifested in the difference of opinion over the penalties for positive drug testing. In June 1986, the NCAA announced that more than 3,000 student-athletes would be involved in drug testing prior to championship events during the 1986-87 academic year. The NCAA Executive Committee initially recommended that both the athlete and the team be barred from advancing in championship competition if the athlete tests positive and has participated in the team's previous tournament play. However, later the penalty was modified to stipulate that the team should not be declared ineligible for championship competition unless the institution knowingly allowed the student-athlete to compete after testing positive.

CASE STUDY: MICHAEL RAY RICHARDSON

In February 1986 the National Basketball Association (NBA) imposed a lifetime ban on New Jersey Nets guard Michael Ray Richardson. The circumstances leading up to that action provide a vivid example of the policy problems of drug use among athletes.

After playing four years of college basketball at the University of Montana without coming close to receiving a degree, Richardson signed a four-year contract with the New York Knicks on September 1, 1978, for $909,000, including a bonus of $149,000 and salaries averaging $190,000 per season. During his rookie season (1978-79), Richardson averaged only 6.5 points and 17 minutes of playing time per game. Following the season he rejoined his wife and daughter in Denver, Colorado, where he played in a summer basketball league. A basketball friend at the time later stated that this was when Richardson first used cocaine. However, Richardson claimed that he didn't start using cocaine until 1981.

From a basketball standpoint, Richardson's second pro season (1979-80) was a success. Early in the season, he won a starting position as the point guard for the Knicks. He went on to average 15.3 points per game, led the league in steals and assists, and was named to the NBA All-Star and All-Defensive teams. However, at the same time, financial problems surfaced. He hired Don Cranson, president of RoundBall Enterprises, as his agent. Cranson confirmed that Richardson's finances were "somewhat of a jungle."

The subsequent report was that Richardson's drug use intensified in the summer of 1980 when he began free-basing cocaine with certain other NBA players. As noted earlier, Richardson later insisted that he didn't have his first experience with cocaine until 1981.

On October 31, 1980, Richardson's contract with the Knicks was extended for three years beyond the original agreement which expired after the 1981-82 season. The contract called for salaries of $300,000, $350,000, and $400,000; a bonus of $75,000; and two loans totaling $158,250.

During the 1980-81 season, Richardson solidified his star status as a basketball player with the Knicks. He averaged 16.4 points per game and led the team in minutes played, as the Knicks won 50 games and a playoff spot. Richardson's personal troubles accelerated during the summer of 1981. His older brother was arrested and later sentenced to 18 months in prison on a felony charge. In July, Rene Richardson, Michael Ray's wife, filed for dissolution of their marriage and custody of their daughter. Richardson also admitted to a friend that he was using cocaine.

The 1981-82 season opened with Richardson still complaining about financial problems. His performance was inept at times in early season, but he also made a typical turnabout. In February he appeared in his third straight All-Star game and finished the season averaging 17.9 points per game, although the Knicks finished last in the Atlantic Division. Richardson thought he deserved a new contract. He hired his sixth agent to negotiate it.

Prior to the training camp for the 1982-83 season, Richardson delivered an ultimatum to Dave DeBusschere, who had recently been hired as executive vice president of the Knicks. Michael Ray said he wanted $500,000 a year or he would not report to camp. He did report, but trouble continued. After first disappearing from camp and later missing a team flight, Richardson was traded to the Golden State Warriors for forward Bernard King. After learning that the Warriors would not renegotiate his contract, Richardson at first refused to report. However, he later changed his mind and reached an agreement with the Warriors, including the payment of $20,600, which he owed as a fine for reporting late. At that time, he denied the drug rumors. He also signed an addendum to his contract wherein the Warriors could terminate his employment if he could not perform due to criminal connection or alcohol or drug addiction.

Richardson's brief stint with the Warriors was troubled. His performance was erratic. In January 1983, the Warriors hired a San Francisco detective agency to investigate his private life, particularly his alleged drug habits. While the investigation continued, Richardson was traded to the New Jersey Nets on February 6, 1983, for forward Mickey Johnson and guard Eric Floyd. The Nets knew about the rumors regarding Richardson's personal life, but there was no confirmed knowledge of drug use.

After reporting to the Nets a day late, Richardson showed signs that his physical skills were not up to par. The principal owner of the Nets, Joe Taub, personally confronted Michael Ray about a drug problem. Again, Richardson denied using drugs. Nevertheless, in March, Taub and Nets Coach Larry Brown made arrangements for Richardson to visit with a doctor at Fair Oaks Hospital, a private psychiatric center in Summit, N.J. Richardson admitted to the doctor that he had free-based cocaine as much as twice a week. The doctor's diagnosis was that Richardson reverted to drugs when suffering from depression.

Richardson finished the season with the Nets, but his troubles continued. He was stunned when Coach Brown accepted a position at the University of Kansas in April. The Nets went on to make the Eastern Conference playoffs but were swept by the Knicks in the first round. Richardson's performance was well below average.

After the season, Richardson was admitted to Fair Oaks Hospital after a meeting with officials of the Nets and a representative from the Life Extension Institute, an agency the NBA utilized to help players with personal problems. Treatment was planned for six to eight weeks, but Richardson signed out after three weeks, announcing that he was cured. He again insisted that his use of cocaine only began when he was traded to the Warriors and that he was now free of drug dependency.

By July 1983 he was again using cocaine. This time he was admitted to the Hazelden Foundation in Center City, Minnesota, for further treatment. He was released in September, and at a Nets press conference later that month he again offered assurance that he was now free of the drug habit. At the same time, the NBA announced the implementation of its anti-drug program. (Details of that plan will be noted later.)

After performing well at the Nets' 1983 training camp, Richardson was using cocaine by October. He expressed his desire to give up pro basketball. Nets' officials again arranged an appointment with the Life Extension Institute, but Richardson failed to show. The Nets placed him on waivers, and the players union subsequently filed a grievance against the Nets and the NBA. This went to arbitration.

Richardson's situation at the time was succinctly described by Bill Brubaker in an article written in 1985.

"I don't want any more part of basketball."
Three weeks before the start of the 1983-84 NBA season, Michael (Sugar) Ray Richardson uttered those words after having quietly left

the New Jersey Nets' training camp, found some cocaine and disappeared into a hotel room, seeking to escape from reality. Though he had been an All-Star three times, he was practically broke, the result of having gone through six agents, 16 cars and untold quantities of cocaine during his five-year pro career. His wife of eight years was pressing for a divorce settlement that would include custody of their only child. His third agent was suing him for $606,000. His addiction to cocaine was worsening, and the Nets would soon cancel the two years remaining on his contract. At 28, Richardson appeared to be finished as a basketball player — and he didn't seem to care. "The life style that basketball has created for me, I can't handle that," he told a friend, Charles Granthan, executive vice-president of the NBA Players Association. "Maybe I'd be better off driving a truck." (*Sports Illustrated*, February 4, 1985, pp. 59-60)

Richardson was admitted to a third rehabilitation center (Regent Hospital in Manhattan, N.Y., a psychiatric treatment center having a special program for cocaine use) on October 14, 1983. He was released on November 1 with the agreement that he return three times a week for urine tests and twice a week for counseling sessions. In December, the Nets agreed to reinstate Richardson at the urging of the NBA. There was concern that other drug-troubled players would be reluctant to enter the NBA's rehabilitation program if Richardson lost in the arbitration process. He was to be given one more opportunity. Grantham offered financial assistance. Richardson's problems now included alimony and child-support payments. His wife had been granted a divorce on November 17.

After marrying Leah Burton in January, Richardson re-entered the starting lineup of the Nets on February 25, 1984. He went on to lead the Nets to their first victory in an NBA playoff series. They defeated the defending champion Philadelphia 76ers, 3-2, with Richardson averaging 20.6 points and 8.6 assists per game. Richardson's fine performance continued into the 1984-85 season. At the beginning of February 1985, he was averaging 19.1 points, 8.0 assists, 5.5 rebounds, and a league-leading 2.8 steals per game. "It's a question of whether a person wants to be a winner or wants to give up," said Richardson at the end of Brubaker's 1985 article. "I'm a winner. I'll be playing basketball until, you know, until the day they kick me out." (*Sports Illustrated*, February 4, 1985, p. 72)

At the conclusion of the 1984-85 season, Richardson was named NBA comeback player of the year. Among other accomplishments, he led the league in steals. In September 1985, he signed a new four-year, $3 million contract. He participated in an NBA anti-drug video, Cocaine Drain and had passed every weekly drug test mandated by the previous contract. The 1985-86 season started much the same. As of December 27, 1985, he was averaging 17.3 points, 7.8 assists, 5.7 rebounds, and 2.9 steals per game. Then, on that date, after attending a team Christmas party, Richardson disappeared for three days. "On December 30, Richardson called his agent, Charles Gruntham, and admitted that for the first time since October 1983, he needed help." (*Sports Illustrated* January 13, 1986, p. 28)

On January 1, 1986, Richardson was admitted to a drug clinic for the fourth time. He entered the Pasadena, California, Community Hospital, the NBA's referral center for drug cases. He was released on January 20 and played with the Nets until February 26. The news was grim by March.

> The NBA last week imposed a lifetime ban on New Jersey Nets guard Michael Ray Richardson after he tested positive for cocaine, indicating his third lapse into drug use in 29 months. Richardson, whose drug problems had taken him in and out of at least four rehabilitation centers over the last three years, was not expected to appeal the ban, which was automatic under the NBA's 1983 anti-drug program but could be rescinded after two years under certain conditions. (*Sport Illustrated*, March 10, 1986, p. 7)

Richardson's case reveals the steps in part of the NBA policy regarding a drug problem. If a player seeks treatment for a drug problem, the NBA pays for rehabilitation and the player is paid under his contract. However, when a player comes forward a second time, he is suspended without pay while undergoing treatment. When there is a third recurrence, whether disclosed voluntarily or not, the player is banned from the NBA.

THE NATIONAL COLLEGIATE ATHLETIC ASSOCIATION

At its 80th annual convention in January 1986, the NCAA passed "Proposal 30 — Drug Testing," to be effective August 1, 1986. Later, that program was summarized (Exhibit 6-1).

During the first half of 1986, the Special NCAA Drug Testing Committee continued to implement the drug testing legislation and provide drug-testing information to the membership. Actions taken by the committee included the following:

1. Determined the protocol for testing events:
   a. Organized the program.
   b. Determined penalties.
   c. Determined the method of selection for drug testing.
   d. Established procedures for collection.
   e. Set up the chain of custody.
   f. Provided for notification procedures.
2. Selected 16 drug-testing crew chiefs, predominantly physicians who volunteered their time to attend the training session in preparation for the testing sessions.

EXHIBIT 6-1. Summary of NCAA drug-testing program

Preface

Among the goals of the program is to provide clean, equitable competition for student-athletes competing in NCAA championships and NCAA-certified postseason football bowl games. The program involves urine collection on specific occasions and laboratory analyses for substances on a list of banned drugs developed by the NCAA Executive Committee and approved by the 1986 NCAA Convention. This list is comprised of drugs generally purported to be performance-enhancing and/or potentially harmful to the health and safety of the student-athlete. The list specifically includes psychomotor stimulants (such as amphetamines and cocaine) and anabolic steroids, as well as other drugs.

Medical code

Any use of a substance currently listed by the NCAA as banned will be considered "doping" and cause for disciplinary action.

Evidence of use of a banned substance will be from analysis of the student-athlete's urine by gas chromatography/mass spectrometry.

The current NCAA list of banned substances has been publicized. In addition, other compounds may be included in the screening process for nonpunitive, research purposes, in order to gather data for making decisions as to whether other drugs should be added to the list of banned substances. The NCAA Executive Committee will be responsible for reviewing and revising the list of banned substances on a periodic basis.

Organization

The NCAA Executive Committee will oversee the procedures and implementation of the NCAA drug-testing program.

The NCAA drug-testing committee will be responsible for supervision of the training of the crew chiefs, who will take responsibility for respective drug-testing occasions.

The drug-testing committee will assign each crew chief to one or more NCAA championships and/or football bowl games. If a subsequent schedule conflict precludes use of the principle crew chief at a particular testing occasion, the drug-testing committee will assign another crew chief or crew for that occasion.

The NCAA national administration will support, coordinate and supply the drug-testing program operations within established policies and procedures. The three NCAA staff members involved in administering the program are Ruth M. Berkey, assistant executive director for administration; Ursula R. Walsh, director of research and sports sciences, and Frank Uryasz, former registrar at Bishop Clarkson College of Nursing, who is in the process of joining the NCAA staff.

Penalties

All student-athletes found to be positive for a banned substance are subject to disciplinary action(s) consistent with existing policies, as designed in NCAA Bylaws 5-2-(b).

Staff members of the athletics department of a member institution or others employed by the intercollegiate athletics program who have knowledge of the use contrary to Bylaw 5-2 by a student-athlete of a substance on the list of banned drugs set forth in Executive Regulation 1-7-(b), and who fail to follow institutional procedures dealing with drug abuse, will be subject to disciplinary or corrective action as set forth in Section 7-(b)-(12) of the NCAA enforcement procedure.

Athlete selection

The method of selecting student-athletes will be recommended by the NCAA drug-testing committee, approved by the Executive Committee, and implemented by the NCAA staff and assigned principal crew chiefs, in advance of the testing occasion. All student-athletes entered in the event are subject to testing.

At NCAA individual/team championships events, the top place-finishers and a random sample of other student-athletes may be selected for drug-testing. All student-athletes participating in the event are subject to testing.

In team championships and certified football bowl games, student-athletes may be selected on the basis of playing time, positions or random selection. The selection will be determined prior to or during the competition. During the competition includes up to one hour following the conclusion of an individual's last participation on any particular day.

If doping is suspected, the crew chief will have the authority to select specific additional student-athletes to be tested.

Student-athletes may be tested on more than one occasion. (*The NCAA News*/July 2, 1986, p. 4)

3. Approved, plans to test approximately 3,000 athletes, including participants in certified post-season football bowl contests for the 1986 football season, the 1987 Division I Men's Basketball Championship and other NCAA Championships.
4. Developed guidelines for selection of laboratories

John L. Toner, athletic director at the University of Connecticut, said, "This program will be able to detect not only the more common forms of anabolic steroids and street drugs (such as cocaine), but also will be fine-tuned to detect the more sophisticated varieties of such drugs, the so-called 'designer' offshoots.

"It is important to realize that many of the drug-testing programs that have been announced are narrow in concept," Toner said. "Some programs may test for so-called street drugs, but do not test for anabolic steroids, and even if they do are not able to detect the so-called designer drugs."

Toner emphasized that the NCAA program is intended to be all-inclusive and the most effective possible. (*The NCAA News*/July 2, 1986, p. 4)

In addition to the "Special NCAA Postseason Drug-Testing Committee," the NCAA also established the "NCAA Drug Education Committee," which has primary responsibility for providing member institutions with information and materials that can be used in starting or improving drug education and testing programs at the institutional level. One of the goals of the committee was to provide information on what various institutions are doing in drug education. Table 6-1 shows the results of a survey conducted by the committee in 1985.

TABLE 6-1. Summary of Results of Drug Education/Testing Survey
(NCAA Drug Education Committee)

1. Does your athletic department currently have in operation a drug/alcohol educational program for student-athletes?
   85 (16%) Yes
   384 (74%) No
   49 (10%) No, but actively planning one
2. Does your athletic department currently have in operation a drug/alcohol education program for coaches and other staff?
   57 (11%) Yes
   431 (83%) No
   30 (6%) No, but actively planning one
3. Do you currently have a plan for treating and rehabilitating student-athletes found to have drug/alcohol dependency problems?
   145 (28%) Yes
   345 (66%) No
   28 (5%) No, but actively planning one
4. Does your athletic department currently utilize a drug testing program for student-athletes?
   54 (10%) Yes
   430 (83%) No
   34 (7%) No, but actively planning one
5. Are coaches and other staff tested along with student-athletes?
   12 (22%) Yes
   42 (78%) No
6. Is there a specific written policy on drug testing given to the student-athletes?
   36 (69%) Yes
   17 (31%) No
7. Do student-athletes sign some type of waiver form pertaining to drug testing?
   37 (69%) Yes
   17 (31%) No
8. Who is informed of the results of any positive tests?

   35 (66%) Student-athlete   *Other*
   35 (66%) Team physician
   40 (75%) Coach   2 (4%) Chief executive
   30 (57%) Athletic trainer   officer
   22 (42%) Director of athletics   1 (2%) Substance abuse
   11 (21%) Parents   coordinator
                                      1 (2%) Director of drug testing

9. What action is taken on the first positive test for an individual (beyond discussing the results with the student-athlete)?

   2 (4%) Removal from team.   *Other*
   31 (57%) Put into counseling
            or drug education   1 (2%) Out of competition
            program.   5 (10%) Talk with coach or
   7 (13%) Suspend from team   physician
            for limited time.   1 (2%) Extra runs/calisthenics.
   10 (19%) Nothing.   2 (4%) Out of school.
                                     1 (2%) Probation, informed
                                             parents, retested.

TABLE 6-1 *(con't.)*

10. This drug testing program is:
    15 (29%) Voluntary
    37 (71%) Mandatory
11. What type of tests do you use?
    16 (30%) Commercial immunoassay-test kit, done by trainer or non-medical staff.
    5 (9%) Commercial test kit, done by team physician.
    11 (21%) Sent to local hospital laboratory.
    21 (40%) Sent to commercial laboratory.
12. What type of confirmation procedure do you for a positive test?
    11 (21%) None.   *Other*
    8 (15%) Repeat test using a
            different test method.   1 (2%) Ask student-athlete.
    23 (43%) Repeat test with same   1 (2%) Send to commercial
            equipment   laboratory
    8 (15%) Use gas chromatography/   1 (2%) Unknown.
            mass spectrometry
13. For what drugs do you test or plan to test?
    33 (40%) Alcohol   82 (100%) Marijuana
    62 (76%) Amphetamines   73 (89%) Other street drugs
    23 (28%) Anabolic steroids   (cocaine, heroin,
                                                 etc.)
                                        6 No answer
14. Do you think student-athletes should be tested for drugs?
    286 (57%) Yes
    137 (27%) No
    77 (16%) No opinion
15. If drug testing were done on student-athletes, at what level or levels do you think it should be done?
    221 (44%) Institutional
    33 (7%) Conference
    121 (24%) National (NCAA)
    108 (22%) All levels
    65 (13%) Should not be done
793 Survey instruments sent
518 Returned
 65% Response rate

The National Collegiate Athletic Association Mission, Kansas EDZ:bb January 31, 1985

After reviewing the results of the survey, the NCAA Drug Education Committee concluded that further efforts should be made to conduct drug testing at the institutional level. The thought was that drug testing is an integral part of drug education. In an April 1986 edition of *The NCAA News* the committee also expressed the opinion that they would be more concerned with street drugs, such as marijuana and cocaine. However, that idea was in conflict with the "draft guidelines" presented by the ACE in May 1986 (Exhibit 6-2).

EXHIBIT 6-2. American Council on Education's Draft Guidelines on Testing Athletes for Drugs

1. The purpose of programs for testing intercollegiate athletes for use of drugs should be to prevent use of performance-enhancing drugs that undermine the integrity of athletic competition. It is undesirable to employ drug testing programs as a means of detecting use of recreational drugs, whether their use is legal or illegal, that are not used to enhance athletic performance.

2. Drug testing programs should be sport-specific. Tests should focus upon drugs whose abuse can reasonably be anticipated because they are used to enhance performance in specific kinds of competition. Testing should also be scheduled to detect use of drugs affecting athletic competition, rather than any use of drugs at any time.

3. The drug testing program should incorporate procedures guaranteeing the accurate identification of each individual's test results and provide for additional verification of initial positive test results through extremely reliable test procedures.

4. The drug testing program should provide students for whom test results are positive with adequate notice and the right to a hearing prior to any adverse action based on the test. The more severe the potential sanction, the more formal must the hearing procedures be in affording the student the opportunity to present information in his or her defense and to challenge evidence and testimony against him or her before neutral hearing officers. Procedures should incorporate a right of review and appeal prior to the imposition of severe sanctions, such as loss of eligibility or rescission of an athletic scholarship.

5. The drug testing program should include procedures protecting the privacy of all athletes. Information disclosed by testing must be restricted to personnel responsible for administering the program. No other release of the information can be authorized without the athlete's written consent or appropriate judicial process.

6. The drug testing program should include written rules governing each step of the program, including: means of selecting for testing; scheduling and collection of samples; the samples; determination that a test result is positive; means of verification of positive results; communication with students and third parties about positive test results; counseling to be provided; sanctions to be imposed for violations of the drug use policy; applicable hearing/due process procedures; and schedule of penalties imposed for particular violations or cumulative violations.

7. The drug testing program should require students to give their written consent to the program prior to their participation in any intercollegiate athletic program. There must at this time be full disclosure to athletes of all facts surrounding the program so that each student can give his or her informed consent.

8. Any college with a testing program should provide full and complete information about the program to all intercollegiate athletic recruits early in any recruitment process (and certainly before any recruit makes a decision upon any offer from the college) and to all students prior to their enrollment.

EXHIBIT 6-2 *(con't.)*

9. The information provided to students should at a minimum include the written program itself; a full description of the purposes of the drug testing program; the procedures for collecting samples; procedures upon determination that a test result is positive, including both verification of the result and the hearing procedures; and sanctions to be imposed for the first and subsequent violations of the drug use policy as determined by the testing program. The information should be clear, complete, and accurate, and acknowledge the risk that information from the testing program may be accessible to third parties.

10. The drug testing program should include procedures for training (and regularly monitoring or retraining) college personnel in all aspects of their responsibilities related to the program, including: testing techniques; the need to adhere to the governing rules and procedures; legal rights and responsibilities implicated by the program; the overriding need for confidentiality of information about drug testing results; and who is to be consulted in the event of any questions or controversies that may arise.

11. Any college with a student athlete drug testing program should also have a policy forbidding any college personnel from providing performance-enhancing drugs or encouraging or otherwise inducing student athletes to use drugs, except as specific drugs may be prescribed by qualified medical personnel for treatment of individual students. The college should also establish and publicize its procedures for handling complaints that staff or faculty has encouraged or induced use of performance-enhancing drugs. Such complaints should be processed by school personnel that are independent of the athletic department and who have full authority to investigate such allegations.

CONCLUSIONS AND RECOMMENDATIONS

At this point it is a bit difficult to predict what the future will show to be the most effective means of attacking the problem of drug usage among athletes. By the time this book is in print, considerably more may be known regarding what is legally permissible and what has proven to be effective. Based on experience to date, only the following generalities can be set forth.

1. Any policy should be aimed at a holistic approach to drug education, drug testing, and drug rehabilitation. The real, long-term key to success is likely to be drug education. In that regard, efforts at the high school level are much more significant than those directed at college and professional athletes. It is also important to keep in mind that drug abuse is much more of a societal problem than an athletic problem.

2. Before proceeding with the implementation of any policy, a sport organization should seek the services of an outside professional agency, specializing in drug education. Heitzinger and Associates of Madison, Wisconsin, is an example of a firm which offers such assistance programs for student athletes.

3. Some form of drug testing would likely serve as a partial deterrent to drug usage. It also seems that random testing would be more effective than regularly scheduled testing. The legality of testing procedures should be carefully considered before any testing program is proposed.
4. All organizations involved should attempt to reach a unified, consistent decision regarding testing for performance-enhancing drugs and/or recreational drugs. Differences noted in 1986 between proposals by the ACE and the NCAA is a case in point. Such differences are also noted between approaches by the colleges and the professional sport leagues.
5. Protecting the privacy of all athletes is integral to the success of any drug education, drug testing or drug rehabilitation program. The news media will make it particularly difficult to carry this out in the sport enterprise, but policy should be first and foremost aimed at that objective.
6. Policies should specify penalties that would deter drug usage by other athletes. The NBA's 1983 anti-drug program was clearly a step in the right direction.

Note: Additional updated information on drug testing can be found in Chapter 20 on pages 319 to 322.

REFERENCES

Brubaker, Bill. "Bittersweet," *Sports Illustrated*, February 4, 59-72.
"Committee Recommends Lessening of Penalty for Positive Drug Test." *The NCAA News* Vol. 23, No. 24, June 11, 1986, pp. 1, 7.
McCallum, Jack. "Life Was Sweet . . . But The Sugar Ran Out." *Sports Illustrated*, January 13, 1986, pp. 26-28.
_____ . "The Cruelest Thing Ever." *Sports Illustrated*, June 30, 1986, pp. 20-27.
"Members to Get More Help with Drug Education." *The NCAA News*, Vol. 23, No. 18, April 30, 1986, pp. 1, 5.
Monaghan, P. "Colleges that Examine Athletes for Recreational Drugs Are on Shaky Legal Ground, Guideline Draft Suggests." *The Chronicle of Higher Education* May 7, 1986, pp. 31-32, 34.
Moore, D. L. and Wieberg, S. "Cocaine Shock Wave Strikes Again." *USA Today*, June 30, 1986, Section C, pp. 1-2.
"NCAA Takes a Firm Stand in Anti Drug Campaign." *The NCAA News*, Vol. 23, No. 26, July 2, 1986, pp. 1, 4.
Nicholi, A. "Will the Losses Shock Us into Strong Action?" *The New York Times*, July 6, 1986, p. 29.
"Scorecard." *Sports Illustrated*, July 21, 1986, p. 7.
"Scorecard." *Sports Illustrated*, March 10, 1986, p. 7.

7

Professional Athletes: Career Counseling

A major, but often overlooked, problem in professional sport involves the career transition period for professional athletes from their athletic careers to second careers. The natural tendency is to focus only on the former star quarterback in the NFL (or similar examples), who becomes a successful television commentator. What happens to the majority of professional athletes following their "playing days" is by and large unknown. Information is largely limited to journalistic accounts of former athletes who encountered extreme problems in retirement. McPherson noted in 1977 that "empirical work of a survey nature is hampered greatly by the very real problem of first trying to locate former athletes, and second obtaining their agreement and cooperation to complete a questionnaire or interview." (p. 2)

In considering this problem of adjustment in an athlete's retirement, it is necessary to first understand the typical professional sport career. Retired athletes are not only those who played the game for several years and chose to retire but also those who are forced to retire due to injury or other reasons. League officials estimate that more than 30 percent of professional athletes are forced into premature retirement due to injuries. A significant number also terminate their athletic careers due to family reasons, poor relations with clubs and/or coaches, and loss of positions to younger players. While very few athletes make it to the professional level, relatively few of those find long-lasting success. Even if they survive the first two years, the average career length for professional athletes is somewhere between five and 10 years, depending on the sport (McPherson, 1977).

Due to the ever increasing injury factor, that figure is even lower today for certain sports. While defending the position taken by striking

NFL players in 1987, Mix reported the average career length to be 3.5 years for football, 3.8 for basketball, and 4.9 for baseball. At the same time, he noted the larger problem involving disabilities among retired players:

> And what becomes of the players when their careers are concluded? They join the ranks of the walking wounded. Part of my current law practice involves representing retired athletes in workers' compensation claims for athletics-related injuries. On the average, veterans of the National Football League end up somewhere between 50% and 65% disabled. The most common source of the disability is a knee injury, which combined with a bad back (for instance) equals 50% disability. Approximately 20% of my clients will be rated 100% disabled. Most of them are unable to even stand or sit for a prolonged period. Total knee and hip replacements are common. Fused spines are a given; chronic searing headaches a plague. (p.55)

The problem area for retiring athletes is the period of transition between professional sport and a new career. This transition phase is handled easily by some, but for many others the change in life style is difficult. Haerle (1975) did an extensive study of the occupational status of major league baseball players. Following are excerpts from some of his findings and conclusions related to post-baseball or second careers for these athletes:

> Perhaps the most interesting and theoretically important career contingency occurs when the major league player is forced to retire from active playing. At a relatively young age, when most of his age peers in other occupations are reaching maturity and stability on the job, the retired player must embark on an entirely new career. In short, this is a crucial 'turning point' in the lifelong occupational career of the professional athlete. . . .
> The trauma of this moment can best be seen as a natural outgrowth of the desire to remain in the game and the lack of planning for a second career. Without going into great detail, the following information on our sample of former baseball players is illustrative. . . . About 75 percent of the 312 respondents reported that they did not even begin to consider retirement until they were in the last quarter of their active career in baseball (thus, in their early to mid-30's). . . .
> When queried about their feelings at the time of leaving the playing career, slightly over half of the 360 codable responses (some gave more than one classifiable answer) were oriented rather nostalgically toward the past. Interview and questionnaire disclosures included regret, sadness and shock with the aging process that brought on the forced decision. . . .
> At the other extreme were those retirees who were future-oriented. About one-quarter of the answers fell into this grouping (with the

remaining responses characterized as a mixture between past and future orientation). The comments of the future-oriented indicated a strong sense of self-confidence and acceptance of the inevitable. (pp. 498-500)

Several variables contribute to this problem of career transition among athletes. First, of all, many professional athletes do not have college degrees. Recent studies have shown that only about one-third of the NFL and NBA players earned college degrees. The situation in the National Hockey League (NHL) is even more severe (Exhibit 7-1). For example, in survey results reported by Blann and Zaichkowsky, 36 percent of the NHL players planned to complete their high school diplomas.

Most professional athletes have worked at their sports nearly year round and thus have no work experience or training in other fields. The length of the schedules and extensive travel contribute to the lack of time for other career pursuits. Furthermore, professional sport managers generally discourage alternative career investigations. This one-dimensional orientation of the athlete begins earlier in life. Blann (1985) summarizes the situation as follows:

Athletes who achieve high level amateur (Olympic) and/or professional sport status do so by committing themselves to training for sport year-round over an extended period of time. By so doing, Olympic and professional athletes may focus on sport to such an extent that, during their development as young adults, they may fail to give adequate attention to educational, career and life plans other than pursuit and attainment of a professional sport career. Several theorists . . . posit that sport participation over an extended period of time, and especially at the 'big time' collegiate, Olympic and professional levels, may result in a one-dimensional mentality which can be detrimental to individuals' development. (p. l)

The high salaries in professional sport also give athletes a false sense of security. Many feel that there is no need to find other careers. When that need is recognized, there is a reluctance to accept lower salaries in other fields. However, the retired "journeyman" athlete usually experiences the most severe financial woes. Due to the relative brevity of a typical career in professional sport, many players are forced to retire without qualifying for pensions.

Finally, coaches and others make decisions for many athletes and control their lives. When their careers are over, these athletes do not have the direction or the ability to make decisions for themselves.

Generally speaking, the problem faced by retiring professional athletes fall into three main areas: financial, psychological, and social. The financial problem has been alleviated to some extent by the overall increase in player salaries and the growing recognition of the need to plan

EXHIBIT 7-1. NHL Survey

At the August, 1985 NHL Players Association meeting we requested permission to conduct a survey of NHL players to determine their career awareness and career needs. In order to conduct this "needs assessment" the Professional Athletes' Career Transition Inventory (PACTI) was distributed to Player Representatives, and 8 NHL teams. Data were obtained from the Player Representatives and 6 NHL teams, a total of 117 players.

Following are highlights of the findings, as well as characteristics of the players completing the survey.

Highlights of Research Findings

1. 85% of the players believe it is important that help be provided them in planning post-sport careers.

Extremely Important	= 50%
Important	= 35%

2. The three programs (out of 5 listed) perceived by players as most helpful to them in planning post-sport careers were:

   Ranked #1 - Seminars and individual counseling programs to help players understand and relate their personal strengths, interests and skills to appropriate careers.

Ranked #1	= 33%
Ranked #2	= 27%
Total	= 60%

   Ranked #2 - Seminars and individual counseling programs to help players develop and then carry out education and career action plans.

Ranked #1	= 34%
Ranked #2	= 19%
Total	= 53%

   Ranked #3 - Seminars and individual counseling programs to help players understand and relate specific education, certification, licensing and other training programs to appropriate careers.

Ranked #1	= 5%
Ranked #2	= 33%
Total	= 38%

3. The two programs (out of the 5 listed) perceived by players as less helpful to them in planning post-sport careers were:

   Ranked #4 - Help in arranging for players to work at jobs part time and during the off season.

Ranked #1	= 22%
Ranked #2	= 14%
Total	= 36%

   Ranked #5 - Help in developing and carrying out job search campaigns.

Ranked #1	= 5%
Ranked #2	= 8%
Total	= 13%

4. 95% of the players believe that the NHLPA should be involved in helping players with post-sport career planning.

Great Deal of Involvement	= 54%
Some Involvement	= 41%

5. 98% of the players think about their sport careers ending.

Very Often	= 40%
Sometimes	= 58%

6. 53% of the players indicate they are delaying planning for a post-sport career.
7. 68% of the players believe their post-sport career will be critical to their life satisfaction after their sport career ends.
8. Only 47% of the players are satisfied that they have managed their finances to provide for adequate financial support for up to 2 years to prepare for and enter a post-sport career.
9. 73% of the players plan to play hockey 5 or more years in the NHL.
   a. The average professional ice hockey career is 5 years
   b. The mode age of the players surveyed was 27 years.

EXHIBIT 7-1 *(con't.)*

10. 36% of the players plan to complete their high school diplomas. The remaining 64% plan to pursue education beyond high school:

Associates Degree	= 19%
Bachelors Degree	= 27%
Masters Degree	= 5%
Law/Doctoral Degree	= 12%

11. Responses to questions included in the Life Satisfaction Scale (LSS) of the inventory showed that the players are exceptionally well-satisfied with their present life situations.

12. Responses to questions included in the Career Awareness Scale (CAS) of the inventory showed that the players have heightened career awareness levels.

Demographic Data on Players

1. Age:
   18 - 22 = 20%
   23 - 27 = 50%
   28 - 32 = 24%
   33 - 37 = 4%
   38 - 42 = 2%
   Youngest = 18 years
   Oldest = 42 years

2. Citizenship:

Canadian	= 77%
U.S.	= 15%
European	= 8%

3. Marital Status:

Single	= 32%
Married	= 65%
Separated/Divorced	= 3%

4. Current Educational Levels:

Less Than High School	= 26%
High School Diploma	= 32%
One Year or Less of College	= 11%
More Than One Year of College	= 12%
Associates Degree	= 0%
Bachelors Degree	= 7%
Masters Degree	= 2%
Law Degree or Doctoral Degree	= 0%

5. Socioeconomic Background (Father's Occupation):

Semi-skilled, Skilled, and Supervisory	= 55%
Clerical and Managerial	= 34%
Professional	= 11%

6. Salary Ranges:

$ 31 — 90,000	= 14%
$ 91 — 150,000	= 33%
$151 — 500,000	= 48%
$501 — 999,000	= 5%

Conclusions

1. The majority of the NHL players expressed a strong need for programs to assist them with post-sport career planning and further, that the NHLPA should be responsible for providing the service.

2. The players felt that seminars and individual counseling programs would be the most effective method of meeting their needs. They were particularly in favor of seminars and counseling focused on:

   a. Understanding their personal strengths, interests and skills.

   b. Developing and carrying out education and career action plans.

(Blann, 1986)

for retirement. Players associations have taken a more active role in guiding the future directions of the athletes. Furthermore, there is a continuing effort by these associations to generate better pension and disability programs to protect retirees in later life.

The psychological adjustment may well be the most acute problem and the most difficult to confront. Athletes may not be able to accept the facts that their skills have eroded or that they cannot match the performances of others, many of whom are younger. They tend to be resistant to relinquishing their playing positions to younger athletes. As in other careers, the individual who retires involuntarily is more resistive and less well prepared for retirement than the individual who makes the decision himself or herself.

The process of sport role socialization begins early. Studies have shown that in childhood the future athlete begins to define the social self in sport terms. This process is reinforced over the years at all levels. The athlete's network includes his teammates, coaches, and other sport personnel. The social life of the athlete has revolved around sport until retirement. The loss of this social network can lead to loneliness. Furthermore, the athlete may sense a loss of self-respect and feel the need to be socially important. Even a senior citizen at age 65 may face a crisis brought about by the damage to his or her social identity. In the case of younger professional athletes, the problem is likely to be more critical because they have been accustomed to the public spotlight and because retirement at age 25 to 35 is less socially sanctioned than it is at 65.

Although many athletes face these kind of problems in making career adjustments, many others have been quite successful in developing rewarding second careers. Why, then, do some make it, while others experience difficulty?

The common denominator among those who have transition problems is lack of planning for retirement. Some professional athletes put off the planning to attempt to stay on with the team and remain associated with the sport. Many lack the education or training for other careers. Not surprisingly, minority athletes as a group have the least amount of preparation and frequently experience the most problems. This explains why career counseling is a growing concern in professional sport.

THE ISSUE

To what extent should league management, team management, or players associations play an active role in helping the retired athlete? What are the obligations of each entity? Players associations have established provisions for retiring athletes as a priority consideration. These associations have stressed the need for counseling programs and career awareness. However, what is the prospect of developing policies whereby leagues and/or teams provide counseling services for their employees?

If there is to be any significant policy regarding career counseling for professional athletes, it will have to result from labor-management relations. Any attempt to provide a league-wide program will have to be negotiated through collective bargaining.

In looking at the history of the labor-management relationship and the current collective bargaining agreements in the major professional team sports, career counseling would not appear to be a high priority consideration for management. As a matter of fact, it is probably not the top priority even for the players associations. The efforts to date have largely centered on attempts to obtain better pension plans, including provisions for former players who retire before any of the current agreements went into effect. In the meantime, with the financial pendulum swinging toward higher player salaries and high operating costs for owners, it seems rather unlikely that the owners would agree to finance a counseling program.

There are programs that offer counseling for athletes outside the management domain. They may offer the real potential for policy in this area. Work with players in the NHL offers one example.

Case Study: The National Hockey League

Among the professional sport leagues, the NHL poses special problems for its athletes in terms of retirement. Although the overall problem has existed for years, current conditions make the problem more acute.

The average career length in the NHL is 4.6 years (McKenzie, 1985, p. 11). This figure is among the lowest of the major team sports. (As noted earlier, the NFL average is even lower, at 3.2 years.) The situation in hockey is complicated by other factors. Junior players who were selected in the 1979 and 1980 entry drafts have come of age and are now competing with relatively young veterans for roster spots. These rookies from the baby boom generation are pushing out the veterans and threatening to lower the average career length even further.

The retirement of the relatively young NHL player is further handicapped by the generally low level of education attained by players in the league. Most junior players who hope to play in the NHL forego college to play in the Canadian Junior circuit where the competition is strong. That situation is changing somewhat with the current upgrading of the college hockey programs in the United States. Nevertheless, NHL players have the lowest level of educational attainment in all of the major professional sports (McKenzie).

Several key individuals and groups are attempting to improve the situation for NHL retirees. One of these is a retired player, Phil Esposito, who established an association and a program to assist in alleviating the problems of NHL players after retirement from the league.

The Phil Esposito Foundation: The Phil Esposito Foundation was established in New York in 1981. Esposito and his board of directors, former NHL players Gordie Howe, Bobby Orr, Lou Nanne, and Roger Vachen, put together a non-profit, tax-exempt organization. The purpose of the foundation was clearly stated by the board at the outset: "This Foundation reflects the problems faced by retired personnel who, during their years of dedicated service, were never offered the professional guidance and support required to prepare them for financial security after their retirement." (*The Phil Esposito Foundation Prospectus*, p. I)

The foundation set up three programs for active and retired NHL players: an Alumni Benefit Program, a Crisis Program, and a Post Career Planning Program. The Alumni Benefit Program was constructed to ease the financial burden of former NHL personnel by providing a major medical insurance plan so that the retired players would always have provisions for medical care. The Crisis Program was designated to help players who suffered financial hardship, drug and/or alcohol abuse, or career adjustment problems. The Post-Career Planning Program is a more formally structured program for career adjustment.

To design the latter program, the foundation obtained the services of Murray Axsmith and Associates of Toronto. The program includes the following components: 1) career assessment, 2) off-season on-the-job training and employment, and 3) job search assistance. Working with career planning experts, the counseling firm conducted a survey of 1,200 former players, coaches, trainers, and officials to provide a basis for the Post-Career Planning Program. A major purpose of the survey was to determine the extent of the career transition problem.

Of the 1,200 surveyed, only 212 returned responses to the questionnaire. The average respondent was 40 years old, married with two dependents, and had been retired from the NHL for 10 years. (*The Phil Esposito Programming Update*, p. 1) Some of the results of the survey are worthy of note:

1) 88 percent of the respondents said they would have utilized a career counseling program, had it been available.
2) Those who experienced difficulties in the first year of career transition indicated they had a lack of preparation, work experience, and vocational guidance.
3) Forty-eight percent of the respondents had made no plans for retirement.
4) Those who prepared for retirement appeared to have a clear advantage over those who had not planned. At the time of the survey, 75 percent of those with preparation were earning $25,000 or more per year. Only 49 percent of those without preparation were at that salary level.
5) Dissatisfaction with their current jobs was expressed by 6 percent of those who prepared. Twenty-five percent of those who failed to make plans for a second career were dissatisfied.

6) Ninety-five percent of those who prepared were employed at the time of the survey, whereas 82 percent of those without preparation were employed.
7) Among all respondents, 56 percent reported that a high school diploma was the highest education level attained and 34 percent had at least taken some college courses.

The survey included provision for comments by the former players regarding their career transitions. These comments produced 15 pages of strong testimony to the fact that a retirement problem exists and that certain programs would be utilized if implemented. Exhibit 7-2 includes some of the comments.

In summary, there was evidence that the players who prepared for a second career had a distinct advantage over those who lacked preparation. Members of the former group made smoother and quicker transitions into second careers, were more satisfied with current careers, received higher earnings, and had a lower rate of unemployment.

Thus, even though the overall response was somewhat limited, the results of the survey reinforced the need for the Post-Career Planning Program, consisting of career assessment, job training, and a job search system. The career assessment includes aptitude testing and an interest survey to evaluate a player's interests and capabilities for the most appropriate second career. The job training consists of classroom training and off-season employment. The job search includes resume development, strategies for appraising the job market, and pooling of possible employment opportunities.

The response of the NHL players to the Post-Career Planning Program was very strong. However, this also points to a major problem faced by the Esposito Foundation. The demand for the services of the program was greater than the foundation could provide. The foundation was simply not equipped to serve the needs of current and former players from all over the United States and Canada from its base in New York. An attempt was made to use career consultants in several of the NHL cities and surrounding areas, which led to a funding problem. As a non-profit organization, the foundation lacked the financial resources to continue to hire career consultants. Attempts to obtain corporate donations were generally unsuccessful, because corporations thought the league should be responsible for career counseling. Nevertheless, in spite of the financial limitations, it is safe to say that the foundation has at least been successful in heightening the awareness of players and related groups to the situation and the problem.

The National Hockey League Players' Association: The group most directly concerned with the NHL retirement situation is the National

EXHIBIT 7-2. Post Career Planning Program Survey of NHL Retired Players
Age 37

You are dealing in a very touchy situation. As a player it is hard to realize what one must do to prepare for the unexpected. Try telling a hockey player that he must study or work in the off season to prepare himself for life, he'll look at you like you have two heads. But until one realizes that hockey is just a short pleasant time in one's life and that there are many, many years left to live and work, there is very little help for them. I don't think a summer job of punching a clock is too hard on anyone, as a matter of fact it trains a person to reality. Best of luck.

Age 50

Players should be more aware of their own personal planning — not only post career, but post family as well.

Although travel is extensive, training should begin during active period as there is a sufficient amount of idle time.

No age given — retired 12 years

Following my retirement it was very difficult to adjust. I always thought that my name, reputation and credibility would automatically open doors and obtain me a job. It opened doors, but it didn't get me a job. I spent 11 years in the NHL and although I thought I was prepared for retirement, I wasn't.

Formal post career planning is an alternative that must be made available to those who wish to pursue it. In my opinion, it will preserve many a person's normal future.

Age 32

The biggest favor this foundation can do is try and get through to the current players these points:

1. Look after the big money now because, unless you are a superstar, the day you retire you are like any other unemployed person — your hockey experience doesn't help land another job.

2. Prepare yourself for another occupation because hockey will not last forever.

3. I repeat. HOCKEY WILL SOON BE OVER. It is much easier to prepare for your second vocation while still playing hockey, rather than scrambling around after you are replaced by a younger player. By this time you may have a wife and family and at this point beggars can't be choosers and you will probably take any job.

Age 36

As far as working after hockey, the Foundation should maybe try to get the members of the various leagues to spend part of their summers with people in different lines of work. Then, maybe they could find something that appeals to them that they could begin to prepare for while playing. I found if I spent all my time with other players, I got a false sense of what life with outsiders was all about.

Age 27

I am still an active player, although I am now playing in France. I have been here for three years now and I enjoy it very much. I read the write-up in The Hockey News about your Foundation and it is about time that something like this is being done. I have been taking courses at Wilfred Lauraier University the last two summers and I hope to finish my business Diploma in the following two summers. If something of a job training program would have been offered while I was playing in the U.S. (five years) I would have definitely taken it up. Personally, I am

EXHIBIT 7-2 *(con't.)*

not looking forward to the adjustment period between my hockey career and my business career. I am however, planning and preparing for it now. Your organization, should you achieve the goals you have set out for your Foundation, can only help to benefit all hockey players.

Age 32

I think that what you're doing is excellent. Looking back on the first part of my career. I wish I'd done many things differently. If this Foundation can help keep things in perspective for current players, and help past players who didn't, then it's done one helluva job.

I took so much for granted when I played and as a result am not as financially stable as I could have been. Especially in farming does a person like to have a little cushion just in case there's no crop.

Without my wife working, the whole situation changes very drastically.
So boys, I wish you luck in getting some players ready for the life after hockey.

Age 36

I think your concept would be of immeasurable aid to young hockey players. One major obstacle would be PLAYER RECOGNITION of future problems. Also, the ego of young players would be affected in that they would not accept that "potential failure" befronts them.

I am almost tempted to suggest that a *forced* program would best suit the young athletes, forced in the sense that the player be made *aware* of the future.

Age 40

I attended university during the off season for the last seven years I was playing. This is a difficult route to follow, especially for people married with families. However, some kind of training is necessary to provide players with some security when their playing days are over.

Age 32

Management should not frown on players 1) pursuing an outside career (retirement) as long as there is no conflict of interest; 2) counselling should be available as to the vocations within and outside of hockey that are available to them after retirement; 3) consideration on the above should be given to abilities, interests, education and experiences (of the retired players) within these vocations; 4) sports psychologists should be employed by all professional teams.

Age 45

I worked at carpenter work every summer during my 14 years as a professional hockey player. I didn't know I would continue this occupation when I retired from hockey during my playing days, but it prepared me for some kind of a future anyways. When I retired from hockey, I decided carpenter work and cabinet making was what I knew best, so that's why I'm doing it now. I think professional athletes should, No. 1, invest their money wisely and save as much as they possibly can. No. 2, spend at least part of each summer or off season learning something about what they want to do when they retire. Every athlete has to retire sometime and it's a very difficult adjustment even when you have another occupation to turn to.

Age 57

I am sure that the participation in off season work experience is the most valuable effort an athlete can make to his future. The importance of the Foundation's activity in this area cannot be overemphasized.

EXHIBIT 7-2 *(con't.)*

Age 33

I think this is a very wise program. I think the biggest problem with hockey players or any athlete is not knowing what one really wants to do when our career ends. In our playing days we get caught up in our own little environment and forget there is another world outside of hockey. If I would have known what I really wanted to do about eight years before I retired from the game, the transition would have gone more smoothly. If players can be helped in making that decision early in their careers, then they can set goals for themselves. After that, it is simply by their own desires and motivation to get there. Basically, if you don't know where you are going you can't get there.

Age 34

Congratulations to you people, as your foundation is a much needed service and a positive step.

Readjusting to the "real world" was not a great problem for me, but for some very good friends of mine it was a very traumatic experience that I believe could have been averted or at least softened. I say the "real world" not only because it is true but I've been out of hockey for five years now and it seems as though it never happened.

The problem of athletes readjusting is going to become more serious in the near future, for a number of reasons. Today a hockey career is considerably shorter than the recent past, and with the confrontation of adjusting at a much younger age the reality of the situation will be staggering. When a player retired at the age of 35, after playing pro for 10 or 12 years he is perceived to have had a fairly successful hockey career. Players retiring today at such a tender age have a degree of a stigma of failure attached whether real or imagined and dealing with that problem is something in itself.

This entire post-athletic career problem that you are addressing is compounded in pro hockey as opposed to other pro sports, and unless dealt with, it will become much more serious. There are teams in the N.H.L. with as many as 95% of their team under the age of 28. Baseball, basketball and football players cannot be drafted until their graduation year in college and teams and dealing with more mature individuals from day one of the pro careers.

Post Career Planning is excellent, but I believe N.H.L. teams require some type of in-house guidance in many aspects for their players. There are teams in the N.H.L. today where the so called leaders or role models are 25 years of age and this situation is not fair to all involved. Where you look at the situation very bluntly, you have 18 to 22 year old boys without a college education (in most cases) earning a considerable amount of money in an "unreal world." I know because I've been in it. Someone has an obligation to explain to these boys that this is a temporary situation, and this is what you should be doing about it. Good luck with the foundation and you have my support.

Hockey League Players Association (NHLPA). Key individuals are the NHLPA executive director, Alan Eagleson, and David Tucker and Scot McFadden, career planning consultants. Tucker and McFadden worked for the Phil Esposito Foundation in its first two years and then formed their own consulting company, which was commissioned by the NHLPA to give seminars to all the NHL teams on career counseling. The program was initiated prior to the 1984-85 season. As in the foundation program, Tucker and McFadden first concentrated on career transition, using aptitude testing to assist in determining the kind of careers the players might be suited for after retirement from hockey.

The Tucker-McFadden seminars also included psychological and social enlightenment toward experiencing retirement. These discussions were aimed at making the players aware of how their social lives would change. Family counseling was also included to help wives and children cope with the changes. In total, the seminars were aimed at creating an awareness of the need for a complete career transition plan.

Player responses to the Tucker-McFadden seminars were enthusiastic. Tucker and McFadden were able to make themselves available to all the NHL teams. At least half the members of some teams attended with their wives, and other teams boasted full attendance. However, financing of the seminars threatens future efforts. Attempting to serve the needs of all NHL personnel presents a tremendous financial burden that the NHLPA finds difficult to support. To make a major contribution in alleviating the career adjustment problem, something on a more comprehensive scale is needed.

Alan Eagleson has continued to work on a more permanent solution to the problem which would be a career counseling policy involving the management of each NHL team. Eagleson hoped to negotiate this matter through collective bargaining with management which began in July 1985. Essentially, the policy would include a whole package of counseling services and retirement benefits. Specifically, Eagleson was calling for lump severance pay, career counseling provided by each team, and continued education programs. The NHLPA estimated the initial cost to be between $12 million and $20 million. Annual costs to maintain the program would total $3 million. These high figures were attributed to the severance pay estimate and the high cost of hiring several career counseling professionals in each NHL city. Eagleson saw the cost being shared by the owners and the NHLPA, but the majority of the cost would have to be covered by the owners.

Although Eagleson viewed the issue as the top one priority for the collective bargaining negotiations, the matter was not brought up in the preliminary negotiations which began in July 1985. All further negotiations were delayed until the beginning of 1986. In August 1986, the NHL players approved a new five-year collective bargaining agreement. Even though a career assistance program was not part of the agreement, at least they gained an improved pension plan. This should help the players through the transition stage.

Hockey players don't always fight. Sometimes they negotiate, meekly. Consider their new five-year collective bargaining agreement with NHL owners, approved by a player vote two weeks ago. In any other pro sport, union and management would have traded contract demands like roundhouse punches until one of the combatants hit the canvas. But the NHL Players Association, never too demanding, went right into a clinch. After some early talk of holding out for broader free-agent rights - "There is a greater chance than ever before that there will be a strike," NHLPA executive director Alan Eagleson had said ominously - the players settled for little more than an improved pension plan and came to terms almost two months in advance of a strike deadline. It was extraordinary. When push came to shove, nobody pushed and nobody shoved. 'Have you ever played hearts?' Asks player agent Art Kaminsky. It's called a laydown.' (*Sports Illustrated*, Aug. 18, 1986, p. 11)

Northeastern University's Center for the Study of Sport in Society

Other efforts have been made to provide career counseling and continuing education for professional athletes. Perhaps the most significant development today is the work directed by Richard Lapchick, who established the Center for the Study of Sport in Society at Northeastern University in Boston, Massachusetts, in 1983. This research center conducts studies of contemporary social issues in sport. Lapchick was greatly concerned about the exploitation of college athletes, mainly blacks, who are not prepared for the non-athlete job market after their professional and even amateur careers in sport end.

One of the center's first programs was aimed at eliminating the main causes of retirement problems. The first of these was the University Degree Completion Program (UDCP), which Lapchick established at Northeastern in 1984 in consultation with the professional sport leagues, teams, and players associations. The program made Northeastern University available as a central location or resource where athletes could complete their college degrees. In addition to academic classes and advising, the program also included career counseling. Fourteen New England Patriot players and 17 members of the Boston Bruins were enrolled in the pilot program in 1984-85.

As a result of the initial success, a consortium was established with other universities to reach as many athletes as possible. Lapchick planned to add five or six universities each year until most cities with at least two professional sport teams would have a UDCP. Agreements were initially reached with the following universities: St. Johns, New York University,

Seton Hall, Temple, Georgetown, Denver University, California State at Long Beach, University of California - Berkeley, and the University of San Francisco.

Under the consortium arrangement, the other participating university agrees to establish a degree completion program similar to Northeastern's and make it available to all professional sport franchises in the area. This might include courses taught at the site of the professional team. The program is administered through an academic unit within the university in cooperation with its athletic department.

In addition, Northeastern provides a special program, called Public Schools Outreach, for the metropolitan area of the participating university. Through this program, professional athletes, under the guidance of UDCP, counsel high school students and younger children on the importance of education and the realities of careers in professional sport. In turn, the universities provide tuition assistance to the athletes for their contributions in the public schools.

The degree completion program is designed to enable an athlete to successfully complete a degree as soon as possible. This begins with special admissions procedures directed toward the athlete's potential as a student rather than at previous academic performance. Also included are special arrangements to facilitate the transfer of credits from other institutions. All the special arrangements must conform to the guidelines established by Northeastern University.

In addition to degree completion, the participating universities also provide career counseling, tutorial services, and a transfer of credits to other consortium members if a player is traded or relocated for some other reason. The athletic department of the consortium member is also encouraged to adopt a plan for its own student-athletes whereby all athletes who entered the university on athletic scholarships since 1975 would be readmitted on a tuition free basis to continue studies as long as they are making progress toward degrees. Each consortium member is also encouraged to regularly prepare and monitor the academic records of all their scholarship athletes.

As with any enterprise of this type, funding is a critical factor. This is where the leagues, teams, and players associations enter the picture. Northeastern University's Center initially made cooperative arrangements with the various players associations as well as the NFL and the NBA providing for funding. Some of the funds are also distributed to the members of the consortium. The members agree not to seek further funds from organizations that help to support the center. In turn, Northeastern agreed to assist members in seeking alternative sources for funding.

Other Career Counseling Programs

Other attempts continue to be made to alleviate the problem of career transition for professional athletes. The New York Giants recognized the retirement problem several years ago and have had their own program since 1981. Giants' management hired Joel Goldberg and his Career Consultants company to develop a counseling program. Similar to the Tucker-McFadden service, Career Consultants provides counsel in job search strategy, resume preparation, and interviewing techniques. Goldberg also provides educational guidance for the players' children. The program is entirely funded by the Giants' management. Also in the NFL, a similar, in-house counseling program was initiated by the Cleveland Browns in 1984 under former player Paul Warfield, director of player relations for the Browns.

In addition to the league-wide efforts in the NHL, career counseling has also been developed at the team level. The Philadelphia Flyers have provided counseling since 1980. The Flyers' management funded the program at a cost of $5,000 per season. This service was written into the "Standard Player Contract" as a benefit to the player. The Flyers contracted with James Johnson of Educational Advisory Services in Philadelphia. Any player who utilizes the service pays a small fee of around $200. Management feels that the players will get more out of the program if they pay something.

At least one other program is worthy of note. This is the program offered by Professional Athletes Career Enterprises, Inc. (PACE), begun in 1982 by Steve Garvey, a player for the San Diego Padres. PACE was based in Barrington, Illinois, with another office in San Diego. However, it developed as a national service, open to all athletes. The company provides placement as well as counseling services, including aptitude testing, free of charge, and sponsored internship programs. PACE receives 25 percent of the first year's salary when the former athlete finds employment through PACE.

PACE also attempted to develop working relationships with the major league baseball players association and the NBA players association. In addition, contact was made with the NCAA, the Big Ten Conference, and the PAC Ten Conference. Similar to the Northeastern program, the intent is to work on the development of degree completion programs for athletes.

POLICY SUGGESTIONS

This is a rather "sticky" policy area because there are no league-wide policies concerning career counseling in professional sport at the present time. The efforts within the NHL probably provide the best example of steps in that direction. Due to the financial structure in professional sport, one even has to wonder whether league-wide policies are feasible. If there are to be any policies, they will probably have to result from collective bargaining agreements. The players associations will have to become more active in pushing management toward policies in this area. At any rate, any solution within the league structures will not be easily identified, because issues such as salaries, television contracts, pension, and drug testing take priority over career counseling in current negotiating.

Therefore, the following suggestions for policy are made with the realization that the goal of league-wide policies for career counseling may not be reached. Nevertheless, any progress may assist in reducing the extent of the current problem.

1. Every professional sport team would be required by the league to provide at least one, and preferably two, career consultants for players.
2. The consultants would be hired by the league with the approval of the players association.
3. The league, the association, and the individual teams would share the cost.
4. The league would aggressively pursue a corporate sponsor or sponsors to provide the funding at the league level. (A precedent here is that Anheuser-Busch has been a corporate sponsor of the PACE program.)

CONCLUSION

Although career transition for professional athletes may be a major problem, it is not a matter that is likely to receive widespread attention. There are a couple of major reasons for the relative indifference to the problem. First and foremost, there is so much focus on the athlete as an athlete. When the playing days are over, the athlete is quickly moved into the background. Also, there is a tendency for professional sport management to feel a responsibility for players only so long as they are employees of the organization. This is true of many business organizations, not just those involved with the business of sport.

Thus, the only real hope is through the various players associations. Collectively, the players must recognize the problem and be prepared to do what is necessary to work toward a solution. There is much to be gained through attention to and cooperation with the efforts of pioneer programs such as the Phil Esposito Foundation, the Northeastern program, and PACE.

REFERENCES

Blann, W. and Zaichkowsky, L. "Career/Life Transition Needs of National Hockey League Players: A Final Report Prepared for the National Hockey League Players Association." June 9, 1986.

Blann, W. "Post Sport Career Planning." Paper Presented at the United States Olympic Academy IX, State University of New York at Plattsburgh, June 26-30, 1985.

Dorfman. J. "Stepping into the Vacuum." *Forbes*, April 30, 1983, p. 134.

Goldbreg, J. *Career Consultants, Inc. Prospectus,* 1985.

Haerle, R. K. "Career Patterns and Career Contingencies of Professional Baseball Players: An Occupational Analysis." *In Sport and Social Order,* eds. D. W. Ball and J. W. Loy. Reading, MA: Addison-Wesley Publishing Co., 1975, pp. 461-519.

Healy, E. "Those Skates Spell Future Shock." *Goal*, Feb. 15, 1982, p. 24.

McKenzie, B. "The End Is Near," *The Hockey News*, March 15, 1985, p. 11.

Mix, R. "So Little Gain for the Pain," *Sports Illustrated*, October 19, 1987, p. 54-69.

McPherson, B. D. "The Occupational and Psychological Adjustment of Former Professional Athletes." Paper Presented at a Symposium on Former Athletes in Later Life, The American College of Sports Medicine Annual Meeting, Chicago, Ill., May 25, 1977.

Northeastern Center for the Study of Sport in Society. *Northeastern University Center Prospectus*. 1983, p. 1.

Northeastern Center for the Study of Sport in Society. "Criteria for Membership in the National Consortium for the University Degree Completion Program." 1983, p. 1.

"Scorecard." *Sports Illustrated*, Aug. 18, 1986, p. 11.

"The Phil Esposito Foundation Overview," *The Phil Esposito Foundation Prospectus*, 1981, p. 1.

"The Results from Retired Players Questionnaire," *The Phil Esposito Programming Update*, 1984, p. 1.

Ward, J. "Athletes Finding Life After Sports." *USA TODAY*, Oct. 19, 1984, p. 2C.

8

Evaluating High School Coaches

There is little doubt that the evaluation of high school coaches represents both an issue and a problem, in fact, various issues and problems. To begin, the topic of evaluation, in itself, poses a series of questions which tend to be issues that lead to problems: 1) Why evaluate?, 2) Who should evaluate?, and 3) How should evaluation be carried out? In spite of these very basic questions, some form of evaluation is necessary within any organization. Before turning to the specific topic of evaluating high school coaches, it seems appropriate to consider the questions involving evaluation generally.

Why should we have evaluation? There are various answers, but selection of any one or determination of priorities only points to the issues involved. Ideally perhaps, the principal reason for evaluating is to improve individual and/or group performance. From this perspective, evaluation can be viewed as a motivating device. The process of evaluation can also be used to coordinate program development by helping to determine strengths and weaknesses. This might lead to adjustments in program assignments. Evaluation is also used as a basis for external critique. There is frequently a need to compare one program with another. The issue here is whether a valid standard of comparison can be established.

On a more practical level, evaluation is used to make personnel decisions (promotions, retentions, dismissals, tenure, and salary increases). Many individuals think this may be the only reason for the evaluation process. The problem is one of finding a valid instrument for this purpose. Finally, evaluation may also be used to fulfill a personal need involving status. To some extent, everyone has a basic need for some feedback in the form of evaluation.

Who should do the evaluation? Superficially, this might seem to be less of an issue. The traditional idea was that evaluation should be conducted by those in superior positions in an organization. In other words, evaluation is carried out through the chain of command. While many individuals still consider this the best or only source of evaluation, at least three other possibilities exist: peer evaluation, self-evaluation, and evaluation by subordinates. There is some thought that peer evaluation may actually be the most valid means of assessment, at least in certain contexts. At the same time, others contend that peer evaluation tends to be biased by popularity. Evaluation by subordinates is a somewhat elusive category. To what extent should student evaluations of a teacher or athlete evaluations of a coach be taken into account? Subordinates will always be involved in evaluation on an informal basis. In terms of policy, the real question revolves around provisions for a formal basis for evaluation by subordinates. Self-evaluation presents less grounds for debate. It is not so much an option but rather a preliminary step in the evaluation by others.

How should the evaluation be accomplished? This is the most difficult question, and it involves additional questions: What is the basis for the evaluation?; and What are the performance standards?. The attempt to answer these questions leads to most of the issues and problems and points to the need for policy development.

THE HIGH SCHOOL COACH

As noted, the process of evaluation is a complicated and controversial topic. When it comes to evaluating high school coaches, the complications are only heightened.

To begin with, the coach represents different things to different people. He or she is called on to be a teacher, trainer, counselor, disciplinarian, manager, and public relations agent. All this is in addition to the up-front need to have a thorough knowledge of the sport. The coach is expected to relate well to a variety of constituencies - students, parents, administrators, other coaches, the news media, fans, and the general public.

The most complicating factor of all is that the coach is employed to win games, even at the high school level, although there may be less pressure here in some cases. Regardless of any evaluation policy employed, the matter of winning and losing is almost certain to enter the picture.

Another unique factor in the attempt to evaluate high school coaches is that they are constant subjects of public evaluation. The effectiveness of the coach is there for all to see during a game or contest. Few people in other walks of life are subjected to the same kind of public scrutiny. The coach is openly evaluated in newspapers, and on radio and television. Parents are among the foremost to assess a coach's performance.

The situation surrounding high school coaching has become even more complex in recent years. Title IX prompted a strong demand for qualified coaches in women's sports. In many cases, women coaches have lacked the qualifications of their male counterparts. The need to hire part-time coaches from outside school systems has increased dramatically due to financial restraints. In some situations, schools have been faced with state and district regulations mandating the hiring of only certified coaches. Tenured, aging teachers have sought release from coaching positions due to burn-out. Low pay for high school coaching is a persistent problem.

The net result of these conditions is that many high schools have been forced to employ coaches with marginal qualifications. It would appear that the need to evaluate high school coaches has increased. Yet, the need only points to the various issues involved. In the attempt to develop policies, a number of questions must be addressed.

1. Should a high school coach be evaluated on the same basis as any other teacher in the school system?
2. Should the performance standards for a high school coach be essentially the same as those for a college coach?
3. How much weight should be given to the won-lost record in assessing a high school coach's work?
4. Should all the coaches in the athletic program be evaluated according to the same standard (e.g., should the head football coach be evaluated on the same basis as the tennis coach?)
5. Should high school athletes be involved in evaluating the work of the coach?
6. What criteria (performance standards) should be used in the process of evaluation?
7. How should the evaluation be carried out?

Some of these questions have legal implications. For example, the Bryan Case in Alabama in 1985 related to the matter of evaluating coaches as teachers:

> William Bryan taught at Weaver High School in Alabama for ten years and had achieved tenured teacher status. He was employed as a head coach for several years and received additional compensation for his coaching duties. After he was notified that his coaching duties were terminated, he contended that his tenured teaching position entitled him to a hearing before the State Tenure Commission regarding his dismissal for coaching, whether he had tenure as a coach or not.
>
> The Court of Civil Appeals of Alabama considered numerous cases similar to the instant case and made two comments:
> 1. The purpose of the Teacher Tenure Act is to protect teachers from cancellation of their contracts or transfers for political, personal, or arbitrary reasons.
> 2. Since a coach is not a teacher, as defined in the Tenure Act, Bryan had no right to a hearing before the Tenure Commission.
>
> It upheld the judgement of the circuit court denying Bryan's petition. (*Bryan v. Alabama State Tenure Commission*, 472 So. 2d 1052 [Ala. 1985]. Appenzeller & Ross, *Sports and the Courts*, p. 5)

Case Study: Burlington, Vermont, High School

The city of Burlington is located in northwestern Vermont on the shore of Lake Champlain. In 1985 Burlington High School was one of the largest secondary schools in the state. However, the city's demographic characteristics had changed in the previous 20 years, reflecting trends in similar communities around the nation. The city lost population, while surrounding towns had grown dramatically. There was a steady decline in the enrollment at Burlington High School from 1,400 students in 1968 to 1,050 students in 1985.

The high school had a tradition of excellence in athletics as well as academics. However, the athletic picture began to change during the 1970s. Part of this can be attributed to the decline in school enrollment. Rice Memorial High School, a parochial school in South Burlington, also affected the situation. During the 1970s at least 100 students per year (many of whom were fine high school athletes) left the Burlington public school to matriculate at the private school. In 1978, Burlington High School's football team was 1-7; the basketball team 7-13; and the ice hockey team had its first losing season in 10 years. Of the major sports, only baseball, under the steady guidance of a long-time coach, had a winning season.

Jim Cardell, the athletic director since 1968, knew that it was time for action by 1978. He recognized that the situation at his school had changed considerably during his directorship. With respect to pay, Burlington teachers had traditionally ranked very high in statewide salary comparisons. The coaches were similarly well compensated for their additional responsibilities. However, there were severe budget problems in the Burlington schools during the 1970s. The athletic program also felt the impact of Title IX, which led to the introduction of five sports for high school girls (soccer, cross-country, skiing, tennis, and track and field) in 1972.

The net result was that the coaching picture changed considerably. When Cardell started as athletic director, he supervised 32 coaches, 26 of whom were regular high school staff members and six of whom were part-time coaches from outside the school system. In 1985, he was responsible for 43 coaches, but only 16 of those were full-time, regular members of the high school staff.

In the meantime, amidst a reduced budget and new challenges, the Burlington athletic program continued to feel the pressure to be successful. Prior to the 1970s, beating Burlington made the season for most of the opponents on its schedule. What action could Jim Cardell take to restore the athletic program to its pre-eminent position?

One possibility would have been to make a special request to the school board, pointing out the need for increased support. However, that was not a particularly feasible solution in light of the teaching staff reductions in the Burlington schools and budget cuts, which had reduced

Burlington's favorable statewide standing in salaries for teachers. The teaching staff went on strike in 1978 as a result of difficulties in contract negotiations with the school board. It seemed unlikely that the athletic program could expect increased support in the late 1970s.

The alternative chosen by Cardell was to work within his own sphere of influence. Specifically, he implemented a formal program of evaluating the coaches of high school sports. Prior to that time, evaluation was largely on an observational basis without set criteria for assessment. In taking this action he had three objectives: l) to maintain contact with and control over the part-time coaches from outside the school system; 2) to support the coaches and improve the overall staff morale; and 3) to use the evaluation to motivate the coaches to put forth their best efforts.

Essentially, three tiers were developed in the program for evaluating coaches at Burlington High School. The first centers around the very specific list of 29 responsibilities of coaches, which is part of the "Job Description - Head Coach" (Exhibit 8-1). Coaches should know what is expected of them and what will provide the basis for evaluation.

The second tier is the "Pre-Season Checklist" (Exhibit 8-2), which is designed to get the season off to a well-organized start and provide for a pre-season, formal meeting between each coach and the athletic director. At this meeting, the athletic director also asks the coach to submit a specific, professional objective for the season. This is a direct attempt to factor self-evaluation into the total evaluation process.

The third tier — the 42-item "Evaluation Report" (Exhibit 8-3) — is the heart of the evaluation program. Items on the report range from the specific duty of ordering equipment to the general responsibility of promoting the sport program. Deciding which of the performance standards are most significant leads to debate, but the establishment of clear standards is a step in the right direction.

In 1985 Cardell reported satisfied action with the results of the evaluation program, which proved to be particularly useful in dealing with the continued need to employ part-time coaches from outside the regular staff. There was also evidence of improvement in staff morale and renewed success of the athletic teams. The ice hockey team won the state championship in 1985. The track and cross-country programs continued to dominate in state competition. The baseball team won two championships in four years. The football program had a consistent .500 record, and the basketball program appeared to be moving in the right direction.

POLICY, POLICY GUIDELINES, AND PROCEDURES

Any attempt to develop policy regarding the evaluation of high school coaches centers around two basic questions: 1) Should there be a systematic, formal system? and 2) If yes, who should be involved in the evaluation process? Once the policy is established, it is then necessary to

EXHIBIT 8-1. Burlington Public Schools Job Description - Head Coach

I. GENERAL DESCRIPTION

To instruct athletes in the fundamental skills, strategy and physical training necessary for them to realize a degree of individual and team success. At the same, the student shall receive instruction that will lead to the formulation of moral values, pride of accomplishment, acceptable social behavior, self-discipline and self-confidence.

II. ORGANIZATIONAL POSITION

The head coach of any athletic activity at Burlington High School is directly responsible to the Athletic Director and the Principal.

III. SPECIFIC RESPONSIBILITIES

1. Will abide by the rules and regulations of the Vermont Headmasters' Association.
2. Will adhere to the policies set forth by the Burlington Board of School Commissioners.
3. Is responsible for assigning all duties to the assistant coaches.
4. Is responsible for the evaluation of the performance of the assistant coaches in their respective jobs and assignments.
5. Is responsible for the conduct and actions of student athletes during all practices, games, and trips.
6. Is responsible for the control of areas involved in each sport, including the locker and shower rooms. The coach must lock up and be the last to leave the building.
7. Will submit recommendations to the Athletic Director as to the teams and officials to be contracted.
8. Trains and informs staff, encourages professional growth by encouraging clinic attendance according to local clinic policy.
9. Is responsible for informing the student-athlete of the rules of the Vermont Headmasters' Association regarding athletic eligibility.
10. Will instruct team members that equipment is to be worn only for the purpose for which it is purchased, namely, for practice sessions and game competition. It is not to be worn at any social event or throughout the community other than athletic sessions.
11. Will provide training rules and any other unique regulations of the sport to each athlete who is considered a participant.
12. Assist athletes in their college or advanced educational selection.
13. Will collect all parental permission forms and forward to the Athletic Director before a student can practice. NO FORM, NO PRACTICE.
14. Will explain the letter award policy to all team members before the first athletic contest.
15. Will clean out the locker room, coaches' office and in-season storage room within five days of your last contest.
16. Will submit to the Athletic Director, no later than two weeks after your last game of the season, a brief report to include the following:
    a. Names of squad members - indicate letter winners, captains, managers, etc.
    b. Schedule played with complete scores.

EXHIBIT 8-1 *(con't.)*

    c. New records set for the season - individual performance, team scoring, etc.

    d. Special honors received by team members.

    e. Complete inventory of all equipment and supplies.

    f. A brief summary of the season and suggestions for improving your program.

    g. Budget request for next season.

17. Will be responsible for maintaining good public relations the news media, Boosters Club, parents, officials, volunteers, fans, etc.

18. Will be accountable for all equipment and collect the cost of any equipment lost or not returned. Arrange for issuing, storing and reconditioning of equipment.

19. Is directly responsible for the supervision of the squad during all practice sessions and games.

20. Will be responsible for the care of the injured personnel until the student has been released to the parent or doctor. Accident report forms must be submitted to the Main Office within twenty-four hours.

21. Will work with the Athletic Director to establish budget needs for the next season. Recommend equipment guidelines as to type, style, color, or technical specifications.

22. Will be responsible for presenting on time all forms and reports pertaining to his/her athletic activity.

23. Will secure all doors, lights, windows, etc., before leaving the building if custodians are not on duty.

24. Will organize and host the end-of-season Awards Banquet.

25. Will be responsible to complete the necessary VHA Tournament application forms and mail them prior to the deadline date. It is imperative that deadlines are met.

26. Will attend seasonal or full coaches' staff meetings called by the Athletic Director.

27. Will assume prime responsibility that all players are properly and safely equipped for the type of activity in which they are engaged, and are thoroughly briefed on safety policy and procedures.

28. Will present to each athlete, a copy of the BHS Athletic Handbook and discuss this with the team prior to the season. Also submit to the Athletic Director and the players copies of any additional rules or regulations governing your particular sport.

29. Will read the BHS Coaches Handbook and follow the policies and guidelines as written.

EXHIBIT 8-2. Pre-Season Checklist

TO: All members of the Burlington High School Coaching Staff
FROM: James Cardell
SUBJECT: PRE-SEASON CHECKLIST

My _____ squad has met the following points and we are ready to issue team uniforms.

_____ 1. All parental permission forms are on file in the Athletic Directors' Office
_____ 2. All physical fitness examinations (physician) forms are in the nurse's office. Students must get their own physicals if they do not take advantage of the appointed time for school physicals.
_____ 3. All players have purchased the school insurance or have insurance coverage by home policy which is indicated on parent's permission forms.
_____ 4. I have reviewed with my squad the BHS Athletic Handbook.
_____ 5. All players have been cleared through the Guidance Office for academic eligibility. The Certificate of eligibility has been completed, typed and signed by the Principal and sent to Vt. Headmasters.
_____ 6. All players have received a schedule of games, a coach's specific set of rules, and they understand that they are responsible for payment for damaged or lost equipment and damaged or lost uniforms.
_____ 7. All parents and players have signed the Athletic Contract to indicate that they have read and understand the student Athlete's Handbook. Contracts are on file in the Athletic Office.
_____ 8. All players understand the criteria to be used for our award system.
_____ 9. I have a medicine kit with supplies and a water container for practices and games.

DATE: _____

HEAD COACH: _____

ATHLETIC DIRECTOR: _____

EXHIBIT 8-3. Burlington High School Athletic Department Evaluation Report

Coach _____ Sport _____ Date _____

Key:1. Excellent   NO - No Opportunity to
      2. Satisfactory   Observe
      3. Needs Improvement   NA - Does not Apply

Organizes practices

Holds punctual practices

Organizes the use of facilities

Has innovative ideas

Instills enthusiasm in athletes

Shows knowledge of sport

Demonstrates and teaches
sportsmanship in all athletic
activities

Provides for individual as well
as group instruction

Helps other coaches become
better coaches

Organizes game procedures

Possesses an adequate knowledge
of his/her sport

Ordering of equipment

Distribution of equipment

In-Season care of equipment

Post-Season collection &
storage

Record keeping

Punctuality of reports

Organizational meetings
with athletes

Organizational meetings
with coaches

Out of season preparation

Has made attempts to upgrade
his/her own personal knowledge
of coaching

Coach's appearance, practice

Attention to safety

Coach's appearance, game

Locker room supervision

Bus conduct and cleanliness

Control of obscenity

Control of discipline

Adherence to training rules

Promotion of Program

Coach Assistants relationship

Coach-Press relationship

Coach-Official relationship

Coach-Athletic Director rapport

Supervises his/her players in
practice and during contest

Coach-Community relationship

Coach-Parent relationship

Ability to take criticism

Concern for total school
program

Loyalty to fellow-coaches

Concern for total athletic
program

Keeps Athletic Director informed
about unusual events

Remarks and Comments:

have policy guidelines and procedures to carry out the policy. Within the framework, the following suggestions are presented with the full realization that a high school staff many not find the time to carry out the entire process. Nevertheless, elements could be selected to fit local exigencies.

Policy

The job performance of high school head coaches will be assessed through a process which involves self-evaluation, player evaluation, and the athletic director's evaluation. The process should follow the guidelines and procedures below.

1. At the beginning of each school year, the athletic director will schedule a meeting to be attended by all coaches. At this meeting, the athletic director will explain the process of evaluation and receive input from the coaches relative to suggested changes in criteria.
2. A pre-season meeting will be held with each coach. Prior to the meeting the coach will complete a self-evaluation and a pre-season checklist. The self-evaluation will be accomplished by filling out a copy of the standardized form for assessing the performance of head coaches (see Exhibit 8-4). The checklist would be similar to that found in Exhibit 8-2 under the Burlington High School case study. Both the self-evaluation and the checklist will enable the athletic director and the coach to identify areas in which the coach sees strengths and areas in which there appears to be room for improvement.
3. For the purposes of observation and assessment of job performance, the athletic director will attend at least two practices and 25 percent of team contests during a season. He or she will keep written notes of the observations.
4. During the sport season, the athletic director will send informal notes of commendation or concern to the coaches, as appropriate.
5. The athletic director will communicate informally at least once per week with each coach during his/her sport season.
6. Sometime around mid-season there will be an opportunity for input from the student-athletes regarding their assessment of the coach's effectiveness. As recipients of the coaching, the players should have that opportunity. At the same time, player evaluation must be kept in perspective due to inherent biases. The mid-season evaluation should be the most appropriate timing in light of the potential bias factor. Player evaluation should be kept relatively short and to the point. Selected items from the complete evaluation form (Exhibit 8-4) might be used to provide the succinct assessment by the players.
7. Also around mid-season, following the player evaluation, there will be another formal meeting between coach and the athletic

EXHIBIT 8-4. Assessment of the Head Coach

Rating Scale Explanations

1 = Critical Problem - needs immediate attention - present level of performance is *extremely unsatisfactory.*

2 = Improvement Required - needs attention by the end of the next season - performance is *below expected level.*

3 = Satisfactory - performance is *at expected level.*

4 = Good - performance *exceeds expected level.*

5 = Superior - performance is *consistently outstanding.*

NA = Not Applicable - no basis for judgment by the evaluator.

A. The coach as a professional:
1. articulates a coaching philosophy that supports the objectives of the athletic department
2. has demonstrated an awareness of current coaching techniques and theories by attending a clinic, conference, workshop, or course relating to coaching in the past five years.
3. has demonstrated a knowledge of safety and first aid techniques by taking a course within the past five years.
4. establishes personal objectives and goals for the sport season and evaluates whether the goals have been met.
5. supports other coaches and sports in the athletic program.
6. demonstrates concern for each athlete's academic achievement.

B. The coach as organizer and administrator:
7. prepares and distributes a pre-season conditioning program.
8. establishes criteria for team selection and informs prospective team members.
9. applies team selection criteria consistently and fairly.
10. prepares for each practice by means of a written practice plan.
11. begins and ends practices on time.
12. follows department and school policy for the timely purchase of safe athletic equipment.
13. provides for proper distribution, collection, care, repair, and cleaning of athletic equipment.
14. submits an equipment inventory to the athletic director within three weeks of the completion of the sport season.
15. participates in budget preparation with the athletic director.
16. operates the program within the allotted budget.
17. knows and abides by school, league, state, and national rules and regulations for the sport.
18. involves athletes in formulating reasonable team rules.
19. communicates team rules - in writing - to parents prior to the first contest of the season.
20. consistently enforces all team rules.
21. provides a safe environment for players.
22. follows proper procedures in the event of an injury to a player.
23. prepares for "away" contests (transportation requests, meal money, etc.)
24. supervises team activities (locker room, bus trips, etc.)
25. meets post-game responsibilities (to team, press, facility, and parents).

EXHIBIT 8-4 *(con't.)*

C. The coach as a person:
   26. is approachable for players to discuss concerns and problems.
   27. provides advice and guidance.
   28. promotes the self-esteem of individual players and the team as a unit.
   29. maintains self-control during times of crisis and stress.
   30. treats game officials with respect.
   31. makes decisions which show reasonable conduct to avoid legal responsibility for liability.
   32. motivates players toward individual and team goals.
   33. sets a positive example in word, deed, and appearance.

D. The coach as technician:
   34. employs up-to-date methods to teach skills and technique (drills, etc.)
   35. demonstrates a sound knowledge of strategy in the sport.
   36. prepares game plans, utilizing the team's strengths and opponent's weaknesses.
   37. provides for individual as well as group instruction.
   38. values the quality of a performance as much as the outcome of a contest.

E. The coach as a staff member works with the athletic director in:
   39. generally keeping the Athletic Director informed about developments and/or potential problems in the program.
   40. attending scheduled athletic department meetings and participating in department activities.
   41. securing parent permission slips, insurance forms, and physical exam verification prior to the first practice of the season.
   42. submitting player participant lists prior to the first scheduled contest of the season.
   43. providing an appropriate end-of-season awards banquet.
   44. cooperating fully with the school's academic requirements for athletic eligibility.
   45. providing for appropriate game management for "home" contests.
   46. submitting an end-of-season report within three weeks of the completion of the sport season.
   47. participating in a process of self-evaluation.
   48. participating in a process to evaluation of the coach by his/her players.
   49. participating in a process of evaluation of the coach by the athletic director.
   50. participating in a process of evaluation of the athletic director by the coach.

EXHIBIT 8-4 *(con't.)*

COMMENDATIONS
(1 full page)

RECOMMENDATIONS
(1 full page)

COACH'S COMMENTS
(1 full page)

_____ Coach
_____ Evaluator

director to review the status of the team and coaching situation at that time. Discussions might center on observations of the athletic director, the coach's assessment of the situation, and/or players' evaluation, as appropriate.

8. Within two weeks after the conclusion of the sport season, the coach and the athletic director will each complete the evaluation form (Exhibit 8-4). They will meet to compare and discuss ratings and to provide the coach an opportunity for input and clarification.

9. Within one week after the above meeting, the athletic director will finalize his/her ratings and will note commendations and recommendations, as appropriate.

10. The finished evaluation will be submitted to the coach and he or she will provide written comments on the form provided.

11. The coach and athletic director will each sign the final document. Copies will be distributed to: a) the coach; b) the athletic director's file; and c) the coach's school personnel file. Signing of the form by the coach does *not* imply agreement with the assessment, but indicates that he or she has participated in the process and has *read* the evaluation.

CONCLUSION

The evaluation of high school coaches is not an easy task. The attempt to evaluate personnel within any organization is difficult under the best of circumstances. The high school situation only compounds that difficulty due to time limitations, tenure structures, and the general debate about assessing teacher effectiveness. To that we add the fact that the high school coach is generally only employed part time for coaching. He or she is either employed as a full time teacher in the school system or has regular employment outside the schools. The question can logically be asked: Is it worth that much effort to assess the high school coach's performance in light of his or her situation in the schools?

With little doubt, the answer is "yes" when one considers the multifarious role of the coach as a teacher, trainer, counselor, disciplinarian, manager, and public relations agent. Furthermore, we know that the coach is constantly being informally evaluated by a variety of constituencies, particularly with regard to the won-lost record of the team. If one truly believes that the coach is there for educational purposes, some type of systematic, formal evaluation becomes paramount.

How should the evaluation be accomplished? That is the most difficult question. After considering the Burlington High School example, I have suggested some guidelines to carry out the basic policy. Parts of the total program of evaluation could be selected to fit local needs and time constraints.

REFERENCE

Appenzeller H. and Ross, C. T. *Sports and the Courts: Physical Education and Sports Law Quarterly.* Vol. 7, No. 3 - Summer 1986, p. 5.

9

Evaluating College Coaches

In the sports-crazy modern world the expert teacher, trainer, developer, motivator of super athletes has become a common phenomenon. But nobody elsewhere stands beside the legendary wizard of the American Big Game. He expresses and symbolizes cultural impulses swirling and conjoined to something like tornadic power: the student *virtu* which invented and evolved the games and took them into the mainstream of college life; the almost hysterical response of the constituencies; the intrusion of the public and exploitation by the media; the expertise of generations of professional sophistication; the sometimes desperate efforts of the institutions to exercise some degree of control. He stands in the eye of the storm; when it blows with him; he is exalted, bestriding the festival, godlike; when it turns and blows the other way, he is strong indeed if it does not tear him to shreds. He becomes, all dimly, the American Vegetation God, watcher of the golden bough, king today, burned tomorrow. We call him "Coach." (*The Big Game*, p. 120)

With that vivid description, Edwin Cady opens his chapter on "Coach." "The Big Game," as referred to by Cady, is American college football and basketball on the NCAA Division I level. Within that context, the evaluation of college coaches follows a simple formula: is he a winner?

Cady contended (and I think most people would agree) that it is the need to win that accounts for many of the abuses and problems in college athletics. However, he also felt that "The Big Game" must and can be controlled. His answer was to provide opportunities for tenure for those high pressured coaches: "I would begin by laying down the firm principle that, as is already largely true for the other sports, nobody among Big Game coaches can get fired for losing." (p. 136) Referring to the nine football coaches and three basketball coaches on a Division I staff, he said: "Why should those twelve apostles of the Big Game, and they only, be without job security, without reasonable expectation of continuance, vulnerable to immolation, the Cinderellas of the academic family and community? The situation is absurd and, because it negates control, disastrous." (p. 137)

Cady's work was published in 1978. Eight years later the situation was much worse. In February 1986, *USA TODAY* published a cover story with accompanying articles about the pressure on college basketball coaches. The following excerpts reveal much about the evaluation and status of college basketball coaches. It is interesting to note that some coaches also suggested that tenure may be the solution to the problem.

> The pressure to win has always been there, but it has risen exponentially with the money that's now at stake. The payoff to a school that makes the NCAA tournament's first round is $165,000. The jackpot is $334,000 for the second round, $500,000 for the regional semi-finals, $650,000 for the regional finals and $800,000 for the Final Four.
>
> "NCAA tournament dollars are so huge it's no longer good enough to be in the top 40," says ESPN analyst Dick Vitale. "If you don't get to the Final Four, you're a failure." . . .
>
> Schools have built big arenas that have to be filled. To get the TV revenue you have to be a winner.
>
> Coaches don't lose their jobs so much because they lose, but because when they lose, they don't make money! . . .
>
> Charlie Moir, Virginia Tech: "There's more pressure than it was 10 years ago. There's more competition to have winning programs. It'll get worse. Everybody wants a winner. You have to continue to win. The answer is getting a good coach, sign him to a long contract and pay him well."
>
> Jerry Tarkanian, Nevada-Las Vegas: "It's like having a gun pointed at your head for four months. You learn to live with it.
>
> "This is very disturbing. There is so much pressure on these coaches. They've been so successful so long, have done so much for the university. It's frightening that this type of pressure is on them." . . .
>
> Ed Tapscott, American: "The pressure to produce is great. Schools make quite of an investment in athletics, they want a return. It's like any business. If you don't turn a profit, you're the odd man out."
>
> Walt Hazard, UCLA: "For years, there's been talk about coaches having tenure. If you have job security, you don't have to worry about your position. But we're in a competitive situation, we're judged on whether we win or lose."
>
> It isn't enough to grumble about how tough their jobs are, coaches say. They want something done to make life easier.
>
> Oklahoma's Billy Tubbs says he thinks coaches should be tenured like college professors . . . "You never see any protection coming in

for a coach, but every time you turn around you see people on coaches," says Tubbs. "How many times have you seen the statement that a coach who runs a clean, program and graduates all his people, that he's going to be tenured like a professor?"

Statistics tell why coaches want tenure. In the last six years, there has been an average of 38 coaching changes each season. Last year was worst of all - 55 job changes, or nearly 20 percent of the 284 Division I basketball jobs. (*USA TODAY*, Monday, February 10, 1986, pp. 2C, 7C. Copyright, 1986. *USA TODAY*. Excerpted with permission.)

While from one standpoint I would like to agree with Edwin Cady and Coach Tubbs, I don't believe it is realistic to think that Division I football and basketball coaches can be considered for tenure as long as "The Big Game" is played under the present set of conditions. In the conclusion to Chapter 2, I suggested that it might be necessary to establish two basic divisions in college athletics - one for programs that offer major commercial events and another for other college athletic programs. Participants in the first division would be recognized as athlete-students, and the coaches would be evaluated on their ability to win, as are coaches of professional sport teams. Participants in the second division would be student-athletes (in the true sense), and the coaches would be evaluated for tenure-like positions. The remainder of this chapter is directed toward policy development for evaluating coaches of student-athletes.

COACHES AND TENURE

The field of higher education in general has traditionally determined the status of its faculty through the terms and conditions of employment. The ultimate reward for those who achieve in teaching, scholarly research, and service to the academic community (and the primary source of status) is tenure. In a 1983 issue of *Newsweek on Campus*, Bill Barol captured the lofty position of tenure by referring to it as "academia's brass ring."

Tenure essentially guarantees employment as long as the institution has funds to pay the salaries and the professor continues to perform in good faith, with competency, and without moral turpitude. Although circumstances such as "bona fide financial exigencies" are acceptable grounds for dismissing tenured professors, in reality, very few get fired for anything.

Tenure is intended to facilitate the pursuit of knowledge by providing individuals with the freedom to follow intellectual inquiry wherever it may lead, without fearing dismissal for upholding unpopular thoughts or beliefs. A problem associated with tenure is that it could influence an individual's professional performance by effectively reducing motivational concerns. Nevertheless, the practice of awarding tenure has long been seen as a necessary component of the educational system. It offers the potential to attract qualified people by providing a significant degree of security, in a profession which often does not pay market value for the expertise involved.

Although the American Association of University Professors (AAUP) has set generally recognized and accepted guidelines for tenure policy, each institution is free to establish its own policy. Earlier in this century, the tone for intercollegiate athletics was directed toward integrating the role of athletics with the larger purpose of higher education by providing tenure opportunities for coaches. In accordance with the primary recommendation of a 1926 AAUP committee on the objectives of intercollegiate sport, coaches were usually full-time members of the general faculty with a seat and teaching responsibility in, but not restricted to, physical education. As faculty members directly involved in the institutions' larger purposes, coaches were afforded the same status and rewards as their academic colleagues. This included academic rank and associated compensation, the right to vote at faculty meetings and serve on elected committees, and the opportunity for tenure.

More recently most institutions have moved away from the idea of making opportunities for tenure available to coaches. The basic difficulty has been one of attempting to evaluate coaches within the framework of traditional criteria for academic achievement. The role of the teacher-coach in the academic community remains a consistent subject for debate. Much of the controversy stems from a belief that coaching is something which can be pursued in addition to academic teaching responsibilities. Furthermore, many argue that there must be this dual pursuit if a coach is to be considered for tenure.

Coaches are in a unique position in the academic community. The occupational subculture of coaches in higher education is one in which they function within the total educational organization but have little in common with the larger group. They may feel alienated from the values and lifestyle of the academic community. In most cases the coach understands that he or she is employed to produce winning teams. However, the faculty outside the coaching subculture do not face this challenge, and the majority do not fully understand a coach's position. The situation becomes more complicated when some type of academic duties are required of coaches.

Anderson (1985) pinpointed the problem when he noted that the dual roles established by appointment to teacher-coach positions carry "exceptions not among those traditionally evaluated to determine faculty performance." (p. 16) He logically explains that as each role becomes more specialized it is more difficult for an individual to function effectively in both capacities. Under these circumstances one or the other roles tends to dominate an individual's attention and energies. Those who choose to emphasize the coaching role (which is a natural choice for a coach) are still subject to the traditional criteria for promotion and tenure. However, these criteria, research and publications, are not logical extensions of the coaching position.

Anderson proposed a model that calls for a continuum of possible positions, depending on the needs of the institution and the interests of the teacher-coach. One end of the continuum represents a position where academic teaching is regarded as the primary responsibility and, consequently, the application of typical criteria for appointment, promotion, and tenure is legitimate. The other end of the continuum delineates a role where there is a major commitment to coaching.

Obviously, the middle part of the continuum, where teaching and coaching receive equal emphasis, presents the greatest difficulty for the individual and the institution. The Division I institutions have by and large stayed away from this gray area by appointing coaches to athletic positions without academic status. This practice continues to be the modus operandi, especially for the high-exposure sports of football and basketball at major institutions. Such an employment mode affords these institutions the flexibility to fire coaches who do not produce mandated results. On the other hand, it also places the coach in the kind of dilemma described by Cady.

The NCAA Division II and III schools are most likely to be caught in the middle territory. Traditionally the Division III colleges have been inclined to follow the policy of hiring coaches who are qualified to teach and appointing them to faculty positions with academic status. However, in recent years, an increasing number of institutions at all levels have moved away from tenure-track appointments for coaches. One reason for the change is that the relatively abundant educational resources of the 1950s and 1960s are no longer available. Declining student enrollments and concomitant financial pressures have forced institutions to re-examine their employment policies. While tenure policies in general have been affected by the changing circumstances, athletic departments are prime targets for cutbacks as the athletic and academic components compete for limited financial resources.

Recent support for the idea of providing faculty status and tenure for coaches has come from various directions. In general, the arguments proceed from the need to do something to alleviate the problems that plague intercollegiate sport. The basic thought is that a coach who isn't under constant pressure to win will be less likely to violate recruiting and eligibility regulations.

There is little doubt that a coach can be evaluated as a teacher, because the coach teaches all aspects of a sport. To be more specific, the coach can be assessed in terms of technical competence, effective communication of information, careful organization of practice sessions, and strategy development during the game. The service criteria also poses no real problem in the assessment of the coach. He or she can be evaluated on the quality of service to the profession, the institution, and the larger community. The "publish or perish" requirement and accompanying research issue pose the major roadblocks in equating the performances of coaches with the achievements of academic colleagues in decisions involving academic rank and tenure.

This much is clear: those concerned with managing college sport programs cannot seem to agree on the most appropriate relationship between athletic and academic life. The issue concerning the academic status of coaches is merely a part of the larger issue. While those institutions caught up in pursuit of "The Big Game" may have passed the point where a consideration of the academic status of coaches is relevant, the vast majority of colleges will have to seriously consider the issue if sport is to continue to be justified from the educational standpoint.

Case Study: A Division III College

Note: The college selected for this case is a small liberal arts college with a rich tradition of pursuing academic excellence. It is also a college which has provided leadership in recognizing the educational role of athletics by appointing coaches to regular academic appointments as faculty members. Names of the college and the individuals involved in this case are not included due to the generally sensitive nature of personnel policies of this type.

As full-time members of the faculty, teacher coaches at the College were traditionally subject to the same policies and procedures that govern the terms and conditions of employment for academic personnel. Individuals are appointed to the faculty under one of three possible scenarios: they may be hired with tenure, they may be hired to a tenure-track position with a decision concerning reappointment and tenure coming after a defined probationary period, or they may be hired to a terminal position which sets forth a specified duration of employment. In the latter two situations, no full-time member of the academic faculty will be retained in his or her teaching position for more than seven years without an appointment with tenure.

A tenure-track appointment is usually made for an initial term of three years with the possibility of attaining a second three-year contract upon reappointment. Reappointment to a second term is based upon a process of review and recommendation originating in the faculty member's department. When an individual is under consideration for a recommendation concerning reappointment or tenure, the chairman of the department formally invites the candidate to present information or evidence that should be considered in an accurate assessment of his or her qualifications or circumstances. The department gathers evidence concerning the individual's teaching effectiveness, scholarly growth, and other contributions, and makes a recommendation regarding reappointment or tenure. This information is then passed for review to the

Committee of Six--the ruling body of the College formed by four elected faculty members, the president, and the dean of the faculty.

While reappointment decisions are important, they are as crucial as the tenure decision. A positive decision for reappointment is essentially "an expression of satisfaction with past performance and of confidence in the faculty member's continued development."

Following the committee's review of the evidence, a recommendation is communicated to the Board of Trustees by the president, acting on his own accord, along with the recommendations of the dean of the faculty, the Committee of Six, and the department. Although the final decision regarding reappointment or tenure rests in the hands of the board, the recommendation of the candidate's department and the considerations of the Committee of Six are the most important components of the process. If the Board of Trustees decides in favor of reappointment, the chairman of the department is called upon to inform the individual of considerations that may enter into a tenure decision. If, however, a decision is made against reappointment or tenure, the individual is granted the option of accepting a one-year terminal contract to maintain employment while exploring future employment possibilities. There are various grievance procedures for candidates to follow if they feel they have been judged unfairly.

The decision on tenure may be made during a faculty member's third, fourth, fifth, or sixth year of full-time service at the college, depending upon previous circumstances. An individual whose first full-time teaching appointment is at the College normally has appointment periods timed so that a recommendation concerning tenure occurs during the sixth year. However, a faculty member who has taught for more than two years at another institution of higher education may stand for tenure in the third, fourth, or fifth year, as agreed upon in writing at the onset of employment. Again, as is the case with reappointment, a negative decision regarding tenure results in a maximum one-year terminal extension.

While the procedure followed in tenure considerations is essentially the same as the procedure for reappointment, the evaluative criteria for tenure are much more specific and stringent. During the tenure process the candidate is no longer viewed as a developing member of the profession but instead must show evidence of leadership in his or her field. A departmental recommendation concerning tenure, which is passed to the Committee of Six, should include evidence of teaching effectiveness (incorporating evidence from students); substantial samples of the candidate's scholarly work, either published or in manuscript form; notice of contribution to the community; and any other information the candidate believes should be considered.

"Institutional considerations" play an important role in all decisions regarding tenure and generally weigh heavily in the deliberations of the Committee of Six and the Board of Trustees. Factors such as the rank structure of the department, the time of retirement of department members, and the fields of competence of the candidate in relation to those already represented in the department are important considerations.

One final area that must be examined before a consideration of the academic status of coaches can proceed is the meaning of academic rank and its relationship to salary, fringe benefits, and certain privileges. Academic rank allows individuals to attend faculty meetings, to have a say on issues that are set to a vote, to serve on elected committees, and to take periodic sabbatical leaves of absence with 80 percent salary payment. The rank of professor is awarded only to tenured faculty, associate professor, to both tenured and non-tenured individuals, assistant professor to untenured faculty members who may or may not be on tenure-track. While the old adage, "a title is but a title," is often accurate, academic rank does provide for some very objective rewards. The salary of a faculty member, and the total value of fringe benefits (health coverage, free tuition for children, second mortgage, etc.) made available to them, are directly tied into a range established for each academic rank.

During the past 15 years the College has experienced various changes and encountered pressures that have affected the institution as a whole and had a significant impact on the athletic department. The dropping of all requirements for physical education challenged coaches to promote voluntary programs of instructional classes and intramural activities. In order to encourage a high level of participation (the backbone of the College's athletic philosophy) a wider range of intercollegiate teams was offered. This development was most pronounced by an expansion in the number of varsity and junior varsity teams, which accompanied the arrival of women through coeducation in 1975.

At the same time, like many other institutions of higher education, the College was under pressure to cut costs. Although the move to coeducation and the effects of financial constraints produced campus-wide problems, nowhere was this predicament more acutely felt than in the athletic department. The same 11 full-time coaches who supervised 26 intercollegiate teams in 1974 had become responsible for 42 varsity and junior varsity squads in 1981. This situation was mainly the result of campus-wide competition for scarce financial resources, for strictly limited faculty slots, and especially for tenure commitments at a time when retirements were low and the tenure ratio was climbing. Desperately needed new positions in the Department of Physical Education could not be justified when every academic department on campus was communicating similar needs.

A further complication centered on the issue of tenure. Understandably, the College did not wish to make too many tenure commitments during a time of financial uncertainty. Many candidates were refused tenure because of institutional considerations. The justification most often given for denying a candidate tenure was that he or she failed to satisfy the criteria. The need to meet the criteria, particularly in the area of scholarly research and publications, became a particularly critical problem for the coaches. Due to excessive coaching responsibilities the teacher-coaches had essentially been forced to abandon the role of the teacher-scholar. At the time, however, seven of the 11 full-time members in the department were protected by tenure, as a result of the policy designed to address the development of teacher-scholars among coaches. The goal had been to keep of the department both symbolically and in its practices related and responsible to the central values of the College. However, now the "Committee of Six" was beginning to feel uncomfortable with the institutional tradition that determined that the status of members of the Department of Physical Education should be identical to that of other academic personnel.

In 1978, following two tenure appointments in the department (the first women and the first minority) concern was expressed about the appropriateness of continuing to apply the traditional criteria for tenure to coaches. The athletic director and the dean of the faculty (an ex officio member of the Committee of Six), lead a comprehensive review of the situation.

The resulting two-page document, titled "A Memorandum of Understanding," modified the criteria for tenure as applied to candidates from the Department of Physical Education and Athletics. The memorandum re-prioritized the three components involved in tenure decisions by recognizing that "it is unusual for a coach to pursue formal academic research as an integral component of his or her professional life." Therefore, the most important criterion for the evaluation of teachers of physical education and coaches was determined to be teaching effectiveness instead of scholarly achievement. This quality was to be evidenced by the normal method of student and peer letters of assessment which considered "the teaching of skills, techniques, strategies, theories; practice and game organization and development; the ability to reach and work with students of varying abilities; analysis of the coach's own team; (and) analysis of opponents." In addition, letters would be invited from peers in the department which focused on the candidate's administration of sports programs: "implementation, especially budget development and control; the development of schedules; home game and travel organization; (and) equipment and facility maintenance." Finally, the memorandum redefined professional and scholarly growth as it should be applied to coaches in the following way:

Among the qualities sought are a continued curiosity about developments in particular sports and in the teaching of physical education, a willingness to take on new sports . . . an extension of the depth of one's knowledge . . . Means to assess scholarly and professional growth include a review of materials used in presentations at clinics, or in lectures, or in articles as well as letters from professional peers about one's contribution to the field.

In essence, the intent of the new criteria for the evaluation of coaches was to call forth a general sense of his or her effectiveness in handling the diverse responsibilities which are unique to the role of the teacher-coach.

The memorandum was presented to the faculty, not as a referendum issue, but as a topic for discussion. When its contents were not questioned, it became a matter of record in the minutes of the faculty meeting, but not as a formal policy approved by the board and entered in the faculty handbook.

With the issue apparently resolved, the department recommended a candidate for tenure in 1981 with the understanding that the criteria set forth in the memorandum would be applied. However, a new administration had taken office and it refused to recognize the unofficial policy. The candidate was denied tenure on the grounds that he failed to satisfy the traditional criteria.

This particular case was viewed as "a red herring" within the department. The coaches felt that the decision of the Committee of Six and the Board of Trustees to deny tenure was not due to the candidate's qualifications, but was a rejection of the practice of assigning athletic personnel to tenure-track positions. Therefore, both College administrators and athletic department personnel decided to re-consider the policy concerning the appointment of coaches. The issue no longer focused solely on the criteria that should be the means for evaluating coaches, but was extended to include the institutional desirability of tenure for coaches.

Ultimately the administration decided that some changes in the traditional pattern were desirable. It was determined, however, that any new policy must preserve the sense of a common enterprise between the physical education department and the academic faculty while recognizing more accurately the necessary differences between the career paths of teacher-coaches and teacher-scholars. The range of alternative policies considered can be delineated by a continuum where one end represents the traditional tenure practice and the other extreme represents a complete move away from tenure-track appointments to various forms of specific contracts.

The latter would allow more flexibility for accommodating the demands placed upon the athletic program by increased numbers and coeducation. A contract system would serve to reduce the conflicts between the needs of athletic and academic programs by allowing for new positions in a situation where faculty seats are strictly limited. It also would make possible the retention of some younger coaches without binding the College to commitments of tenure.

However, a contract system would seem to remove academic faculty from any significant role in the process of evaluating coaches. With the elimination of the tenure decision, there would probably be no institutional evaluation of coaches. Consequently there would seem to be no clear assurance that coaches on contract would be protected from alumni or administrative pressures to win at any cost. The parties involved agreed that such a situation would be undesirable. The College sought and eventually arrived at a middle course--one that offered many of the advantages of increased institutional flexibility which the full system of contracts provides, but one that still preserved much of the coherent sense of common purpose and the protection of coaches from undesirable pressures which the system of tenure insures.

A new policy was formulated and presented to the Board of Trustees in a paper titled "Recommendations for the Reorganization of the Department of Physical Education." Exhibit 9-1 includes the five main points addressed by the policy, which was approved by the board in 1982.

This new policy did not affect members of the department who already enjoyed tenured status (eight of the 11 current members of the department). The three non-tenured individuals who were hired under the old policy were given the option to stand under the old system or to move into the new contract system. A significant effect of the new policy is the allowance for the addition of two desperately needed positions.

Overall the College took a major step in providing more flexibility in the conditions of appointment for coaches, while at the same time offering some security for coaches. In doing so, the College may have developed a model for other Division III institutions.

SUGGESTED POLICIES AND GUIDELINES

In a division or college featuring student-athletes, there must be policies which are aimed at evaluating coaches from a broader perspective than the win-loss column. In essence, the coach has to be evaluated as one who has academic status even though that status is not identical or directly parallel to that held by faculty in the traditional academic disciplines. Using the case study as a basic model, the following policies and guidelines are suggested for evaluating coaches of student-athletes:

1. *The Gestalt* quality of the coach will be assessed*: Due to the multifarious nature of his or her responsibilities, the coach should be assessed as a whole person. Much of the evaluation will be informal. Such informal processes would include frequent one-on-one conversations between the athletic director and the coach, during which the latter's self-appraisal is reviewed and critiqued by the athletic director and performance standards are set. Even though the focus will be on the "Gestalt," certain specifics can be identified under the general assessment. These specifics fall under three major categories: 1) coaching abilities per se (this

(* As used here the "Gestalt" implies that the role of the coach is more than can be identified through an identification of specific responsibilities. It is the whole which transcends particulars.)

EXHIBIT 9-1. Revised Policy for Appointment of Coaches

1. An Extended Probationary Period Of Twelve Years

Because coaches typically begin their teaching careers at an earlier age than academic faculty, it seems desirable to have a longer period in which to evaluate the effectiveness of the coach in early employment. Besides achieving this goal, a twelve-year probationary period also addresses the need to retain some younger coaches who would contribute the vitality that often diminishes in a department that is staffed year after year by the same personnel.

During the extended twelve-year probationary period coaches are hired to an initial three-year contract. Reappointment to a second three-year contract is made by the Trustees upon the recommendation of the president after he has received the recommendations of the department and the "Committee of Six" (as was previously the case for all faculty). Reappointment to a third and fourth three-year contract is done similarly. Coaches coming to the college who have had experience elsewhere are ordinarily expected to serve at least six years before coming up for their major evaluation.

2. A Major Evaluation In The Twelfth Year

During the twelfth year — or any year after the sixth year depending on the previous circumstances of the individual — a coach can be recommended by the department for appointment to a Senior Contract. Failure to receive a positive recommendation at this stage results in a one-year terminal contract offer, a procedure that is followed in each of the earlier appointments.

This recommendation is reviewed in the same manner as are tenure recommendations concerning academic faculty — by the president of the college and the "Committee of Six" before action by the Board of Trustees. Such a process attempts to insure that athletics are not placed completely outside of the control of the academic component of the college community.

3. The Senior Contract - A Four-Year "Rolling Contract"

Once approved in the major twelfth-year evaluation, a coach receives a four-year Senior "rolling contract" with the understanding that it will be renewed annually for another four years unless there is clear reason for discontinuing the contract. Such clear reason would be the loss of effectiveness as a teacher or coach by the individual or a change in the financial circumstances or educational priorities of the college. Nevertheless, any consideration of non-renewal must be reviewed by the department, the "Committee of Six," and the Board of Trustees, and such a review can be initiated by any one of the three.

4. The Option To Grant Tenure

Due to the institutional need to insure continuity in the standards and tone of athletics at the College, administrators decided that it was desirable to have a significant core group of "senior" faculty on tenure in the department. Therefore, the College retained the option to grant tenure to selected members of the department who have Senior Contract status. As a basic guideline, the College defined a significant core group to be approximately 50 percent of the "senior" personnel in the department. The procedure for such a tenure consideration continues to follow the same guidelines as for academic faculty, but a negative decision does not affect the individuals status under a "rolling" Senior Contract.

EXHIBIT 9-1 *(con't.)*

5. Elements Of Faculty Status

    Members of the Department of Physical Education continue to enjoy many of the benefits of their previous status, but they no longer are awarded faculty status. The reason for this change was twofold: most members of the department openly expressed that such status was not what they sought, and many academic faculty felt threatened by the new system for employing coaches. The academic personnel feared that if the contract system was allowed to creep into the faculty, it would eventually grow to consume their status. However, members of the Department of Physical Education did express a concern about maintaining a level of compensation comparable to that for members of the College community. Hence, the department was given the authority to set up a review committee to annually evaluate the fringe benefit package and salaries of athletic personnel under the contract system to assure that they stay in line with academic faculty who are at the same approximate stages in their careers.

    includes abilities as a teacher); 2) managerial abilities; and 3) abilities in professional and public relations.

2. *Three-year appointments and an extended 12-year probationary period*: Unless it is a temporary or special appointment, the coach will initially be appointed under a three-year contract. Subsequently, the coach will be considered for reappointment every three years during the total probationary period of 12 years. Thus, the decision to terminate the employment of the coach can be made at the end of the third, sixth, ninth, or 12th year if he or she does not meet the performance standards under the "Gestalt" assessment. Failure to receive a positive recommendation at any one of the three-year stages will result in a one-year terminal appointment.

3. *Consideration for a "Senior Contract"*: The major evaluation of the coach will be conducted at the end of the 12th year of employment at the college. The one exception to this would be that a coach could be given a period of credit time for previous collegiate coaching experience at another institution. The 12th year is the pivotal year in the evaluation process because at this time a decision will be made as to whether the coach will be offered a "Senior Contract." This is a four-year "rolling contract," awarded with the understanding that it will be renewed unless there are valid reasons for terminating the employment. As examples, the decision may be made to drop the sport program, or the coach may decide to give up coaching. The latter would be particularly critical if other legitimate responsibilities were not available for assignment within the department. Evidence of overall coaching effectiveness, professional growth, and contribu-

tion to the college community will be major factors in considering the coach for a "Senior Contract."

4. *Modified faculty status*: Coaches will have faculty status except for the opportunity to obtain tenure in most cases. The exception to the latter would be in a case where the coach has achieved what Cady terms as "Artist-In-Residence" status. That is, a coach with a long and distinguished record of achievement and service to the college might be awarded tenure as a special recognition. However, coaches would have academic rank with full privileges, including comparable salaries, fringe benefits, the right to vote at faculty meetings, and the right to serve on significant college committees. Depending on the specific faculty structure of the college, the initial appointment could be made at the rank of lecturer or instructor with eligibility for appointment to assistant professor at the end of the sixth year and to associate professor when a "Senior Contract" is awarded. Appointment of a coach to full professor rank would only be made in those exceptional cases where tenure is awarded.

CONCLUSION

There are no simple answers to the question about how college coaches should be evaluated. Only this is clear: the coach has to be evaluated in a way that is consistent with the objectives of the collegiate athletic program. If those objectives involve student-athletes in the true sense, the coach must be evaluated accordingly. Basically, this means that the coach must be evaluated on a basis that is somewhat akin to the basis used for traditional faculty. On the other hand, the coach has total responsibilities and a role that are *very* different from those of the typical faculty member. Therefore, the evaluation must proceed with certain significant modifications while retaining the basic faculty status.

REFERENCES

Anderson, E. W. "The Faculty-Coach." *Journal of Physical Education, Recreation, & Dance.* August, 1985, pp. 16-18.
Barol, B. "The Threat to College Teaching." *Newsweek on Campus*, October 1983.
Brady, E. "Pressure Building on Coaches." *USA TODAY*, February 10, 1986, Section C, pp. 1, 2, 7.
Cady, E. H. *The Big Game: College Sports and American Life.* Knoxville: University of Tennessee Press, 1978.
Porto, B. L. "When Coaches Are Teachers, Athletes Will Be Students." *Liberal Education*, Vol. 70, No. 3, 1984, pp. 231-233.
Richardson, H. D. "The Academic Status of Coaches." *Athletic Purchasing and Facilities.* August 1979, pp. 47-48.

10
Part-time Coaches

One of the more significant changes in staffing athletic programs during the 1970s and 80s has been the use of part-time coaches at both the high school and collegiate levels. Obviously, the decision to employ part-time coaches is first and foremost based on financial considerations. The passage of Title IX in 1972 brought about the need to employ additional coaches for women's sports. At the same time, athletic departments were facing inflation and reduced budgets. The relative significance of salaries in budget allocations made the move toward part-time coaches a logical necessity in many situations.

Before proceeding with an analysis of the problem, it is important to note that there are various categories of part-time coaches. They share only the common characteristics of reduced responsibility and compensation. Part-time coaches range all the way from the volunteer coach who is in an auxiliary role on a temporary basis without compensation (more likely to be found at the high school level) to the coach with a primary appointment as a coach with some other additional responsibility in the athletic department. In between those two extreme, part-time positions, one also finds other part-time coaches who may be 1) college athletic administrators who also coach, 2) university graduate assistants, 3) high school classroom teachers who also coach, 4) personnel outside the school or college who have other occupations, or 5) interns.

THE PROBLEM

When one considers the range of part-time coaching categories, it becomes difficult to generalize about the nature of any problem. However, the following dimensions of an overall problem may be evident whenever a coach is a part-time volunteer or employed for less than half time as a coach.

1. Part-time coaches may have less loyalty toward the athletic department and less respect and concern for the facilities and equipment.

2. They have a reduced time commitment to the overall program. This becomes critical in terms of carrying out certain administrative duties necessary in the management of a team (recruiting, scouting, or budget management). Of course one can also find part-time coaches who actually serve full time. That poses a problem for the coach and may lead to low morale.
3. They often have a poor understanding of the institution's position on the role of athletics and athletic policies and procedures.
4. Due to reduced availability, a severe lack of communication may develop between part-time coaches and administrators. However, part-time employment is rarely the only reason for communication problems.
5. Frequently, a part-time coach may be restricted in terms of overall qualifications. He or she may have the necessary athletic background but lack knowledge in the areas of health, athletic training, and safety.
6. Athletes may feel neglected by a part-time coach. The coach may not be available for advice and counseling mentor.
7. There tends to be a high turnover rate among part-time coaches. When the coach remains for only one season, one year, or a couple of years, there is a lack of stability on the team and a lack of continuity in the athletic department.
8. Administrators may feel less need to evaluate part-time coaches due to the turnover rate. This may lead to a general reduction in standards.
9. Due to the general lack of availability, part-time coaches are not easily integrated or accepted by the full time staff.

THE ISSUE

When viewed from the standpoint of the administration, there are advantages as well as disadvantages in employing part-time coaches. Many of the arguments for and against are similar to those involving part-time faculty generally.

Arguments For Part-Time Coaches

1. From the viewpoint of administrators, the number one reason to employ part-time coaches is finances. The move to part-time coaches, like part-time faculty, results from cost-benefit analysis. Faculty in a school or college and coaches within an athletic department represent the principal labor cost.
2. Part-time coaches offer greater flexibility in determining workloads and making personnel decisions such as reappointments and terminations.

3. In many situations, a part-time coach makes the difference between retaining or dropping a sport program. This may well be one of principal arguments for employing a part-time coach.
4. Part-time coaching often provides a young person an entry into coaching or the sport management field. This sort of advantage is particularly manifested in graduate assistants and interns. Regardless of the particular form, the idea of the apprentice is very much related to part-time coaching.
5. Major studies on part-time faculty point to certain motivational advantages in part-time teaching. "Studies suggest that most individuals teach part-time for positive rather than negative reasons and find a relatively high level of job satisfaction." (*The NEA Higher Education Journal*, p. 55) "Studies argue that part-timers experience lesser levels of dissatisfaction because their reasons for teaching are clearly defined." (Ibid., p. 56) There is reason to believe that those two conclusions regarding part-time teaching would apply to part-time coaching as well.
6. Part-time coaches are particularly useful as assistant coaches in many situations. As a matter of fact, if it were not for some part-time coaches, there would not be assistants. The full-time head coach would likely view the part-time assistant with considerable favor.

Arguments Against Part-Time Coaches

1. Various dimensions of the problem with part-time coaches were identified earlier. Collectively these are the principal arguments against employing part-time coaches. However, the opposition to part-time coaching also comes from other directions.
2. From a conceptual or symbolic standpoint, the employment of part-time coaches (particularly as head coaches) reflects negatively on the central role of coaches in an athletic department. (This is related to the opposition to part-time faculty in light of the central role of faculty in institutions of higher education.) In essence, the part-time coach can be viewed merely as "cheap labor."
3. The gradual move toward more part-time coaches can be seen as a threat to job security in the athletic department. Beyond that, there may be an overall threat to professional advancement due to the general reduction in full-time positions at all institutions.
4. Perhaps the strongest argument against the employment of part-time coaches is that there tends to be a lack of continuity or stability in the sport program. This is particularly true when there is a part-time head coach. The athlete is most affected. He or she may feel that the sport lacks administrative support.

5. Continued and increased use of part-time coaches tends to reduce the salary base within the department. The general disparity between full and part-time salaries is well documented. Once the shift is made to part-time positions, it is difficult to get funding for restoration of full-time positions. There is typically an erosion of the salary structure.

SOURCES FOR PART-TIME COACHES

Each part-time coach presents his or her unique set of circumstances in terms of being integrated into the total structure of the department. When an athletic director has a need to make a part-time coaching appointment, what options are typically available? At the college level, at least five sources can be identified.

1. *Faculty members outside the athletic department*: These are faculty members who have primary appointments in one of the academic departments in the college or university. A history professor may have an extensive background in tennis, or a geology professor may have been a competitive skier in his or her college days. There can be considerable advantage in this kind of part-time coaching appointment. Communication may be facilitated because the faculty member has an office on campus and is likely to be more accessible to students and administrators. The fact that these individuals are already faculty members helps to alleviate the problem of orientation to the institution.

2. *Individuals from the community at large*: This category of part-time coach is not otherwise employed by the college or university, but lives nearby. The individual may have previous coaching experience or may be a former, accomplished athlete who seeks an involvement with coaching. The appeal of this source of appointment is the potentially rich source of talent "out there." Limitations could include lack of orientation to the college, availability, communication, and program stability. However, if the individual is well established in the community, this type of appointment may offer some stability to the program because he or she is more likely to remain in that setting.

3. *Graduate student assistants*: Within universities this tends to be one of the more common and acceptable sources for part-time coaches, particularly as assistant coaches. Obviously, this source is limited to institutions offering graduate programs. There are distinct advantages to this form of appointment. From the perspective of the graduate student this is *the* means of entry into the coaching field, and gaining the necessary experience. This may also be the principal means for the student to finance a graduate education. For the department, the graduate assistant offers a rich potential

source of enthusiasm and energy. The limitations to this source of appointment are the relative lack of experience of these part-time coaches and the constant turnover. This does not facilitate program continuity or stability. Also, the source is "cheap labor," which has certain negative aspects.

4. *Student interns*: This source may well offer the greatest potential for future development. By and large, the interns are college graduates who have been college athletes and are now enrolled in graduate programs (usually sport management) at other institutions. The internship is necessary to fulfill master's degree requirements. The advantages and disadvantages of this form of part-time coaching are similar to those involving graduate assistants. However, certain additional advantages can be noted. Employment of student interns is not restricted to universities that offer graduate programs. As a matter of fact, the intern may be contracted from an academic program in sport management to any collegiate athletic program. The internship gives the student contacts with at least one other institution and often provides a means of entry into the field. Furthermore, the internship often combines administrative and coaching requirements. This provides training in the complete functioning of an athletic department.

5. *Administrative staff members in the athletic department*: These are part-time coaches who hold other primary assignments within the athletic department. This could be an assistant athletic director who also coaches the golf team or the ticket manager who coaches the tennis team. The clear advantage is that the individual is likely to understand department and institution policies and procedures. The most apparent disadvantage may be time commitment to the sport and the team. Depending on the particular arrangement, there could also be problems with administrative partiality and relationships with other coaches.

In the spring of 1985, 21 of 50 randomly selected Division I institutions responded to a survey regarding the sources for part-time coaches and the reasons for this type of employment. Sources for part-time coaches are described in Table 10-1.

Information from this limited survey pointed to the following conclusions and reactions to part-time coaching.

1. Among the available sources, athletic directors rely most heavily on employing part-time coaches (both head coaches and assistant coaches) from the community at large. Athletic directors who responded said they preferred these individuals because they did not have conflicting commitments to the athletic department and were more stable. The athletic directors also noted a "larger

TABLE 10-1. Sources of Part-time Coaches

Source	Part-time Head Coaches	Part-time Assistant Coaches
1) Faculty member outside the department	19	9
2) From the community (outside the college)	41	95
3) Student assistants	4	48
4) Interns	0	18
5) Athletic staff (administrative)	0	4
TOTALS	64	174

opportunity for unearthing new talent." One institution indicated its best type of part-time coach was the independent businessman or woman who did not wish and could not afford to be full-time. The next most popular choice is the young, "just give me an opportunity to get started" type, who understands that the position is, and will remain, part-time.

2. The survey showed that a relatively large number of faculty members were part-time head coaches. The athletic directors often preferred this source of part-time coaching because the faculty tended to have organizational skills that allowed accommodations for reduced time. In general, the athletic directors also felt these faculty coaches were more "in tune" with college philosophies, more reliable, and easily accessible. On the other hand, the available pool of faculty for part-time coaching positions tends to be very limited.

3. Students and interns are employed rather extensively as assistant coaches. The basic reasons are in line with the advantages of these sources noted earlier. However, the survey revealed that work/study funds, as a supplement to regular budget allocations, were another significant reason for employing students as assistant coaches.

Case Study - A Four College Area

This case study is based on information obtained during the spring of 1985 from four institutions of higher education located in a specific geographic area, within a 15-mile radius. They include one large state university and three private, small colleges. Names of the institutions and athletic personnel are withheld due to the confidentiality of some of this information. General profiles of the institutions are as follows:

University A
State university
Enrollment - 19,478 undergraduate students
            - approximately 4,000 graduate students
NCAA - Division I
28 intercollegiate sports (in the process of dropping seven sports).
Five part-time head coaches
22 part-time assistant coaches

College B
Private, coeducational college
Enrollment - 1,550
NCAA - Division III
30 intercollegiate sports
Seven part-time head coaches
Five part-time assistant coaches

College C
Private, all-female college
Enrollment - 2,500
NCAA - Division III
15 intercollegiate sports
Three part-time head coaches

College D
Private, all-female college
Enrollment - 1,950
NCAA - Division III
12 intercollegiate sports
Two part-time head coaches

   In analyzing this four-institution, comparative case, the focus is on the employment of part-time head coaches. There are 17 among the institutions involved, compared with 27 part-time assistant coaches. The focus on the part-time head coach is warranted because many of the problems inherent in employing part-time coaches manifest themselves with head coaches rather than with part-time assistants. For example, an assistant coach rarely has to communicate directly with the higher levels of athletic administration. The basic channel of communication is from the head coach to the athletic director. The head coach is responsible for defining the responsibilities and orienting the assistants. In essence, the part-time employment is more or less built into the structure for assistant coaches.
   Although there are obvious differences among these institutions, certain common denominators emerge in assessing reactions to having part-time head coaches. Interviews with athletic directors at the four

institutions revealed the following common reactions, with some differences as noted.

Qualifications of Part-time Coaches: Administrators from all four institutions gave similar responses concerning desired qualifications for a part-time head coach. They sought a coach with at least a bachelor's degree, and preferably a master's. However, in each situation, due to the available pool of applicants, all indicated that they fell short of their preferences. In general, part-time coaches with master's degrees also held other jobs in the community. The remainder were mostly students working toward their master's degrees.

There was also consensus among the athletic directors regarding the other desired qualifications: high expertise and knowledge of the sport, ability to teach appropriate skills, ability to manage a team, ability to interact well with athletes and administrators, and previous coaching experience. In terms of the latter qualification, the institutions once again fell short. For example, at the three colleges less than half of the part-time coaches had any previous coaching experience, and at all four institutions only three of the part-time coaches had previous collegiate coaching experience. This is another case of living with the realities of the available pool for part-time positions.

Responsibilities: Expectations regarding responsibilities of part-time coaches were also found to be much the same among the four institutions. The part-time coach was expected to carry out those functions related to his or her specific sport. Generally, this excluded teaching assignments, committee memberships, and regular office hours. Work was performed during the duration of the specific sport season. Most of the part-time coaches went to faculty/staff meetings whenever possible, although this was not required. The coaches were expected to do the necessary administrative paperwork, but there were lower expectations for the more time-consuming jobs, such as recruiting and scouting.

Evaluations: Policies concerning the evaluation of the coaches were also essentially the same at the four institutions, with slight variations, particularly between the university and the three colleges. The university representative stressed that ultimately the win/loss record was the bottom line for coaches. At the three colleges, teaching skills, administrative skills, and interaction with the athletes were used as the principal criteria for evaluation. These criteria were considered prior to any reappointment. However, all the institutions indicated that evaluations are rarely written and tend to be quite informal. Athletic directors at two of the colleges stated that they assessed and evaluated their coaches throughout the season by attending games and practices. (It would appear that this might be more applicable for full-time coaches. Few part-time coaches noted that the athletic directors came to observe their games or practices on a regular basis.)

As another dimension of the overall evaluation process, the athletic administrator from the university also referred to student-athlete complaints. If a coach was neglecting his or her duties or doing something unusual, the athletes notified the administration promptly.

Initial Orientation: Initial orientation for part-time coaches was considered quite weak at all four institutions. The university did very little in this regard. The coaches were more or less left on their own to determine departmental procedures. New coaches usually obtained information and assistance from coaching colleagues. The athletic director from College B also admitted that his orientation for part-time coaches was "flimsy" and that the orientation should be stronger. New coaches (full or part-time) were informed of the college's philosophy, with emphasis on the academic pressures among the students.

At College C, the athletic director gave all new coaches a booklet which contained information and procedures on specific matters such as equipment care, facility usage, uniform distribution, vehicle usage, meal policies, and safety policies for practice and competition. The material also included clarification of certain basic responsibilities for a head coach: budgeting, recruiting policies with admissions, speaking engagements, attending conference meetings, and advising athletes on academic matters. Although the booklet was quite thorough and useful, it was clearly geared toward the full-time coach who was generally available and expected to carry out diversified assignments. There was no indication as to how the part-time coach was expected to relate to the total structure. None of the administrators had policies that would regularly monitor the work of part-time coaches, especially during their first seasons.

Institutional Comparisons: The foregoing represents most of the common elements in part-time coaching at these institutions. However, some differences can be noted in the reasons for employing part-time coaches as well as the problems. These differences are largely related to the specific natures of the institutions involved.

University A: The university offered 28 intercollegiate sports. In light of that number, it was not surprising that there were five part-time head coaches, six part-time assistant coaches, and 16 graduate assistants. The head coaches were in wrestling, women's cross country, men's skiing, women's skiing, men's tennis, and women's tennis. The number of years that these part-time coaches had been at the university varied from one to 26 years. The primary occupations of these coaches were equally as varied. At the time of the survey, the university announced that it was dropping seven sports from the intercollegiate program. It is interesting to note that five of the seven were coached by part-timers.

The assistant athletic director at the university stated that the main reason for using part-time coaches was finances. A part-time coach typically received less than one-third of a full-time coach's salary.

Primary problems in having part-time coaches included lack of communication and a high turnover rate (with the one exception of the coach with 26 years tenure). High turnover results in less commitment to recruiting, scouting, and program building.

College B: The college had seven, part-time head coaches. They were all hired within the past two years, and the majority had no previous coaching experience. Four of the coaches had recently graduated from college, and three were employed elsewhere in the community. The part-time head coaches were in ice hockey, men's crew, women's crew, women's volleyball, wrestling, men's skiing, women's skiing, and women's squash.

The athletic director at the college said that the major reason for employing part-time coaches was due to a faculty freeze of 150 faculty positions in the overall college. The athletic department already had its allotment. A full-time addition could not be made until a coach resigned or was not reappointed. Also, the philosophy at the college was to have a large and diversified intercollegiate athletic program specifically geared to serve the needs of student-athletes. With 30 intercollegiate sports, the department lacked the resources to cover all the sports with existing faculty.

Having the part-time coaches understand institutional philosophy, athletic department philosophy, and academic pressures were considered to be the number one problem. There were difficulties in educating these coaches regarding the NCAA and conference regulations. A lack of continuity in the program due to high turnover of part-time coaches was also listed as a problem.

College C: The main reason for using part-time coaches at this college was also finances. However, the number of part-time coaches had actually been reduced in recent years. After taking the job, the current athletic director strengthened the program by adding some full-time positions. He did this by hiring coaches who had expertise in more than one sport. Part-time coaches remained in squash, skiing, and gymnastics. The latter was historically a part-time position. In general, there was more stability in the part-time positions at this college, compared to other colleges in the area.

The athletic director identified divided loyalties as being the main problem with part-time staff. Attendance at meetings and communications in general were difficult. Continuity was not a problem due to the fact that the part-time coaches were relatively well established in the community.

College D: The college had only two part-time coaches in 1985 and in recent years. These coaches were in diving and crew, both with a fair amount of seniority. The athletic director stated that she did not like utilizing part-time coaches due to the usual problems and the specific philosophy of the athletic department. Coaches at the college were required to have backgrounds in physical education, and the athletic director found it difficult to obtain part-time coaches who met the qualifications in that area. By hiring part-time coaches, the athletic director felt she was compromising important standards. This was viewed as the major problem in employing part-time staff members.

Reactions of Part-time Coaches: The case study also included interviews with selected part-time coaches at these four institutions. Although the part-time coaches also varied in their responses, the following generalities can be noted.

1. Most of the part-time coaches said that orientations to the athletic programs were non-existent or insufficient. They tended to seek advice from the full-time coaches. The consensus was that their work during the first year would have been considerably easier with more structured orientation programs. At one of the institutions, the coaches said they were not even given a tour of the facilities when they first arrived.
2. The part-time coaches agreed that communication was a major problem. They were not required to meet regularly with any member of the administration. Several of the coaches indicated that they made it a practice to speak with the athletic director or an assistant on an informal basis.
3. The part-time coaches commonly perceived a lack of support for their particular sports. The overall communication problem probably contributes to this type of perception as does the choice of part-time leadership.
4. The prevalent feeling among the part-time coaches was that the athletic departments did not recognize or show appreciation for their efforts. This was particularly manifested in the compensation levels. This frustration is understandable in light of the overall demands in being a head coach. A part-time coaching position can very easily become full-time without commensurate compensation. However, in addition to the compensation factor, the part-time coaches also expressed concern about intrinsic rewards, such as recognition, opportunity for advancement, and a sense of importance.

Case Study Conclusion: This comparative case study of four institutions of higher education reinforces general concepts about some of the problems associated with part-time coaching. It is also clear that the specific nature of part-time coaching is largely institutionally defined. For example, the case study reveals some differences between the state university and the three smaller, private colleges. If there is a common problem, it may be the lack of communication between part-time employees and the regular staff. Financial limitations are another common denominator in employing part-time coaches. Regardless of any problems or issues, there is every reason to believe that part-time coaches are here to stay, at least for the foreseeable future.

POLICIES & POLICY GUIDELINES

Due to the fact that part-time coaching is now an integral component of the collegiate athletic structure, it seems desirable and necessary, to facilitate the integration of these coaches. The following policies and guidelines are suggested for college athletic departments in general, recognizing that there will always be variations from institution to institution due to local and periodic exigencies.

1. *Policy: Selecting and Hiring*
   The screening process for selecting and hiring part-time coaches will be comparable to that employed in obtaining full-time staff members.
   Guidelines
   a. General, minimum qualifications for all coaches should include: 1) a thorough knowledge of the sport, including the rules and regulations; 2) a demonstrated ability to teach the skills for the sport; 3) a knowledge of safety procedures; and 4) the ability to relate to athletes, coaching peers, and administrators.
   b. Whenever possible, part-time staff members should be selected from among individuals who are already established in the community. This enhances the possibility of having stability in the program. It would be highly preferable to recruit qualified coaches from other academic departments because these individuals already understand the institution orientation.
   c. When considering individuals for assistant coaching positions, particular attention should be given to internship candidates who generally comprise an available pool of young, enthusiastic coaches with great potential for development.

2. *Policy: Orientation*
   Due to the general problem of communication, special attention will be given to a structured orientation program for all coaches, including those who are employed part-time.
   Guidelines
   a. All new coaches should have a thorough tour of the athletic facilities as well as other college facilities that may be utilized.
   b. Information about institutional philosophy and athletic policies should be presented.
   c. Each coach should receive written copies of departmental procedures (e.g., team travel arrangements, equipment distribution, and laundry procedures) as well as applicable conference rules and regulations.

d. Whenever possible, another coach should be appointed to serve as a mentor to the new coach particularly for the part-time employee.

e. In an early meeting between the athletic director and the new coach, the responsibilities and expectations for the position should be clearly defined, preferably in a written agreement, signed by both parties.

3. *Policy: Communication*

Specific steps will be taken to facilitate continued communication with and among coaches in the department.

Guidelines

a. Every coach would be expected to attend a regularly scheduled departmental meeting on at least a monthly basis.

b. The athletic director should follow an open door policy on an available basis.

4. *Policy: Evaluation*

The basic format for coaches' evaluations will be management by objectives.

Guidelines

a. Evaluation should be based on performance standards determined by the athletic director and coach prior to the sport season.

b. In a regularly scheduled meeting between the athletic director and coach, the performance of the latter will be assessed at the conclusion of each season and prior to any reappointment.

c. Any extenuating circumstances or unexpected variables should be taken into account when making the evaluation.

d. The evaluation meeting should be followed by some form of formal, written evaluation signed by both the athletic director and coach. It becomes a part of the employee's record.

5. *Policy: Reward*

The department will take steps to recognize that reward for professional accomplishments involves more than pay increases and promotions.

Guidelines

a. Part-time coaches should be invited to all departmental functions that are attended by full-time staff members.

b. Whenever possible, there should be an annual dinner or luncheon to recognize part-time coaches.

c. The sports information director should be alerted to the need to publicize the achievements and success of part-time coaches.

d. Part-time coaches should also have the opportunity and encouragement to grow professionally through attendance at workshops, clinics, and other professional meetings.

e. The athletic director should attend selected home games and practices for all coaches, including those who are employed part-time.

REFERENCE

Lightman, M., Katz, E. and Helly, D. D. "The Literature on Part-Time Faculty." *Thought & Action: The NEA Higher Education Journal.* Vol. III, No. 1, Spring, 1987.

11

Evaluating College Officials

Who is the most condemned, central, and yet, least known, individual in the sport enterprise? The answer: the official. Once the whistle blows, next to the athlete, the official is the person at center stage. The work of the official is a critical determinant in the quality of the game. Yet, we do not know much about officials other than the fact that they are constant targets for criticism by coaches, athletes, and fans. The news media is replete with accounts about athletes and coaches. Yet, relatively little is written or said about officials, except for references to bad calls.

Information about how officials are evaluated is also scarce. When it comes to college officials, the situation is particularly complex, because evaluation procedures vary greatly. In terms of the national picture, the only certainty is that each conference evaluates its officials differently. Some conferences employ rating systems, while others do not. Those conferences having rating systems differ in the ways they use the ratings. There also are considerable variations from sport to sport.

The weightings assigned to components of the evaluation are not uniform. A survey of supervisors of football and basketball officials for selected conferences was conducted in 1985. The conferences surveyed were the Pacific 10, Big 8, Southwest Conference, Pacific Coast Athletic Conference, Southeast Conference, Big 10, and the Eastern Collegiate Athletic Conference (ECAC). Results showed a number of divergences.

1. In general, the conferences employed some combination of the following components in evaluating officials: ratings by coaches, supervisors, outside observers, and fellow officials; film evaluation; book exams; and "general value."
2. The weight assigned to the coaches' evaluations varied from 0 percent in Big 10 basketball to 60 percent in ECAC basketball.
3. An observer's rating had a weighting of 40 percent in Big 10 basketball, contrasted with no weighting in Big 8 basketball or Southwest football.

4. The Southwest Conference was the only conference to use a film evaluation, giving it a weighting of 25 percent.
5. The value given to the rating by the supervisor of officials ranged from a low of 10 percent in Pac 10 football and basketball to a high of 70 percent in Big 8 basketball.
6. Two conferences, the Pac 10 and ECAC, gave some weight to the evaluations of fellow officials.
7. The Pac 10 was the only conference which had the same rating system for both football and basketball.
8. The ECAC was the only conference to use book exams in evaluating officials, giving this component a weighting of 25 percent for football only.
9. The ECAC also factored in a "general value" component with a weighting of 15 percent for football and 20 percent for basketball.
10. Some conferences permitted officials to review the ratings, whereas others did not. Still others permitted only partial reviews, to maintain confidentiality on the ratings of coaches and conference supervisors.

THE ISSUE

These differences point to the major issue: To what extent should policies be developed that are aimed at providing more uniformity in evaluating officials? Another dimension to the issue, and a problem in this regard, concerns independent schools with no conference affiliations. Many games involving independents are worked by officials from different conferences. Based on the way in which these officials are evaluated, are they all calling the game essentially the same way?

Although not directly aimed at evaluation, the NCAA has taken a step in providing more uniformity for basketball officiating. Separate clinics are held for men's and women's basketball at various locations and are attended by coaches, officials, and administrators.

Basketball officiating clinics conducted by the NCAA this year apparently met with overwhelming approval, if a series of interviews conducted by *The NCAA News* is any indication.

"I thought the clinic I attended (for men's basketball) was refreshing," said Lou Bonder, men's basketball supervisor of officials for the Atlantic 10 Conference. "I believe this program is a needed change from conferences trying to give the same kind of clinic every year. I think the NCAA should be complimented for taking the lead in an effort to improve officiating nationwide." . . .

"I was impressed with the fact that we will now be hearing the same interpretations (of rules) nationwide," said Johnny Overby, supervisor of men's officials for the Big Eight Conference. "The game is called differently in different parts of the country because rules are interpreted differently. I believe these clinics are a great start toward developing officiating consistency in both the men's and women's games. Also, for the first time ever, all Division I supervisors of officials assembled for a meeting in Kansas City. That should prove extremely valuable." . . .

Dave Gavitt, Commissioner, Big East Conference: "It is hard for me to be totally objective, since I chaired the special committee on improving officiating, but I believe these clinics made a big start toward doing that." . . .

"When this program initially was drawn up, those of us who worked on it were a little concerned with the reaction we'd get from conference supervisors of officials . . . we wondered whether they'd feel threatened by all this. Actually, their reaction is proving quite the contrary. The support we have received throughout the country has been absolutely encouraging." (The NCAA News, No. 17, 1986, pp. 1, 11)

The NCAA officiating clinics do not necessarily mean that college basketball is moving toward greater standardization in evaluating officials. However, it is a step toward assessing officiating from a national perspective. The clinics are aimed at developing officiating consistency which should be a factor in improving the evaluation process.

In the 1985 survey regarding college officiating, supervisors of officials and coaches responded to questions about the evaluation process. Their answers, some of which follow, point to the complexity of the issue:

Is there a more effective way to evaluate officials? (Responses by various supervisors of officials)

I don't know - maybe films or tapes could be more helpful.

We have tried several other systems - this is the best.

Possibly film study and evaluation - the extra cost may be counter-productive.

Yes - use observers only. Keep coaches out of the ratings - they are not objective in some cases.

Yes, by good qualified observers - the problem is qualified observers.

Are officials being evaluated in the best possible way? If not, how would you change the system?
(Responses by selected basketball coaches)

No - Need more input from coaches and a broader use of video-tapes.

Yes - We have a good range of perspectives. I would, however, rank the officials based on performance and let them see where they stand in relation with each other and compensate the good ones with bonuses.

No - Involve a checklist with room for discussion by each coach after every game. At the very least coaches would have regular input instead of waiting until the end of the season - or worse yet until they believe they've been wronged.

No - Grade them on a week to week basis.

No - I think there is a bias between most evaluators and officials (play favorites) plus there is not enough evaluators to see all the officials equally in game situations.

No! I would evaluate each official by someone from the Big 10 office and the coaches and then see the results.

Take the politics and "good old boy" theory out of the officials group. The right to hire and fire for poor work is the right of any business or administrative group.

No - We need something public - coaches must talk to the media and answer questions about every move and decision we make. It makes us review everything we do - this keeps us sharp. Somehow officials need something like that - they tell each other "good job."

No way. What evaluation that is done is weak at best. I would require each official to review a tape of his game and have the supervisor of officials view tapes of games that are requested by coaches.

(Responses by selected football coaches)

No. I would eliminate conference officials - all officials would have to pass a national test with national standards. There would be one governing body split up into different sections so that the cost of travel would not be too expensive. They should have regional representatives evaluate the officials on one common ground and one common test because in the current system, different conferences call different things according to the way they interpret the rules.

No - More evaluating should be done by the conference commissioner of officials and a board of officials by using films of the game.

I would have an exchange of evaluation crews. The Big 10 could send a group to evaluate another conference and so on.

Yes and no. Current coaches and observers ratings are good but the supervisor must become active in the true evaluation of all officials and the ability of his evaluators. The supervisor must continue to move up and develop new officials and move down or out those officials that are constantly poor in judgment, mechanics, and game control.

I think those officials who take time to study the film do a much better job.

I have 3 suggestions:
1. Put numbers on the officials so they can be identified more easily.
2. A strong board of officials - 2-3 men who evaluate officials from game film on a weekly basis.
3. Grading of officials by coaches from game films on a weekly basis.

Probably not, but haven't studied it.

No. I would put together a committee to evaluate them weekly and give them a weekly grade. If they fail, they drop out.

No. Hire full time evaluators who use film for evaluation and teaching.

Should coaches have the right to blackball officials if they are unhappy with their performance in a particular game?
(Response by selected football and basketball coaches)
Only if the coach can back up his complaints with tapes to prove his point.

Yes, it is the practice in many high school situations. I would like to feel all coaches are only interested in consistent, fair officiating. I think it would force them to be consistent.

No, blackballing is not the answer.

Yes, but not for just one particular game, but over the course of the season. The concentration level will increase, but they also may become more timid and not blow the whistle at all.

Yes, coaches should have the right to blackball any official if that official is not competent. Hopefully, this will make them aware that they will be held accountable for their performance. We have a policy that lets coaches rest two officials each year, but we do not have the authority to fire them.

The right to blackball an official should only occur after the season is over and the officials are rated for their season performance by the Board of Officials and coaches. A coach's blackball should take effect for the following season. If there are a number of negative votes, the official should be fired.

I think something should be done to discuss the reason for trying to blackball the official, if that is an option. There is an appropriate time after the season to discuss this with the supervisor of officials.

This situation should be handled with discretion. It would probably be the course to take only if and when poor judgment and performance occurs as a pattern and not on the basis of one game.

Many coaches, after a particular, blatant, bad call would immediately blackball anybody after the game. Consistent bad calls indicate an incompetent official that should be blackballed.

Coach should be able to request an official not to call their games. It should not affect the performance of an official. If it did, he should not be officiating.

No, you could probably blackball one a game and soon you'd run out of officials.

Some people believe that college officiating needs younger and fresher blood. Do you believe that age is an important factor for officials' performance levels?
(Responses by selected football and basketball coaches)

No. Experience is more important, in my opinion.

We need more young officials - but take away the retirement age - health should determine the retirement.

No, ability and performance are the important criteria.

No, age is a state of mind. If an individual is physically able, alert and excited about his assignment, then he has the makings of a good official.

I believe that many officials tend to stay too long. A constant influx of new people is desirable, yet it is very difficult for young men to get a start.

I have a concern that older officials are kept beyond their prime years. They should be used as a resource to help in the training of younger officials. I am concerned about injury to older officials. The game is so much faster.

Age isn't that important - rather, it is their conditioning. Some 50-year-old men are in better shape than men in their 30's.

Should conference officials be allowed to officiate outside of their respective conferences?
(Responses by selected football and basketball coaches)

Absolutely. In some big intersectional contests, it is most desirable, in my opinion.

Yes, - the rules should be interpreted the same, and officials are supposed to be impartial.

The home team should supply the officials. There should not be any split crews.

If you're talking split crews from two different conferences of competing teams, it is probably a necessary evil.

It is best to keep your officials in your conference. The evaluations are constant and I feel a relationship develops that helps all concerned.

No. There is a problem of favoring their conference.

They should be allowed to officiate outside their conference for professional expertise.

Yes. In fact, a constant mixture of officials is worth experimenting with again. Certain officials seem to be intimidated by certain coaches over a period of years.

In your opinion, what is the greatest problem facing college officials today?
(Responses by various supervisors of officials)
Media "hype" on selected plays and calls as well as over reaction by public opinion in potentially volatile situations.

We must improve the image of basketball officials. The greatest indictment of our intercollegiate basketball programs is that so few former varsity players want to officiate after their playing days are over.

Lack of respect from coaches, fans, and media.

News media looking to create some sensational sidelines to games. Instead of *reporting* the facts of the contest, some reporters are creating problems by going to players for quotes on officiating.

They are used too often as scapegoats. It is always an official's error that costs a game - never a coaches' or team's. Also a general lack of understanding on the coaches' part of the rules and what an official does.

There is a difference of opinion when the topic of official evaluation is addressed by a coach and by a supervisor of officials. Any generalities seem to be more or less along the following lines: 1) more attention should be given to game films and videotapes in the evaluation process; 2) television commentators pose a problem in assessing the performance of officials; 3) officials should be evaluated at the end of the season; 4) experience is a more important factor than age in quality officiating; and 5) there is need for more standardization in selecting and evaluating college officials.

A Case Study: The 1985 Men's NCAA Division I Basketball Tournament

For several reasons, the 1985 men's NCAA basketball tournament provides an appropriate case study. The records and assessment of the 1985 tournament are readily available. It kind of marked the climax to the development of the NCAA tournament as a premier event. The tournament began in 1939, just two years after the National Invitational Tournament, which was the prestige tournament of that time. There were 16 teams in the first NCAA basketball tournament. Over the years, the number of teams has steadily increased. With that increase and added television coverage, the publicity, visibility, and revenues have expanded accordingly. The 64 teams in the 1985 tournament represented another major step in the development of a classic sport event.

Any NCAA basketball tournament dramatically portrays the need to effectively evaluate officials, due to high stakes visibility, and pressure. A basketball official faces a difficult challenge at best whenever he is officiating, and when a possible $400,000 or more rests on a single call, the importance of evaluation is magnified. How were the officials selected and evaluated for the 1985 tournament?

Of the 64 teams in the tournament, 29 earned automatic bids through conference championships. The remaining 35 teams were "at large" selections made by the NCAA's Men's Basketball Committee, comprising athletic directors from nine Division I institutions. A total of 96 first round officials were needed because there were 32 games with three-man officiating crews. Each conference with an automatic bid was also allowed to select an official to work one of the first round games. The Men's Basketball Committee selected the remaining 67 at large officials after receiving a list of recommended candidates from the supervisor of officials for each conference.

It was understood that supervisors would only submit the most qualified candidates for consideration. The committee made its selections by evaluating the background sheets submitted by the conference supervisors. These background sheets essentially provided information on 1) the colleges which the official attended, 2) previous experience in post-season tournaments, 3) other conferences for which the official worked during that season, and 4) the ranking of the official in the conference for the season. After the committee selected the 67 at large officials, the officials were then classified into three categories.

"A" Officials: These officials have considerable tournament experience. For the most part they have been involved with a minimum of six to seven NCAA tournaments with at least two appearances in the "Final Four." In 1985, Hank Nichols from the Atlantic Coast Conference fell into that category, having been involved in 12 tournaments and five finals.

"B" Officials: This category of official typically has limited NCAA tournament experience. In most cases these officials have worked approximately two to four tournaments, although they generally had not advanced beyond a regional final. A 1985 example was Ben Dreith of the Big 8 Conference. He had worked three tournaments and one regional semi-final.

"C" Officials: Although these officials have no NCAA tournament experience, they are regarded as having excellent potential. Through dedication and hard work, they have come to the attention of their conference supervisors.

The process of selecting and categorizing officials was completed before the final field for the tournament had been selected. Once the field was completed, assignments to the first round were made.

Assignment of Officials: The assignment of officials to particular games is a critical function of the NCAA Men's Basketball Committee. This is why it is important to have the preliminary categorization of officials. The committee intended to assign three-man crews with an official from each category. Tom Gernstedt, assistant executive director for the NCAA Tournament, explained that the assignment system was designed to bring parity to the crews and insure balance among the tournament officials.

Another dimension of the system was that an official would advance as a member of a crew rather than as an individual. By establishing crew advancement, the committee hoped to address a complaint expressed by the NCAA Division I Basketball Advisory Committee on behalf of coaches who felt that the tournament had become an "officiating tournament." The thought was that officials were blowing the whistle too often and too tightly because they had to be noticeable in order to advance.

In making the actual assignments, the committee also had two other principal goals. The first of these was to stress regions and not conferences through the cross assignment of officials. Rather than considering an official to be from the Pac 10, he was instead assigned as a representative from the western region. CBS, who had the television rights to the 1985 tournament, was instructed to refer to the officials by regions, and not by the conferences with which they were associated.

The other goal was to avoid any emotional ties of officials to teams to the greatest extent possible. Thus, an official who had worked four or five games for a particular team during the regular season would not be assigned to a tournament game involving that team. Through proper cross assignment, the committee also aimed at eliminating ties to a particular region. Therefore, it was not unusual to see a crew comprising eastern, midwestern, and western officials working in the southeast region. This kind of assignment pattern also proved useful in evaluating officials.

Evaluation and Advancement: Evaluation of officials for the 1985 tournament was conducted by at least four individuals for each region, representing different perspectives.

1. *A Member of the Men's Basketball Committee:* This individual was also responsible for obtaining the other evaluators and serving as the chair when the members met to evaluate the tournament crews.
2. *A Member of the NCAA Rules Committee:* This appointment was designed to provide competency in evaluating an official on knowledge of the rules.
3. *A Supervisor of Conference Officials:* The supervisor added the dimension of being able to evaluate overall game control by the officials involved.
4. *A Non-Active Division I Basketball Coach:* This was an individual who has another perspective on the role of the coach in a game environment. The former coach offered insights on the pressure of the tournament environment.

Prior to the start of each game, the evaluators positioned themselves around different areas of the arena. Each official was evaluated according to eight guidelines (Exhibit 11-1). Although no specific weight was assigned to each of the guidelines or criteria, the combined assessment was used to rank the officials.

Following the conclusion of each game, the four evaluators compared their ratings. The obvious purpose was to determine who should advance to the next round. The complication, of course, was to compare one crew with another crew when officials advance as a crew. Some deviation in the general structure of advancing crews can be noted in the 1985 tournament. The design was as follows:

Round One - The highest rated crew will advance. A second crew may advance or a crew can be made up of the remaining individuals if there is not a second crew with a high rating.
Round Two - Following the second round, the Men's Committee decides which three officials should advance to the regional semi-finals. These three officials can either be a crew or three individuals, whoever is evaluated the highest.
Regional Semi-Finals - At this point there are eight crews remaining. The four highest rated crews will move on to the regional finals.
Regional Finals - The highest rated crew from the four regions will move on to the national semi-finals. A second crew may advance or three individuals may advance, depending on the evaluation.
National Semi-Finals - Of the two remaining crews, the highest ranked will move on to the finals. (Note: This was not followed in 1985. Due to the poor evaluation of both crews, three individuals were chosen for the final game.)

EXHIBIT 11-1. NCAA Men's Basketball Championship Officials Rating Card

Tournament and Location _____

Date _____ 19____

NCAA Basketball Committee Representative _____

Officials (Names)

_____   _____

_____   _____

_____   _____

Guidelines for Ranking Officials

Consistency—calls the same at both ends of the court and throughout the game

Mechanics—signals, voice, whistle, moving, anticipating, switching

Judgment—guarding, hands, post play, screening, goal-tending

Decisiveness—firm, clear, controlled

Game control—players on court, coaches and bench personnel, official table

Reaction under pressure—calls the tough play, personal and game control

Manner—handling players, coaches, poise, friendly, courteous, alert

Appearance—uniform neat and proper, condition

RANKING OF OFFICIALS

1. _____   4. _____

2. _____   5. _____

3. _____   6. _____

Rating by _____

1985

SUGGESTED POLICIES

The following policies are suggested for Division I football and basketball, with the understanding that such policies would have to be modified for other levels and other sports. Obviously, these are suggested as optimum policies. Restrictions and exceptions might be necessitated due to limitations in time, finances, or both.

1. All Division I football and basketball officials would be required to belong to a national officials organization, which has a primary purpose of evaluating officials. The organization would be under the direction and guidance of the NCAA with implementation of policies through the supervisor of officials for each conference.
2. All independent officials would be required to join an independent officials conference, which would appoint a supervisor of officials, who would act in the same capacity as any other conference supervisor of officials.
3. Each official would be evaluated for every game he works. The evaluation would be based on the following standardized sources:
   Outside Observers - 40 percent (observer to be certified through the National Officials Organization)
   Supervisor of Officials - 25 percent
   Coaches - 20 percent
   Fellow Officials - 15 percent
4. Each conference would employ a rating system for the purpose of ranking their officials at the conclusion of the season. The areas for rating and relative weight distribution would be as follows:
   a. Composite Game Ratings (supervisor, coach, peers, observer) - 35 percent
   b. Game Management - 15 percent
   c. Rules Exam (mandatory one per year) - 15 percent
   d. Clinic Attendance (mandatory one per year) - 5 percent
   e. Physical Condition - 10 percent
   f. Mechanics Exam (mandatory one per year) - 15 percent
   g. Conduct and Appearance - 5 percent
5. Officials would be penalized for falling below certain percentages in the composite rating according to the following provisions: (Imposed the following season)

   Below 85 percent
   Basketball: three-game suspension
   Football: one-game suspension

   Below 75 percent
   Basketball: six-game suspension and one additional clinic must be attended

Football: two-game suspension and one additional clinic must be attended

Below 60 percent
Basketball & Football: will not be allowed to officiate any conference games for a one-year period. Must receive a positive reevaluation by a conference supervisor (based on performance at other levels) to be reinstated.

6. Officials would be required to review game films bi-monthly with the conference supervisor of officials. The primary purpose would be to use the films as a teaching tool. At this time, overall game control would also be evaluated.

7. At the conclusion of the season there would be a scheduled time for all coaches in the conference to meet with the supervisor of officials to discuss the officials' performances. Game films and videotapes would be utilized for clarifications.

8. Officials would be required to meet with the supervisor of officials at the conclusion of the season. The supervisor would give each official his ranking and discuss the criteria for the evaluation. At the same time, the supervisor would outline areas to work on for improvement next season. The official would also be given the opportunity to discuss circumstances that may have already affected his performance.

CONCLUSION

The quality of officiating is an important element in high quality games in organized sport. The need for having the best officiating increases proportionately to the level, complexity, and structure of the sport. In spite of the significance of highly organized sports in the college today, there is a marked lack of uniformity in terms of the way in which officials are evaluated. The suggested policies are aimed at providing greater uniformity. Implementation of such policies may not be entirely feasible due to limitations in time or money. However, this is a case where it is not necessary to adopt the whole package in order to bring about improvement. The policies are suggested as parts that might contribute individually or collectively in attempting to improve the quality of college officiating.

REFERENCE

"No Disputed Calls at NCAA Officiating Clinics." *The NCAA News*, Vol. 23, No. 41, November 17, 1986, pp. 1, 11.

12

Spectators: Control of Violence

On May 29, 1985, at the European Cup soccer final in Heysel Stadium in Brussels, 38 people died and 437 were injured after "hooligans" from Liverpool, England, attacked fans of Juventus, the soccer team of Turin, Italy. The shocked reaction to this horrible event was expressed throughout the world. Unfortunately, the problem of spectator or fan violence at sport events is far from new, and it is not confined to nations of modern Europe. The following are a few of many examples in the history of sport.

- 532 B.C. — 30,000 Roman spectators died in rioting associated with a chariot race.
- 1910 — 19 people left dead in Nevada, following Jack Johnson's knockout of Jim Jeffries.
- 1962 — 340 people injured and hundreds of cars damaged in a riot following a championship high school football game in Washington, D.C.
- 1965 — Eight people stabbed following a high school regional tournament basketball game in Detroit.
- 1982 — 25 policemen sent to the hospital after attempting to control a brawl between Florida and Florida State fans following a football game.
- 1984 — one man shot and at least 80 people injured when Detroit Tiger fans burned and overturned cars outside Tiger Stadium after a World Series victory.

What is new is a growing awareness that something must be done to alleviate the problem. Most sport administrators regard fan violence as a very significant problem that will become more severe if preventive action is not taken. The terrible event in Brussels might not have occurred if effective crowd management had been employed.

In addressing the problem of fan violence, it is important to note that the extent of the problem varies from sport to sport, depending on the nature of the sport and conditions surrounding a particular sport event.

Sports violence is most likely to occur at team events involving traditional rivals, say researchers. Aggression tends to increase the bigger the crowd and the hotter the weather, and is worse at night than during the day. According to a 1979 study of 39 professional baseball games, 77% of the fights in the stands occurred in the least expensive seats; 69% happened at night; and 70% in the last four innings, when alcohol had taken hold.

Open seating (or, as in Brussels, open standing) also contributes to fan violence. (*Sports Illustrated*, June 10, 1985, p. 27)

Effective policy development must take into account the causes of the problem. Very few incidents of fan violence result from a single, isolated cause. Any combination of the following factors is more than likely to be instrumental.

1. Excessive consumption of alcohol or drugs
2. Poorly designed and operated facilities
3. Intense rivalries, including media hype of such rivalries
4. Tensions within the crowd resulting from competition for goods or services
5. Violence on the court or playing field
6. Contagion and anonymity of the crowd
7. Close and involuntary contact with strangers
8. Disdain for authority
9. Untrained and overjealous security forces
10. Unpopular calls by officials

When considering the causes and complexities surrounding fan violence, one must also recognize that violent behavior is not manifested in a single, simplistic manner: categories of fan violence can be identified. There is rowdyism or what might be termed "hooliganism" in England. This typically occurs regardless of what happens on the field of play. Acts of rowdyism include invading the playing field, hurling objects at the players, and stealing or vandalizing property in or around the stadium or arena. Another category is found in acts of hostility. These result from such tensions as officials' calls, game losses, intense rivalry, or intergroup conflict along ethnic, class, or religious lines. (The Washington, D.C., high school football episode is an example of the latter.) The third category of fan violence, exuberant celebration, includes destroying property, threatening innocent spectators, and even committing assaults. The aftermath of the 1984 World Series victory by the Detroit Tigers is a vivid example of this category. Management must distinguish among these three categories; anticipatory measures should assume different forms, depending on the category involved.

A wealth of literature and research documents the psychological and sociological forces behind fan violence. The topic has been a favorite for those who study sports from the perspective of social psychology. Explanations range all the way from the unconscious nature of crowd reaction to alcohol consumption. Some analysts have stressed the tension-filled atmosphere of a sports setting, while others point to the frustrations of losing and perceived injustices.

There is some consensus that no single precipitating factor is more inclusive and widespread than the effects of excessive alcohol consumption. The addition of alcohol to any of the other factors is similar in effect to pumping fuel on a fire. "Nobody has ever suggested that a good way to calm down a crowd is to fill it to the gills with strong drink," said Gilbert and Twyman. (Sports Illustrated, Jan. 31, 1983, p. 68) Yet, beer is sold in 61 of the 63 arenas across the country that serve major professional teams. (p. 67) Don Guenther, manager of Rich Stadium in Buffalo, estimated that 99 percent of the arrests at Bills' games are alcohol related. (p. 67) If sport managers are to seriously undertake a preventive posture against the problem of spectator violence, the realities of alcohol-related causes can not be minimized.

MARKETING IMPLICATIONS

Any policy aimed at the control of spectator violence in sport has definite marketing implications. The stated goal of many professional sport franchises is to provide "family entertainment." It is a noble concept but one that is not always achieved. For some franchises, it is mere lip service.

One of the principles of sound sport marketing is to mesh the facility image with the product and consumer image to produce a balanced, consonant relationship. Each image reinforces the other. Thus, a family entertainment package aimed at a father with three children will not be an effective marketing strategy if the facility is unclean and dimly-lit, with dark allies that serve as havens for rowdy teenagers. The relative importance of the facility image is repeatedly stressed by those who probe the causes of fan violence. The conclusion is that there is a tendency toward good behavior when spectators are in facilities that are clean, comfortable, and convenient. A facility with a poor image reflects on the team and consumer image, thereby influencing the type of crowd the facility draws. Irving Goldaber, a fan violence expert, advises that it could even be significant to present the illusion of a well maintained facility:

. . . Even the illusion that management is concerned with the amenities seems to have a good effect. Goldaber advises clients, not entirely facetiously, that if they have only $50 for crowd-control innovations, they should employ two men, dress them in immaculate white coats, give them brooms and set them to furiously and conspicuously sweeping. Whether they sweep up any dirt is beside the point. (*Sports Illustrated*, Jan. 31, 1983, p. 72)

The way in which management markets the team can also be a significant factor restricting violent behavior among fans. The team image is important. Presenting the "All-American" image (e.g., the Dallas Cowboys) attract a different kind of fan than a posture that depicts the "bad guys" in the sport. In terms of crowd control, there is little to be gained by promoting the idea that a team leads the league in penalties or hyping the rough play of a given player. Ice hockey is a vivid example of a sport wherein the promotional efforts tend to work against crowd control.

Special promotions can also be instrumental in determining the kind of spectator who is attracted to a sport event. A "family entertainment" package is not consistent with promotions such as "Disco Demolition Night" or "25¢ Beer Night."

One final marketing implication is worthy of note. Security can be enhanced through a coordinated public relations approach, extending from security guards to ticket sellers, to parking attendants, to coaches and players. Consumer satisfaction is one of the more effective ways of minimizing the problem of spectator violence.

LEGAL CONSIDERATIONS

To date, the problem of fan violence has presented relatively few legal ramifications in the form of lawsuits against facilities and management. Cases such as *Toone* v. *Adams* (1968) and *Townsley* v. *Cincinnati Gardens* (1974) determined that, as far as spectators are concerned, the facility is no guarantor of safety and owes only a standard of reasonable care for the spectators.

Nevertheless, in an increasingly litigious society, legal concern about fan violence hangs like a cloud over the head of facility managers who chose to ignore the problem. If an innocent bystander is injured in a brawl outside the stadium where there is little lighting and/or no security, could the victim successfully sue the facility, the team, or both? Might there be doubt about reasonable care in the following incident?

The New England Patriots' fans have a long and sorrowful history of drunkenness and violence at Sullivan Stadium in Foxboro, Mass. . . . Facing that fact — and the unhappiness of Foxboro's town fathers about rowdiness at games — the Pats' management announced before the '84 season that only low-alcohol beer would be available at the concession stands. Violence at games diminished noticeably after that, but during the season-ending 34-23 win over Cincinnati two weeks ago, regular beer as well as the low-alcohol brew again flowed from the stadium's taps, and trouble returned with it. Eighty fans were arrested, and many others were ejected from the stadium;

the Pats had been averaging fewer than a dozen arrests during home games this season. The worst incident occurred after the game when a mob of fans tore down a metal goalpost and carried a section of it out of the stadium. The section came in contact with a high-power line, and five men holding the post were hospitalized with serious burns. Four of them admitted to police that they had been drinking before and during the game.

Patrick Sullivan, the Patriots' G.M., said the regular beer could be returned if unused but the low-alcohol brew could not, and 'the concessions man was more worried about the bottom line.' In a promise that must sound all too familiar to the people of Foxboro, he said it wouldn't happen again. ("Scorecard," *Sports Illustrated*, Jan. 6, 1986, p. 7)

The threat of legal action also has serious implications for franchises that lag behind the rest of the league in upgrading the "reasonable standard of care." If all but one stadium provides ramps for spectator entry and exit, does that change the picture for the single stadium in which a patron is seriously injured while falling down the stairs? As more facilities adopt preventive approaches to the problem of crowd control, facility managers who remain in the dark ages could increasingly find themselves in court.

Finally, this matter of reasonable care may also be applied to violence on the field. If, as some experts think, there is a link between fan violence and on-field violence, management could reasonably be expected to take steps to control actions on the field. While there are limitations to management's ability in this, some franchises seem to be ahead of the game in providing a more effectively controlled environment.

CONCEPT OF ANTICIPATORY MANAGEMENT

When considering fan violence, the sport manager has three basic alternatives: ignore the problem and hope that it will not materialize, react to the problem and take remedial action when the need arises, or anticipate the problem and plan for crowd control measures to alleviate its extent and severity.

Within the past 10 to 15 years there has been a growing recognition that the latter is really the only viable alternative. Managers need an organizational structure to prevent problems to avoid being forced to react after the fact.

Major league baseball has taken steps to implement a preventive approach to spectator violence. In 1975 former Commissioner Bowie Kuhn initiated security seminars, which have since become yearly events. A survey of major league baseball security directors was conducted in 1985. The *vast majority* of the respondents characterized their policies as preventive in nature. The foremost instrument in that regard is the training of the security staff. It is also not surprising that alcohol consumption was overwhelmingly ranked as the number one cause of fan disturbances. "Tensions within the crowd" and "teenage rowdies" also ranked high. Selected comments from the survey returns illustrate actions taken in the direction of anticipatory management.

"The environment controls the types of problems that you encounter. However, I believe that you can educate your public to minimize the security problems at your park."

"We take into consideration some of these factors in preparation for an event for baseball: day of the week, time of the game, weather conditions, group sales from suburban areas, team performance to date, score of the game and many times you react on intuition, on a 'hunch.' . . . Contrary to beliefs, . . . football games (Sundays) present less crowd control problems than baseball."

"Stay on top from the beginning, make public examples of violators. When the rest see that you mean it they have two choices. It works!"

"We train our people as service oriented and to defuse a problem before it explodes into a more volatile situation. Many considerations involved in regard to 'prevention' crowd control include: attendance projections; opposing team, past problems, location of certain known 'problem groups,' etc."

"Last year was the first year that we adopted the 'preventive' security philosophy. We had a great deal of success with it. Our arrests were down to 7 last year, as opposed to 67 the previous year."

Case Study

There seems to be little doubt that the more positive, preventive approach to crowd control has replaced the reactive, "fire-fighting" approach that long characterized the operation of professional sport leagues and franchises. However, few are as advanced as the American League Texas Rangers baseball team in implementing the concept of anticipatory management.

From the time the Texas Rangers moved to Arlington, Texas, in the winter of 1973, until the winter of 1984, the stadium was owned by the city of Arlington. The stadium's concessions were also controlled by the city. Due to Arlington's ownership, the security during all sporting events (and in this case, baseball games) was controlled by the city's police force. A representative of the Rangers described the police force's control as being "highly reactive." The police did not take action until the law was broken, and, generally the action only followed flagrant violations. The city's ownership of the concessions presented an accompanying problem, since the city's apparent priority was making money from the alcohol sales.

In the winter of 1984, the Rangers purchased the stadium from the city of Arlington and, in the process, gained control of the concessions. The Rangers and Mat Stolley, director of maintenance and crowd control, were faced with three alternatives for the future:

1. retain the Arlington police force to serve as stadium security;
2. create an in-house security force and maintain a reactive crowd control philosophy and "bottom-line" mentality on alcohol sales; or,
3. create an in-house security force and adopt a "preventive philosophy."

The Rangers chose the third course of action. In discussing the decision, Stolley stressed the city's demographics. For a preventive approach to be successful, one has to know the clientele. The policy developed by the Rangers was based on the following demographics and characteristics:

1. Arlington is a "nice neighborhood" of 200,000 people.
2. Arlington does not have a mass transit system.
3. Arlington does not have the groups "that tend to give you trouble."
4. Rangers' crowds are "very family oriented, especially compared to Boston or New York crowds."
5. The Arlington area has become a melting pot of Americans (often in transit) who bring to the area their loyalty to other American League teams. "Sometimes the ratio of Ranger fans to opposing team fans is about 60-40," noted Stolley, "and much of our fan disturbances arise from tensions and conflicts over team loyalty, depending on which team is winning and losing."

The decision to establish an in-house security force and to adopt a "preventive philosophy" was based on two primary considerations: economics and control of the security force. In 1983, the season prior to the change, the Rangers spent $180,000 for the services of the city's police force. That season there were 67 arrests during baseball games at Arlington Stadium and, said Stolley, "about 99 percent were alcohol-related."

In implementing a "preventive philosophy" for the 1984 season, the Rangers' proceeded with five major thrusts.

1. *Emphasis on the education and training of the in-house security force*: This process includes a 10-hour training program, during which the Rangers deal with a variety of matters, ranging from

recognition of potential trouble spots, to arrest and detention of violators, to security staff rules and regulations, to how to approach the crowd." See Exhibit 12-1 for a summary of the curriculum. Similar topics are covered in the Chicago Cubs' Crowd Control Training Manual for 1985 (Exhibit 12-2).

2. *Emphasis on Public Relations*: The security training sessions include an emphasis on public relations. The curriculum (Exhibit 12-1) provides for discussions of image, corporate representation, spirit of the law, letter of the law, and low profile enforcement. According to Stolley, "Seventy percent of the job is PR, making yourself available, visible, and being polite."

3. *Presenting a non-threatening image*: This concept goes hand-in-hand with public relations. The Rangers' security officers do not carry guns or otherwise present themselves in an intimidating manner. As Stolley points out: "Anyone can hire a bunch of gorillas who tell you to 'sit down or I'll break your face.' I tried that one and it didn't work." The approach taken by the Rangers is part of the "low profile enforcement" in the training program. On the other hand, it is also important to note that the particular approach must be adopted to make-up of the crowd and the context of the franchise. For example, a few years ago, the Boston Red Sox, in Fenway Park, hired responsible college football players to "relate" to unruly, college-age, spectators. That was successful in the context of that particular situation.

4. *Creating a command-post communication system*: The Rangers established a system wherein one of every three security personnel communicate via walkie-talkies to each other and to the central command post, a booth which provides an unobstructed view of the entire stadium. It should be noted that a similar, command-post communication system is used in most professional sport facilities.

5. *The alcohol factor*: By obtaining control of the concessions operation, the Rangers also gained the opportunity to decide when alcohol sales will be terminated during the game, as well as the option of "shutting off" sections of the stadium that pose potential fan violence problems. Like most other pro sport facilities, the "law" prohibiting fans from entering the stadium with alcohol in cans, bottles, or thermoses is strictly enforced. The Rangers also considered the possibility of establishing an alcohol-free "Family Section," as several franchises have already done. Stolley noted that "our overall goal is to create a family atmosphere *everywhere* in the stadium." He added that the Rangers would be willing to try the "Family Section" if necessary. However, the crowd demographics and facility layout in Arlington reduce the need to move in that direction.

EXHIBIT 12-1. Texas Rangers Baseball Club Security Training School
Topics Covered
   I. Curriculum Introduction
      Training Objectives
      Curriculum Review
  II. Public Relations
      Image
      Corporate Representation
      Spirit of The Law
      Letter of The Law
      Low Profile Enforcement
 III. Corporate Policies
      Rules and Regulations
      Appearance
  IV. Law
   V. Arrest and Physical Detention
      Laws of Arrest — Physical Detention
      Physical Contract
      Civil Liability
      Physical Contact
      Procedures
  VI. Crowd Control
      Formation Recognition
      Disbursement
 VII. Radio Procedures and Codes
VIII. Forms — Documentation
  IX. Field Exercise
      Intoxicated Fan
      Criminal Trespass
      Ticket Scalpers
      Physical Detention
      Physical Removal
      Arrest

While this example is not a complete description of the factors involved in a preventive crowd control policy, it includes the major components of effective crowd management in any large facility: an educated and trained security force, a positive public relations approach, a useful system of communication, and a controlled alcohol-sales arrangement.

Joe Shirley, director of stadium and security for the Atlanta Braves, has identified a much larger number of considerations for a complete training program, noted in Exhibit 12-3. This illustrates the extent to which sport managers are taking positive steps toward alleviating the problem of violence among spectators.

The results of the Texas Rangers' implementation of a preventive crowd control policy is best illustrated in numbers. As noted earlier, in

1983 (the last year of the Rangers' "reactive" policy) the Rangers spent $180,000 in security, and there were 67 arrests. For the 1984 season, the club cut the costs in half and witnessed a dramatic decrease in the number of arrests (seven) and evictions. According to Stolley, "the mood of the crowd is definitely getting easier to control. We've gotten the message across that we won't tolerate obnoxious drunks anymore." The bottom line is that the Rangers have obtained more for less through implementing a preventive policy. They have made great progress toward attaining professional sports' elusive goal of providing "family entertainment in a family atmosphere."

POLICY GUIDELINES

The case of the Texas Rangers illustrates some key considerations in the development of a preventive crowd control policy to cope with the problem of fan violence.

First is the need for adaptability. Demographics, facility layout, and such factors as when games are played, must be considered before an effective policy can be developed for a particular franchise. For example, the Chicago Cubs' security director has noted that fewer problems are encountered in Wrigley Field due to day baseball. The Rangers' Stolley also stressed the adaptability factor: "The things we've done here in Texas are different from the way we might have handled the crowd control situation in Detroit or New York."

Second is the need to gain, or retain, a significant amount of control over the management of the facility and its concessions operation. As was

EXHIBIT 12-3. Stadium Security and Crowd Control

CROWD CONTROL STRATEGIES
  Creating a buffer zone
  Use of exits and entrances
  Videotaping crowd activity
  Handling hostile attendees
  Manpower visibility
  Photography applications
  Importance of using signs
  Emergency power/lighting
  Stage construction logistics

THE POLICE ROLE
  Foot and motorized patrol
  Mounted and air patrol
  Using decoy squad
  Community liaison
  Policy on arrests

IN-HOUSE SECURITY ROLE
  Post assignments
  Post responsibilities
  Liaison with peace officers

EMERGENCY STADIUM EVACUATION
  Importance of preplanning
  Bombs, fire or bad weather problems
  P.A. system control
  Gate control

TRAINING NEEDS

STADIUM SECURITY
  Vehicle/pedestrian traffic flow
  Protection of VIPs
  Bomb threat searches and evacuations
  Threats against players
  Key control
  Limiting clubhouse access
  Demonstrations and pickets
  Confiscating cans, bottles etc.
  Handling fan intrusions on field
  Protection of game umpires/officials
  Breaking up fights
  Lost and found: property and people
  Handling terrorist activity
  Medical aid

MEDICAL NEEDS
  Medical staff needs
  Logistics of communications
  Transporting injured attendees
  Needed reporting system

TERRORISM
  The stadium as a terrorist target
  (Hostage, extortion, kidnapping
  and armed attacks)
  Role of Federal, state and local police

GATE SECURITY
  Entry and egress control
  When should gates be opened?

significantly illustrated in the Rangers' case, it wasn't until the club gained control of facility management that a preventive crowd control policy became a reality.

Third is the realization that training an in-house security force and halting alcohol sales at critical times could reduce the potential risks to the francise in spite of the fact that both actions might initially appear to be costly.

The Texas Rangers case study serves as a solid example and source of inspiration for the development of appropriate policy for other sport franchises and arenas. At least four objectives can be identified in setting forth the need for such policy: 1) to insure the safety and welfare of spectators, 2) to minimize angry confrontation; 3) to maximize spectator enjoyment, and 4) to emphasize sportsmanship.

The policy guidelines which follow are aimed at the implementation of an overall policy of preventive crowd control. They are also specifically geared for professional sport franchises who want to provide family entertainment packages. Even though fan violence is not restricted to the professional sport setting, it is an appropriate place to begin in establishing standards for the spectator sport environment at large.

One final caution. Any policy can only realistically be aimed at alleviating the problem of spectator violence. The problem will never be eliminated. The thoughts of Leonard Koppett offer an appropriate frame of reference.

Major sports events definitely provide an excuse for unruly crowd behavior. But so does anything else that gathers a crowd and stimulates excitement. To expect a promoter, whose financial existence depends on being able to stimulate excitement in large groups of people, to screen his ticket buyers for stable character and good manners is a wee bit unrealistic.

Violence, as a vicarious thrill, is part of the appeal of spectator sports. As an implement of play, it is fundamental to most games. As a by-product of crowd behavior, it's unavoidable. . . . (*Sports Illusion, Sports Reality*, 1981, p. 243)

1. Each facility's security staff should participate in a minimum, 10-hour training seminar, conducted by a league-approved, staff of experts in the area of preventive crowd management techniques. The curriculum should include: legal considerations, corporate policies, arrest and detention techniques, public relations considerations, post-game reports, and a field exercise session.
2. Each facility should operate an effective "command post," controlled by the facility's security director. The chain of command should be carefully defined, including duties and responsibilities of security guards, ushers, ticket takers, and first-aid personnel. All should be trained in how to properly react in an emergency situation.
3. The security director should file a weekly report documenting all serious incidents; providing accurate data on causes of the incidents and the number of arrests and evictions; and commenting on the general effectiveness of the preventive policy.
4. The alcoholic beverage situation should be carefully controlled. This would include at least the following control measures: a) spectators are prohibited from carrying any alcoholic beverages into the facility, whether the beverage be in cans, bottles, or thermoses; b) any patron caught while attempting to smuggle alcoholic beverages into the facility should be banned from attending that game; c) alcoholic beverages should be sold only at

concession stands; d) a customer should be limited to the purchase of no more than two beers at one time; e) facility staff members should exercise the right to deny sales to a patron for reasons of intoxication or general rowdiness; and f) each league or conference should agree on a specified, reasonable time at which all alcohol sales will be terminated. This agreed upon time would be the limit, but individual franchises could shut off sales earlier at their own discretion.

5. Close attention should be given to the physical layout and maintenance of the facility. Illegal and dangerous obstructions should not be allowed. Turnstiles should be located with care. Graphics should be used advantageously to help spectators find quick and safe entry and exit. Ticket lines should be controlled. Aisles should be kept clear. Concerted effort should be directed at maintaining a clean facility.

6. Some form of preventive security council should be established within each league. This council would have both regulatory and advisory functions and would consist of the league's security director, an expert in the area of fan violence, a marketing expert, legal counsel, and team representatives. Task of the council should include: a) evaluating weekly reports submitted by each franchise's security director; b) conducting bi-yearly inspections of each facility during an event; c) establishing and enforcing penalties for franchises that repeatedly fail to implement effective preventive policy as recommended by the council; and d) charting the long-range progress of the preventive crowd management policy.

7. Each league should conduct a yearly seminar, arranged by the council, to review the successes and failures of the previous season, to present new and improved crowd management techniques, and to generally share experiences and ideas.

8. Each league should take a solid and positive public relations approach to spread the word about the nature of its preventive policy. This is based on the recognition that, in general, 95 percent of the spectators present no security problem. With the assistance of a marketing/advertising firm, the league could devise an ongoing public relations campaign designed to inform and educate sport fans (and to discourage miscreants); to stress the bold stand against spectator violence; and to portray the sober and safe, yet exciting, nature of the facility atmosphere. Each league should gain the backing of the local and national news media. For example, the council could provide the media with numbers, illustrating the success with the policy. A strong public relations approach, highlighting the preventive policy, should assist in returning the game to the vast majority of civilized fans.

9. Each franchise should establish a committee consisting primarily

of fans and management representatives. This committee could identify past and present problems in the stands and encourage management to take additional preventive measures.

CONCLUSION

The control of violence among spectators is another problem in which any solution is more of a journey than a destination. As noted, a certain amount of unruly behavior will always be a by-product of attendance at events involving large crowds. If there is anything at all unique about sport crowds, it probably is to be found in the idea that violence on the field may transfer to spectators.

A preventive policy of crowd management must be implemented from a multidimensional stance, involving a number of people with different roles and responsibilities. This is why the suggested policy guidelines extend from the league level to the individual franchise and include responsibilities for a variety of people: security guards, ushers, ticket-takers, first-aid personnel, and parking attendants. Preventive crowd management is a unified approach, and effective communication is the key to success. Actions taken under the preventive policy can have long-term legal and marketing benefits which far outweigh any immediate advantages of a reactive policy.

REFERENCES

Gammon, C. "A Day of Horror and Shame." *Sports Illustrated*, Vol. 62, Issue 23, June 10, 1985, p. 27.
Gilbert, B. and Twyman, L. "Violence: Out of Hand in the Stands." *Sports Illustrated*, Vol. 58, Issue 4, January 31, 1983, p. 72.
Koppett, L. *Sports Illusion, Sports Reality*. Boston: Houghton Mifflin Company, 1981.
"Scorecard." *Sports Illustrated*, Vol. 62, Issue 1, January 6, 1987, p. 7.

13

Financing International Athletes

According to guidelines set forth by the International Olympic Committee (IOC), each international sport governing body can define who is eligible to compete as an amateur in its sport. This has led to a continuing debate about the parameters of amateurism and significant differences in interpretation of the rules among sport groups and competing nations.

In the United States, the situation is further complicated by the relatively unique structural arrangement for the administration of amateur sport programs. The United States Olympic Committee (USOC) and individual, national sport governing bodies (NGBs) are independent from the federal government and, hence, rely solely on corporate and private funding. Without government backing, the NGBs have no strong and consistent support mechanism. At the same time, there is pressure for subsidization of U.S. amateur athletes in order to make them competitive with the "state supported" amateurs of Eastern Europe. Essentially, this is the problem. The obvious answer is corporate sponsorship. However, that approach also raises various issues.

ISSUES

While the NGBs and the USOC have basic control over event sponsorship, their control over individual athletes and teams sponsored by corporations is limited. For example, what assurance does the USOC or an NGB have that an athlete who competes for a corporate sponsor will not have contractual obligations which either jeopardize his or her eligibility or preclude the athlete from competing in an NGB sponsored event (due to scheduling conflicts). The overriding policy issue becomes this: how can an NGB insure honesty and integrity to the "Olympic ideals" in light of corporate sponsorship?

Before attempting to develop any policy, it is important to keep in mind that three principal parties are involved, each with a distinct and different perspective:

> *The NGB*: which must develop the policy aimed at insuring that U.S. athletes remain eligible under international rules through control of corporate sponsorship;
>
> *The athlete*: who is served by policy that insures his/her eligibility while, at the same time, looks toward the financial benefits of corporate sponsorship; and
>
> *The corporate sponsor*: which is looking for a return on the financial investment but must be nurtured and controlled.

This tripartite relationship represents a tricky balance problem. The control of corporate involvement is a legal issue, a marketing problem, and, from the NGB standpoint, a managerial problem.

From a legal standpoint, the issue centers around an attempt to determine when an NGB's involvement in the process constitutes an invasion of the athlete's private business and financial affairs. How much "say" or control can an NGB exercise when an athlete is under contract with a corporate sponsor?

The marketing problem stems from the need for the NGB to be sensitive to the marketing demands of investing corporations. Corporate sponsorship of amateur sport is a clear case of marketing through sport. For example, in return for its investment in U.S. amateur cycling, the Southland Corporation expects certain benefits in terms of publicity and name association. In developing any policy, an NGB must insure that an investment in sport sponsorship remains attractive. The potential for corporate sponsorship has increased significantly in recent years.

> The nation's companies, checkbook in hand, are scrambling to underwrite the nation's pastimes. Disenchanted with the high costs and sagging ratings of TV sports, corporations are going beyond 30 second TV spots and directly sponsoring events, teams and even entire leagues to promote their products. The estimated annual cost: $1 billion, at least triple the amount of five years ago.
>
> Although the strategy isn't new, it has gained considerable momentum since the 1984 Summer Olympics in Los Angeles. Largely because of Peter Ueberroth's success in making the games profitable by attracting corporate support, sponsorship has now acquired a cachet in board rooms. (*The Wall Street Journal*, Wednesday, June 25, 1986, Section 2, p. 33)

Varying conceptions of amateurism pose both an issue and a managerial problem. The IOC and international governing bodies are constantly modifying the guidelines for determining amateur status. It appears that the actions taken by the NGBs have usually been reactive in nature. When a change in definition of amateurism is set forth, an NGB responds accordingly. There is a need for anticipatory policy that is flexible enough to adjust to minor changes in definition and sufficiently effective to encompass and control the situation.

Consistency in policy is also a part of the overall managerial problem. Among sports, this is nearly impossible because of the differences among international federation rules. However, efforts must be made to address consistency between governing bodies within a given sport (for instance, between the NCAA and an NGB). In cases where athletes compete on both the collegiate level and the international/Olympic level, efforts must be made to minimize differences in policy.

Olympic Job Opportunities Program

The Olympic Job Opportunities Program is sponsored by the USOC to encourage career-oriented employment of elite athletes by granting time off for competition and training without loss of full-time pay or benefits. The program was conceived in 1977 by Howard Miller, former president of Canteen Corporation. It is the USOC's approach to financially supporting athletes so they may compete against government-subsidized athletes of communist countries. The USOC is emphatic in stressing that the athlete is paid for a job in this program, not for being an athlete. The policies that apply to this program are noted in Exhibit 13-1.

A Case Study: The Athletics Congress

Any one of the national governing bodies might be used as a case study to show how an individual sport attempts to cope with the problem of financing its international athletes. However, the efforts by The Athletics Congress (TAC), the NGB for track and field, provide a particularly significant example. It is one of the largest and highly organized governing bodies in the United States. Track and field also has a high degree of visibility and popularity at the international level. Consequently, the sport is very marketable in terms of attracting potential corporate sponsors. Track and field also lends itself to corporate sponsorship of individuals and teams, such as Bud Light Track America, Athletics West, and Athletic Attic, among examples in the United States.

TAC was established as the national governing body for track and field in the United States as a result of the Amateur Sports Act of 1978. It was officially formed in 1979. Since its inception, TAC has been designed "by and for" the athletes of track and field. The concerns of the athletes are considered of primary importance. For example, Edwin Moses, world record holder in the 400-meter hurdles, was the first active athlete from

EXHIBIT 13-1. Olympic Job Opportunities Program

POLICY STATEMENT

Pursuant to the relationship of _____
and the United States Olympic Committee, relative to participation in the Olympic Job Opportunities Program, the following is understood and had been agreed upon:

— The United States Olympic Committee encourages career oriented employment of OJOP participants granting time off for competition and training, without loss of full-time pay or benefits. Details of employment and scheduling needs must be negotiated with each athlete individually.

— The United States Olympic Committee guarantees the "Olympic potential" of the athlete, based on national and international rankings and the recommendation of the National Governing Body Authorized OJOP Applicant Endorser for the athlete's sport. This does not guarantee that the athlete will definitely qualify for the Olympic Team, but it does, however, guarantee that at the time of endorsement, and unless otherwise notified, that the athlete had been identified as a strong candidate for the Olympic Team.

— If at any time the athlete's rankings no longer qualify him/her as an "Olympic potential," the participating corporation and the athlete will be notified. At that time, the athlete's status should become that of any other company employee who can be retained or terminated.

Requirements relative to terminology, marks/logos, and publicity follow:

Terminology: When referring to the Olympic Job Opportunities Program, the term, "United States Olympic Committee's Job Opportunities Program," should be used.

The USOC strongly encourages use of the phrase:

"(*Participating corporation's name*) is proud to participate in the United States Olympic Committee's Job Opportunities Program."

Marks/Logos: No United States Olympic Committee marks or logos may be used at any time. (This may not apply to corporate sponsors of the U.S. Olympic Committee.)

Publicity: All external publicity (ie. press releases, athlete appearances, paid advertising) must have prior USOC approval.

Please direct press inquiries relative to the Olympic Job Opportunities Program to:

Sheryl Abbot, OJOP Coordinator
United States Olympic Committee
1750 East Boulder Street
Colorado Springs, CO 80909
(303) 632-5551

Special Conditions: APPROVAL

The policy as outlined in this statement are understood and are considered agreed upon.
Date: _____
Approved by: _____
Title: _____

any nation to be elected as an official representative to the International Amateur Athletics Federation (IAAF).

TAC must work within the established guidelines of the IAAF, the international governing body of track and field. Specifically, IAAF rules related to the financial aspects of eligibility basically determine the TAC policy on financing amateur track and field athletes in the United States. The following IAAF rules are particularly applicable:

Rule 14: This rule covers the allowable "expenses" for an amateur track and field athlete. The daily allowance for out-of-pocket expenses of an athlete must not exceed U.S. $10 or its equivalent in other currencies, payable for the minimum time that the athlete is required to be absent from normal residence. Other allowable expenses are for transportation costs, travel insurance, meals, lodging, and a subvention for hardship for the minimum time that an athlete is required to be absent from normal residence. Participating athletes in International Invitation Meetings specifically sanctioned by the IAAF Council may receive a specially authorized per diem allowance of up to $50 or its equivalent in local currency.

Rule 15: This rule establishes limits on the equipment and services which may be provided athletes. Assistance is limited to sports equipment and clothing; insurance coverage for accidents, illness, disability and personal property; cost of medical treatment and physiotherapy; payment for coaches and trainers authorized by the national governing body; and expenses allowable under Rule 14.

Rule 16: According to this rule, with the approval of a National Governing Body, an athlete may receive a subvention to assist him in the expenses incurred in training for or participation in competition - basically, cost-of-living stipends.

Rule 17: This rule outlines provisions for "Athletic Funds," which are basically trust funds, coordinated through the NGB. The key point here is that the funds must be held, controlled, and administered by the NGB. Regulations for usage require the approval of the IAAF. Athletes become ineligible for competition if any monies are paid to them or disbursed at their request, except under Rules 14, 15, and 16.

Rule 53: This rule covers conditions of ineligibility for international competition or domestic competition under the NGB. Certain parts of the rule apply specifically to the financial aspects which will result in ineligibility:

(1) The athlete is ineligible if he or she has competed in any sport or has taught, trained, or coached in any sport for any pecuniary reward other than awards won in competitions approved by the IAAF Council. An exemption to this is granted to physical educators. In addition, the IAAF Council has the power to declare an athlete to be eligible if he received pecuniary rewards in a sport other than track and field, if it is satisfied that the practice of that sport is not of direct help for any track and field events. In other words, a professional athlete in another sport could be declared eligible. For example, it was under this provision that Renaldo Nehemiah, then wide receiver for the San Francisco 49ers, attempted to regain his eligibility with the IAAF in 1984. Even though a three-man IAAF arbitration panel ruled that football was no help to track, the IAAF Council ignored that determination and continued the ban. Eventually, Nehemiah obtained his reinstatement in July 1986 after he wrote a letter to the IAAF, confirming that he was through with football and would abide by IAAF rules. Later, in August 1986, the IAAF broadened its interpretation to extend eligibility to any professional athlete outside of track and field.

(2) The athlete is ineligible if he or she has at any time been financially interested in any athletic meeting in which he or she is entered, except where there is a contract with the National Federation.

(3) If the athlete writes, lectures, or broadcasts for payment on the sport of track and field without the permission of the NGB, he or she is ineligible.

(4) An athlete can also lose eligibility by allowing his or her name, picture, or athletic performance to be used for advertising. An exception is when this is connected with a contract for sponsorship or equipment entered into by the athlete's national governing body, wherein the payment or benefit goes to the national governing body. After deducting any percentage considered appropriate, the NGB can pay the remaining part of such sponsorship payment to an athletic fund (trust fund). (This is the key provision for policy development by TAC.)

(5) The athlete loses eligibility if he or she displays on person, while competing, any advertising material other than the accepted name of his or her club or organization. Also, advertising material may not be taken on to any arena or course. The rule basically applies to clothing and traveling bags. It is designed to prevent the athlete from selling personal advertising space.

(6) Ineligibility results when an athlete accepts directly or indirectly any money or other consideration for expenses or loss of earnings, other than what is permitted under Rules 14, 15 and 16.

(7) The athlete is ineligible if he or she uses the services of a commercial agent, sponsor, or manufacturer to plan, arrange, or enter into negotiations on his or her behalf in connection with the athlete's athletic program.

The concept of "athletic funds," or trust funds, for competing amateur athletes, under IAAF ruling, is a direct result of the TAC/Trust program of The Athletic Congress. This trust fund program was proposed by TAC in 1982 and received IAAF approval. Essentially, it was an effort to bring monetary payments to competitors "above the table." The trust funds legitimize payments but control the methods of collection and distribution of monetary rewards.

TAC recognized that an amateur athlete participates in sport as an avocation rather than a profession. Although this may be a commonly accepted interpretation, amateur participation is not necessarily non-productive in terms of earnings. TAC contended that Soviet and other Eastern European athletes were being fully subsidized and supported by the state while training and competing as amateurs. The trust funds idea was TAC's free market answer to subsidization. For some time, rumors persisted of "under the table" prizes and appearance fees paid to track and field athletes. TAC's management of trust funds provided athletes with the ability to obtain "legal" financial benefits without jeopardizing their amateur status according to International interpretation. The basic mission of the TAC/Trust program is straightforward: it allows an athlete to put prize money in trust in his or her name and retain his or her eligibility to compete internationally as an amateur.

The individual parties hereto are athletes who may receive prize money and other financial rewards by virtue and as a result of their athletic activity. The individual parties wish to continue to be eligible to enter and compete in international amateur athletic events notwith-standing their receipt of prize monies or other financial rewards in such competitions. The Athletics Congress of the USA, Inc., as the national governing body for the amateur sport of athletics, pursuant to the Amateur Sports Act of 1978 (36 USC 371), in an effort to reflect the views of such athletes, has obtained the approval of the International Amateur Athletics Federation of the trust to be created hereby as a method of protecting the amateur status of such athletes and all other amateurs of the United States of America competing with them. (The Preamble of the "TAC/Trust Agreement")

The TAC/Trust sanction is basically a license granted free of charge by TAC to a meet director which allows the director to pay money for competitors. Various kinds of payments can be made; one stipulation is that a TAC/Trust sanction has been issued. There is no limitation on what can be paid and how it is to be paid, other than channeling the money through the trust fund network to insure compliance with IAAF rules. Exhibit 13-2 provides guidelines issued by TAC in 1985.

From the trust fund, athletes can draw funds allowable under IAAF Rules 14 to 16 for cost-of-living expenses while in training and competition. To make a withdrawal, athletes submit a written request to TAC. This kind of control helps insure that athletes are receiving funds from the trust only within the allowable IAAF limits.

Athletes may choose to withdraw the total amounts in their names in trust if they declare themselves professional, surrender membership in The Athletics Congress, and accept life suspension from amateur status. Otherwise, the principal amount in trust will earn interest until an athlete decides to retire from competition as an amateur. At that time, the amount can be withdrawn in total. The Athletics Congress does not take a percentage of the money from the trust, and there is no financial reward for TAC in this program.

TAC/USA Athlete Sponsorship Program: TAC's other response to IAAF guidelines was the establishment of the TAC/USA Athlete Sponsorship Program, which was approved at the 1982 TAC national convention. Essentially, it authorizes athletes, their representatives, and/or their clubs to freely solicit and negotiate with sponsors toward agreements that enable participation in advertising and promotional activities on behalf of a sponsor's product(s) and service(s) and/or to become engaged in related employment or contractual services for which direct compensation can be authorized. This conforms to IAAF Rule 53 which allows athlete advertising if it "is connected with a contract for sponsorship or equipment entered into by his national governing body."

To maintain the eligibility requirements of both IAAF and TAC rules an Athlete Sponsorship Program Agreement (ASP) must be completed (Exhibit 13-3). This letter outlines the specific terms (monetary, duration, etc.) of the agreement between the sponsor and the athlete. The program allows a corporation to become a "National Sponsor of The Athletics Congress," thus permitting use of the national governing body's athletes in advertising under IAAF ruling.

Under the program there is direct solicitation of and negotiations between potential sponsors and an athlete, his or her representative, and/or his or her club. The potential sponsors may be national, regional, or local. Additionally, TAC may serve as a conduit towards bringing a potential sponsor and an athlete together for the purpose of such negotiations. The fee structure is a matter to be determined between the athlete and the sponsor.

Exhibit 13-2. Quick 7 Easy Guidelines To TAC/USA Rules About Money and Agents

Question: What kinds of payment to athletes are allowable under IAAF and TAC/USA rules?

Answer: All kinds. Payments are called by lots of different names. It doesn't matter: they're all legal and don't have to be paid under the table. By the way, the rules call such payments, ATHLETIC FUNDS. TAC/USA feels best about prize money systems such as endorsed by ARRA. But the rules permit all payments so long as a TAC/Trust sanction has been issued to the event paying the funds.

Question: What's a TAC/Trust sanction and how do I get my race TAC/Trust sanctioned?

Answer: No problem here. The TAC/Trust sanction is free for the asking. Just call the TAC/USA national office in Indianapolis and ask for John Jackson. He'll do the rest. (317-638-9155).

The TAC/Trust sanction is your license to pay money. What you pay and how you pay it is your business. TAC/USA needs to know about it, that's all.

Question: If all I do is pay appearance money and don't pay prize money, why should I get a TAC/Trust sanction?

Answer: Paying money under the table endangers the eligibility of athletes. That's foolish in today's day and age when every athlete has the right to earn compensation and still stay eligible. But for you, Mr. or Ms. Race Director, there's a more compelling reason. If you pay under the table, then you're at the mercy of the commercial representative who is involved in your recruitment process. If you pay under a TAC/Trust sanction then recruiters play it by the rules, or they don't play it at all. Think about that and your best course of conduct is obvious.

Question: What's in it for TAC/USA?

Answer: Not a thing. Except that when we all pull together our sport stays in the hands of sports people. And that means TAC/USA is fulfilling its statutory role under the Amateur Sports Act of 1978. Since we take federal statutes seriously, that's good enough reason to do it the right way.

Question: Does my bookkeeping get screwed up if I use a TAC/Trust sanction?

Answer: Absolutely not. You pay expense money as you always have. You pay clinic and promotional money as you always have . . . except that you need a TAC/USA approved letter agreement to cover yourself with your athlete. And athletic funds get paid to "TAC/Trust for the benefit of (athlete)." You send, TAC/USA one report and your covered. Foreign athletes' checks are paid to their federations unless they have TAC/Trust accounts, in which case they're treated the same as U.S. athletes.

Question: Where are the rules about all of this?

EXHIBIT 13-2 *(con't.)*

Answer: Right in the rule book, where they belong. Look up IAAF Rule 17, take a gander at the TAC/Trust sanction application and skim through the TAC/Trust instrument. Pretty soon (we've been promising for a while) we'll have all the rules in one place. But any time you need help call Alvin Chriss (516-482-1133). It's one stop shopping.

Question: Isn't it true that if I get a TAC/Trust sanction every runner in the event has to have a TAC card?

Answer: Only athletes who get paid need a TAC card. No rule requires every runner in a TAC/USA sanctioned event to have an athlete's registration card. It is true that TAC/USA wants all athletes to register with TAC/USA, but that's voluntary and a measure of support. It's not mandatory and there's no intention to ever make it so.

Question: Can't a race work with an agent or a recruiter to help fill its field?

Answer: A new IAAF rule prohibits an athlete from using a commercial representative to plan or execute his or her athletic program (IAAF Rule 53 (v)). An older IAAF rule limits the negotiation of entry into an international event either to the athlete's federation or club. The IAAF and TAC/USA are taking steps to enforce these rules. At track meets, meet directors are working under these rules, but on the road it's a mixed bag.

Question: But athletes need agents, and races find it easier to recruit a field by working through an athlete's representative. What are we to do?

Answer: That's a legitimate concern. The answer lies in setting up ethical guidelines and give them the force of rules. Then representatives and race directors will know how to act. And athletes won't be exploited.

Question: But how will you enforce those rules? Won't they be ignored in the competitive quest for money and prestige?

Answer: Right now representatives can ignore rules because TAC/USA has no jurisdiction over them. If they do something wrong, all that TAC/USA can do is penalize an athlete or deny a race director a sanction. Those are poor choices and make TAC/USA unpopular. Part of the answer is to register representatives with TAC/USA after obtaining an agreement that a condition of the registration will be to comply with applicable rules. But in the last analysis the cooperation of the race director community is the essential ingredient. Unless race directors will refuse to work with any representative except a registered representative, then the rules will be scraps of paper. But if you respect the registration process, victory is assured.

Question: When is all this going to happen?

Answer: It's happening now. By the end of 1985 it will be an accomplished fact.

Question: What do you do in the meantime?

Answer: You act as if these new rules are already in place. When TAC/USA rules are broken and conduct is unethical, don't just put it away in the back of your head. Tell TAC/USA's Al Chriss. We'll act. Depend on it.

At the request of an athlete, TAC forwards the standard "Letter of Agreement" to a potential sponsor. This letter, which is submitted to TAC, must be accompanied by a release from the athlete (Exhibit 13-4), indicating his or her agreement to serve as a spokesman for the sponsor.

TAC reviews the agreement to determine conformity with IAAF and TAC rules. The athlete is notified of any required revisions, and it is the responsibility of the athlete to initiate a new "Letter of Agreement," when required.

Sponsorship fee payments are made to TAC, which retains 10 percent of the first $5,000 when the agreement is initiated by an athlete and 10 percent of the total amount if TAC initiated the contact between the corporation and the athlete. This also is in accordance with the stipulation of IAAF Rule 53 that "any resulting payment or benefit goes to the national governing body." The IAAF ruling allows that after an NGB has deducted a percentage "considered appropriate," the remainder may be disbursed to an athlete's athletic fund, in this case, TAC/Trust. Funds may also be disbursed to the athlete's club, if that club has current membership status. In that case, the club must agree to only make disbursements to the athlete which represents allowable expenses for training and competition as detailed in IAAF Rules 14 to 16.

In essence, TAC has allowed corporations to become "National Governing Body Sponsors" under international rules for the express purpose of promoting the sponsorship of individual athletes by these entities. By working within IAAF rules, TAC has opened a new avenue for the financing of America's amateur track and field athletes.

Case Study Conclusion: Through both the TAC/Trust program and the TAC/USA Athlete Sponsorship program, TAC has done a fine job of working within the parameters set forth by the IAAF. In both cases, TAC receives very little monetary reward for its involvement. The small percentage of funds from the Athlete Sponsorship Program is taken to remain within the guidelines and rules of the IAAF. It appears that TAC has addressed the legal implications and ramifications quite well.

Due to the flexibility afforded them, athletes are not likely to view TAC's involvement in the financial process as an invasion of personal affairs or as a restraint on their ability to conduct private business. In fact, TAC has done everything within its power to facilitate and expedite corporate involvement within allowable limits.

At the same time, TAC has addressed the marketing concerns of its corporate sponsors . TAC efforts have contributed to more aboveboard marketing through track and field and have increased the marketing opportunities for prospective sponsors. By playing an actual role, TAC lends a certain amount of credibility and professionalism to the sponsorship process. While attempting to insure that the amateur standing of the athlete is not placed in jeopardy, TAC works closely with sponsors of teams and individuals to make the sponsorship venture profitable.

EXHIBIT 13-3. Agreement/Athlete Sponsorship Program (to be typed on Sponsor's letterhead)

The Athletics Congress/USA
P.O. Box 120
Indianapolis, IN 46206

     Attn: Martin E. Weiss
            Director of Communications and Marketing

Gentlemen:

The purpose of this letter is to confirm the understanding between___Full___ ____Corporate Name____ ("FCN") and the Athletics Congress/USA ("TAC") with respect to FCN's participation in TAC's Athlete Sponsorship Program ("the Program").

> Note: FCN as utilized herein represents a two or three-letter acronym applicable to the sponsor's Full Corporate Name.

The Term of this Agreement shall be from ___month/day/year___ to ___month/day/year___ ; conformation of this Agreement by TAC is also an acknowledgement that the ___$0,000.00___ fee for this one-year period has been paid.

> Note: Upon request, TAC will provide the language for a paragraph to be inserted here reflecting any renewal option — including dates and fees — upon which the athlete and sponsor may have agreed.

We understand that such participation in the Program entitles FCN to utilize the services of ___name of athlete___ in connection with the advertising and promotion of FCN products/services (whichever is applicable) so long as said athlete is currently registered with TAC and has filed a release with TAC stating his/her (whichever is applicable) willingness to participate in the Program. TAC warrants that such participation will not endanger the amateur status of said athlete.

We also understand that:

(1) While participation in the Program entitles FCN to utilize photos of the athlete, and make reference to his/her (whichever is applicable) athletic performance, no reference may be made to Olympic performance(s) or the Olympics themselves.

(2) FCN is obligated to submit all advertising and/or promotional copy and art relating to said athlete's participation in the Program to TAC for its prior approval, which approval will not be unreasonably withheld.

(3) In the event that said athlete's participation in the Program requires him/her (whichever is applicable) to make public appearances on behalf of FCN, said athlete will be provided with transportation, lodging, meals and per diem by FCN that is commensurate with junior executive level — or, upon proper documentation, will be reimbursed therefor.

EXHIBIT 13-3 *(con't.)*

(4) FCN represents that this Agreement constitutes the only agreement involving the services of _____ name of athlete _____ to FCN, and that there will be no additions or revisions hereto without the prior consent of TAC, and that there will be no other payments reflecting the athlete's services other than the fee set forth herein.

Note: In the event that a consulting or services agreement is entered into between the company and the athlete, said agreement must be submitted to TAC along with the ASP Agreement —in which event (4) is to read as follows:

(5) FCN represents that this Agreement and a services/consulting (whichever is applicable) agreement of even date herewith which has been reviewed by TAC constitute the only agreements which FCN has relating to said athlete. FCN agrees that there will be no other agreements or additions or revisions hereto without the prior consent of TAC, and there will be no payments other than those identified hereunder or in said services/-consulting (whichever is applicable) agreement.

It is also expressly understood that while FCN's participation in the Program makes it a National Sponsor of TAC, no reference to the fact of that status may be made by FCN in any of its advertising or promotional materials; the same exclusion pertains to utilization of the TAC logo and other marks.

Upon TAC's acknowledging the receipt of this letter, the arrangements described herein shall be binding upon the parties.

Sincerely,

By _____

  (name to be typed)
  (title to be typed)
  (full corporate name to be typed)

Acknowledged this _____ day of _____

THE ATHLETICS CONGRESS/USA

BY _____

  Ollan C. Cassell
  Executive Director

Exhibit 13-4. Athlete's Release/Athlete Sponsorship Program

The Athletics Congress/USA
P.O. Box 120
Indianapolis, IN 46206

    Attn: Martin E. Weiss
          Director of Communications and Marketing

Dear Marty:

I hereby agree to participate in the TAC Athlete Sponsorship Program as a spokes-man for _____Full Corporate Name_____ ; I understand that my name, photo-graph and athletic accomplishments, other than Olympic, may be utilized in connection with advertising and promotion under this Program without endan-gering my amateur status.

I further understand that this sponsorship is for the period month/day/year through ___month/day/year___ , and that my participation authorizes TAC to make distribution of the funding involved as indicated in D (7) of the Operating Proce-dures for the Athlete Sponsorship Program.

                          Signed _____
                          Date   month   day   year

Finally, TAC has also demonstrated that it has the capacity to exercise strong management control of the situation while providing financial opportunities for its athletes. This is particularly important in light of the recent upsurge of third party agents or representatives in the area of track and field. TAC, through its policies, has positioned itself in the corner of the athlete, providing information and assistance as needed. By simultane-ously addressing the needs and concerns of athletes and corporate sponsors and maintaining firm monetary control over the financial dealings with track and field, TAC has established itself as a model for NGB involvement in the process of corporate sponsorship and financing of amateur athletes.

POLICY GUIDELINES FOR NATIONAL GOVERNING BODIES

The efforts by TAC provide a solid example of what can be done to finance international level athletes and conform to international policies and rules. This is not the only example of success by a national governing body in the United States.

Earlier in this chapter, reference was made to the sponsorship of amateur cycling in the United States by the Southland Corporation. The

United States Cycling Federation (USCF) was able to attract Southland as a primary sponsor from outside the cycling industry. USCF has worked with Southland in coordinating sponsorship efforts which include national and international teams, development programs, and sponsorship of competition. More recently, there has been some questioning as to whether Southland made the right decision in sponsoring cycling due to its remote relationship with that sport.

> The best arrangement, according to corporate executives and so-called sports marketing consultants, are those where sport's participants and fans match up well with a company's customers. . . .
> But hyping the corporate name through sports can backfire. Perhaps the biggest problem, consultants say, is a inability to link the company and its sport in the consumer' mind - and to their buying habits.
> Southland Corporation, for example, sponsors cycling. But what is the connection, asks Ms. Ukman, (President of International Events Group, which publishes Special Events Report, a newsletter that tracks event sponsorships) between cycling and the company's 7-Eleven convenience chain? "They never figured out a way to use it to get people in the stores," she says. According to one consultant, Southland has cut back its commitment to cycling; a company official declined to comment on Southland's sponsorship efforts. (*The Wall Street Journal*, Wednesday June 25, 1986, Section 2, p. 33)

Nevertheless, the efforts of TAC and other national governing bodies clearly demonstrate that corporate sponsorship is the major answer to the problem of financing U.S. athletes who compete at the international level. Based on efforts to date, the following are suggested as policy guidelines.

1. General: A national governing body's primary objective is to insure that participating athletes remain eligible under international rules. At the same time, an NGB in the United States should seek to attract corporate sponsors. The attempt to coordinate corporate involvement includes the following dimensions:
   a. *Legal*: To identify all legal ramifications of its policies, the NGB should seek professional legal counsel before their enactment. Policies and rules proposed and formulated by members of the body should be subjected to close legal scrutiny in an effort to eliminate any potential gray areas. This helps to reduce the possibility that the NGB will be placed in a reactive stance to potential legal problems.

b. *Marketing*: If financially possible, an NGB should establish a position for a full-time marketing coordinator for its sport. This will help to address the marketing concerns of potential corporate sponsors and aid in attracting them. If a full-time position is not feasible, the NGB should coordinate activities through a professional marketing consultant. A consultant can help to prepare a sponsorship package that is attractive to both the NGB and a corporate sponsor.

c. *Managerial*: An NGB should attempt to solicit athlete input and feedback before policy is enacted. This serves to establish a communications link with the athletes so the NGB will not be perceived as adversarial. The overall managerial goal is accepted control.

d. *Consistency*: To address the consistency problem, NGB should attempt to obtain feedback from the appropriate collegiate governing bodies when applicable. This specifically applies to any sport offered at both the intercollegiate level in the U.S. and at the international level. Also, if the sport is contested professionally, the NGB should make every effort to inform professional bodies of the explicit and implicit expectations and allowances of the policy. Effective communication with the colleges and professional leagues can be a major step in maintaining a consistent approach.

CONCLUSION

As long as there are international rules designed to preserve the idea of amateurism at that competitive level, financing international athletes in the United States will continue to be a problem. I am very much inclined to agree with the thoughts of Leonard Koppett when he proposed "Abolish Amateurism" in *Sports Illusion, Sports Reality*. Of course, Koppett wasn't suggesting that there would no longer be amateurs in the total sport enterprise. He was saying that the attempt to preserve the amateur status does not make much sense with respect to major commercial events, which certainly includes international sport competition.

Nevertheless, one is still faced with the reality that the IOC and the international sport governing bodies continue to have the power to set and enforce rules aimed at preserving an amateur status. Consequently, there continues to be a need to develop policies with the persistent problem of financing athletes who compete at the international level. Until someone initiates a bolder approach, the efforts by TAC and others are commendable. Under the present structure, the only real answer seems to be controlled, corporate sponsorship.

REFERENCES

International Amateur Athletic Federation, *Official Handbook*, 1985-86.

Koppett, L. *Sports Illusion, Sports Reality*. Boston: Houghton Mifflin Company, 1981.

Lowenstein, R. and Lancaster H. "Nation's Businesses Are Scrambling to Sponsor the Nation's Pastimes." *The Wall Street Journal*, June 25, 1986, p. 33.

The Athletics Congress. "Quick and Easy Guidelines to TAC/USA Rules About Money and Agents." Indianapolis, 1985.

_____ . "TAC/USA Athlete Sponsorship Program". Indianapolis, 1985.

_____ . "The Preamble of the TAC/Trust Agreement." Indianapolis, 1982.

United States Olympic Committee. "Olympic Job Opportunities Program." Boulder, Colorado, 1985.

14

Title IX and Women's Sport Programs

No person in the United States shall, on the basis of sex, be excluded from participation in, be denied the benefits of, or be subjected to discrimination under any education program or activity receiving Federal financial assistance. (Section 901(a) of Title IX of the Education Amendments of 1972)

On July 1, 1972, the above provision of Title IX became Public Law 92-318. In subsequent years this legislation was to have a major impact on athletic programs for women in the United States. However, the effect was not immediate, and there were various stages of development as well as one major setback.

To begin with, athletic programs were not specifically referred to under the original Title IX legislation. As a matter of fact, there was strong opposition to the inclusion of athletics based on the revenue-producing element in certain intercollegiate athletic programs. Due to the efforts of the Department of Health, Education, and Welfare (HEW), athletics was included in 1974 in accordance with the contention that sports and physical education were an integral part of education. The Education Amendments of 1974 specifically stated that:

The Secretary (of HEW) shall prepare and publish . . . proposed regulations implementing the provision of Title IX of the Education Amendments of 1972 relating to the prohibition of sex discrimination in Federally-assisted education programs which shall include with respect to intercollegiate athletic activities reasonable provisions considering the nature of particular sports.

These regulations to implement Title IX became effective July 21, 1975. Institutions were required to complete self-evaluations of their programs and activities by July 21, 1976, but they had an "adjustment period" until July 21, 1978, to bring their athletic programs fully into line with the regulation. However, the Title IX regulation did not mandate a specific process for evaluating or modifying athletic programs to assure equal opportunity for women and men.

In December 1978, HEW released a proposed policy interpretation in response to criticism about the vagueness of the regulations. It was not until December 1979 that the Office of Civil Rights finally released the policy interpretation for Title IX.

In essence, the amended Title IX regulation provided a broad mandate for equal athletic opportunity. The general requirement was set forth in section 86.41(a).

> No person shall, on the basis of sex, be excluded from participation in, be denied the benefits of, be treated differently from another person, or otherwise be discriminated against in any interscholastic, intercollegiate, club or intramural athletics offered by recipient, and no recipient (institution) shall provide any such athletics separately on such basis.

The regulation was designed to provide equal opportunity for both sexes in athletic programs yet permit separate teams for contact sports and team selection based on competitive skill. In determining whether equal opportunities are available, the HEW's Office for Civil Rights would consider the following 11 factors:

1. **Select sports and levels of competition which effectively accommodate the interests and abilities of both sexes**: HEW's 1975 "Sports Memorandum" specified:

> "Determine the interests of both sexes in the sports to be offered by the institution and, where the sport is a contact sport or where participants are selected on the basis of competition, also determine the relative abilities of members of each sex for each such sport offered, in order to decide whether to have single sex teams or teams composed of both sexes. (Abilities might be determined through try-outs or by relying upon the knowledge of athletic teaching staff, administrators and athletic conference and league representatives.) . . .
>
> In determining student interests and abilities . . . educational institutions as part of the self-evaluation process should draw the broadest possible base of information. An effort should be made to obtain the participation of all segments of the educational community affected by the athletics program, and any reasonable method adopted by an institution to obtain such participation will be acceptable."

2. **The provision of equipment and supplies**: Institutions may not discriminate on the basis of sex in providing necessary equipment, supplies, and uniforms. However, the regulation does not require that exactly the same equipment be bought for women and men or that the equipment for women's and men's teams be replaced at exactly the same time. The intent is that there should not be widely different standards for purchasing or replacing equipment.

3. **Scheduling of games and practice times**: The function of scheduling practice times and games should be centralized in one institutional committee or office. In scheduling, women's teams and men's teams should have equal opportunity for both the most "desirable" and "undesirable" times. Whenever possible, women's and men's games should be scheduled concurrently or in tandem.

4. **Travel and per diem allowance**: The intent is that there will be an institutional policy which assures that busses, cars, and other vehicles are equally available to women's and men's teams and that both female and male athletes receive the same per diem allowances, including the amounts allowed for lodging, meals, and other expenses.

5. **Opportunity to receive coaching and academic tutoring**: Title IX does not require that an identical number of coaches be assigned to women's and men's teams. However, the number of coaches per team must be determined by objective standards, such as the nature of the sports or the number of participants, rather than by the sex of the participants in a particular athletic program. Also, an institution should provide academic tutoring or other academic services for all students, with a clear institutional policy to assure that female and male athletes have equal access to these services.

6. **Provision of locker rooms, practice and competitive facilities**: Under Title IX all facilities must generally be available without discrimination on the basis of sex. Locker rooms, toilets, showers, and other facilities available to women and men must be comparable. A close inspection of the facilities which women's and men's teams use, as well as a careful analysis of the access of each female and male team to various facilities and any related services, is necessary in order to assess whether or not there is discrimination in this area.

7. **Provision of medical and training facilities and services**: An institution should have a single standard for both female and male athletes regarding the type, nature, and extent of medical, health, and training facilities which are provided by the institution. This provision also includes equal and comprehensive medical insurance programs.

8. **Provision of housing and dining facilities and services**: An institution is required to examine a number of aspects in housing and dining services and facilities to determine if those available to female athletes are

comparable to those available to male athletes. Carrying out this provision begins with the need to determine if any athletes receive any special, different, or preferential treatment regarding housing or dining services or facilities. If there is any difference, it is necessary to evaluate how equal opportunity can best be provided.

9. **Publicity**: Institutions are expected to centralize and closely coordinate the publicity and/or public relations services for both women and men, taking care to assure that these services are provided in a non-discriminating manner and that women's teams and men's teams have equal access to these services.

10. **Assignment and compensation of coaches**: In section 86.41(c) of the Title IX regulation, the "assignment and compensation of coaches" was listed as one of the factors which would be considered in determining whether or not an institution is providing female and male athletes with overall equal opportunity. Of course, a number of other prior federal and state regulations prohibit any employment discrimination on the basis of sex. For example, Title VII of the 1964 Civil Rights Act prohibits all employers, including those that do not receive federal monies, from employment discrimination on the basis of sex, race, color, religion, or national origin. In terms of this section of Title IX, an important point was that the three-year "adjustment period" that applied to athletic programs affecting students did not apply to employment discrimination in these programs.

11. **Financial aid to athletes: athletic scholarships**: The Title IX regulation (in section 86.37(c)) set the following standards for judging Title IX compliance with regard to athletic scholarships:

> (1) To the extent that a recipient (institution) award athletic scholarships or grants-in-aid, it must provide reasonable opportunities of such awards for members of each sex in proportion to the number of students of each sex participating in interscholastic or intercollegiate athletics.
> (2) Separate athletic scholarships or grants-in-aid for members of each sex may be provided as part of separate athletic teams for members of each sex to the extent consistent with this paragraph and (the athletic section of the Title IX regulation).

The Title IX regulation did not require institutions to duplicate their men's athletic financial aid program for women. Nor did it deny individual institutions the flexibility to develop their own women's and men's athletic programs, as long as an institution's total program ensured both women and men an equal opportunity to compete in athletics in meaningful ways. Title IX compliance regarding financial aid is determined by the overall "reasonableness" of the financial aid available to participants in the women's and men's athletics programs, rather than by the specific aid provided to each student or in each sport.

In summary, the Title IX legislation was first and foremost aimed at providing equal opportunity for both women and men. At the same time it recognized certain exceptions that related to the very nature of athletic programs. Berry and Wong (1986) identified some of the exceptions or complications succinctly:

> The policy interpretation contained some very strict guidelines for OCR to apply in assessing Title IX compliance, including the following:
> 1. The exemption of football and other revenue-producing sports.
> 2. 'Sport-specific' comparisons as the basis for assessing compliance.
> 3. 'Team-based' comparisons (grouping sports by levels of development) as the basis for compliance assessments.
> 4. Institutional planning that does not meet the provisions of the policy interpretation as applied by OCR.
>
> The policy interpretation also outlined certain nondiscriminating factors to be considered when assessing Title IX compliance. These factors include differences that may result from the unique nature of particular sports, special circumstances of a temporary nature, the need for greater funding for crowd control at more popular athletic events, and differences that have not yet been remedied but which an institution is voluntarily working to correct. In the area of compensation for men's and women's coaches, OCR assessed rates of compensation, length of contracts, experience, and other factors, while taking into account mitigating conditions such as nature of duties, number of assistants to be supervised, number of participants, and level of competition. (pp. 218-219)

THE GROVE CITY COLLEGE CASE

A setback came with the much discussed "Grove City College Case," legally identified as "Grove City College v. Bell." A decade of progress in achieving equality between men's and women's athletics was at least slowed by the U.S. Supreme Court ruling on February 24, 1984, that Title IX was intended to apply only to education "programs and activities" that receive direct federal aid.

The case involved a major issue in Title IX, regarding the scope of the legislation and the programs to which it is applicable. Debate over the issue centered largely on the "programmatic approach" vs. the "institutional approach." In other words, did Title IX apply only to specific departments that receive direct funding or to any department in an institution that benefits from federal assistance? In the Grove City case, the decision was for the former, that Title IX is program-specific. Consequently, receipt of federal money by one college department does not mean that the entire institution has to comply.

The case began in 1977 when Grove City College, a small, Presbyterian, liberal arts college in Pennsylvania, filed suit in district court against HEW. Terrel H. Bell was the commissioner of education in HEW at the time; thus the suit came to be known officially as Grove City College v. Bell.

HEW had requested that the college execute an assurance of compliance with Title IX as a recipient of federal funds. The college argued that it should not be subject to Title IX because it received no direct federal funds. Grove City had earlier declined to participate in the Regular Dispersement Scheme (RDS) of HEW, which would provide funds to be distributed to students as financial aid on a need basis. However, the college did enroll students who received funds directly under the Basic Educational Opportunity Grants (BEOGs) or Pell Grants. The college had no control over such disbursements.

When Grove City College refused to execute the assurance of compliance, HEW initiated proceedings which declared the college and its students ineligible to receive BEOGs. The college and four of its students filed suit in district court, which ruled that the student aid could not be terminated even though the BEOGs constituted federal financial aid. Later, the decision was reversed by a court of appeals, which held that indirect as well as direct aid was covered under Title IX. The court of appeals also ruled that the college was in the program even though the Title IX language was program-specific. However, the Supreme Court disagreed in its final decision, ruling that only those programs directly receiving federal funds were subject to the regulation of Title IX. This meant that Title IX jurisdiction was limited to the financial aid office.

In the final analysis, neither side really won. Grove City College was hurt by losing the Pell Grants for its students. (The college responded with private financial aid through what it called the Student Freedom Fund.) The college also became sensitive about a common perception that it discriminated against women in its athletic or sport programs.
From the beginning, the intent of Grove City College was to resist federal interference, not to denounce equal opportunity. The Department of Education (established independently in 1980) lost the partial applicability of Title IX to athletic programs.

Following the Grove City case, there were mixed but generally pessimistic reactions concerning the future prospects of women's sport programs. One year later (1985), some of the responses were as follows:

> Two steps forward one step back. That's the reality of women's athletics today, one year after the U.S. Supreme Court, in its now historic "Grove City College" decision, re-interpreted Title IX and threatened to undo a decade of progress in achieving equality between men's and women's athletics.

"We're in the same position now that we were before the 1970's," says Donna de Varona, a former Olympic gold medalist and now president of the Womens Sports Foundation.

"It's true that there is more support for and acceptance of women's sports than ever before, but the mechanism that opened those doors (Title IX) is gone and we've already seen some erosion of women's opportunities in sports." . . .

While everyone involved waits for Congress to make the next move, the status of Title IX enforcement remains uncertain. The Department of Education's Office of Civil Rights has either closed or suspended some 60 Title IX cases since "Grove City," says public affairs liaison Thomasina Rogers. Harry M. Singleton , assistant secretary for Civil rights, told a Congressional committee recently that several cases remain unresolved because the department's jurisdiction was curtailed by "Grove City." . . .

"We must have some enforcement mechanism for Title IX," says Bell. "Colleges and universities have responded during the past few years and, with few exceptions, there has been substantial compliance. But without the ability to enforce Title IX, I believe we will begin to see a deterioration in compliance." . . .

Ruth Berkey, assistant executive director of the National Collegiate Athletic Association (NCAA), says there are enough safeguards in place among NCAA institutions to prevent slippage

"From the NCAA point of view, I don't think the "Grove City" decision will have any effect," says Berkey. "Whatever happens with the pending legislation, the NCAA is going to continue to support women's athletics as it always has." . . .

Despite the failure to provide teeth for Title IX in the last Congress, Auchincloss (Eva Auchincloss, executive director of the Women's Sports Foundation) is convinced that some sort of legislation will pass this time around.

"I'm optimistic because I can't believe they wouldn't pass something. It's like voting against motherhood," says Auchincloss. "How can you be against equality?" (Athletic Business, May 1985, pp. 10-16)

THE SITUATION IN 1988

Three years later, four years after "Grove City", and 16 years after the original Title IX, the situation surrounding women's sports is still unpredictable. Assessment can begin by listing significant improvements in the status of sport programs for women since 1972.

The Plus Side

1. Girls' participation in high school sports increased from 300,000 athletes in 1972 to 1.8 million in 1986.
2. During that same period, women's participation in collegiate sports increased from 16,000 to 92,200 athletes.

3. Institutions have made growing and substantial financial commitments to women's athletics. For example, in 1972, the University of California at Berkeley had a budget of $5,000 for women's athletic programs. The 1986-87 budget was $1.9 million.
4. The average number of womens' sports per college increased from 5.61 in 1978 to 7.15 in 1986.
5. The 1987 estimate was that 800 colleges were offering a total of 10,000 scholarships to women athletes.
6. An increase in spectators for women's college athletics can be noted. At the University of Texas at Austin more than 3,500 season tickets were sold for the 1987 basketball season with an average of 5,290 fans per game.
7. Some inroads have been made in television contracts for women's athletics. In late 1986 the women's athletic program at the University of Minnesota signed a television contract for $25,000 to cover five women's athletic events in 1987.
8. There is evidence of increased proficiency among women athletes. Women's performances in the 1984 Olympics improved, in some cases surpassing what men were doing in the 1960s Olympics.

There is little doubt that the impact of Title IX has been tremendous. Yet, there was still much room for improvement in status of women's sports as of 1987. In some respects, women's athletics had lost more than it gained.

The Minus Side

1. In 1972, over 90 percent of the women's intercollegiate athletic programs were administered by female athletic directors. By 1986, that figure had dropped to 15.21 percent, and 31.9 percent of all intercollegiate athletic programs did not have a female involved in administration. *Sports Illustrated* (Sept 29, 1986) provided further documentation of this kind of change:

In 1972, 90% of the coaches and administrators in women's college sports were women. Ten years later the National Collegiate Athletic Association took control of women's collegiate sports. Now 49.4% of all women's college teams are coached by men, and 90% of the Division I athletic programs for men and women have been merged and placed under the direction of men. Eileen Livingston, 56, of Duquesne is the only female athletic director of both men's and women's programs at a Division I college. (p.56)

2. Such loss in administrative control of sport by women is not restricted to college athletics. *Sports Illustrated* went on to summarize the total situation involving women administrators in the sport enterprise.

What is going on? The revolution is over, the battle won. Women athletes have long since taken their positions on playing fields across America. The power structure for women's sports is in place, a perfect pyramid, broad at the base, thanks to Title IX, visible from great distances, thanks to the spotlight trained on individual athletes. Yet who sits astride this pyramid? Who has the power to build, to change, to pick up a telephone and say, "Do it now?" Men, that's who.

Men control the IOC, the USOC, the NCAA, the International Tennis Federation, the United States Golf Association and the Jockey Club, just to mention a few of the organizations that determine the athletic destinies of women. And still women are losing ground. (pp.56,58)

3. During a period in which there have been steady and consistent cuts in athletic department budgets, many institutions have dropped an equal number of men's and women's teams, and equal dollars have been cut. The effect is disproportionate in light of the comparable status prior to the cuts.

4. The percentage of intercollegiate women's teams coached by women has dropped considerably. Acosta and Carpenter (1987) did a nine-year study on women and sport. Following are some of the results in comparing the situation in 1977-78 with that in 1985-86:
   - The total percentage of women's teams coached by women dropped from 58.2 percent to 50.6 percent.
   - There were 18 sports in which more men were coaching contrasted with six sports in which more women were coaching.
   - The percentage of women basketball coaches dropped from 79.4 percent to 61 percent.
   - The percentage of women softball coaches dropped from 83.5 percent to 68.0 percent.
   - Even the percentage of women's field hockey coaches dropped from 99.1 percent to 97.1 percent. (USA TODAY, March 18, 1987, p.1c)

5. In some cases, there are wide discrepancies in coaching salaries. Selected 1986 data for college basketball coaches include the following figures.
   - The average salary for women's Division basketball coaches was $33,109 - $23,381 less than the average men's salary of $56,490. (Of course, it should also be noted that more than 21 million people attended Division I men's basketball in 1985-86, while the women drew 1.5 million during the same season.)
   - In many cases, the head coaches of women's basketball made less than men's assistant coaches.
   - Instead of a $100,000 shoe contract (common among the top

men's coaches), women's endorsement contracts range from $500 to $15,000.
- ● - There was also a wide discrepancy in the amounts which were earned from summer camps. (*USA TODAY* Dec 10,1986, pp 1,2,10c)

In the spring of 1987, the controversy regarding the future of women's athletics was still prominent. Proponents of the status quo were inclined to point out the significant progress in women's involvement in sport during the past 10 years. Any minuses were largely attributed to the very high public and mass media interest in male sports. Yet many women feared that they were about to lose most of what had been gained. Women's rights advocates looked to the federal government for renewed protection. The feeling among many people was that it was critical for the U.S. Congress to restore Title IX to its original strength to insure continual growth and equality in women's sports program.

The shift in control of the U.S. Senate in 1987 offered new hope that Congress would press the Civil Rights Restoration Act. However, not all officials agreed that federal legislation was the answer for civil rights or that Title IX needed more teeth. Doug Bandow, a senior fellow at the Cato Institute presented an opposing view:

> The laws no longer even focus on basic equality. Title IX, for example, has been used to force schools to spend equivalent amounts of money on women's and men's athletic activities. But the simple fact is that men's sports are more popular and more remunerative, so it makes sense for schools to invest more in those programs. It surely isn't the federal government's role to decide how much universities should spend on sports. . . .
>
> Bills to overturn the Grove City decision have reassuring names, like the "'Civil Rights Restoration Act," but in reality such proposals would violate the civil rights of far more people than they would protect. The greatest danger to individual freedom comes from the government, not private institutions like Grove City College. So the more we restrict Uncle Sam's power to meddle, the better off we all are. (USA TODAY, Tues. Feb. 10, 1987, p. 10A. Copyright 1987, *USA TODAY*. Excerpted with permission.).

CASE EXAMPLES

During the fall of 1986, seven institutions were contacted in an effort to determine what actions they had taken in response to Title IX and where their athletic or sport programs for women stood at that time. The following is a small but diverse sampling of situations at the institutional level.

University A

Public university - Southeast
Student body: 3,500
NAIA member
Varsity athletic teams : six men's, four women's

At this university, the most significant influence of Title IX was the increased funding for women's sports, including scholarship allocations for selected women's teams. Other areas, such as facility usage, were little affected. There were nine male head coaches and one female head coach. Men coached women's volleyball, tennis, and softball. No women were coaching men's teams. The athletic director indicated that the department did not have a particular policy regarding Title IX compliance.

University B

Public university - Far West
Student Body : 23,500
NCAA Division I member
Varsity athletic teams - 11 men's, six women's

Scholarship allocation was the major effect of Title IX at this university. In compliance, based on the percentage of athletes, scholarships are equally allocated to women and men. The total funding of programs is very much influenced by the allocation for revenue-producing sports for men. The department employed 16 head male coaches and three female head coaches. Men coached women's teams in gymnastics, cross country, track and field, tennis, and fencing. No women coached men's teams. Aside from the general compliance with Title IX, there was no specific department policy in this area. Due to budgeting constraints, the department had recently dropped the women's golf program.

University C

Private university - Northeast
Student body : 6,500
NCAA Division I member
Varsity athletic teams - 21 men's, 19 women's

Scholarship allocation was not a factor at this institution since it does not offer athletic scholarships per se. The large number of varsity athletic teams reflects the university's commitment to a broad-based athletic program. Eighty-five teams are sponsored by the athletic department. The institution apparently viewed Title IX as a real spur for equal opportunity in athletics. Compliance policies and procedures were in place, as manifested in funding and facility usage. The only real disparity seemed to be in the ratio of men and women coaches. Of course, as noted earlier, any difference here is not related to Title IX compliance. Of the 40 head coaches, only six were female. In other words, 13 of the 19 women's varsity teams were coached by men. There were no women coaches for any of the men's teams.

University D

Public university - Northeast
Student body: 3,900
NCAA Division II member
Varsity athletic teams — 12 men's, 12 women's

Among the seven institutions surveyed, this one appeared to have the most identifiable policies which were directed toward Title IX implementation. There were definite guidelines for budget review to equalize and regulate the total budget. Facility usage was based on a specific rotation system. A formula was used to equalize scholarship allocations and to act as a check system. However, once again, there was a vast difference in the number of male coaches and female coaches. There were 15 male head coaches, compared to three female head coaches.

University E

Public university - Northeast
Student body : 19,500
NCAA Division I member
Varsity athletic teams - 11 men's, 12 women's

Title IX compliance was basically checked by the scholarship allocation process. This may be largely attributed to the fact that the institution was selected for a compliance review by OCR in 1983. The review showed that the university was not in full compliance in terms of athletic financial assistance. Full compliance was achieved within the next two years. Aside from that, the institution had a strong history of commitment to women's athletic programs, reflected in comparable programs, facility usage, or other funding. Policies were in place very early as a result of a Title IX task force appointed by the dean of the school of physical education in February 1976. Nevertheless, this university also showed the disparity in the number of women head coaches. There were only two female head coaches with each coaching two sports as the head coach.

University F

Private university - Midwest
Student body: 6,500
NCAA Division I member
Varsity athletic teams - 11 men's, 10 women's

The university is somewhat unique in that the impact of Title IX was relatively minimal due to a heavy commitment to all intercollegiate athletic teams prior to the 1970s. Aside from the inevitable differences involving the revenue-producing sports, all the intercollegiate sports, including those for women, had more or less been sponsored on the same basis. All the sports had the NCAA maximum scholarship allocation in 1986. Furthermore, the facilities were more than adequate to provide equitable use, again reflecting the university's commitment to a total athletic program. Of the 16 head coaches, two were female. Men were coaching the women's teams in fencing, volleyball, basketball, swimming, and track.

College G

Public college - Northeast
Student body: 7,000
NCAA Division III member
Varsity athletic teams - 10 men's, 10 women's

Title IX had a very direct impact on the athletic program at this college. The primary change occurred when women's athletics were separated from the physical education department and merged into an integrated athletic program. Of the seven institutions in the survey, only this college had a woman coaching a men's team. She was an assistant coach for men's tennis. A more significant difference at this institution is that there was only one male coach for women's teams -- a man who coached the women's track and cross country teams. The basic policy regarding funding was that corresponding sports are funded equally. Facility usage among men and women was equally scheduled according to time and percentage of usage. Scholarship allocation was not applicable because it was a Division III college.

Conclusions From Case Examples

These case examples more or less reinforce what is generally known about the institutional impact of Title IX. The institutions were first concerned about meeting the specific requirements for compliance. This was particularly manifested in the concern about proportionate scholarship allocations for women and men. In most cases, there was no particular need expressed for policy development beyond meeting the requirements of Title IX. Quite obviously, the most direct impact was on the need to provide additional funding for women's sports. The basic difference among institutions can be found in the degree to which they were committed to a total sport program for men and women prior to the time that Title IX became effective. The disparity between the number of female and male coaches is the most glaring shortcoming in the drive to provide equality among sport programs for women and men. This can largely be attributed to the fact that male applicants for coaching positions have considerably more sport experience than the female applicants.

SUGGESTED POLICIES

Basic policies for women's sport programs were determined by the federal government through the policy interpretation of the athletic component of Title IX. By and large, institutions had only to demonstrate that they were in compliance. Regardless of any limitations or debate in the future, it is also evident that sport programs for women are now well established at the high school and collegiate levels. In order to insure continual progress, the following policies are suggested for areas that still need improvement.

1. The concerns and priorities of women's and men's programs will be accorded equal weight in arriving at unified, institutional policies for both women's and men's athletics.
2. The funding process for women's and men's athletics will be centralized with the intent that women and men have equal representation and decision-making authority.
3. The recruitment of female and male athletes will be coordinated through a single office so that travel expenses and other resources might be more equitably shared.
4. All equipment, supplies, and uniforms for both women's and men's teams will be purchased from a central institutional fund and the control of these items will also be centralized.
5. The function of scheduling practice and competitive events and facilities will be centralized in one institutional committee or office, with representation from both the women's and men's athletic programs.
6. Special opportunities will be provided for women graduate assistants and interns to serve as apprentices to female or male coaches to develop coaching skills.
7. The publicity and public relations services for both women and men will be centralized, and some joint public relations events will be held for women's and men's teams.

CONCLUSION

In terms of increased participation of girls and women in scholastic and collegiate sport programs, the impact of Title IX is here to stay. The "Grove City" decision resulted in a temporary setback, but this was more symbolic than real. Whether or not there is need for or there will be additional federal legislation is open for question at this writing. This much is known: institutions have to develop or maintain policies aimed at improving the quality of women's involvement in sport programs. Perhaps the biggest need is to find and employ more qualified women coaches and administrators. This is not really a policy area, as such. It can only be accomplished by sensitive and dedicated administrators who have the responsibility for staffing athletic programs.

Note: Additional updated information on Title IX can be found in Chapter 20 on pages 322 to 323.

REFERENCES

"After Grove City." *Athletic Business.* Vol. 9, No. 5, May 1985, pp. 10-16.

Ballard. S. "The Most Powerful Woman in Sports." *Sports Illustrated*, Vol. 65, No. 14, Sept. 29, 1986, pp 56-68.

Bandow, D. "We Don't Need a Law; It Would Discriminate." *USA TODAY*, February 10, 1987, p. 10A.

Becker, D. "Discriminating Fans Keep Women No. 2." *USA TODAY*, December 10, 1986, Section C, pp. 1-2, 10.

Berry, R. and Wong, G. M. *Law and Business of the Sports Industries*, Volume II. Dover, MA: Auburn House Publishers Company, 1986.

Garratt, L. "Women's Sports Need Federal Protection." *USA TODAY*, December 12, 1986, p. 12A.

Lopiano, D. A. "Participation is Up, Role Models Missing." *USA TODAY*, February 10, 1987, p. 10A.

Shuster, R. "Women's Sports Still Man's World." *USA TODAY*, March 18, 1987, Section C, pp. 1-2.

U. S. Department of Health, Education, and Welfare, Office of Education. *Competitive Athletics: In Search of Equal Opportunity*, 1976.

"Women's Athletics: A Clouded Forecast." *Athletic Business.* Vol II, No. 3, March 1987, pp 20-25.

15

Dropping and Adding College Sport Programs

One of the more difficult decisions to be made by a college athletic director involves the dropping or adding of sports. Of the two, the former is particularly difficult. Yet, every year athletic departments throughout the nation are forced to eliminate sports from their programs.

This matter is a vivid example of the need to manage change. The environment surrounding college sport is constantly changing. Economic conditions, legal requirements, and NCAA regulations have all changed rapidly in recent years. The difference between an effective manager and an ineffective one is often seen in the ability to manage change. The latter tends to manage reactively. Crisis management becomes the name of the game. In essence, situations are dealt with after they become problems.

Economic conditions are the principal factor in any decision to drop sports from all athletic programs. A senior college sports survey in 1985 showed declines in the sponsorship of seven men's collegiate sports: wrestling, gymnastics, golf, tennis, track, baseball, and swimming/diving. From 1981 to 1984, the number of senior colleges offering men's programs was up from 1,217 to 1,279. However, during the same time the total sports offered was down from 8,806 to 8,502. In 1981 the average senior college offered 7.24 men's sports programs. By contrast, in 1984 the average was down to 6.65. (*Athletic Business*, January 1985, p. 20) In addition to financial considerations, lack of interest and safety were also cited as reasons for dropping sports.

The political/legal environment also brings about program changes. Title IX is beyond a doubt the most significant factor behind any program additions in recent years. For example, the above survey also revealed the number of women's sport programs increased from 6,290 to 6,833 (a net gain of 543) between 1981 and 1984. During the same period, 147 senior college institutions offered women's sports for the first time. In 1984 they sponsored an average of 5.35 women's sports per school. The only declining women sports for the period were field hockey, golf, and gymnastics. Finances *were probably* also the major factor here.

NCAA legislation has been the other important factor in program additions. Section 4 under Article 11 of the NCAA Bylaws sets forth sports sponsorship criteria. Until recently, member institutions were required to sponsor a minimum of eight men's sport programs and three women's sport programs. During the 1984 NCAA Convention, the association voted to require Division I members to sponsor six women's sports by 1986 and eight by 1988. At the 1985 convention this was further modified to require eight sports for women as well as men by 1986 for all *Division I-A* football playing institutions. This new regulation affected some 30 universities.

When one adds the need to increase the number of women's sport programs to the financial restraints, the reason for decreasing the number of other sports is readily apparent. Far too often, decisions about adding or dropping sports fall within the crisis category. This is precisely why there is the need for policy development in this area.

THE ISSUE

A basic philosophical question beyond any legal requirement must be faced when an athletic manager considers the addition or elimination of a sports program. Is it more desirable to strive for excellence in selected sports or to offer a more comprehensive and diversified program? One's initial response might be to wonder why this has to be an either-or consideration. Is it not possible to proceed from the assumption that a department should attempt to pursue excellence in all sports? The answer again is found in finances. If there are sufficient funds to do both, there will be no problem and no issue. However, most institutions are not in that kind of comfortable situation today. Basic choices about the direction of the total program have to be made.

The answer to the key question can be found by considering the objectives which have been set forth for the athletic program. However they may be worded, the possible objectives essentially fall into one of the two categories: image objectives and educational objectives.

The image, status, or reputation objectives are first and foremost aimed at gaining external support for the institution even though the internal effects may also be extensive. Quite clearly, most Division I football and basketball powers operate from this stance. Just think of the visibility basketball has provided for Villanova and Georgetown and football for Alabama and Oklahoma. Lacrosse, a so-called "minor" sport, has enhanced the image of Johns Hopkins. This kind of externally directed objective points to the choice of striving for excellence in selected sports.

The other category of objectives might be called educational. These are directed internally, aimed at broadening the educational opportunity through sport for the entire student body. The objectives proceed from the assumption that participation in a sport program is an integral part of the educational process. In contrast with the image category, the educational objectives require a more comprehensive and diversified program so that more students can benefit from the intercollegiate sport experience.

A survey of institutions throughout the country will reveal that a few are in the fortunate position of being able to pursue excellence in selected sports *and* offer a comprehensive program. However, a growing majority face decisions about dropping sport programs. In such cases, policy is needed to determine what should be dropped. Legislative requirements to add sports dictate the same need for established policy.

THE PROBLEM

The problem is particularly manifested when a decision is made to drop certain sports. Generally speaking, it is always easier to increase than it is to delete. The exception, of course, is that financial restraints may prohibit any additions. Nevertheless, once a program is in place it is a most sensitive matter to get it removed without offending parties with vested interests. Up front the problem in dropping a sport is acute with regard to the direct impact on athletes and coaches. Neither of those groups can be expected to be objective when a decision is made to drop their sports. Beyond that, the political ramifications involving the reactions of alumni, boosters, trustees, and various other supporters are almost certain to be extensive. As with the overall issue, the problem also points to the need for sound policy. There must be a basis on which to make and justify critical decisions. A consideration of criteria for adding, dropping, or retaining sports is a logical place to begin.

Criteria

The criteria actually provides the basis for policy development in this area. A criterion is a standard for correct judgment. As an administrator, how does one know whether he or she has made the correct decision? Furthermore, how can that decision be justified? The absence of criteria or questionable criteria will receive most of the criticism when a decision to add or drop a program is announced. Any sign of arbitrary decision making will prompt an outcry that will reflect poorly on the athletic department. Predetermined criteria should be used as the basis for any decision. Sound criteria, based on program objectives, will go a long way toward minimizing negative reactions and possible legal complications.

Following are criteria which might be used as a basis for policy development regarding the addition or deletion of sports. Except for the first, these are not necessarily listed in order of importance. The relative weight of the criteria will have to be determined within the context of the given institution. That is the first step in establishing policy.

1. *Legal concerns:* One must start with this criteria. NCAA Bylaws set forth sponsorship requirements regarding the minimum number of sports that must be offered for men and women. As noted earlier, this has been an important factor in many Division I sport additions in recent years. Both the Bylaws and Title IX are aimed at promoting balanced programs for men and women. In terms of specific implementation, the ensuing issue becomes one of determining equity versus equality.

2. *Needs and interests of the students:* Ideally, this would rank as an important criterion for most institutions. However, it is perhaps the most elusive among the various standards. A form of market research can be done with the students viewed as the consumers of the athletic department's programs. Such research would include the use of surveys, informal feedback, and continuous observation.

3. *Current/potential, Cost/success ratio:* This is a complicated criterion which ranks near the top of the list for many institutions. Basically it involves an assessment of what has been achieved in relationship to the funds spent on the program. Determination of success is a judgment call. Nevertheless, a ".500" or better record over a five-year period is a place to begin. For conference schools, relative cost might be assessed within the budget range of conference competitors. Potential cost/success ratio is likely to be based on the current ratio unless there are significant changes which indicate a shift.

4. *Current/potential facilities:* Anyone close to a sport program knows that the quality of the facility is a significant factor in the success of the program. When it comes to adding or dropping sports, both the current and potential facility situations have to be taken into account. Several questions must be addressed. How do the facilities compare with those of comparable institutions at the same level? What are the sub-par facilities? Is there adequate practice space? What are the possibilities for obtaining new facilities? Which sports have facilities that provide a special quality dimension to the total program? Which facilities are no longer adequate for use under current conditions?

5. *Current/potential staff qualifications:* One has to assess the current staff profile. Are some of the coaches particularly well established in their present positions? In some institutions there may be a certain number of tenured coaches on the staff. In most cases it would probably make less sense to drop a sport that has a

tenured coach. Based on comparable competition, what are the measures of relative success among the coaches? Are there part-time coaches on the staff? All other factors being equal, it is easier to drop a sport with a part-time coach. What are the financial limitations in adding new coaches to the staff? Are retirements anticipated in the near future?

6. *Regional and Climatic Considerations:* The decision to add or drop a sport can also be based on the region or climate in which the institution is located. The matter of regional popularity of certain sports should be taken into consideration. It would be unlikely for a college in the Baltimore or Long Island area to drop lacrosse. By the same token, a college in Minnesota or Massachusetts without an ice hockey program might well consider adding that sport. The climatic criterion extends beyond regional popularity. Spring sports such as baseball, softball, golf, and tennis have extensive national popularity. Yet, a decision to drop one or more of these sports could be based on the relatively short time available for spring semester play in a northern region of the country.

7. *Current/potential, competitive context:* What is the available competition in a given sport? Furthermore, what is the potential for adding new opponents? In some cases, these questions may also represent an important criterion for decision making on the scope of the total program. Economic considerations obviously factor into this kind of assessment. Are there an adequate number of potential opponents within a reasonable distance from an economic perspective? Sports offered by other conference schools can be a significant factor. For example, if more than 50 percent of the conference schools offer a sport, this might provide a basis for retention or addition.

The Process

Well established criteria provide the key to policy regarding changes in the total sport offerings. However, the process in implementing these changes may be just as important. Thus, once the criteria are established, there is also need for policy to control the process. In developing such policy, certain factors should be taken into account.

Most importantly, there is a need for political sensitivity. In particular, any decision to drop a sport program has either direct or indirect effects on a variety of interest groups, including athletes, coaches, parents, boosters, trustees, and administrators. Collegiate sport, particularly in the public sector, exists in a bureaucratic structure which tends to be hierarchically regulated. The built-in, top-down management style is a primary constraint. Policy must be directed accordingly. The athletic director is responsible for representing all parties, from the trustees to the coaches and athletes. The process can be a political balancing act for the director.

Dropping or adding sports has implications for a program's public relations. How the media and the general public view the athletic department's actions can affect the overall program. Public opinion regarding athletics is a powerful force in educational institutions. It is important to maintain a positive image for the purposes of athletic recruitment, athletic contributions, and the overall welfare of the institution.

Special consideration should be given to those directly affected by the decision, specifically the coaches and athletes. Two-way communication is vital to the effectiveness of the process. Coaches and athletes should be informed in advance of any final decision, and they should have the opportunity to provide feedback. They should understand the precise reasons why their program is being dropped. There is something amiss when the coach and athletes of a sport to be dropped are the last to know. By that time, they really have no choice but to file their protests and ask for reconsideration. Whenever possible, there should be ample time between the decision and implementation for those directly involved to make alternative plans.

CASE STUDIES

Before proceeding to any recommended policies, we will consider the challenges faced by two institutions that needed to change their sport offerings. Although these are actual cases, names are disguised due to the sensitivity of coping with this kind of problem. Both cases represent state universities, each having a student population of approximately 20,000.

University A

At the time the decision was made to drop seven sports from the program, this university offered 28 varsity sports. In 1981, University A was second among all NCAA Division I athletic programs in terms of the number of sports offered. Even with the drop from 28 to 21, the university would be offering a relatively high number of sports for a Division I program.

Much of the strong reaction against the decision can be attributed to the tradition and basic philosophy of the athletic department, which prided itself on offering a comprehensive and diversified program for the educational benefit of the student body at large. In addition to the extensive intercollegiate offerings, the intramural sport program was also sponsored by the athletic department. The athletic director stated that the plan to drop sports did not reflect a change in philosophy. He contended that they were simply taking into account the reality factor — the financial situation within the department.

Other people, especially coaches and athletes of the sports to be dropped, had different opinions. One of the coaches stated bluntly that a state university should not drop any sports. His opinion was supported by a writer from his hometown newspaper who said that the department should be adding rather than dropping sports. "A state university should have everything under the sun," he stated.

On the other hand, a local sportswriter who regularly covered the university's athletic program, applauded the decision. His point was that a college athletic program in the 1980s cannot continue the "fun and games" of 20 years ago. From his perspective, the decision was overdue. The plan would put more emphasis on the revenue-producing sports and bring University A more in line with its competitors and other major college athletic programs.

The decision by University A's athletic department clearly reflects typical issues and problems. To better understand the reasons for the decision, it might be well to review the chronology of events leading to it.

A decline in University A's win-loss records was a primary cause of the problem. Not all of the teams were experiencing a decline in success level; in fact several of the women's teams (particularly, field hockey, soccer, and lacrosse) had been very successful. The problem was in the relative lack of success in the three sports which had spectator interest and media attention at University A: men's football, basketball, and lacrosse. The latter's popularity could be largely attributed to an exceptional record over a period of several years. However, in 1983 the lacrosse team's record fell to 5-10. Even more critical, the men's basketball team had experienced five consecutive 20-loss seasons prior to 1983. The culminating blow came in the fall of 1983 when the football team finished a poor season by losing to a state rival in the state capital city by a score of 31-14. That event caught the attention of trustees, legislators, and alumni.

During the winter of 1983-84 a change in attitude about University A's athletic program was evident among people in power. The president informed the trustees that he was continuing to receive "expression of unhappiness" about the status of the athletic program from alumni and the legislature. He urged the trustees to find more about the nature of the problems and determine how they might be solved.

Ironically, the athletic department had attempted to gain higher level support for needed athletic changes, but the efforts were met with apathy. Proposals for football tuition waivers and doming the stadium were not well received by the board of trustees. The latter proposal would have been particularly beneficial for the basketball program because it included provision for a major basketball arena within the stadium. Recruiting for basketball was limited by a sub-par facility. The tuition waiver proposal was predicated on the fact that the athletic scholarship fund was projected to run out of money by 1986.

Yet, in spite of the previous indifference, in the winter of 1983-84 the trustees demanded that the athletic department develop a plan to make its major sports more competitive. What kind of options were available? One might suggest that an option would be to preserve the status quo, do nothing. Yet, that was hardly realistic under the circumstances. The more viable alternatives are described below.

1. *Obtain the necessary funds to keep all programs, while raising their competitive support.* This appeared to be the ideal solution, but according to the athletic director additional funding was unlikely from the possible sources. Student fees were already relatively high at the university, with a significant percentage going toward the support of the athletic program. Furthermore, there was considerable student reaction against recent fee hikes on the campus. Possible alumni/booster contributions merely reflected the old "chicken and the egg" problem. Contributions tend to increase as teams win more games. At any rate, University A could not look for much from this source at that time. Additional funding could not be anticipated from the state legislature through the trustees due to the need to upgrade other programs on campus. The trustees also had recently authorized an increase in athletic funding for improving the facilities. Another possibility might have been to charge admission to sport events in addition to football and basketball games. By and large this would again involve mostly students. Due to the relatively high student athletic fee, this option was ruled out. Additional television revenue could not be projected. The university was a *Division I AA football* school. Television revenue had been very limited in the past. The Supreme Court television ruling against the NCAA further limited any potential in that regard. The long and short of the matter is that none of the possibilities were promising.

2. *Drop down to NCAA Division II or III.* From one standpoint this would appear to reduce the pressure to be more competitive. The university could certainly compete more successfully at a lower level. But University A was not only a large state university, it was *the* university of the state. It would be unthinkable for many people (trustees, alumni, boosters) to see University A drop out of Division I.

3. *Cut back administrative support.* Pursuit of this alternative would also conflict with the more competition posture sought by the trustees. According to the athletic director, University A was already operating at the "bare bones" level. If anything, there was a need to add administrative staff members.

4. *Cut programs.* As noted in the introduction to this case study, this route was ultimately selected. Here also, options were available. The junior varsity programs could be dropped, but this option was eliminated from consideration due to the minimal savings involved. In 1982-83, the athletic department sponsored 11 junior varsity programs at a cost of $14,000. Subsequently, the

football and softball junior varsity programs were dropped, bringing the cost down to $8,000. In 1984 the number of student-athletes participating in junior varsity programs at University A was about 100. This left the choice of dropping varsity sport programs. Seven sports were selected for change from varsity to club or intramural status.

The Plan: Dropping the seven sports was only part of the total plan presented by administrators in the athletic department. The complete plan outlined below was predicated on a number of contingencies in the effort to alleviate mediocrity and bring the athletic program in line with the growing recognition of academic excellence at University A. Steps to be taken were the following:

1. Increase the number of tuition waivers.
2. Increase the football scholarships from 55 to 75.
3. Provide three levels of scholarship support with corresponding expectations.
4. Renovate the field house.
5. Build an ice skating facility.
6. Hire more staff: strength coach, academic advisor, fundraising promoter, and more assistant coaches.
7. Reduce the number of sports offered.

The last received the most attention because of its controversial implications, particularly in light of the other steps calling for increased expenditures. Table 15-1 shows the projected savings of $75,000 resulting from the removal of seven sports from varsity status. Critics readily pointed out that the figure represented a "drop in the bucket" in comparison to the funds to be spent in upgrading the major sport programs.

Criticism was also directed toward another part of the plan, that involving the administrative expectations for all sport programs with their corresponding scholarship support. This breakdown is displayed in Exhibit 15-1. In essence, three classes of athletic citizenship were established, and a fourth class was eliminated.

Earlier in this chapter we noted some criteria which might be employed as a basis for policy development to guide changes in sport offerings. Exhibit 15-2 lists the actual criteria used by University A in its decision to drop seven sports. Similarities between the two sets of criteria can be noted. How are these criteria reflected in the rationale for dropping each of the seven sports?

With regard to all seven sports, one overriding theme should be noted — the relative lack of visibility in comparison with most of the other sports in the total athletic program. This was reflected in the retricted amount of media attention and spectator interest. Undoubtedly, this had an effect on the decision.

TABLE 15-1. Projected Savings From Moving The Following Intercollegiate Sports To Club Status*

Sport	Projected Savings
Golf (M)	$ 7,000
Golf (W)	3,600
Ski (M)	8,900
Ski (W)	7,800
Tennis (M)	6,400
Tennis (W)	10,500
Wrestling	21,600
Subtotal	$65,800

Additional Savings:

Less frequent travel van replacement	$ 4,500 per year
Miscellaneous: awards, pictures, student coverage, postage, office supplies, training supplies	4,700 per year
Total Estimated Savings	$75,000

*No cost assigned to the considerable amount of administrative time spent in administering the seven programs; i.e. affirmative action searches, eligibility, clearance, scheduling.

The Process: Having made the preliminary decision, the athletic administrators had to obtain approval and implement the plan. Implementation posed a new *problem.* Late in the winter of 1983-84 the plan was presented to the athletic committee of the university's board of trustees and to the university's top administration. Both groups approved the plan. The coaches were the next to be informed in May 1984, when the athletic administration gave a lengthy presentation on the problem of University A's mediocrity in athletics and the need to become more competitive. Then the coaches of the sports involved were informed that their sports were to be dropped to club status the following year.

There were two very different perspectives on the implications of that meeting. The athletic director stressed that the coaches were told that it was a "proposed" plan, not final at that time. By contrast, the coaches felt they received the word that their teams were "dead."

Following the coaches meeting the plan was announced to the news media. The timing of the announcement is also worth noting. In late May students at University A are either busy with final examinations or gone for the summer. The student newspaper was not being published. This averted much conflict from students. However, the timing caused problems for incoming recruits and current team members of the sports to be dropped. Late May was too late to obtain scholarships from other institutions.

EXHIBIT 15-1. University/Administrative Expectations

Level I: Maximum scholarship support as allowed by the NCAA.

MEN'S FOOTBALL
- Conference supremacy
- National championship contention IAA

MEN'S BASKETBALL
- Conference-highly competitive
- Periodic championship contention

MEN'S LACROSSE
- Top 10 in country annually
- National championship contender

WOMEN'S BASKETBALL
- Conference-annual championship contender

Level II: Scholarship aid in varying degrees.

WOMEN'S FIELD HOCKEY
WOMEN'S SOCCER
- Highly Competitive in Region
- National Recognition Contention

WOMEN'S LACROSSE
WOMEN'S SOFTBALL
- Highly Competitive in Region
- National Recognition/ Contention

MEN'S SOCCER
MEN'S XC/TRACK
- Respectable in Region Atlantic 10

MEN'S BASEBALL
- Respectable in Region Conference

Level III: In-state tuition waivers.

COMPETITIVE IN RESPECTIVE DIVISIONS

Swimming	Men, Women
Gymnastics	Men, Women
Volleyball	Women
XC/Track	Women

Level IV: Change of status from varsity to club or intramural.

Golf	Men, Women
Tennis	Men, Women
Ski	Men, Women
Wrestling	Men

During the summer of 1984 there was a great deal of lobbying by the coaches, athletes, and other concerned parties. Numerous letters were received by the athletic department and the trustees of the university protesting the "change of status" plan. Pressure and concern over prior commitments and the need to give affected athletes time to relocate

EXHIBIT 15-2. Criteria (Factors in Decision-Making Process)

1. Number of participants/students served by the program.
2. Number of constituents served by the program.
3. Media attention.
4. Current/potential success of program with the resources available.
5. Title IX considerations.
6. Spectator interest.
7. Facilities.
8. Full-time personnel.
9. Scheduling.
10. Image.
11. Commitments to coaches, student-athletes.

Wrestling: One major problem with wrestling was the record. In the two seasons (1982-84) prior to the decision to drop wrestling, the team compiled a record of 1-27-2. The fact that the coach was only part-time, had been at University A just 4 years, and had a contract expiring in June, facilitated the decision. Another instrumental factor was the recognition that many schools across the country were dropping wrestling. *The NCAA News* reported that wrestling had been on the decline for seven consecutive years. Among approximately 860 NCAA institutions in 1983-84, only 342 sponsored varsity wrestling.

Men's/Women's Tennis: University A had not been strongly committed to tennis. The facilities were adequate but not ideal for varsity purposes. Both teams had relatively new (one to two years) part-time coaches. Team records between 1982 and 1984 were poor to mediocre: women, 13-21, and men, 19-15.

Men's/Women's Golf: The cost per number of people served was probably a primary reason for deciding to drop golf from the program. Over the period 1982-84, men's golf averaged 13 team members with a record of 4-10, while women's golf averaged eight players with a 13-8 record.

Men's/Women's Ski: Skiing was a prime exception to the mediocrity problem. Both teams had demonstrated considerable success. The men had a 140-17 record, and the women a 120-0 between 1982 and 1984. Their part-time coach of 26 years indicated that they won with "boring" regularity which contributed to a lack of publicity. Travel distance was a definite factor behind the decision to drop skiing. It was the only sport in which home contests occurred more than 50 miles off campus. Sponsorship of the sport was also declining nationally. In 1983-84, only 46 NCAA member institutions sponsored men's ski teams, and there were only 36 women's teams.

prompted the trustees to give the teams a temporary reprieve. The seven teams were reinstated for two years through a special trustee reserve fund. Reinstatement occurred in mid-August, soon before school was to start. The seven teams competed during the 1984-85 academic year with terminal status in mind. The men's and women's teams of golf, tennis, and ski were scheduled to lose varsity status after their 1985-86 seasons. Wrestling was terminated after the 1984-85 season due to the expiration of the part-time coach's contract in June. In May 1985 students on campus, led by the athletes involved, made a further effort at reinstatement through a "save our sports" protest. However, the decision to drop the sports remained firm.

University B

In the fall of 1982, University B merged its men's and women's athletic departments. The merger made an impact on the following areas: 1) organizational structure and job descriptions, 2) coaches, 3) sports, 4) facilities, and 5) budget. Recommendations for each of these categories were developed by the Athletic Merger Committee, which included: the associate provost, the assistant director for women's athletics, the chair of physical education for women, the men's tennis coach, the women's ski coach, the associate director for men's athletics, and the controller for men's athletics.

That committee's recommendations regarding sports are the focus of this case. The committee established the criteria to be used for justifying the inclusion of any sport within the intercollegiate athletic program, guidelines for arrangements for athletes in sports to be dropped, and recommendations with rationale for the dropping of women's ski and field hockey and adding women's golf. These recommendations are found in Exhibit 15-3.

Although the recommendations were adopted, they did not receive much support from coaches and others involved. This was apparent in memoranda from the coaches to the academic vice president and provost of the university. Following is a summary of ideas expressed in the letters of objection to the proposals.

1. The coaches expressed considerable concern that the decisions on dropping and adding of sports were taking place only in the merger committee without input from the department.
2. Skiing and field hockey represented two high quality teams. It would be disastrous to drop these teams before others have been developed to a comparable level of performance. The positive visibility and publicity for skiing and field hockey had reflected university's commitment to excellence in women's sports.
3. The decision to drop skiing and field hockey was not consistent with the criteria used for justifying the inclusion of any sport in the program.
4. Traditionally, field hockey is a top women's sport in the United States, much the same as football is a prime men's sport. Furthermore, field hockey is an Olympic sport. The women athletes in field hockey at least needed an opportunity to compete for selection to the olympic team.

EXHIBIT 15-3. Selected Recommendations Regarding Sports At University B

1. Criteria to be used for justifying the inclusion of any sport within the intercollegiate athletic department.
   a. Facilities available
   b. Climate
   c. Opportunities for competition
   d. General appeal to citizens of the state
   e. Pool of athletes available to play the sport
   f. Cost of operating the sport
   g. Equitable opportunities for participation by male and female student athletes
2. It is recommended that women's skiing be dropped in the fall of 1982. The reasons for this recommendation are the following:
   a. Practice and competitive facilities are marginal.
   b. Competition does not exist in the conference.
   c. The pool of in-state athletes who compete at the high school level is small.
   d. The cost of operating the sport is high, because long-distance travel is necessary for competitive schedule.
3. It is recommended that women's golf be added effective fall 1982. The reasons for this recommendation are the following:
   a. The university has practice and competition facilities.
   b. Four schools in the conference compete in golf.
   c. Ninety-eight high schools in the state have interscholastic golf programs for women.
   d. The cost of operating golf is low.
   e. Golf has the potential for becoming self-sustaining.
   f. Golf can be used to promote intercollegiate athletics.
4. It is recommended that the fall of 1982 be the last year of competition in women's field hockey. The reasons for this recommendation are the following:
   a. The pool of in-state athletes who compete at the high school level is virtually non-existent.
   b. Nationwide travel is required to have a competitive schedule.
   c. The cost of operating the sport is high because of travel and out-of-state scholarship costs.
5. For athletes in sports recommended to be dropped, the following guidelines should apply:
   a. Generally, the NCAA guidelines for scholarships (one year continuation) should be followed.
   b. Because of the extraordinary circumstances involved in dropping women's skiing, any ski team member who is a sophomore in good standing as of spring semester 1982 will be eligible to receive two more years of scholarship.

It is interesting to note that neither university listed criteria for dropping or adding sports in their policy statements prior to these decisions. However, University B had established procedures (Exhibit 15-4).

EXHIBIT 15-4. University B's Procedures for Adding or Deleting an Intercollegiate Sport Activity

Addition of a Sport
  Procedure
  1. Only sports activities which have been registered with Campus Recreation, and actively and effectively functioning as a club sport or a former varsity sport will be considered for addition to the intercollegiate sports program.
  2. Sponsors and/or members of the team should request consideration of their activity and its development as an intercollegiate enterprise through both the Athletic Director and the Chairman of the Athletic Council in writing.
  3. The activity petitioning for inclusion as an intercollegiate sport shall make a presentation to the Athletic Council at which time they will develop their plan for implementation, i.e. budget, facilities, competition, coaching staff, participant staff, alumni support, etc. All matters relating to inclusion in the Intercollegiate Athletic Department will be shared with both the petitioners and the Athletic Council and in the presence of the petitioners.
  4. Following consideration, the Athletic Council will recommend to both the Athletic Director and the President of the University a position in regard to the addition of the sport activity.

Deletion of a Sport
  Procedure
  1. The Athletic Director will present for review of the Athletic Council the rationale for the recommendation from the Athletic Department to delete and/or de-emphasize any intercollegiate activity. No sports activity will be *eliminated* without review by the Athletic Council, and if requested, presentations by the sponsor, coach, and/or members of the activity affected.
  2. If a recommendation for change of status of a sport is to be presented to the Athletic Council, this will be specifically listed as an item on the agenda sent out to Council members prior to the meeting.

POLICY GUIDELINES

We have now arrived at the important question: What kind of policy can be developed by an athletic department to facilitate the decision-making process when there is a need to make a change in program offerings (i.e., sport sponsorship). The two case studies should offer some testimony to the fact that the central issue can be resolved and the subsequent problem minimized if there is a policy in place when the decision has to be made. The case studies also reveal the need for policy to guide the process.

The following points are not designed to be specific policy statements. Rather, they are guidelines for the development of policy within the context of a given athletic department. A particular policy can only be developed at the institutional level. The divergent nature of collegiate athletic programs precludes the possibility of national policy in this area.

1. There must be a strong correlation between the policy and the objectives of the athletic program. As noted earlier in this chapter, an institution basically has two choices when it comes to establishing objectives in sports programming. The sports programs are either educational in nature or they are externally directed at enhancing the image of the institution. A combination of objectives is possible when finances permit. However, most institutions will have to make a choice between a broader based program and one which is highly selective in sport offerings.
2. Definite criteria should be in place when the time comes to make a decision regarding the addition, retention, or deletion of sports. Problems are likely to occur if the criteria have to be determined at the time the decision is made or applied after the fact. The more effective policy provides a rank order listing of criteria to be considered. Legal concerns should be the number one criterion for every college or university program. Beyond that, each institutional policy should provide a rank order identification among those possibilities described earlier:
   Needs and interests of the students
   Current/potential, cost/success ratio
   Current/potential facilities
   Current/potential staff qualifications
   Regional and climatic considerations
   Current/potential, competitive context
3. A set procedure should be established for adding a sport to the intercollegiate athletic program. Once again, the specific policy to control that procedure will have to be determined within the context of the institutional structure. However, it is reasonable to expect that a sport would have met the test of being a successful club sport. The groups seeking varsity status for the sport would be required to submit a formal petition through the appropriate channels. In many institutions, the initial screening of petitions might be done by an athletic council or a similar body. A petition would include a detailed plan for implementation covering such matters as budget, facilities, competition, coaching staff, and participation base. Petitions would be considered in accordance with the pre-established criteria for determination of sport offerings.
4. A policy would also be needed to modify the procedure for adding a sport in those cases where legal requirements precipitate the addition. The NCAA legislation increasing the required min-

imum number of women's sports would be a prime example. In such cases, the policy might outline a procedure for soliciting petitions for varsity sport status.

5. Deletion of a sport should be controlled by a policy which sets forth the review process when an apparent need arises. In most cases the athletic director will initiate the recommendation for deletion. There should be a provision for requiring support for the recommendation. Whether the reasons are financial or based on other factors, the athletic director is most likely to have access to the necessary information. Those directly involved, particularly coaches, should have the opportunity to provide input early in the review process. Prior to submitting the recommendation through the administrative channels, there should be a complete preliminary review by an appropriate advisory body, probably the athletic council in most institutions. At every step in the process, the recommendation should be assessed in accordance with the pre-established criteria for determination of sport offerings.

6. Whenever possible, there should also be a policy controlling the deletion of a sport through a "phasing out" period. In most cases, this would likely be a one- or two-year extension period for any relocation of athletes and coaches. Provision must also be established for determining scholarship aid for athletes when a sport is dropped from the program.

CONCLUSION

The issue of dropping and adding sports will exist as long as there are collegiate athletic programs. This is one of the more difficult issues to be faced by an athletic director. It is important that athletic directors stand ready with the policy and competence to make the decision and carry it through in a professional matter. The initial key is the pre-established criteria for determination of the sports to be offered. Beyond that there is need for policy to control the process of change.

REFERENCES

National Collegiate Athletic Association - 1985-86 Manual.
"Sports Sponsorship Rises in All Divisions." The NCAA News, February 27, 1985, pp. 1, 16.
"The Athletic Business Senior College Sports Participation Survey." Athletic Business, January 1985, pp. 20, 23-24.

16

Promoting Non-Revenue Sports In The Colleges

Sport promotion on the collegiate level is a relatively new activity, having developed over roughly the past 10 years. Promotion includes the associated activities of marketing, fund raising, and merchandising. Don Canham, athletic director at the University of Michigan, was one of the first to recognize that sport promotion requires a multifarious approach. In addition to his efforts in enhancing football ticket sales in the 1970s, he also merchandised a variety of products identified with Michigan football. His success became a model for university athletic programs throughout the country.

Promotion of non-revenue collegiate sports is an even more recent development. For purposes here, a non-revenue sport is any sport that is not considered potentially profitable for the institution. There are no extensive gate receipts or television revenue, and the activity is not primarily aimed at spectator attendance and support. Basically, the non-revenue sports are all sports other than football and men's basketball, with a few exceptions, such as ice hockey in Michigan, wrestling in Iowa, or baseball in Florida and Texas.

Much of the interest in promoting non-revenue sports can be attributed to the expansion of women's athletics and the financial crunch which threatens the continued existence of a diversified sport program. Most women's sports are in the non-revenue category, and the men's non-revenue sports have been caught in the squeeze between the women's expansion and the ever-growing popularity of revenue-producing sports.

THE ISSUE

The central question is this: should an athletic department make a special effort to promote a non-revenue sport? The rationale behind the promotion of a major revenue-producing sport is quite simple. The potential for significant financial support for the institution is great. But what is to be gained from promoting a non-revenue sport? While the coach of any given sport might be interested in its promotion, the reasons for promoting are not always that apparent from a departmental perspective. After all, there are repeated claims that sport programs should be offered purely in an educational context. What does that tell us about the desirability of making special efforts to promote non-revenue sports?

Once a decision is made to promote non-revenue sports, other questions also emerge. Which sports should be promoted? Does the department promote all sports, a selected few, or only one? Answers are likely to be dependent on a number of variables.

The overall consideration is the potential for development of various sports with the department. The status of facilities and staff, both present and planned, are principal determinates. The geographic location of the institution is also critical. For example, it is easy to see why Johns Hopkins University decided several years ago to promote lacrosse, and why efforts are made to promote women's basketball in Iowa. Another significant consideration is the competitive success of the various sports. Quite obviously, it is easier and more logical to promote sports with proven records of success.

At least one other factor may influence a decision regarding the specific nature of promotion in the non-revenue category. This revolves around the status of revenue-producing sports in the institution. It would be more difficult to promote a non-revenue sport that is in direct competition with a major revenue producer at the same institution. This might explain why the University of Vermont chose to promote soccer where there is no intercollegiate football program.

THE PROBLEM

Deciding to promote and what to promote brings one to the problem: how can the promotion be most effectively accomplished? One way to solve the problem involves the use of "Management by Objectives" (MBO).

Deegan and Fritz (1975) identify three classes or categories of job related goals or objectives: routine (regular), problem-solving, and innovative. Routine objectives are concerned with normal work output, and they are set forth to meet a standard. With a problem-solving objective, the current results are below par; the objective is aimed at finding a solution. An innovative objective involves something new, a change, with the intent of adding benefits. (p. 160)

Any effort to promote a non-revenue sport is both problem-solving and innovative in nature particularly the latter. The very nature of a non-revenue activity indicates that one is dealing with something that is not inherently promotional. Essentially, it is a new endeavor. However, at the same time, the promotion will not be easily accomplished.

Deegan and Fritz also identify nine steps in a problem-solving model:

1. Identify the problem area.
2. Determine the present unsatisfactory level.
3. Define a reasonable desired performance level.
4. Isolate the difference between the present and desired levels.
5. Brainstorm possible causes of the problem.
6. Decide which causes are the most crucial.
7. Identify alternative solutions.
8. Evaluate proposed solutions.
9. Make commitment to time and action plan. (pp. 197-198)

These steps will be applied in an analysis of a hypothetical analysis of a Division I institution's situation at the end of the chapter.

CASE STUDY: UNIVERSITY OF CONNECTICUT

In 1969 when Coach Joe Morrone arrived at the University of Connecticut in Storrs, the soccer program existed in relative obscurity. The schedule traditionally included the better teams in New England. However, in some 40 years of soccer at UConn, the teams only had four or five years of significant success. No scholarships were offered to soccer players, and there was not an organized recruiting effort. Games were played in an open area without any bleachers. In Morrones' first year as coach, the team played on a field that was converted swampland. As the head coach, Morrone also found that he had to line the field. This was the status of soccer at UConn in 1969.

Three basic choices were available to the coach. He could maintain the status quo by carrying out his coaching responsibilities without giving any special attention to promotion and development. This may well have been completely acceptable to the athletic administration at UConn. They did not view the status of the soccer program as a particular problem. Soccer was not a priority, and there was no reason to consider promotion at that point. However, preservation of the status quo was unacceptable to Morrone.

To change the situation, he had a choice of two options. He could focus his efforts internally by working within the department and university structure to obtain support for better facilities, equipment, schedule, indoor and spring play, scholarships, and staff additions. Eventually, those developments materialized. But, Morrone basically chose a third action alternative — to embark on a long-term development program by working both internally and externally. Much of the external work helped in obtaining the internal support. External development included the formation and development of the Mansfield Youth Soccer Association, the Connecticut Junior Soccer Association, the Connecticut Soccer School, the Friends of UConn Soccer Club, and the overall support to generate gate receipts.

Underlying all these public relations, promotional, and fund-raising activities was the dual objective of developing soccer, in general, and UConn soccer, in particular. Morrone realized that the soccer program would have to be built on a firm foundation to achieve a pattern of success. This takes time. The record shows that it took from 1969 until 1980 to establish a broad base of support. In essence, a non-revenue sport became a revenue producer through the promotional effort. The steps along the way are worthy of note.

1. In 1969 Morrone worked for and received an electric scoreboard and three rows of bleachers to accommodate spectators.
2. The Connecticut Junior Soccer Association was formed in 1970. This was accomplished through the combined effort of Morrone and Al Bell, who had previously organized a youth group of four teams in Hartford. Morrone recognized that the organization could improve soccer in the state, work as a potential feeder system to the UConn soccer program, and develop spectator interest. He wrote the constitution and served as the association's first president for eight years.
3. The same year, 1970, Morrone also organized the Mansfield Youth Soccer Association. He enlisted sponsors for eight teams and worked with the recreation department to recruit parents of the participants as coaches. The teams played at the halftime of UConn games. This resulted in more fans for UConn soccer and contributed to goodwill in the community. This developing local support group included parents who were faculty at UConn and business people in Storrs and Mansfield.
4. An indoor soccer tournament also was initiated by Morrone in 1970. This was the first of its kind in the nation, and subsequently it has developed as the largest. Beginning in 1981, Metropolitan Life Insurance Company agreed to sponsor the tournament. More than 50 different colleges have participated over the years, and since 1978 it has been a 32-team tournament. Tele-Media has also televised segments of the tournament in local area. This has been another step toward increased visibility for the UConn soccer program.
5. Spring practice, including some informal games with other colleges, was instituted in 1970.
6. Morrone began the Connecticut Soccer School in 1970. He brought in high school coaches to work at the school, which

sought to improve the level of coaching, impart Morrones' philosophy of coaching, and add to the visibility of UConn soccer. A recruiting benefit also developed. Camps were promoted through nationwide advertisements in all major soccer publications. Typically, only one-half of the campers were from Connecticut. Having campers and eventually players all over the country coincided with the UConn schedule of intersectional games to promote a program with national scope.

7. Finally, Morrone's 1970 thrust at gaining external support for the program was manifested in the formation of the Friends of UConn Soccer. As with most clubs of this type, the basic idea was to provide a link among former lettermen and other interested people to support the advancement of UConn soccer. Initially the club was strictly a Morrone endeavor. Funds generated went through an account number in the alumni association. Over the past several years the club has developed into a true "friends club," running independently of Coach Morrones' leadership. The club purchased video tape equipment (soccer was the first sport at UConn to use video as a teaching tool and a recruiting aid) and office furniture, and laminated and mounted certificates for players awards. The club also hosts post-game dinners for both teams after Sunday games, conducts youth soccer games before and at half-time of most home games, sponsors raffles, and maintains a hospitality tent for fans during games. The club also covers costs for the annual awards banquet, the printing of players' names on game shirts, rings for players who play in the "Senior Bowl," the stationary with UConn soccer logo, and a newsletter which is published four to six times per year.

8. In 1973 Morrone initiated the first intersectional soccer game in New England. St. Louis University, a perennial national power, came to Storrs to play UConn. Since then, UConn has scheduled intersectional games each season. Objectives of this schedule are to improve player performance through a stronger schedule, give UConn national visibility, and to gain more consideration in the voting weekly polls and in the tournament selection at the end of the season.

9. Through the efforts of Morrone, a fence was constructed around the game field in 1976. This gave UConn the capability to charge for attendance. Initially only intersectional games required a paid admission, and the receipts were used to pay guarantees to visiting teams. The next step was to charge for all adult admission. From there the move was to eventually charge all fans for all games. Paid admission has developed to a point when UConn has gone from general admission to reserved sections to having reserved seats. The combination of the fence and admission

charges appear to have helped boost the budget allocation for soccer. For example, one plane trip per year was authorized for the soccer *team*. Trips were made to Texas in 1983, South Carolina in 1984, and Indiana in 1985.

10. The first scholarship for soccer was offered in 1976. By 1985 the number of scholarships for the soccer program was increased to eight.

11. Although there were various modified forms of a game program earlier, the UConn soccer program came out with its first bona fide, printed game program in 1977. Costs, which have risen considerably in recent years, are largely covered by program advertisements.

12. ESPN televised five UConn soccer games on a national basis in 1981.

13. Also in 1981, UConn hired a full-time assistant soccer coach and a full-time secretary for the soccer program.

14. Revenue from gate receipts, parking, and concessions totaled over $100,000 in 1981.

15. To avoid scheduling conflicts with football, the weekend soccer games were moved to Sundays beginning in 1982.

16. In 1984, the UConn soccer team played their first home game away from home — the New Britain game. This game, played on a weekday, drew 6,200 spectators.

17. All home and away games for soccer are now broadcast on the UConn radio station.

The action alternative pursued by Coach Joe Morrone at the University of Connecticut is a vivid example of how a non-revenue sport can be promoted. What can one conclude from this case? First, careful planning is necessary to employ a promotional strategy. To achieve any degree of success takes time, and there are many building blocks along the way. Second, staffing is a crucial factor in the decision to promote a non-revenue sport. That is not to say that the University of Connecticut necessarily hired Coach Morrone with the promotional potential in mind. Nevertheless, it is very clear from this case that the role of the coach is pivotal if a non-revenue sport is to be promoted. Third, real promotion takes place through persistence, patience, and a long-term developmental strategy. The chronology of events related to the UConn soccer program is testimony to that fact. Finally, building a broad base of support through a solid public relations effort is integral in its success. UConn soccer would not be at its present level without the support of the larger community. Tables 16-1, 16-2, and 16-3 are partial indicators of the degree of success in promoting soccer at the University of Connecticut:

TABLE 16-1. Comparisons — Season Records & Tournaments

Year	Wins	Losses	Ties	Tournament Appearance
Pre-Morrone				
1962-1968	37	44	5	None
Morrone Era				
1969-1972	21	32	3	None
1973-1976	65	11	3	Four NCAA appearances
1977	9	11	1	None
1978-1981	79	16	4	Four NCAA appearances 1981 National Champions
1982-1983	31	12	8	NCAA Final Four twice
1984	14	9	1	NCAA appearance

TABLE 16-2. Player & Coach Recognition

Player Recognition:
Professional Players: 16 Players
Hermann Trophy (Nation's Top Player): One player (1980)
All American Players: Five players (two times)
                          Four players (once)
Senior Bowl: (Top seniors in nation; game began in 1972):
                          Eleven players
All New England: One player (four times)
                          Four players (three times)
                          Eight players (two times)
                          Ten players (once)
All NEISL: One player (four times)
                          Five players (five times)
                          Seven players (two times)
                          Eleven players (once
Coach's Recognition: 1980 NSCAA New England Coach of the Year
                          1980 and 1981 NEISL Coach of the Year

TABLE 16-3. Attendance Records

Year	# Games	Total Home Attendance	Avg. Home Attendance
1981	18	53,900	4,146
1982	15	64,320	4,288
1983	17	64,535	3,796
1984	16	58,160	3,635

Attendance — Leading NCAA Soccer Playing Schools — 1984

School	Avg. Home Attd.	NCAA 2nd Round Attd.
Connecticut	3,635	6,948
Indiana	2,200	2,500
Duke	2,000	NA
Penn State	1,720	NA
San Francisco	1,350	NA
Fairleigh Dickinson	1,200	4,010
Columbia	1,000	1,900
Clemson	842	2,177
St. Louis	775	1,500
Virginia	750	1,855
UCLA	500	1,500

Note: Figures supplied by respective schools.

SUGGESTED POLICIES FOR A DIVISION I INSTITUTION

Following the outline and guidelines for the Deegan-Fritz model, we can hypothesize the particulars in problem-solving for a Division I institution and arrive at policies. To a certain extent, these policies may also be applicable for Division II and III institutions. However, in most cases the potential for significant promotion is restricted to Division I programs, and efforts in that regard are more consistent with the revenue-producing thrust.

1. *Problem area*: The athletic department is dissatisfied with the current level of support for its non-revenue sports.
2. *Present unsatisfactory level*: The lack of general support is manifested in low student participation, limited spectator appeal, and little news media coverage. Due to budgetary restrictions, the department is in a position wherein it may be forced to drop some of the non-revenue sports due to unfavorable comparisons with other (more lucrative) sports. Part of the problem is that the developing women's sports programs have received relatively little attention from students, faculty, administrators, alumni, and the media.

3. *Reasonable desired level*: The department desires to retain its present level of offering 21 intercollegiate sports (12 for men and nine for women). There is a particular need to provide greater visibility for developing women's sports. However, at the same time, the promotional effort should be extended to all the non-revenue sports, with emphasis on one or two sports that show promise for national recognition.

4. *Difference between present and desired level — The Problem*: By and large the promotional effort to date has been restricted to the revenue-producing sports (men's football and basketball). Any promotion in the non-revenue area has been more incidental than by design.

5. *Possible causes*:
   - unfavorable comparison with popular, spectator, revenue-producing sports
   - administrative apathy in the non-revenue area
   - student apathy in the non-revenue area
   - athletic staff apathy in the non-revenue area
   - general lack of competitive success in the non-revenue sports
   - lack of staff orientation toward promotion
   - qualifications of the coaches
   - environmental restrictions (facilities)
   - general apathy toward the women's sports
   - lack of alumni support
   - insufficient news media coverage

6. *Most likely causes*:
   - unfavorable comparison with popular, spectator, revenue-producing sports
   - administrative apathy in the non-revenue area
   - qualifications of the coaches

   Explanation for the choices: In this hypothetical situation, we conclude that the above three causes of the problem are the most crucial because the other possible causes can ultimately be attributed to one or more of these three. The unfavorable comparison with the popular, spectator, revenue-producing sports is the overriding consideration. Consequently, any promotion of a non-revenue sport will require a special effort. However, the record also shows that some athletic administrators are also more generally inclined toward promotion then others, and that coaches also vary considerably in their willingness to promote. In most cases, apathy on the part of students, alumni, and staff may be attributed to attitudes and actions of administrators and/or coaches. The same can be said for any general lack of competitive success. There may be a certain amount of inherent apathy toward the developing women's sports, but their situation is not that different than those of the other, non-revenue sports. The facilities may also be sub-par in some cases, but that brings one back to the lack of administrative support. If facility improvement is not possible, the need to drop the sport may be justified. Any deficiency in news media coverage may ultimately be attributed to all of the foregoing considerations. Reporters clearly reflect the level of the promotional effort.

7/8. *Alternative solutions and evaluation*:

   a. *Reducing the emphasis on the revenue-producing sport.* This is not one of the better solutions, either from a cost or feasibility standpoint. It is doubtful whether this could be accomplished without losing considerable alumni support and having a negative effect on the image of the institution. Furthermore, the non-revenue sports are largely financed from sports that produce revenue. Any reduction in revenue-producing sports would only magnify the problem.

   b. *Analyze the products.* This is a prime step in most marketing strategies. What it means here is a careful assessment of the potential for each sport within the total program. Promotion starts with a quality product. In the case of sport, this is generally manifested in being able to successfully compete at the existing level. Having a quality coach and talented athletes is the key. Geographical priorities and restrictions and schedules must also be taken into consideration. The product analysis may show that one or two of the non-revenue sports should be targeted for special promotional efforts. The major limitation of this alternative is that it may only further contribute to an unbalanced program and result in the need to drop certain sports. Women's sports could be at a disadvantage because of their recent development. At any rate, women's sports will also require a special promotional effort.

   c. *Set new performance standards for coaches.* Another possible way to promote non-revenue sports is to make promotion one of the performance standards for coaches. Obviously, having a competitive team is the place to begin. Beyond that, the coach would be expected to carry out various other promotional activities, such as establishing a strong alumni network. In addition to the alumni, maintaining a larger group following is another key to success in promotion. Mike Palmisano, director of promotions, marketing and special events at the University of Michigan, recommends building a group of alumni and interested business people. According to Palmisano, baseball is a top, non-revenue sport at Michigan because the coach is particularly adept at public relations with the general public, groups of supporters and the news media.

There would appear to be a couple of possible limitations in this third alternative. Not all coaches have the personalities required for successful promotion. Also, some coaches may work at a disadvantage due to the absence of tradition or status in their sports.

d. *Hire a professional in marketing to organize special promotions.* A fourth, major alternative would be to hire a professional person in marketing or advertising who is specifically responsible for promoting non-revenue sports. This requires an increase in the budget allocation for salaries, and there is no guarantee that the investment will pay off. Palmisano (1982) identifies several possible special promotions developing a theme for a team, recognition days, special clubs, alumni events, social tournaments, appreciation days, and special advertisements. Lopiano (1980) cites additional possibilities that have proven successful: establishing a support group for each sport, hosting a major annual event for each sport, hosting a minimum of one national championship a year (when feasible), and highlighting individual athletes as opposed to the entire team.

Not every Division I institution will be in a position to employ a professional solely for the purpose of promoting non-revenue sports. The resources for various special promotion efforts will also vary considerably from one institution to another.

9. *Action plan*:
   a. *Performance Standard for coaches*: Demonstrated ability to promote their sport will be one of the performance standards for the selection and evaluation of coaches. In the long run, this standard will be a measure of total coaching effectiveness because the quality product is essential for successful promotion.
   b. *Special consideration for women's sports*: At least one or two women's sports will be targeted for special promotional efforts. Although women's sports will also be promoted on the basis of product analysis, there is a need to take into account the differences in the stage of development for women's sports.

CONCLUSION

We began by discussing this topic of promoting non-revenue sports as being both an issue and a problem. In the final analysis, it would appear that the latter is the prime consideration. There is not much of an issue regarding the promotion of a non-revenue sport, *provided* that sport is deserving of promotion. The problem is essentially twofold: (1) determining what should be promoted, and (2) assessing how this can be most effectively accomplished. Hopefully, product analysis will contribute to solving the first part of the problem, and the second part will be approached with promotion as a performance standard for coaches. The University of Connecticut case study is a vivid testimony of the significant role of the coach in promoting a non-revenue sport.

REFERENCES

Deegan, A. X. and Fritz, R. J. *MBO Goes To College*. Boulder, Colorado: The Regents of the University of Colorado, 1975.

Lopiano, D. A. "Selling Women's Athletics: Realities and Potentials." *Athletic Purchasing and Facilities*, October 1980, Vol. 4, No. 10, pp. 8-14.

Palmisano, M. "Promoting Your Non-Revenue Sports." Athletic Purchasing and Facilities, April 1982, Vol. 6, No. 4, pp. 84-86.

17

Facility Funding

There seems to be little doubt that fine facilities are essential if a school is to offer a high-quality sport or athletic program. While it is true that the athlete is the top priority in highly organized sport, and the participant is the number one consideration in recreational sport programs, it is also true that the ability to attract, retain, and develop the athlete or recreational participant is directly dependent on the quality of the facilities. This is another "chicken and egg" situation. One of the reasons that Syracuse University has fine basketball teams is that players are attracted by the idea of playing in the Carrier Dome. On the other hand, the success of the team contributes to funding for facilities.

Facility funding for sport programs is a broad topic because one finds a wide scope of facilities utilized by diverse sport organizations. These facilities range from large arenas and stadia for major spectator sports to small specific facilities for recreational participation. The organizations using these facilities may be professional sport teams, individual professional sports, private clubs, corporations, the military, community recreation programs, and schools or colleges. The latter category, schools or colleges, will be the focus for examination in this chapter. Policies are particularly critical in this area due to the need to compete for institutional funds. Also, school and college sport facilities tend to run the gamut in terms of type and size. The consideration will largely center on college sport facilities, but many of these points apply equally as well to elementary and high school facilities.

THE PROCESS

Funding athletic or sport facilities is a complex process that requires careful organization and planning. It involves identifying and justifying needs, locating the sources of funds, preparing a financing plan and, finally, mounting a drive to secure the funding.

The first step may often be overlooked. Policymakers must review the institutional policy toward sport, athletics, and physical education to ascertain the goals or objectives of the institutions in this area. To a large extent, this will determine the necessary facilities and the possible funding.

Such review would include emphasis on different kinds of activity, participation of specific groups, potential community participation, and possible relationships with neighboring institutions.

With respect to funding for a facility, one of the steps is the formation of a development team. The development program is a two-stage operation requiring a preliminary survey to establish funding potential followed by a formal fund-raising campaign. The team charged with mounting a development program should comprise individuals who will administer all phases of the project, including a member of the institution management/planning unit, a marketing/public relations person, a financial consultant, and one or more administrators from the athletic department.

When there is a need for a specific fund-raising campaign, it is often desirable to use one or more consultants to assess the funding potential, develop a financing plan, and orchestrate a drive for funds. George Casey (1982) presented guidelines as to when, why, and how professional counsel should be used in a fund-raising campaign.

> Seeking professional counsel should be considered when the objective is in the range of $200,000 or more. While this figure is somewhat arbitrary, it should be recognized that the costs per dollar raised will be higher for a campaign at this level than for a much larger objective. . . .
>
> Professional counsel normally conducts a fund-raising appeal more speedily and economically than the client's staff. Wide experience and training equip the fund-raising professional to determine the most effective and cost-efficient procedures for a campaign. . . .
>
> A major advantage of employing a firm specializing in fund-raising counsel is 'back-up' service. If, for any reason, the campaign director becomes incapacitated, a competent replacement is available, avoiding a delay should the institution be forced to seek a substitute. . . .
>
> The presence of accredited professional counsel with a known record of success tends to create an air of confidence. . . .
>
> It is better practice to select professional counsel early in the planning process than to wish later that more time were available. If your organization is not ready for a campaign, you will be so advised. The professional firm can assist you in getting ready. (pp. 70, 73-74)

Another early organizational step is to evaluate the need for either new or improved facilities within the context of the institution's total operation. There are relatively few occasions when a totally new facility is clearly mandated from the outset. Most institutions will begin by carefully assessing existing athletic facilities to determine whether they are adequate to meet the needs of the program. (This tends to be particularly critical for recreational sport facilities at institutions that are trying to meet increased demands for space.) Many existing facilities have become obsolete due to the greater participation of women in all sports and the necessity to meet the needs of special groups, especially participants with handicapped conditions.

David L. Finci, director and senior vice president of the Eggers Group, which specializes in sports facilities planning, (1980) offered the following advice regarding the bottom line, cost data, financing, and project budget estimate.

> The information gathered must be translated into cost data, which must go beyond the actual costs of initial alterations to the physical structures or new construction and include operations and maintenance costs over the projected planning period.
>
> While alterations to existing mechanical and electrical systems may ultimately result in more efficient operations, these economies must be weighed against the costs of making such changes and compared with the life cycle costs of building anew. Assessing the costs of alterations is a complex business. Generally speaking, one can assume that if the costs of alterations approaches 50 per cent of the cost of new construction, then it does not make sense to embark upon them.

Other information must also be obtained during the preliminary planning. There should be a survey of the attitudes of students, faculty, staff, administrators, and other users regarding the existing facilities and programs. The extent of such a survey will largely depend on the specific nature of the projected facility. Research into future programs and trends is also needed. What is being done by other institutions in terms of facility development? What kind of changes are taking place locally, regionally, and nationally in terms of program development and sport popularity? Finally, and most importantly, the preliminary planning or organizational process is completed by identifying the possible sources of funding and assessing the intensity of competition for funds. This includes marshalling support for the programs from units inside and outside the institution. Such groups would likely be the student government association, the alumni office, faculty senate, related cultural groups, and various community organizations.

Possible Sources of Funding

When competing for funds, an athletic department must justify the need for a facility and demonstrate a viable plan for financing. The potential sources of funding vary greatly, depending on the nature of the institution. Generally speaking, the following sources may be available:

1. Institutional funds: These are funds specifically appropriated for facilities. The appropriation would come from the state in the case of a public college or university, from the school district for a public school, or from the trustees for a private institution.

2. Revenue from intercollegiate athletic events: This source applies to relatively few institutions in terms of the entire collegiate spectrum.
3. Special fund raising drive: In many cases, this is basically in the form of alumni support. However, this source is by no means limited to alumni for most institutions.
4. Student fees: As noted later, this is a growing source of funding particularly for recreational facilities.
5. User fees: This was typically used more frequently outside the school and college environment, but the potential for development is also there in this setting.
6. Corporate funding: This may also be tied in with the special fund-raising drive.

There are other possibilities, depending on the institution. The above appear to be the more viable alternatives. Nevertheless, the situation has changed considerably in recent years. Robert Bronzan, an athletic facilities consultant for APER Consulting Services in Danville, California, (1984) identifies what appears to be the major change.

Until some 12 years ago, two major sources existed for funding athletic, recreation, and special spectator event facilities on state college and university campuses. The nation is dotted with institutions who received state monies to construct stadiums, arenas, gymnasiums, natatoriums, tracks and other types of sports-related facilities. This source has virtually disappeared, however, except for Sun Belt states currently experiencing population and economic explosions. Economic and political signs point to continued austerity programs for most states.

The other major funding source in the past was the Department of Intercollegiate Athletics (Men). Some institutions, private and public, enjoyed profitable athletic programs in football and basketball. Surplus funds were channeled to construct facilities which have been used also for recreation and fitness programs. However, during the past decade a limited number of athletic programs have realized a profit. The causes are many, but leading are inflated operational costs, increases in the number of intercollegiate sports sponsored, particularly the addition of women sports, and the issuing of grants-in-aid to more students. (p. 18)

Student Fees: Bronzan said that the real answer for many institutions, particularly for recreational sport facilities, is to provide facility funding through student fees. Even though construction for athletic and physical education facilities has lagged because of budget cuts, there has been a surge in recreational facility construction. Incoming college freshmen, reflecting a societal trend, have become more involved in sports, exercise, and fitness programs. Thus, they are willing to dig into their pockets to fund such facilities. On an increasing number of campuses, students have voted to assess themselves additional fees to fund the construction of recreation centers. The facilities are usually financed through long-term notes. Such fees have ranged all the way from $10 to $80 per year, depending on the scope of the project and the term of the financing.

Programs financed by these self-assessed student fees also reflect a change in terms of an emphasis on "open recreation," as opposed to intramural sport or club sport. Again, this reflects a societal trend away from the more highly structured sport activities to individual exercise and fitness pursuits. The shift has also affected the role of administrators, who recognize that when students fund a facility, they also expect to have a direct voice in determining design, operational policies and practices, and program content.

Bronzan cautioned that the groundwork must be carefully laid if facilities are to be funded from the student fee source. Approval is usually by means of a referendum, but there are many earlier steps. A referendum campaign should probably begin at least three years before the voting year. This provides time to identify and nurture the facility need with three successive freshman classes, using selected student leaders who recognize the need and favor student financing. This is largely accomplished through a "Central Campaign Committee," which includes representation from various components of the institution. Strategy and tactics are very important in planning such a campaign, including the timing of the referendum. Bronzan suggests two time periods which may prove to be advantageous. One of these is six to eight weeks after the registration for the fall term, a time during which students tend to be enthusiastic and are more likely to have a feeling of financial security. At this point in the academic year, there is also less time for the opposition to get organized. The other time might be about three to four weeks prior to the end of the academic year. Seniors are thinking about graduation, and the fees will not apply to them. The students generally are also more likely to be thinking about final examinations than mounting opposition to a fee structure.

User Fees: Another type of fee structure is increasingly employed in providing funding for recreational sport facilities. This is the user fee, which may also be called the "pay as you play" or "pay as you go" fee. In the educational setting, the essential difference between the student fee and the user fee is that the former is an across-the-board assessment of all students, regardless of the extent to which any individual or group may use the sport facilities. Within the past 10 years, the user-pay concept has been implemented frequently in municipal recreation programs, but there is potential for utilizing this kind of fee in the school and college context.

Perhaps the most significant factor in this form of facility financing is to have definite policies that determine the fee structure and are applied consistently. For example, this kind of fee is particularly applicable to private groups who wish to rent the facility. Beyond that, various questions arise. Should students be assessed user fees, particularly if they have already been assessed through a general fee structure? Should faculty and staff be required to pay user fees? If so, should the fee structure be set at a different level than it is for other users? Some groups or programs may receive preferential treatment in using the facilities. Should the fee structure be set accordingly? An institution may also decide that it should charge lower rates for beginners programs than it does for advanced programs, working from the assumption that it has an obligation to introduce people to various sport activities.

Aside from the differences among users, there is one other major complication in having user fees as a source of facility funding: to determine the amount of the assessment for any given group. What are the real costs in providing and operating the facility? The number of users has to be related to the total costs. That can be most difficult to determine, particularly in the school or college setting. How much does it cost to keep the building or other facility open? Facility costs must be distinguished from program costs. Administrators need accurate cost assessments in order to establish an appropriate scale of fees.

Corporate Funding: The two previous funding sources particularly apply to recreational sport programs, even though student fees are also assessed to fund spectator sport facilities. Another possible option for major funding of spectator sport facilities is corporate funding, although this is also very much related to the special fund-raising drive and alumni contributions. Of course, either of the latter two possibilities extend beyond corporate funding per se.

There is little doubt that corporate funding is one of the more effective means of promoting and generating revenue in the sport enterprise generally. With respect to facility funding, the potential is enriched by the possibility that the business firm may have the opportunity to support and have its name identified with a specific, permanent project. One cardinal rule of thumb more or less applies to any form of corporate involvement. If an institution can show benefits from a company's involvement, the company is likely to get involved, if it has the money.

There is a cloud on the horizon, however, in terms of the future possibilities for corporate support. Reductions in tax incentives may hurt college athletic fund-raising. The 1986 IRS decision (Ruling 86-83) limits tax deductions to athletic programs, if the contribution is tied to the donor's ability to gain preferential seating at athletic contests. Furthermore, the 1986 Tax Reform Act limited the tax deduction for business entertainment expenses to 80 percent. Most threatening, in terms of its impact on new stadium construction and renovation, is the three-year phase out of tax deductions for skyboxes. By 1989, annual leases on skyboxes will be no longer deductible. The situation at the University of Oregon provides a case in point in terms of how tax reform might severely limit corporate funding.

Bill Byrne thought he had it all figured out: 54 skyboxes at $25,000 a year for 10 years would bring in enough extra revenue to give the University of Oregon's Autzen Stadium a facelift, and add 13,000 needed seats to boot.

That was B.T.R. (Before Tax Reform), when a skybox lessee could blithely write off the cost of his or her box as a tax-deductible business expense. Under the Tax Reform Act of 1986, those deductions will be phased out by 1989.

Today, the Oregon athletic director's plans are considerably more restrained. The skybox plan has been scaled back to 22, and only 11 of them are spoken for, although Byrne originally had 20 commitments. For now, a shell large enough to contain all 22 skyboxes will be constructed, but the future is uncertain enough that Byrne says he will finish each box as it is needed. . . .

Other revenue will be generated by setting aside reserve preferential seating for supporters who contribute at least $1,500 to the Oregon athletic program.

Even that strategy - a tried and true method of fund raising is not as simple as it once was. Under IRS Ruling 86-83, contributions to athletic programs may not be tax deductible if the contribution entitles the donor to purchase game tickets that would not be available to him or her otherwise.

The IRS ruling requires the recipient institution to determine how much, if any, of the contribution is deductible.

In Byrne's case, he has a number of long-term season-ticket holders already occupying seats in the preferential-seating section. Those patrons will be able to keep their seats under a grandfather clause. In the meantime, Byrne will have supporters who paid $1,500 to $2,000 for the right to buy tickets sitting next to people who paid for nothing but the ticket itself. Out of that, Byrne is expected to come up with a coherent policy under which donors can claim their tax deductions.

"It's been an administrative nightmare," says Byrne. (*Athletic Business*, May, 1987, p. 22)

Overall, there tends to be some difference of opinion among athletic directors regarding the impact of the change in tax legislation. In general, the private institutions depend more on fund raising than the state colleges and universities. However, their alumni may also be more loyal and may continue to contribute without the tax incentive. A further complication is adverse publicity for college athletics, resulting from scandals in certain programs. In the final analysis, whether it be corporate funding or broader means of fund raising, the bottom line is to develop and maintain good personal relationships with the supporters of the athletic program.

CASE EXAMPLES

There is no single formula for facility planning or facility funding. Although all college athletic departments face a continued need to upgrade their sport or athletic facilities in some way or another, the common ground ends there. Probably the only other similarity is that there is always some resistance to providing money for new athletic facilities, due to the belief that classrooms, laboratories, and libraries should have priority on college campuses. Beyond that, planning and funding sport or athletic facilities depends on the nature of the program and the institution. The following case examples illustrate some of the differences and complexities.

The Ohio State University

Starting in 1984, the athletic department developed a 25-year master plan to provide up to $79 million worth of facility improvements by adding new facilities and renovating existing facilities. This master plan, completed in January 1986 at a cost of approximately $200,000, calls for a two-phase construction schedule: the "Scarlet Phase," to be completed by 1990, at an estimated cost of between $41 million and $45 million; and the "Gray Phase," to begin in 1991, projected to cost between $27 million and $34 million. Facility renovation would include about $15 million to $20 million for the Ohio Stadium which was completed in 1922.

The funding for all these new or renovated athletic facilities will come from a university-wide capital campaign aimed at raising $350 million for a variety of academic, athletic, and extracurricular facilities. This master plan is for a 25-year period. Prior to this development, the athletic department had not undertaken a major facility project in 20 years.

The principal-in-charge of the facilities plan was architect Dennis Wellner, vice president of Hellmuth, Obata and Kassabaum Sports Facilities Group (HOK). He noted that the funding for the athletic facilities was facilitated by the tie-in with the $350 million for academic and service facilities for the entire university. Another member of the department (master planning) team was Robert Bronzan, who also had the valuable background as a teacher, coach, and athletic director. (*Athletic Business*, Jan. 1987, pp. 18-23)

UCLA - The Wooden Center

The university's major spectator arena, Pauley Pavilion, was built in the late 1960s. At that time, the plan was to add two complementary buildings in the future. One of these, a building for athletic department administrators, was built. The second, a recreational sport building, did not materialize as planned.

Another feasibility study for this second building was conducted in 1977, a time when funds for the University of California system were being constricted by the state government. State funding would not be available. The only real possibilities for funding this building were private financing through a fund-raising effort and student-assessed fees.

It was also apparent that a fund-raising drive was not likely to be successful if the building was only intended for recreational purposes. Potential donors preferred to support the intercollegiate athletic program. The answer was to extend the Wooden Center building project to include additional athletic facilities. That stimulated the support of the boosters, who contributed $2.5 million. The remainder of the total cost for the building was financed by bonds underwritten by the student-assessed fees. After the first student referendum failed in 1977, a second referendum passed overwhelmingly the following year.

Ground for the Wooden Center was broken in late 1980. The building was completed in 1983 at a cost of $80 per square foot or $8 million. It is a facility which includes two gymnasia, racquetball and squash courts, a gymnastics room, recreation and intramural office space, activity rooms and underground parking for 450 cars. (*Athletic Business*, May 1986, pp. 38-45)

Gustavus Adolphus College - The Lund Center

This comprehensive facility is an excellent example of funding through alumni support. The building includes a "multisport forum," an ice arena with seating for 1,200, a natatorium, gymnastics studio, five handball/racquetball courts, a weight room, wrestling room, and various support facilities. The forum also has spectator seating for 3,000. The $10.8 million, 220,000 square-foot complex was completely funded with private funds. Short-term financing of $3 million at 8 percent was used to get started. The remainder of the funds were generated through foundations and personal gifts. There were 5,000 individual gifts. These included a $1 million contribution from the Russell T. Lund family as well as three other private donations of more than $600,000.

Even the operational funds are not derived from student fees. There is an on-going alumni solicitation program with pledges from those who support this kind of campus activity.

The athletic department increased the number of varsity sports from seven to 23, many of which were for the women's program. In addition, the building has become a social center for the campus, with a strong interest in open recreation. The building was designed to put particular emphasis on separating intercollegiate events from intramural and open recreation activities. (*Athletic Business*, Jan. 1986, pp. 34-37)

The University of California at Berkeley-Recreational Sports Center

This $13.5 million facility was completed in 1984. As early as 1958, the need for such a facility was recognized. However, it was not until 1981 that the regents authorized interim financing during construction after 61 percent of the voting students (51 percent of the student body), in a campus-wide referendum, voted to assess themselves an annual fee to amortize the cost of building construction. The requirements for approval were that at least 25 percent of the students must vote with at least 55 percent voting in favor of the mandated fee.

An extensive promotional campaign was used to gain student support for the referendum. This included two campus-wide surveys to determine student interest in the proposal and the possibility of student financing. During the final three months preceding the referendum, student leaders and staff members from the department of recreational sports intensified the promotional effort.

The construction costs of the building are entirely funded from the student fee with the students being assessed $28.50 per semester. The fee collection began when the facility was completed and will remain in effect for the duration of the 30-year revenue bonds used to provide the funds for the project.

The "multi-use" concept was central in designing the facility. However, this did not include provisions for a major spectator facility. The building was clearly established to have recreational programs as the functional priority. As with other facilities of this type, the recreational sports center also serves as a social gathering spot for students.

Due to the source of funding, students had a major role in determining the type of building that was constructed. They also had input in developing policies and continue to be a major voice in the operation. (*Athletic Purchasing* and *Facilities*, June 1981, pp. 42-46 & *Athletic Business*, Dec. 1985, pp. 24-27)

Concordia College - Outdoor Track

This NCAA Division III college had conducted a track and field program for several years without having its own outdoor track facility. The base project for an outdoor track was completed in 1979, but the college was unable to add a quality synthetic top surface due to other priorities in the general budget.

In January of 1983, the college administration gave approval for a special fund-raising drive to finance the completion of the track through the Letter Club. The latter was not the typical booster club but, rather, an organization of alumni athletes.

This special fund-raising project for the track was designed not to conflict with the regular fund-raising efforts of the college's development office. The drive was targeted toward letter receivers and other supporters of the athletic program who were more likely to support this kind of project. The idea was to obtain relatively small contributions from as many people as possible.

The initial goal for the drive was set at $200,000. This could be reached by obtaining a $500 pledge from each of 400 people. The pledge was called a "meter" to relate to the 400 meters of the circumference of the track. Potential donors were encouraged to at least buy a "meter" for $500. Further incentive was to buy two "meters" and thus become a member of the college's "C-400 Club." (The latter had been established in 1955 for the purpose of college development generally. A member of the club pledges to contribute $1,000 to the college over a four-year period.) Either type of pledge could be paid over a four-year span. Of course, pledges of all amounts were accepted, and these ranged from $5 to $1,000.

A special letter, outlining the needs for an all-weather track, was sent out to the target group of alumni. This was followed by a phon-a-thon by which local alumni contacted other alumni through long-distance calls.

The results were very successful. By the end of May 1983, $146,000 had been pledged. The total cost of the track was projected at $173,000, and construction began in August. The track was completed and dedicated at the Homecoming on October 1, 1983. At that time, the amount pledged had risen to $163,000. (*Athletic Business*, June 1984, pp. 104-106)

Babson College - The Babson Recreation Center

Babson College, a small college with an undergraduate enrollment of only 1,250, was able to build a $1.5-million multi-use recreation center and athletic complex in the mid 1970s through unique financing.

The 92,000-square-foot facility includes an ice hockey rink with a 1,500 seating capacity, eight indoor tennis courts, saunas, locker rooms, pro shop, snack bar, a first aid room, and a nursery.

The idea for the center arose from the need for a hockey rink both for Babson College and the Wellesley, Massachusetts community where the college is located. The college had more than 200 acres of unused land, jointly owned with Babson Reports, Inc. In searching for a location for a hockey rink in Wellesley, the Babson Recreation Center, Inc. (BRC) approached the college with an offer to buy or rent a 26-acre piece of land.

The decision was to rent the land with the following financial arrangements for the center. The stock in BRC was distributed three ways: 1) 25 percent is owned by the college from its endowment; 2) 25 percent is owned by the Babson Organization, Inc., a holding company for the business interests of the late Roger Babson, the founder of the college; 3) 50 percent is owned by sports-minded investors in the community. The center was expected to realize a profit by the second year of operation through memberships in the tennis facilities and rental of the ice rink.

For the college, the plan was advantageous. It built an athletic complex on the campus for only a 25 percent investment in the common stock. The college also receives rent for the use of the land and dividends as a stockholder. The investors made a profit. There was even a benefit for the taxpayers in Wellesley because the land for the center was previously tax exempt.

The circumstances surrounding the case may be somewhat unique to Babson, particularly the availability of such land and the corporate relationship. Nevertheless, the case offers a stimulating example of what can be done through innovative facility funding. (*Athletic Purchasing and Facilities*, October 1978, pp. 63-64)

Fredericktown, Ohio - High School Field House

The field house on the high school grounds in Fredericktown, Ohio was recognized as a "Facility of Merit" in 1982. The complex is valued at $175,000, but the cost was about $85,000.

No school or taxpayer funds were used in building the facility. Funding was through the Fredericktown Boosters Club. This began in the mid-1970s with the creation of the "200 Club," which contributed $4,000 a year to the Booster Club. The boosters also operated a concessions trailer at the county fair, local produce shows, and home football games. Other funds were generated through donations from individuals and business organizations. For example, one firm matched any donation of $25 or more from an employee.

The key to the low construction cost and the value of the facility was donated materials and labor. Total construction time was four months, and all the labor, except for block and brick work, was donated.

This 4,700-square-foot complex is used for all spring sports and football. Also included in the building are a training room, a large concession area, ticket rooms, and locker rooms. (*Athletic Purchasing and Facilities*, August 1983, pp. 44-46)

CONCLUSION AND POLICY GUIDELINES

The case examples and other information presented in this chapter should demonstrate that facility funding is a fairly elusive policy area. A policy for funding facilities does not neatly fit the typical conception of the nature of policy making. In the first chapter we noted that policy development is the continuous process of making significant, standing decisions on recurring matters. Athletic facilities are not built every day or even every year or every five years on any given campus. In addition, the various possibilities for facility funding are determined by particular situations in colleges and universities. It is most difficult to propose general policies for facilities funding. Nevertheless, the following policy guidelines are parameters which might prove useful to any collegiate or high school athletic department in developing a long-term stance toward facility funding.

1. Facility funding cannot be separated from facility planning. In most cases, the potential sources for funding are dependent on the type of facility planned and when it is planned.
2. Facility planning, and thus facility funding, should begin with an assessment of the institutional philosophy toward athletics, sport, physical education, recreation. Such philosophy will determine the planning, and the planning will determine the funding.
3. Very early in the planning or organizational process, it is important to establish a development team which will have the responsibility for mounting a development program. Such a team should include a core of members who will manage all phases of the project as well as specialty consultants and representatives from various campus interests.
4. Professional counsel can be very important, if not absolutely essential, in facility funding. The institution should seek consulting services to assess the funding potential, develop a financing plan, and orchestrate a drive for funds.
5. Before any planning can proceed, the need for the facility must be established. Basically, this is the justification procedure. There should be a comprehensive, detailed evaluation which compares existing facilities with projected demands and optimal criteria. In some cases, the evaluation may show that the solution to a facility problem may be a combination of upgrading existing facilities and adding some new construction.
6. Even though there are various forms of multi-use facilities, the primary use of the facility should be the basic determinant in developing a financing plan. A building which is first and foremost designed for recreational sport use would be funded differently than one that is intended for spectator sport. In recreational sport buildings, financing policies are more likely to be directed toward student fees and/or user fees, while spectator facilities offer real potential for alumni support, corporate funding, and other forms of special fund-raising drives.

REFERENCES

"A Community-Built High School Athletic Center." *Athletic Purchasing and Facilities*, Vol. 7, No. 8, Aug. 1983, pp. 44-46.
"A Legacy Lives On: The John Wooden Center." *Athletic Business*, Vol. 10, No. 5, May 1986, pp. 38-45.
"A Place of Their Own." *Athletic Business*, Vol. 9, No. 12, Dec. 1985, pp. 24-27.
Bauman, M. "Unique Financing Provides Babson College With a New Athletic Complex." *Athletic Purchasing and Facilities*, Vol. 2, No. 5, Oct. 1978, pp. 63-64.
Bronzan, R. T. "Student Fees: A New Source for Funding Facilities." *Athletic Business*, Vol. 8, No. 3, March 1984, pp. 18-22.
Casey, G. R. "Using Professional Counsel in Your Fund-Raising Campaign." *Athletic Purchasing and Facilities*, Vol. 6, No. 3, March 1982, pp. 70-74.
"Comprehensive Facility Is Pride of Small College." *Athletic Business*, Vol. 10, No. 1, Jan. 1986, pp. 34-37.
Finci, D. L. "Need New Facilities? Don't Overlook the Old." *Athletic Purchasing and Facilities*, Vol. 5, No. 3, March 1981, pp. 24-30.

"How to Work With a 'Corporate Partner.' " *Athletic Purchasing and Facilities*, Vol. 5, No. 3, March 1981, pp. 24-30.

"How Will you Fund Your Athletic Facility?" *Athletic Purchasing and Facilities*, Vol. 4, No. 6, June 1980, pp. 31-36.

Manning. B. "Creative Planning: Berkeley's Recreational Sports Complex." *Athletic Purchasing and Facilities*, Vol. 5, No. 6, June 1981, pp. 42-46.

"Masters of Their Fate." *Athletic Business*, Vol. 11, No. 1, Jan. 1987, pp. 18-23.

McCuaig, K. "Seeking Facility Fees that Make Sense." *Athletic Business*, Vol. 8, No. 11, Nov. 1984, pp. 36-41.

Pipho, A. "New Track Fund-Raiser Targeted Athletic Alumni." *Athletic Business*, Vol. 8, No. 6, June 1984, pp. 104-106.

"Recreation on Campus: The New Building Boom." *Athletic Business*, Vol. 9, No. 4, April 1985, pp. 10-16.

"Scandals and Taxes." *Athletic Business*, Vol. 11, No. 5, May 1987, pp. 20, 22, 24-25.

18

Priorities For Facility Usage

Whenever a facility is to be shared by more than one program or various components of a single program, a three-part policy question always has to be addressed: *who* should be allowed to use *what*, and *when*? The answer becomes a matter of establishing priorities for facility usage. Such priorities are particularly significant in school and college sport programs due to the diversified nature of these programs and the prominence of multi-use facilities.

In the college environment one usually begins with the need to determine priorities among the three major components of the total sport program: instructional classes, intramural activities, and intercollegiate athletics. That traditional division is even further complicated today by the popularity of "open recreation." In the area of intramural activities, the facilities manager must make scheduling decisions regarding highly organized competitive events and informal sport participation.

Priorities can only be established after determining the institutional standards in the total sport program. Every institution has specific needs or goals regarding the balance between competitive intercollegiate athletic events, on the one end of the continuum, and relatively unstructured recreational sport programs, on the other.

In a few Division I institutions, determining priorities for facility usage may not be a problem. Due to the revenue from gate receipts and television contracts, these select universities are able to offer diversified sport programs without particular attention to priority usage. Nevertheless, few colleges or universities are able to completely separate the use of facilities to the extent that a certain building is only for recreational use whereas another is clearly used as an intercollegiate athletic arena. In the vast majority of institutions, the matter of priorities for facility usage is an important policy area.

Policy decisions on facility usage priorities must first and foremost be based on the institutional stance toward this realm of student activity.

What are the basic choices? Also, what is the possible rationale for granting any one activity preferential treatment?

1. Intercollegiate Athletics: This area is given top priority in the vast majority of institutions, even though there may be a reluctance to admit to this stance. For universities with "high powered" athletic programs, the rationale is simple and clear. The revenue-producing sports provide not only the income to support the entire sport program but also the visibility to enhance the image of the institution. For many other colleges and universities, establishment of a priority in this area may be more complex. Intercollegiate athletics does provide selected athletes the opportunity for the pursuit of excellence. Beyond that, athletics can serve as a major point of institutional identification for both students and alumni. Depending on the specific nature of the institution and the athletic program, that in itself may be sufficient reason to give top priority to intercollegiate athletics.(Of course, another complication in this area is that involving priorities for facility usage among the various athletic teams. In the case of a revenue-producing sport the decision is not that difficult with the possible exception of priorities among men's and women's sports. Yet, for most sports, the total impact of each sport will have to be carefully assessed. In large athletic programs, the matter of junior varsity sports poses a further complication. For example, should a junior varsity sport have precedence over intramural or club sport activity?)
2. Club Sport Usage: The basic rationale for establishing a priority in this area is that a club sport tends to be much more student-centered. Most club sports are initiated and controlled by students. Club sports also provide many of the benefits of intercollegiate athletic programs, excluding visibility. If a facility is primarily funded through student fees, the priority of club usage may be rather clearly established. As with intercollegiate athletics, there is no magic answer regarding how to determine priorities for usage among various club groups. The total impact of each club sport has to be assessed.
3. Intramural Sport Usage: This aspect of the total sport program offers the distinct advantage of offering organized, competitive sport activities to a relatively large percentage of the student body. As with club sport, intramurals are likely to be student-centered and will probably receive higher priority in facilities financed through student fees. Two possible limitations may be factors in lowering the priority in particular institutions and situations. Intramural sport does not provide the same kind of extension or competition offered through a club sport program,

and the popularity of the more structured intramural program may be reduced by the growing interest in "open recreation."

4. Instructional Class Usage: Based on the premise that schools and colleges exist primarily for the purpose of offering formal instruction for students, there is always some logic in deciding that an instructional class should receive top priority among various components of the total sport program. That position has considerable merit at the theoretical level, but before college priorities can be established in this area, other factors have to be considered. Many college students have acquired various sport skills and knowledge prior to entering college. Also, it can be argued that the education in sport and through sport is not necessarily best facilitated through the instructional class.

5. Drop-in Usage: This possibility for sport facility usage was identified earlier under the concept of "open recreation." If student interest in various forms of exercise and fitness programs is strong, this is very likely to be the top priority among the student-centered options. Some of the case examples in the previous chapter clearly indicated that this would be the top consideration if the facility is financed through student fees.

6. Rental/Special Group Usage: This possibility involves the use of facilities by external groups. In most cases, this type of usage will rank rather low, if not at the bottom, of the priority scale. The exceptions might be if a user fee is an important factor in facility financing or if the facility was built through a joint effort between the college and the community. The case of Babson College (see Chapter 17) is an example of the latter exception.

PRE-DESIGN OF MULTI-PURPOSE FACILITIES

The matter of establishing policies for facility usage cannot be separated from facility planning. Due to the group demands for multi-purpose facilities, one of the current trends is to utilize the "pre-design" services offered by architects. These services typically include space programming and scheduling. There is always one up-front question in any pre-design activity: what is the purpose of the facility? In the case of multi-purpose facilities, this question is not easily answered.

The process of pre-design begins with the establishment of a planning committee representing the interests of various potential user groups. Such a committee should have a leader who is not associated with the user groups and can provide more objective opinions regarding various needs. After the needs and interests of the groups are identified, the architect joins the committee. In most cases, there are conflicting interests. The architect meets with representatives of each user group and guides them through the process of defining specific needs.

Pre-design is not the magical answer to all problems and issues involving priorities for usage. Most decisions have to be made on a day-to-day basis. Programs are constantly changing in popularity and emphasis. There also are extenuating circumstances or emergencies that may negate any pre-design plan. All the variables are more or less demonstrated by the case examples which follow.

CASE EXAMPLES

Priorities must be determined among sports; among male, female, and coeducational sports; and among instructional classes, intramural activities, and intercollegiate teams. It is most difficult to be specific about a set of priorities that will be appropriate for any given institution. There are too many variables due to differences in program objectives and existing facilities. In the long run, the institutional philosophy should be the prime determinant. The following case examples demonstrate how some institutions have approached this policy area.

Temple University

In 1978, Temple University in Philadelphia developed its priority scheduling system (PSS). It is an excellent example of an attempt to accommodate diverse campus groups as well as to meet the needs of the off-campus community. The PSS operates through a facilities committee chaired by a facilities coordinator. The facilities committee determines the initial priority order for space assignments for each different facility. The facilities coordinator serves primarily as a communicator and acts as a problem-solver and referee in case of conflicts.

The PSS concept operates under the premise that each user group has the control of some space in a given facility for a specified period of time, assigned by mutual consent through the committee. A master schedule is developed by the facilities coordinator, who identifies the priority user group for each facility for each available block of time. Any remaining blocks of time are then made available to university and community groups on a first come, first served basis. This is done with the approval of the program director who controls that space. The entire framework for PSS is summarized as follows:

- Priority Scheduling System is designed to identify and assign program space for maximum and efficient use of all facilities.
- Facilities Committee is made up of representatives of all major user groups, plus facilities coordinator.
- Facilities coordinator chairs committee and oversees implementation of scheduling system.
- Facilities Committee assigns priority for each facility.
- Priority schedule is developed for each facility area based on priority order and available time blocks.

- Facilities coordinator draws up master schedule.
- Each user group 'controls' its assigned time block and space.
- Unused or under-utilized time slots available for use by other groups by request.
- User group with priority on requested time slot approves or denies request.
- Facilities coordinator attempts to resolve conflicts or brings disputes to the committee.
- Priority schedule includes agreement clauses to cover foreseeable scheduling problems.
- Priority schedule also used as basis for determining contributions of each user group to equipment maintenance budget. (*Athletic Business*, March 1986, p.61)

Vincennes University

Vincennes University is a junior college in Vincennes, Indiana with an enrollment of 3,000 students. Its major indoor sport facility is called the "Physical Education Complex," reflecting both the strong emphasis on physical education at the university and the fact that the facility was built with a federal grant for education. Michael L. Ross, who was hired as director of the facility before its completion, recognized the need for a policy handbook to define specific usage guidelines.

Policies were established with the approval of the university's administration. Essentially these policies reflected the following usage priorities.

1. Physical education for the students
2. Intercollegiate athletic teams
3. Recreational programs for students, faculty, and staff
4. Community programs

Excerpts from Vincennes "usage policy handbook" (Exhibit 18-1) provide an excellent example of how sound policies can be developed.

Springfield College

Springfield College is a vivid example of the importance of having priority policies in place whenever there is a crisis involving facilities. The college was founded in 1885 as "A School For Christian Workers." Its name was changed to The International YMCA Training School in 1890 and, later, to The International YMCA College in 1912. In 1953, the institution adopted the present name of Springfield College. The institution has consistently fulfilled its primary purpose of educating students for service oriented professions. In the area of sport and exercise, Springfield's reputation for preparing physical educators is well established.

The college faced a crisis on May 10, 1979, when the Memorial Field House was condemned. That field house was originally constructed as a "drill hall" at the Naval Training Center in Sampson, New York. In 1942 it was brought to Springfield and reestablished at a cost of $160,000. Prior to

EXHIBIT 18-1. Vincennes University Physical Education Complex - Excerpts from
Usage Policy Handbook

Statements of Objectives by Priorities
1. To provide health, physical education and recreation classes for Vincennes University students.
2. To provide athletic opportunities for Vincennes University sponsored athletic programs.
3. To provide free time recreational facilities for the university students, faculty and staff.
4. To provide recreational facilities for community adults and families.
5. To provide facilities for Vincennes University sponsored activities.

Statement of Philosophy
   The Physical Education Complex at Vincennes University is primarily for the use of its students, faculty and staff. The educational pursuits of the students are the first priorities. Aligned with their structured educational classes, the facility is so organized as to satisfy the recreational needs of the university affiliated persons.
   Since it is sometimes necessary to exclude some interests for the pursuits of others, the administration attempts to provide the most educational and recreational opportunities for the most people in a wholesome and safe manner.
   Abuse or ill use of the facility will not be tolerated.
   Secondly, it is felt that since this facility will accommodate more than just the university community, the administration attempts to offer recreational opportunities to the community at large with restrictions of priorities.

Administrative Organization
   There is to be a Building Coordinator under the administration of the Division of Health, Physical Education and Recreation.
   Since physical education is the stated primary objective of the facility, classes will always take priority, with athletics and intramurals next. Students' recreation generally begins at 3 p.m. on weekdays in all areas except the main gym floor and gymnastics area. The main floor is closed for recreation because of the potential damage to the finish. The complex closes at 10 p.m., with the pool closing at 9 p.m.
   Faculty and staff can use any recreational facility that is open with the exception that they do not disturb a class. Faculty and staff have exclusive use of the handball courts from 4 to 6:30 p.m. each weekday and the noon hour each weekday.
   Since it is impossible to offer classes and recreational opportunities to students, faculty and staff, and community, while at the same time have the facility closed for special events, there area severe limitations regarding scheduling of special events in the P.E. Complex. Overscheduling negates possibilities for night classes as well as recreation.

Criteria for Special Scheduling
1. All special scheduling must be oriented to Vincennes University students.
2. Regular traditional campus events will receive first priority.
3. All scheduling must be approved through the building coordinator's office at least one month in advance.
4. Any activity which can be accommodated by Beless Gym or Green Auditorium will be scheduled there first.
5. Charges for scheduling will include cost of maintenance crews.

Students
1. All students are members by having an I.D. card.
2. Any student enrolled at Vincennes University for six credit hours or less may pay the "Faculty and Staff" fee of $7 for the use of the facilities in the Physical Education Complex.
3. Lockers and towels are provided but each student is to provide his own combination lock.
4. Students have out-of-town guest privileges with a maximum of two per visit per student.
5. Any married student enrolled may buy a membership for their spouse for a fee of $7.

Faculty and Staff Athletic Club
1. Faculty and staff may buy an Athletic Club membership for their families for $15 a year and for an individual for $7 for one year.
2. Lockers and towels are provided but each member is to provide his own combination lock.
3. Faculty and Staff have unlimited guest privileges with discretion.
4. A faculty and staff person is determined by the fact that person received a check from Vincennes University.

Equipment Checkout
1. Equipment may be checked out of the equipment room by presenting and leaving an I.D. card for the equipment.

EXHIBIT 18-1 *(con't.)*

2. *Members are required to sign a card stating the conditions of the equipment and accepting responsibility for repayment of full price if the equipment is damaged by normal use or misuse.*

Main Gym Floor

The main gym floor is used for athletic contests, supervised men's and women's basketball practices and intramural events. Athletes must be accompanied by a coach and wear clean gym shoes to use the floor. The floor is closed to all other activities with designated exceptions because of excessive wear unsupervised play causes. Free play is frequently available on the upper deck basketball areas and Beless Gym offers a wood floor for recreational play.

Gymnastics Area

The gymnastics equipment and workout area is for physical education activity classes and recreation. Recreational time is set up for certain evenings and weekends each semester. There is always a supervisor in charge during these times. The area is not open any other times.

Weight Room

The weight room is used for physical education classes, recreation and Vincennes swim team practice. It is open daily for personal use. Weights are to be used in the correct manner. Any abuse will result in loss of privileges for the individual.

Handball Courts

Handball courts are open to all members. Faculty and staff have priority use from 4-6:30 p.m. daily. Sign-up for reservations starts at 1 p.m. each day. Persons may sign up at the courts to use them one hour. Any person is not to be in the courts more than one hour during times that other persons desire to use them.

Badminton and Tennis

The indoor badminton and tennis courts are available for use any time there are no classes or team practice going on. The same area accommodates recreational basketball; consequently, when the numbers demand, the area will be used for basketball.

Pool

The pool is open at designated open hours. There are separate times for faculty, staff and students' usage for which the community members are excluded. The community members' time is considered open to all categories.

Information Board and Monthly Calendar

A monthly calendar is in the main hall to tell what events will be happening in the Complex for planning. An information board keeps a day-to-day plan as to when different areas of the Complex are available.

Special Scheduling

The P.E. Complex is used for special events of Vincennes University such as the Miss V.U. Pageant, convocations, basketball games, Dad's Weekend, etc. Many of the recreational areas are closed during these times. A monthly schedule is available in the main hall so persons can adjust their schedules.

Requests for special scheduling should be made to the P.E. building coordinator.

I.D. Check

There is an I.D. check at the front door of the Complex during recreational hours. I.D.'s honored are as follows:

Faculty and Staff Athletic Cards
Vincennes University Athletic Club cards
Vincennes University current student cards

Guest Passes

The Athletic Club cards, other than student cards, are sold to adults 18 years old and older. If a family membership is bought, then the parents must accompany children under 18 years old. No card, consequently, no admittance, is available to persons under 18 years old.

Summer Schedule

After May 15, the Physical Education Complex goes on a summer schedule. The building is open from noon to 8 p.m. with the pool open from 4 p.m. to 8 p.m. The complex is closed on weekends. (*Athletic Purchasing and Facilities*, Nov. 1980, pp.68-69)

1979, plans called for a 50,000-square-foot addition to the facility, as part of the college's capital development campaign. However, it was necessary to drop that plan and demolish the building after inspection revealed that the "arch construction" did not meet minimum building code requirements. Subsequently, a new 5.3 million dollar physical education complex was built and dedicated on October 31, 1981. In the meantime, the college faced a major facility problem over a two-year period.

Prior to the condemnation, the priorities for use of the field house were well established: 1) physical education classes, 2) intercollegiate athletics, 3) intramural sport activities, 4) other college use, and 5) outside group use. Springfield College offered some 110 physical education skill courses to more than 2,300 students. Ninety percent of those courses depended on full or partial use of the field house. The college also sponsored 19 varsity sport teams at the time of condemnation. Each of those teams made some use of the field house. Intramural use of the facility involved eight separate activities in 1979. There was also a substantial time allotment for open recreation and some occasional use by outside groups.

When faced with the facility crisis in 1979, there were few alternatives. Physical education classes were the first consideration. The accommodation was made by using other building space on campus in addition to one off-campus facility. Quite naturally, the accommodation for the intercollegiate athletic teams was not as simple. It was necessary to use other facilities in the greater Springfield community. However, once again, any available space for practices or locker rooms was assigned after the physical education allocation. The intramural sport program was severely affected during the winter months. The strategy was to have an entirely coed operation involving half-court basketball, volleyball, stickball, floor hockey, and swimming during the late evening hours. The arrangements discouraged most potential participants. Open recreational use of the facilities was essentially not available.

Springfield College was able to maintain its two top priorities during the time of a facility crisis: 1) to offer classes for physical education majors and other students, and 2) to have a wide variety of competitive, intercollegiate athletic teams at the small college level.

Other Institutions

A limited survey of other colleges and universities during the period of 1985 to 1987 indicates that establishing priorities for facility usage is a rather elusive policy area. Representatives of most institutions seem to agree that it is important to have policies; yet, in most cases these policies are not in writing.

Results of the survey indicated that physical education classes have the top priority among the majority of institutions. However, that can be misleading. There may be a tendency to suggest that physical education is the top priority even when it is not. There is always an advantage in identifying a department with educational pursuits first. There is also a time factor to be considered. It is not very difficult to assign number one priority to physical education classes between the hours of 8 a.m. and 3 p.m. The real crunch in determining priorities comes when the same time period must be assigned for a multi-use facility.

Some of the respondents indicated that intercollegiate athletics had the top priority whenever there was a conflict in desired time for use of a facility. Due to the very nature of athletics, this is probably a straightforward response. The size of the institution and the overall nature of the program are also important factors in assessing any response in this regard. Physical education classes are minimal or virtually non-existent in some institutions. In others, physical education is still a requirement for all students. Those colleges with strong programs for physical education majors are also likely to have a different set of priorities.

Another conclusion from the survey is that intramural and recreational activities are typically identified as the third priority, after physical education and athletics. Whether or not the policies are in writing, there may be some logic in that response. Nevertheless, there is also a complication. In this chapter and the previous chapter, I noted a recent shift in student interest toward the "open recreation" programs. At many institutions, there may be a need to re-assess priorities.

CONCLUSION AND POLICY GUIDELINES

Among the various policy areas considered in this book, the matter of priorities for facility usage may be the most paradoxical. From one standpoint, it would seem very important to have policies at an institution with a multiple use facility. Yet, it appears this is not a prime policy area for many colleges and universities, since a fair number of institutions had no written policies.

I am inclined to believe that there is a need for written policies wherever there is a multiple-use facility. The following guidelines are suggested for determining priorities for facility usage.

1. The policies should reflect the institutional philosophy toward the entire realm of sport, athletics, physical education, and physical recreation. (Note: Other terms could also be used to identify this entire realm of student activity but the names are not really that important. The significant factor is that there are different kinds of specific activities under the general umbrella, and a determination has to be made as to which activities have priority whenever there is a conflict.)

2. Policies should be established by a facilities committee, which has representation from all potential user groups on campus. The

committee should include some combination of students, coaches, teachers, and administrators.

3. The committee should be chaired by a facilities coordinator who serves as a communicator and facilitator and who is available to resolve any unexpected conflicts daily.

4. The source or sources of funding for the facility should be an important factor in determining priorities for use. For example, with a facility exclusively funded from student fees, there is logic in granting the top priority to an intramural sport program or an "open recreation" program.

5. There should be some flexibility in the scheduling patterns to accommodate extenuating circumstances. Scheduling requires "situational sensitivity."

6. Whenever a new facility is built, the pre-design process (utilizing professional services) should be an important fact in determining initial priorities.

REFERENCES

Fitzgerald, L. E. and Chambers, R. L. "Scheduling Diplomacy." *Athletic Business*, Vol. 10, No. 3, March 1986, pp. 58-61.

Hartzell, R. "Scheduling Requires Situational Sensitivity." *Athletic Purchasing and Facilities*, Vol. 7, No. 9, Sept. 1983, pp. 24-28.

Parsely, J. D. "Solving the Facility Scheduling Puzzle." *Athletic Business*, Vol. 11, No. 1, Jan. 1987, pp. 72-75.

"Planning a Facility? Don't Just Design It - Pre-Design It." *Athletic Business*, Vol. 8, No. 6, June 1984, pp. 8-16.

Ross, M. L. "A Case Study in Usage Priorities." *Athletic Purchasing and Facilities*, Vol. 4, No. 11, Nov. 1980, pp. 66-69.

19
Marketing Golf

At this point, the reader might logically ask two questions: why golf and why marketing?. More to the point, why does a book on policy development include a chapter on marketing golf?

The answer to the first question is that golf is used here only as one example. Any one of several leisure time sports could have been selected. Golf is appropriate in that it attracts a relatively large number of participants, first-hand spectators, and television viewers.

Why is marketing included amidst the various policy areas which have been discussed thus far? The simple answer is that there is a need for marketing policies in the sport enterprise. This need is based both on the encompassing nature of marketing and the increased significance of marketing in contemporary society. In concluding his work, Buell (1984) targets the function of marketing most succinctly and appropriately:

> People who have not studied or practiced marketing usually think of it in terms of its promotional aspects, particularly selling and advertising. One of the purposes of this book has been to help you realize that marketing is far more than promotion. You should now be aware that marketing is the key to the entire process of securing and satisfying customers. Carried out well, this process results in profits for a business and the achievement of purpose by a nonprofit institution.
>
> In a free market economy consumers have a variety of choices as to how they will satisfy their needs. Therefore, those institutions that survive are the ones that are most efficient at identifying and fulfilling the needs and wants of consumers and user organizations. In one way or another, every part of a producer's organization serves the organizational purpose of creating and retaining customers. Marketing management is the catalyst for these activities. It identifies market needs and wants, helps marshall the organization's resources to produce desired products or services, and persuades potential customers to buy because its offerings will satisfy them. (p. 616)

The persistent problem for those who market golf is that golf has to compete with other leisure time activities for a share of the entertainment dollar. What can be done by the golf industry to increase, or at least maintain, the current share of the leisure time dollar?

Two interrelated objectives must be considered. One is to increase the number of golf participants. The other is to increase the number of golf fans. The golf equipment manufacturers are the group most concerned with increasing the number of golf participants. Efforts directed toward golf spectators are a major focus of organizations such as the Professional Golfers Association of America (PGA) TOUR, Ladies Professional Golf Association (LPGA) TOUR, and the Seniors TOUR. Marketing success in one area will positively affect marketing efforts in the other.

In marketing golf, it is also important to understand a distinction that applies to marketing any sport: the difference between marketing *of* sport and marketing *with* sport. The former activity deals with increasing a sport's ticket sales and public consumption; the latter involves using sport as an effective tool for marketing consumer products. Both of these concepts are integral to the development of an industry-wide, marketing policy for golf.

As one example of marketing *with* golf, the marketing department for the PGA TOUR is primarily concerned with increasing the involvement of corporations in sponsoring professional golf tournaments. Efforts are directed toward outlining the potential benefits of corporate affiliation with the PGA TOUR. This begins by describing the demographics of the consumers of the PGA TOUR product. Since upscale Americans are the primary consumers of professional golf, it behooves the marketing department to solicit affiliations with companies interested in reaching this population. Thus, we find affiliations with such companies as Buick, Manufacturers Hanover, Merrill Lynch, and AT&T. In marketing terms, this is known as establishing "the hook." There would be little benefit for the PGA TOUR to solicit corporate affiliations with companies that manufacture products intended for the blue collar population.

THE GOLF INDUSTRY

Before proceeding with a more detailed discussion of policy development for marketing golf, it is necessary to describe the entities that make up the golf industry. The following seven organizations are very much involved in marketing golf. This listing is not all-inclusive, but these organizations identify the key sources for marketing the sport.

The National Golf Foundation

The National Golf Foundation (NGF) is the "umbrella" organization for the entire golf industry. It was formed in 1936 to be the information source for the game's development. Through the NGF, the collective resources of the golf equipment manufacturers and leading golf associations can be channeled. Essentially, its purpose is to promote golf for the benefit of all involved.

The services provided by NGF include the following: l) industry data and research materials, 2) market research information, 3) information on golf course development and operations, and 4) educational and player development. NGF services are not limited to these four areas, but they provide the nucleus for the organization's work.

The industry data and research materials include golf consumer reports, national golf participation surveys, and other statistical profiles. Through interviews with golfers throughout the country, the consumer reports provide golf equipment manufacturers and golf associations with information regarding current equipment usage and future preferences.

NGF's market research services are designed to provide professional responses to various research questions that arise in the golf enterprise. This category includes the field service research and mailing list services. The former is a network of field research offices designed to undertake both private market research and ongoing major NGF research projects; the latter is the most comprehensive mailing list on golf facilities in the United States. The NGF is constantly developing new information sheets on specific subjects pertaining to various phases of golf facility planning, financing, operation, statistics, activities, and research.

Through the education and player development program, a library of instructional films and publications is available for golf teachers. This vast source of instructional information has earned the NGF a reputation as the organization that teaches golf teachers. Included in this program are in-service workshops as well as summer teaching seminars.

Professional Golfers Association of America

Earlier, reference was made to marketing efforts of the PGA TOUR. That organization will be used as a case study later and should not be confused with the Professional Golfers Association of America (PGA of America). The PGA of America and the PGA TOUR are two separate entities. Perhaps their closest link is the common goal of attempting to market golf in the most effective manner. The PGA TOUR is a tax-exempt membership organization (technically a trade association or business league) made up of independent contractors (players) "formed for the purpose of regulating, promoting and improving the business of golf." (PGA TOUR Annual Report, p. 34) The PGA of America is an association made up of head club professionals who manage the nation's 12,000 or more golf facilities.

Qualifications for membership in these two organizations are independent of each other. A successful player on the PGA TOUR would not automatically qualify as a PGA club professional. By the same token, a successful PGA club professional is not necessarily qualified to be a PGA TOUR competitor.

In terms of marketing golf, it is noteworthy that the PGA of America, the PGA TOUR, and the NGF do not compete. Each of these three leading organizations share the goal of promoting golf's continued growth and prosperity by attempting to make the game as much fun as possible for as many Americans as possible. There is no real conflict of interest.

The two most significant contributions of the PGA of America are the education of club professionals and the annual merchandise show. To become a Class A Club Professional, one must go through an extensive educational and screening process that includes passing written examinations as well as displaying adequate golf skills. Among other topics, the written examinations cover the development of human resources, turf and grass maintenance, club repair, teaching techniques, and golf cart maintenance. Preparation for the examination is provided through the PGA Business School, which offers two intense one-week learning sessions.

At the annual PGA Merchandise Show exhibitors include clubmakers, clothing designers, and various accessories firms. The typical four-day show has steadily resulted in record attendance, sales, and registered exhibitors in recent years.

Ladies Professional Golf Association (LPGA TOUR)

Next to the PGA TOUR, the LPGA TOUR is probably the most visible golf organization. The development of the two tours has been very similar. The LPGA TOUR was chartered in 1950 and has experienced extensive growth and increasing financial stability since its inception. In 1975, Ray Volpe took over as LPGA TOUR commissioner, after three and a half years as vice president of marketing for the National Hockey League. During his seven-year reign, LPGA prize money increased from $l.2 million to $6.4 million annually, and tournament purses increased on the average from $50,000 to $176,000. John D. Laupheimer relieved Volpe as commissioner in 1982 and continued the expansion.

The LPGA TOUR and the PGA TOUR do not view each other as competitors. Each has a product that is viable in its own right. The main source of revenue for the LPGA TOUR is corporate sponsorship. The LPGA TOUR purses are not as large as those offered by the PGA TOUR due to smaller television contract revenues. Aside from that difference, the men's and women's tours are essentially equal in revenue generation.

The LPGA TOUR has demonstrated leadership in two important areas. In 1981, the TOUR became the first, non-team professional sport to implement a player retirement plan. This "non-contributory fund" was established to provide some retirement security for LPGA members. The men's TOUR followed suit in 1983.

As another innovation, the LPGA offered professional golf's first bonus points system through the Mazda-LPGA Series. This series awards the top performer (based on money winnings) in Mazda-sponsored events a $125,000 bonus at the conclusion of each season.

Seniors TOUR, Mini-Tours, Allied Association of Golf, International Golf Travel

At least four other organizations deserve mention in an effort to identify the scope of the golf enterprise. The **Seniors TOUR** was initiated by the PGA TOUR. The precedent for this was a yearly event titled "The Legends of Golf." Its success served as an inspiration for developing the Seniors TOUR as it is today. Through a very successful marketing program, the Seniors TOUR enables significant and recognizable golfers who are more than 50 years old to remain in the public eye. Corporate sponsors as well as television companies have apparently concluded that the Seniors TOUR is a viable product, evidenced by their extensive involvement. Some golfers have earned more money in a couple of years on the Seniors TOUR than they did while on the professional golf circuit. Several of the older players on the PGA TOUR can hardly wait to turn 50, so they can compete on the Seniors TOUR.

The **mini-tours** are professional golf's version of the minor leagues. While there is no direct affiliation with the PGA TOUR, there is no intent to expand or compete with it either. The main objective of the mini-tours is to provide players an opportunity to see if they have the qualifications to play on the PGA TOUR. A high percentage of the players who have competed on the PGA TOUR gained entry through the mini-tours. Unlike the other professional golf tournaments, revenues at the mini-tour level are derived from entry fees paid by players. Corporate sponsors have not provided revenues because they do not see the mini-tours as viable marketing opportunities.

The Allied Association of Golf is similar to a "think tank." Representatives of the major golf organizations (PGA of America, PGA TOUR, NGF, and others) meet twice a year to discuss how to market and promote their sport. Topics include the development of junior golf programs and solicitation of corporate sponsorships. The basic purpose is to maintain a line of communication among those who share the common interest in marketing golf.

From the marketing perspective, at least one other golf organization is significant -- the **International Golf Travel** (IGT), founded by Bruce Osborne in the San Diego area. The organization has two basic functions: to arrange and coordinate travel for golf professionals who compete overseas, and to organize golf travel vacations for recreational golfers. Osborne began the vacations by working out an arrangement with local club professionals whereby they were offered cash commissions for getting their members involved in using the services of IGT.

A CASE STUDY: THE PGA TOUR

In developing policy for marketing golf, the PGA TOUR stands out as the prime example among the various golf organizations. The TOUR took an aggressive stand by establishing a properties division with the explicit purpose of marketing an organization composed of independent contractors -- the golfers.

It is a difficult to pinpoint the exact origin of the PGA TOUR. There were various golf tournaments throughout the United States in the early 1900s, but these tournaments could hardly be considered the beginning of the tour. They were individual events with no particular affiliation. However, beginning in the late 1920s, the concept of the tour began to crystallize through the legendary names of Bobby Jones, Walter Hagen, and later, Sam Snead. Resorts, hotels, and corporations were beginning to take notice of the potential commercial value of golf. After World War II, the TOUR became more structured. With names such as Byron Nelson and Ben Hogan emerging into public view, the prospects for growth were apparent.

The next phase of the TOUR's growth took place in the 1960s when three important elements arrived on the golf scene: Arnold Palmer, Jack Nicklaus, and most importantly, television. Telecasts of PGA TOUR events inspired many people to try the game and sent purses skyrocketing from rights fees paid by television companies.

With the public's increased interest in golf, the PGA TOUR grew rapidly. In the past 10 years, the number of tournaments on the PGA TOUR has more than doubled, total prize money has nearly tripled, and contributions to charity have quadrupled. With this kind of growth, the PGA TOUR realized that it needed to expand into the marketing aspects of its product. This was accomplished in 1982 when PGA TOUR Properties, Inc. was formed as the centralized marketing and licensing arm of the PGA TOUR.

The establishment of PGA TOUR Properties, Inc. (hereafter, the marketing department) was beyond a doubt the most significant step in marketing professional golf. One of the primary functions of the marketing department is defining a target market for the PGA TOUR. Essentially this involves the process of identifying the potential product consumers. Through market research, the PGA determined that its primary consumers are not only spectators but also golf participants. These consumers invest both time and money into a favorite leisure time activity. For example, over 17.1 million golfers played approximately 425 rounds of golf in 1982. During that year approximately $5.5 billion was invested in the golf facilities and $1.2 billion spent on golf equipment. From such data the PGA TOUR concluded that its principal target market is the economically upscale sport consumer. After researching the demographics of golf fans, the following conclusions were reached in 1984.

- Incomes are relatively high, with 47 percent earning in excess of $35,000 per year.
- They are well educated, as 53 percent have attended college a median of two years.

- The median age is 42.5 years.
- They are typically in the prime of their working lives.
- Overall, they are affluent, well educated, and leaders of business and industry who make many influential decisions.

Thus, a key factor in the PGA TOUR's success has been identifying the product consumers and directing the efforts toward reaching that segment of the population. Attendance at TOUR events is not really that impressive compared to that of other professional sport events. The growth of the PGA TOUR can be attributed more to the quality of the consumer than any quantitative consideration. By attracting these economically upscale consumers, the PGA TOUR has been able to present a very well defined audience to its potential advertisers and corporate sponsors, which in turn has considerably enhanced the value of the product offered.

A marketing advisory committee has been formed to keep the tour players informed of the various activities of the marketing department. This is actually a subcommittee of the tournament policy board which consists of four players, three independent directors, and three PGA directors. Essentially, the role of the committee is to facilitate a line of communication between the players and the marketing department.

The development of the PGA TOUR marketing department has not been smooth. From the standpoint of the TOUR's administrative headquarters, it has been a success. From the standpoint of some players and their agents, the merit and goals of the marketing department are viewed with reservation. The reason for this discrepancy is a fundamental disagreement regarding the role of the marketing department.

The marketing department has taken control of the legal rights to sell and promote the name of the PGA TOUR. A major vehicle toward achieving this end has been the development of business relationships with top tier corporations. As far as promoting the name of the PGA TOUR is concerned, this has been very successful. Yet from the players' point of view, these corporate relationships are viewed as potential individual endorsement contracts. Therefore, some players have viewed the activities of the marketing department as being in direct competition with them in the market for negotiating endorsement contracts and corporate affiliations.

When the marketing department was initiated in 1982, these problems between the players and the marketing department were more prevalent. After its inception, the marketing department had to demonstrate its potential benefit for the players. More specifically, there was a need to arrive at an understanding that the benefits to players were relatively indirect and that they would accrue over a course of time.

The PGA TOUR policy board publishes an annual report that outlines what it does to promote the game of professional golf. Revenues generated from the efforts of the marketing department have increased every year since its inception ($2.7 million to $6.1 million in 1985). These increases in revenues from the marketing department have contributed to the increases in TOUR purses.

The royalties and license fees that corporations pay the TOUR's marketing department have also been allocated to help fund the recently formed Player Retirement Plan, designed to benefit active participants on the TOUR by setting aside sums of money each year to be distributed later as deferred compensation. The allocation of this deferred compensation is based on points accumulated in relation to the number of cuts made throughout a career.

By increasing the involvement of corporations, or bringing new companies into tournament golf, the marketing department has carved a significant niche for itself as an integral part of the TOUR's quest to broaden the base of public support for golf. The TOUR board believes that as the activities of TOUR marketing increases, the chances for individual endorsements and promotional opportunities for players will also increase. The theory behind this contention is that in the long run membership will benefit substantially more from corporate relationships the marketing department is able to negotiate as a representative of the entire PGA TOUR. These top tier corporations are, in most cases, "untouchable" by the TOUR players individually. As an entity representing the PGA TOUR, the marketing department can present more lucrative and comprehensive packages. These packages can only be matched by the superstars in golf, whose names are as recognizable as the PGA TOUR itself. Consequently, the superstars are, for the most part, the only ones who can be hurt by the solicitation of these corporate relationships. It appears that the PGA TOUR has adopted an attitude that reflects a larger concern for the expansion of the game of golf, rather than the gains that may be pursued by individual players.

In summary, the growth and development of the marketing department has been the major project of the PGA TOUR in promoting the game of professional golf. While there are still those who oppose the existence of a marketing department, overall the players have accepted the marketing department and the functions it performs on their behalf.

Stadium Golf

Another project to broaden the base of professional golf has been the concept of "Stadium Golf," or Tournament Players Clubs (hereafter TPCs). TPCs are a new concept in golf course design whereby the spectators are given as much consideration as players with regard to golf course construction. These courses are designed to not only test a golfer's skills, like any other championship course, but also to give the spectators a chance to sit back, relax, and enjoy the golf action.

This innovative idea in golf course design was the brainchild of PGA TOUR Commissioner Deane Beman. During Beman's tenure, he has constantly investigated new ideas that might enhance the game of professional golf. As Beman contemplated possible ways of expanding professional golf's base of support, he concluded that the facilities for professional golf tournaments were inadequate for spectators and sponsors. In an article published in the November, 1984 issue of *PGA Magazine*, Beman offered the following assessment of the state of professional golf facilities:

> When you go into a stadium to watch a football or basketball game, somebody will come up and down the aisles selling you a Coke while you're seated. But with golf, spectators are walking five or six miles around a course. This puts us at a great disadvantage. We were looking at the idea of comfort versus an entire day filled with walking and standing five deep along the fairways to watch the players. Our feeling was: How can we enhance the enjoyment of the spectator and let him feel like he got real value for his dollar? This whole concept evolved over a period of time. We looked at different sporting facilities and tried to figure the best way to make this as much a spectator event as it can be without destroying the whole concept of tournament golf as we know it at the professional level. (p. 30)

Professional golf's answer to the problem of inadequate facilities are the TPCs. In 1978, the first TPC was constructed in Ponte Vedra Beach, Florida. According to Vernon Kelly, the TOUR's director of TPCs, these courses benefit more than the spectators. They are also a source of revenues for the PGA TOUR, along with being a non-rental paying site for PGA TOUR events. They also are able to accommodate more spectators than regular golf courses. Soon after opening the TPC of Connecticut, an estimated 60,000 spectators attended the Sammy Davis Jr. Greater Hartford Open. In 1984 Commissioner Beman projected that any TOUR event held at a TPC might expect a 50 to 100 percent increase in gallery. Beman's long range goal is to have 20 to 25 TPCs completed by 1995.

Vantage Scoreboard

When R. J. Reynolds Tobacco Company became involved with the PGA TOUR in 1981, the speed and accuracy of posting information and scores at PGA events took on an entirely new dimension. The days of reporting scores at events by receiving information through walkie-talkies and then posting the appropriate numbers by hand, are long gone. The Vantage Scoreboard is golf's answer to the electronic scoreboard. The board provides current scores, biographical and statistical information, special reports, and messages to fans and players over the entire course. It is also adapted to a wide variety of weather conditions.

This venture is partially financed through fees paid to the PGA TOUR by the R. J. Reynolds Tobacco Company. Along with the Vantage

Scoreboard, R. J. Reynolds also sponsors the Vantage World of Golf Centers located at most of the TOUR events as well. The Vantage World of Golf Center is a promotional feature located on the premises of a tournament. It consists of a media center that offers past highlights of the PGA TOUR, instructional films, live tournament action, rules-of-golf videotapes, and a putting and simulated driving center.

There are two drawbacks in having a tobacco company as the major sponsor of this venture. For legal reasons, no one under the age of 21 is allowed to enjoy the facilities provided in the Vantage World of Golf Centers. This conflicts with the TOUR's effort to broaden the base of support for golf by getting youngsters involved. Secondly, a handful of players have contended that allowing their names to appear on the Vantage Scoreboard is an implied endorsement of R. J. Reynolds Tobacco Company. These problems are being investigated by the PGA TOUR. Nevertheless, the PGA TOUR considers the Vantage Scoreboard and Vantage World of Golf Centers great successes in upgrading facilities at professional golf tournaments to a level that is competitive with counterparts in the professional sports industry.

Various Corporate Affiliations

As mentioned earlier, the solicitation of corporate affiliations has been one of the key vehicles used in marketing the PGA TOUR. Affiliations with such corporations as Mastercard International, Buick, and Van Heusen provide examples of different arrangements that contribute to the mutual benefit of the TOUR and the corporate sector.

The license agreement with Mastercard International designates Mastercard as the "Official Card of the PGA TOUR." The grant to Mastercard includes the use of PGA TOUR trademarks in connection with the promotion, advertising, marketing and sale of Mastercard's licensed services. Additional benefits granted to Mastercard International include corporate membership privileges at TPCs; Pro-Am spots at certain tournaments for employees, clients, and prospective clients; and a list of PGA TOUR players' addresses for use in promotional activities for purposes of the agreement. For these benefits, Mastercard International pays PGA TOUR Properties $100,000 per year for the length of the contract (three years), and agrees to spend at least $500,000 per year in golf-related advertising.

Buick and similar corporations offer the potential for individual endorsement contracts. Players and their representatives have been inclined to question whether the activities of the marketing department are always in the best interest of the players on the TOUR.

The corporate affiliation with Van Heusen is an agreement that allows the use of the PGA TOUR's logo on apparel manufactured and sold by Van Heusen. This affiliation is an example of the marketing department negotiating money right into the players' pockets. For the use of the logo,

Van Heusen pays the marketing department a 4 percent royalty fee on all sales of the apparel. By wearing the Van Heusen apparel that displays the PGA TOUR logo, Van Heusen has established an $83,000 pool of money for competitive distribution among the participating players. The winner of the pool at the end of the year (based on official money winnings) receives a $25,000 bonus, second place $20,000, third place $15,000, fourth place $13,000, and fifth place $10,000.

Other Marketing Activities

The marketing department of the PGA TOUR has also developed other programs which demonstrate the potential scope of marketing golf or any other sport.

The TOUR and Diversified Products (DP) established an arrangement that might be considered the first significant attempt to determine whether there is any correlation between playing "good" golf and being physically fit. In 1985, Lanier Johnson, director of marketing for DP, noted the status of golf in the area of fitness: "Until now, progressive resistance training has been accepted and employed with success in every major sport except golf." (*Golf Magazine*, Jan. 1985, p. 114)

That situation is changing due to the joint efforts of the TOUR and DP. The latter provides a mobile fitness training center that is 45 feet long and expands to a width of 25 feet when parked at the PGA TOUR sites. The trailer is equipped with an exercise room that includes weight equipment, a training room, whirlpool, massage table, and a player lounge furnished with a television, stereo, and a full line of nutritional products. As the bottom line in professional golf, the players are the focus of this marketing endeavor. Commissioner Beman noted that the affiliation with DP has generated one of the more positive responses during his position as commissioner.

Another marketing department idea has resulted in the "TOUR Statistics Program," designed to generate another source of spectator interest in golf. It is patterned after the fan interest in batting averages, earned run average, and other statistics in baseball. Golf also lends itself to various statistical, special interest, features such as the highest percentage of drives in the fairway, fewest putts per round, and the longest drive.

POLICY GUIDELINES AND CONCLUSIONS

Based on this case study and other developments in the golf industry generally, what conclusions can be reached regarding policies for marketing golf? The following are suggested as general guidelines for policy development. Overall, they are aimed at broadening the base of public support for golf. At the same time, these guidelines are viewed as being equally applicable for any individual, leisure time, sport which has potential for a large participation base as well as spectator appeal.

1. Further attention should be given to the development of junior golf programs. Participants in these programs are the golfers and golf spectators of the future. The link between participation and spectatorship in golf has been fairly well established.
2. The target market should be established by obtaining the necessary demographic information. Golf is one of those sports which will always have somewhat limited attraction due to the financial aspects of the game. However, the market is there. It just has to be more fully tapped. The market cannot be equated with that of a mass participation sport.
3. Continued efforts must be made to improve the lines of communication among the various golf organizations. Basically, they are not in competition with one another. They have the common goal of obtaining a larger share of the leisure time dollar.
4. There should be a continued effort to further develop the corporate involvement with the sport of golf. Corporate involvement with sport is one of the most significant changes in the entire sports industry during the past 10 years. Due to the financial and social nature of the game, golf stands out as one of the prime areas for a corporate relationship.
5. Pursuant to the last point, it is quite clear that golf is a vivid example of the potential for marketing with sport as well as marketing of sport. The marketing activities in golf should always employ the two-pronged approach.

Note: Additional updated information on Marketing With Sport can be found in Chapter 20 on pages 325 to 327.

REFERENCES

Annual Report to the Membership. Ponte Verda, Florida: PGA TOUR, 1983.
Buell, V. P. *Marketing Management: A Strategic Planning Approach.* New York: McGraw-Hill Book Co., 1984.
Diehl, M. "TPC's - Deane's Dream." *Golf Magazine,* January 1985.
Foley, P. "Stadium Golf . . . Boom or Bust?" *PGA TOUR Magazine,* November 1984.
Hersey, S. "Fitness Craze Hits the PGA TOUR." *Golf Magazine,* January 1985.
Marketing With Professional Golf. Ponte Verda, Florida: PGA TOUR, 1984.
Official 1984 PGA TOUR Media Guide. Ponte Verda, Florida: PGA TOUR, 1983.

20

Conclusion and Updates

In the introduction to this book, various characteristics of policy development were identified. One of these is that policy development is directed toward a dynamic social process in a changing environment. That has never been more evident to me than at this time. Some of the issues and problems continue to be debated almost daily. The matter of drug testing is a classic example of the changing dynamics. Nevertheless, I will attempt to draw some conclusions regarding the territory which has been covered. At the same time, there will be an effort to update those areas which appear to be in a particular state of flux.

ATHLETICS AND HIGHER EDUCATION

Among all the topics which have been considered, those related to the relationship between athletics and higher education appear to be the most critical and controversial. The need for sound policies in this area is acute. The status of the college athlete is obviously the common focus in the topics of recruiting violations, college admissions, "Proposal 48," normal degree progress, and drug usage. What kind of policies can be developed to improve the status of the college athlete in line with the purposes of higher education? Other policy areas, including the evaluation of college coaches, relate to this central concern.

Concern about the relationship between athletics and higher education has reached an all-time high. Some would like to think that colleges are on the threshold of making significant changes in defining that relationship. Yet, this problem has persisted throughout most of this century. One can read statements from the 1920s that sound as though they were made today. It seems to be one of those situations where everything changes and yet nothing changes. Excerpts from two *Sports Illustrated* reports, six months apart, following two NCAA conventions in 1987, offer prime evidence.

313

THE REFORMATION

Since 1983, reform has been a byword in college sports. First, the NCAA approved Proposition 48, which mandated a minimum grade-point average and standardized test scores for entering Division I athletes. Next, the newly formed NCAA Presidents Commission, a 49-member body, pushed through tougher penalties for rules violators; these included the 'death penalty,' which can cost a school that is a repeat serious offender an entire program. At last week's NCAA convention in San Diego the reform bug became an epidemic as athletic directors actually vied with their presidents to see who would pass the next piece of reform legislation. . . .

Some of these measures were passed by the eager delegates despite a plea from the Presidents Commission that action on them be deferred. The commission announced that it hopes to correct the imbalance between college athletics and academics at a special convention in Dallas in June. "We want to look at this thing more holistically," said University of California Chancellor I. Michael Heyman. . . . Looking further down the road, Heyman went so far as to urge the "mutual disarmament" of the biggest college athletic programs.

Before reform became all the rage, such talk was sacrilege. These days, it's all one hears at NCAA gatherings. (*Sports Illustrated*, Jan. 19, 1987, p. 9)

NOTHING DOING

The news out of the special NCAA convention in Dallas last week was that there was no news. It was ostensibly a cost-cutting session called by the Presidents Commission; yet, with one exception, all measures designed to de-escalate big-time college sports were defeated, and the member schools even restored two men's basketball scholarships that had been trimmed at the last convention. "We made a mistake by calling this thing," said University of Maryland Chancellor John Slaughter, the Chairman of the Presidents Commission. "We presidents had not done enough homework."

Still, there was a silver lining to the convention, which, incidentally, cost the NCAA an estimated $1.8 million to stage. The commission inaugurated an ambitious 18-month forum, involving both coaches and administrators, to examine the role of intercollegiate athletics. . . .

The NCAA blew a small opportunity last week, but the forum is at least a start. Clearly, something must be done to restore integrity to college sports. Two days after the convention closed, an internal investigation into the Virginia Tech basketball program revealed that not a single basketball player admitted to the school between 1981 and 1983 had graduated. (*Sports Illustrated*, July 13, 1987, p. 15)

It seems that everything is still very much at the talking stage and is likely to remain that way for some time. At the Dallas convention, 10 speakers offered widely disparate viewpoints to approximately 1,200 representatives in the three-hour forum. The forum was designed that way, to stimulate provocative discussions that might lead to sweeping reform by January 1989. Speeches ranged all the way from the University of Michigan's "Bo" Schembechler's impassioned defense of football as one of life's great experiences to the extreme suggestions of Chancellor Heyman. Among those suggestions were that athletic scholarships be awarded only on a need basis, freshmen ineligibility for college athletes, the abolition of football bowl games, and minor leagues for professional football and basketball in lieu of the college training grounds. Few observers expect to see these suggestions adopted.

Frank discussions of philosophical differences are a rare occurrence on the floor of an NCAA convention. Some of the delegates expressed frustration about the fact that dialogue had replaced hard legislation. Nevertheless, the NCAA Presidents Commission seemed to be encouraged by the overall response to the initial forum. An "Ad Hoc Committee on the National Forum" was appointed to evaluate the forum and to make plans for further sessions.

At this point, three additional forums are planned. The next would be held in conjunction with the NCAA's 82nd annual convention in January 1988 in Nashville, Tennessee. That session would focus on economic considerations in athletics, including various cost and revenue factors and the concept of revenue sharing or distribution. This would be followed by another special national meeting in June 1988. Tentative topics include the NCAA membership structure and appropriate bases for financial aid to student-athletes. The final session is planned in conjunction with the annual NCAA Convention in January 1989. The proposed agenda would include the topic of freshmen eligibility and the results of the various in-depth studies dealing with the student-athlete's experience in comparison with that of the non-athlete student. The ad hoc committee also recommended that the NCAA contact the American Institutes for Research to develop a plan for conducting the studies.

The outcome and net effect of these plans remain to be seen. Some of the answers may be better known by the time this book is in print. College presidents must be credited for showing a willingness to consider the larger picture. The reservations are that it may be "just talk" and that there are external forces that may preclude the possibility of any significant actions.

RECRUITING VIOLATIONS

As of August 1987, 21 institutions were under NCAA sanctions for various violations of the NCAA rules. In three cases, sanctions had been imposed within the previous six months. "Improper recruiting" was cited as the grounds for action in 15 of the cases. Another prominent reason for the probations was "improper benefits to athletes," which also relates to recruiting.

The most widely publicized case was that of Southern Methodist University, the first institution to receive the so-called "death penalty" for violations regarding the conduct of its football program. SMU was placed on probation with the following sanctions: 1) a complete cancellation of the football schedule in 1987; 2) only seven games permitted in 1988, none at home; 3) loss of all new scholarships in 1987-88, and 15 in 1988-89; 4) no post-season or televised games in 1988; 5) only five assistant coaches permitted through 1989; and 6) players subject to financial audits through 1990.

Will such harsh action tend to deter others who would ignore the rules? What, if anything, can be done to control the efforts of overzealous boosters? In January 1987, delegates to the NCAA convention took corrective steps. Effective August 1, 1987, boosters are barred from all recruiting, on or off campus, including writing letters and making phone calls to prospects. Football and basketball recruiting seasons were also cut in half.

Yet, not everyone is convinced that the answer is to be found through additional NCAA legislation. A much more extreme approach was proposed by John Bryant, a Dallas democrat in the U.S. House of Representatives and a SMU alumnus. Reacting to the disclosures about his alma mater, Bryant introduced "The Intercollegiate Athletics Integrity Act of 1987," which would make it illegal to pay a college athlete beyond the allowable benefits. An individual found guilty could be fined up to $100,000 and imprisoned for up to one year. An institution taking a willful part in the crime could be penalized by loss of federal funding, including student loans.

NCAA officials reacted with skepticism on two grounds. Government intervention in the area might create more problems than solutions. For example, a criminal investigation might serve only as a deterrent in cooperation efforts between the NCAA and an athletic department. Also, there was doubt whether the federal law enforcement agencies would give a high priority to prosecuting a crime in this area.

Others in the collegiate athletics believe that the answer to control of recruiting practices is not to be found either through the NCAA or federal intervention. Fred Miller, the athletic director at San Diego State, makes the following argument.

> "I am not impressed by the federal track record," says Miller, referring to proposed legislation by Bryant that would make it a federal crime to pay college athletes above and beyond their prescribed grant-in-aid limits.

Bryant's proposal, "like the current NCAA system, is based on punishment, not on prevention, and as such it is bound to fail," says Miller. "We've been adding more and more investigators and more and more legislation for the past 50 years, and it still hasn't solved the problem." . . .

"You have to get the people who are involved in the system to work toward a solution," says Miller. "Athletic directors as a group have not met that responsibility, and as such they should be criticized, but it's not too late for them to come to grips with it."

Miller believes change will occur naturally as more athletic programs are headed by professional administrators and fewer by "good old boys.". . . .

PEER-REVIEW AUDITS. As a tool to make institutional self control work, Miller suggests that athletic programs periodically undergo independent peer-review audits. . . .

In his ideal scheme of things, all NCAA institutions or, at the very least, those Division I schools with major football and basketball programs, would go through the process.

Auditing teams could consist of two or three professional observers who are closely acquainted with the workings of intercollegiate athletic programs. These professionals, Miller says, could be drawn from the associate director level, the coaching ranks, or persons "on top of the recruiting system."

Miller also says athletic programs need to put "some teeth in the system by rewarding coaches who do well on the audit." (*Athletic Business*, June 1987, pp. 24-25)

Thus, at this time, it appears that there are three potential sources of control in the attempt to alleviate the problem of recruiting violations: 1) the NCAA, 2) institutional self-control, 3) federal law. The first two are employed. The only question here involves the degree of success. How large is the problem? It seems rather unlikely that the third choice, federal intervention, will become a reality. Possibly a further solution will emerge from the forthcoming NCAA forums. On the other hand, this could persist into the 21st century.

PROPOSAL 48

Proposal 48, later modified as Proposal 16, and Bylaw 5-1-(j) when it became official, went into effect on August 1, 1986. It stipulates that entering college athletes must have a minimum score of 700 on the combined College Board SAT test (or at least a 15 of 36 score on the American College Test) and at least a 2.0 high school grade point average in 11 core courses. Under Proposal 16 this was modified for the first year to allow an SAT of 660 or an ACT of 13, if the score was balanced by a GPA of

2.2 or above. Likewise, a 1.8 GPA could be balanced by a 740 SAT or a 17 ACT. Those athletes not meeting the minimum criteria may neither compete nor practice during their freshman year. The athlete may receive a scholarship from the institution, but he or she then forfeits a year of athletic eligibility.

As expected, the initial effect of this legislation was severe. On August 3, 1986, *The New York Times* reported the results of a survey of Division I colleges and universities on the effects on male football and basketball players who had received athletic scholarships for the following year. More than 200 of these athletes, one out of every 20 selected, failed to meet the new minimum standards. Several of these were among the most highly recruited athletes for football and basketball. In almost all the cases, the failure to qualify was due to the test score requirement.

Various options were pursued by the athletes and institutions involved. Those with sufficient grades were eligible for scholarships. Some of these accepted scholarship offers and sat out their freshmen years, making them eligible for three years of competition instead of four. Others chose to attend a junior college rather than miss a year of competition. Still others opted to pay their own college expenses as freshmen to avoid losing the year of eligibility at the four-year institution. This raised concern that boosters would finance the first year through "under the table" payments.

Prior to the implementation of Proposal 16, the NCAA announced that it had launched an extensive six-year study to determine the total impact of the new standards. As many as 100,000 records will be examined from 1986 to 1992 for some 25,000 Division I athletes who enter college from 1984 through 1988. As was true with the passage of Proposal 48, the presidents of the predominately black colleges were once again in opposition because the study would not include a sample of athletes who did not qualify under the new rules.

In May 1987, the NCAA released its first official statistics on the results of the first-year implementation. Key results from a survey of 250 Division I institutions were reported as follows:

1. Of the 250 institutions, 168 reported that a total of 599 "partial qualifiers" had registered at their institutions. A partial qualifier is one who has at least the minimum high school grade point average of 2.0 but who fails to meet either the test score or core-curriculum requirement.
2. Of the 250 institutions, 38 reported that a total of 85 "non-qualifiers" were registered at their institutions. A non-qualifier has met neither the 2.0 nor the core curriculum or test score requirements.
3. Of the 599 partial qualifiers, 372 received athletic scholarships, while 227 are paying for education by other means. (As noted earlier, a non-qualifier cannot receive an athletic scholarship.)

4. Of the 599 partial qualifiers, 254 were football players, 198 of whom were on athletic scholarships.
5. Of the 500 partial qualifiers, 90 were basketball players, with 62 of these receiving athletic scholarships.
6. Test scores were the stumbling block for the vast majority (424) of the 599 partial qualifiers.
7. Of the 424, 299 were black, 104 were white, and the remainder were from other racial groups.

A representative of the NCAA noted that it was unfortunate that there is a no way to obtain data on non-qualifiers who did not matriculate. In terms of that which was reported, the black presidents found support for their contention.

> Joseph B. Johnson, president of Grambling State University and an outspoken critic of the standards, said last week that the survey only proved further what he and other black college presidents had been saying for years.
> "It is a racist rule that was instituted by racist people intent on denying black kids an education," he said. "It is totally unfair, and they knew it even before the rule was adopted. The NCAA's own study showed that many black athletes who had graduated in the past would not have been eligible under Proposition 48." (*The Chronicle of Higher Education*, May 13, 1987, p. 44)

One other item is worthy of note, unfortunately involving Southern Methodist University. On August 12, 1987, *The Chronicle of Higher Education* reported on a situation involving a basketball recruit at SMU. When the recruit, Larry Johnson, first took the SAT's in October 1986, his combined score was below 500. After re-taking the test in February 1987, he improved his score by more than 300 points. President A. Kenneth Pye announced that he would personally review the circumstances surrounding this case. One has to wonder how many other irregularities surround the implementation of this controversial component of Proposal 48.

DRUG TESTING

The NCAA instituted its drug testing program in late November 1986, with the Division I Men's and Women's Cross Country Championships and continued with the testing of football players in all three division championships and on several bowl-bound Division I-A teams. The tests were not announced in advance. In the playoffs for the division championships, 24 players on a winning team could be tested. This included the nine defensive and nine offensive players with the most playing time, plus six others selected at random.

Winners in the quarterfinals of the Division II and III championship tournaments were the first football players to be tested. Five players failed the drug tests. They were suspended for 90 days and barred from participating in semifinal or final games in the tournament. The report was that four of the five used anabolic steroids and the fifth apparently took unacceptably large doses of a commonly used over-the-counter decongestant.

Late in December, the NCAA announced that its drug-testing efforts were proceeding according to plan. Crew chiefs administering the tests reported that they were received positively. NCAA administrators expressed confidence.

Around the end of 1986, the results of the testing of bowl-bound football players were made public. According to the rules, the 22 players who played the most minutes during the regular season and 14 randomly chosen reserves from each bowl team could be tested for anabolic steroids and some 80 other drugs. Actually, only the participants in 10 major bowls were tested due to a shortage of top-quality labs and testing personnel.

As one would expect, the results of testing these football players was widely publicized, with the feature case being that of Oklahoma linebacker Brian Bosworth. The cover of the January 5, 1987 issue of *Sports Illustrated* read, "The Boz Flunks Out." Eleven other Division I football players were also identified as being ineligible to participate in their teams' postseason bowl games. All 12 tested positive for anabolic steroids. According to the report, a total of 21 college football players had tested positive either from the division playoff teams or the bowl teams.

Following the testing, John Toner, chairman of the NCAA committee on drug testing, continued to express satisfaction with the effort and optimism for the future.

> "I'm happy and quite encouraged. We wanted to test at all 19 bowls, but logistically we just couldn't. . . . We will have at least one more lab next year. It's possible we will test more bowl teams next year. Our plan is to eventually test everybody going to a bowl game." (*Sports Illustrated*, Jan. 5, 1987, p. 25)

The enthusiasm of NCAA officials regarding the drug-testing endeavor was not necessarily shared by the colleges. From the time it was established, the NCAA policy has been under attack from civil libertarians and others who contend that mandatory testing, without reasonable suspicion of drug use, violates the privacy rights of athletes. The central thrust is the shift of focus from legislation to litigation. Some of the action has been restricted to the institutional level. However, in recent cases, the NCAA has also been more directly involved.

Reaction against drug testing was first manifested in December 1986 at the University of California at Berkeley. Faced with a threatened lawsuit by the American Civil Liberties Union (ACLU), the university rescinded its policy requiring all athletes to undergo urine tests for drug use in order to compete on varsity teams. The suit was planned on behalf of the Associated Students of Berkeley and an athlete who objected to the tests. In February 1987, Miami University of Ohio also announced that it had postponed random drug testing of student-athletes as a result of legal concerns raised by both students and faculty.

The first direct involvement of the NCAA was in the Stanford University case. Simone LeVant, a diving team captain at the university, won an injunction on March 11, 1987 to permit her to compete in the Division I Women's Swimming and Diving Championships without being tested.

Perhaps the most significant ruling to date was that involving the drug-testing program at the University of Washington. The program was scheduled to go into effect on August 12, 1987, and would have been one of about 130 that have been adopted by various colleges or universities. Once again, the suit was sponsored by the ACLU. Two University of Washington athletes filed the suit in July 1987. A Superior Court judge ruled that the Washington program violated the Fourth Amendment and the Washington state constitution's privacy-protection provisions. More significantly, he also issued a temporary restraining order against the NCAA's testing of Washington's athletes for drugs. In granting the restraining order, Judge George T. Mattson said the NCAA policy "suffers from even more constitutional deficiencies" than the University of Washington's. The ruling was considered significant because it was directed against an entire program rather than toward individual protection, as in the Stanford case.

In August 1987, a Superior Court judge in California has allowed Stanford to join as a third party in a lawsuit filed by some of its athletes, challenging the legality of the NCAA's testing program. On August 26, Stanford won a temporary restraining order which would prevent the NCAA from requiring that Stanford obtain written consents to drug testing from its athletes as a condition for participating in intercollegiate athletics. The constitutionality of the testing policy will have to be decided. In defending its policy, the NCAA argues that athletes have no constitutional right to compete in NCAA events. If they wish to compete, they must abide by the association's requirements, including drug testing. The only thing which seems clear at this point is that the final decision will be made in the courts.

In the meantime, one must also recognize that the NCAA's drug-testing program is only one component of a broader, drug-education program. The association has developed a videotape on drug and alcohol abuse, brochures carrying the anti-drug message, seminars for college athletic officials, and a speakers bureau to address athletes on the dangers of drug and alcohol abuse. As part of its television contracts, the NCAA also makes its anti-drug pitch on television, with five dozen 30-second commercials featuring highly visible athletes. Estimates are that the association would spend $430,000 on such activities for the academic year 1986-87, contrasted with $750,000 for the drug-testing program during the same year.

TITLE IX AND WOMEN'S ATHLETICS

In essence, the Supreme Court's narrow interpretation of Title IX removed much of the pressure on colleges to continue expanding women's sport programs. Before the Grove City decision, colleges faced the threat of lawsuits if their programs did not comply with Title IX. After the decision, that threat diminished considerably. Immediately, the Office for Civil Rights dropped its investigation of 64 Title IX complaints. In the next three years only 30 Title IX complaints were received, with just six filed in 1986.

The net effect was that leaders in women's sport programs joined a broad coalition of civil rights groups in lobbying for passage of the Civil Rights Restoration Act of 1987. At this time, the prospects for passage of that bill remain uncertain. It is entangled with the regulation of abortions and other emotional controversies. The bill has been generally opposed by the Reagan Administration.

Leaders in women's athletics contend that much of the momentum has been lost in the attempt to advance their programs. Before Grove City, there was not equality among programs. Now, at best, women's programs were placed in a maintenance situation. Other changes only added to the concern. There was increasing interest among men in coaching women's sports, and a growing tendency to combine men's and women's athletic departments with the merged department being administered by men.

On the other side of the coin, one can also look to the significant progress which has been made in upgrading the status of women's involvement in sport or athletics during the past 15 years. In some cases, this even applies to the governance structure for the administration of women's and men's programs. Milverstedt reports on the structure implemented in the Pacific 10 Conference in 1986. This might serve as a model for other conferences.

> On the first level of the conference governance structure, administrators for both the men's and women's programs conduct their business separately through their own administrative committees, acting in concert with conference staff. . . .
> The next step is a joint administrative committee, composed of the athletic directors and the PWAA's (primary women's athletic administrators), (each with an equal vote), which meets to debate matters affecting both the men's and women's programs.

Certain issues are then advanced to a council, made up of all the administrators, plus the faculty representatives from each institution, and the faculty representatives then cast their votes for referral to the presidents, who make the final decision....

"It has worked exactly the way it was designed," says Hedges (the PWAA at USC). There is every opportunity on the committee and in the council for people to speak and express their opinions, and no one is reticent to do so.

. . . If all this sounds too Pollyannish, it may be comforting to some to learn that the system has not been without its controversial issues.

A case in point was the position the conference chose to take on grant-in-aid reductions. There were differences of opinion, but when a proposal was adopted--a recommendation to reduce football scholarships from 95 to 90--it was Roby's (the PWAA at Arizona) suggestion that led to the accord.

"When the (NCAA) Presidents' Commission proposed cuts in the number of grants awarded to different sports, they omitted football," says Hansen (the Pac-10 commissioner), "and our women's administrators felt that was unfair."

The women, says Hansen, believed the decision to exclude football from the cuts violated an agreement, established when the NCAA program for women was founded, that "there would continue to be a certain proportionality between men's and women's scholarship opportunities. Our men agreed that, philosophically that was fair, and that's why we put in the proposal." (*Athletic Business*, August, 1987, pp. 25-26)

Will the Pac 10 structure indeed serve as a model for other conferences or sport organizations? Is there need for further federal legislation to provide for more equity among women's and men's sport programs? These questions remain unanswered. This much can at least be said. The status of college athletic programs for women has been advanced considerably during the past 15 years in spite of any limitations due to the Grove City decision.

HIGH SCHOOL ATHLETIC ELIGIBILITY

In recent years there has been a rash of state legislation and proposals to raise the academic standards governing eligibility for participation in high school sports and other extracurricular activities. Among all the legislation of this type, none has caught the attention of more people than the Texas Law known as "No pass, no play."

The law, "House Bill 72," was enacted by the Texas legislature in 1984. It set a rigid standard: any student failing any course in a six-week grading period is ineligible for participation in extracurricular activities for the following grading period. At the same time, the minimum passing grade was raised from 60 to 70. At the time of passage it was considered to be the toughest statewide legislation of its type.

The no pass, no play rule was only a small part of a much larger bill, directed toward educational reform. The need for such reform was recognized by Governor Mark White due to the state's standing as 46th in the nation in student achievement test scores. The governor appointed an education study commission, which presented numerous recommendations for reform. The strong emphasis on athletics, namely football in Texas, was identified as part of the problem.

Public reaction to the much larger educational reform package was dwarfed by the response to "No pass, no play." Many students, including those in non-athletic extracurricular activities, were severely affected by the new law, but the largest outcry resulted from the effect on high school football in Texas. An estimated 15 percent of the high school football players were ineligible for the 1985 season.

High school coaches led the opposition to the rule. They basically pursued an old argument that athletics was the scapegoat for the larger woes of education. Opponents also generally argued that an overall grade point average is a better standard for eligibility than performance in a single subject. Another objection was that the law would only discourage students from taking the more challenging courses. Many also felt that the six-week ineligibility period was too long.

The law was also attacked from the standpoint of its discriminatory effect on minority students. In 1986, a Houston attorney surveyed about 300,000 students in 200 Texas school districts. He found that 19 percent of the white students had failed at least one course, contrasted with 32 percent of black and 31 percent of the Mexican Americans failing a course.

The reaction to higher standards for athletic eligibility in high school has also been linked to Proposal 48 or technically, NCAA Bylaw 5-1-(j). Obviously, both are designed to motivate athletes to academic achievement. Yet, critics argue that such standards hurt those who need sports the most, those who are struggling academically. It is also interesting to note that some leaders in high school athletics do not view the high school eligibility standards and Proposal 48 in the same light.

> Others, like Warren Brown, who monitors eligibility for the National Federation of State High School Associations, say that high school sports, unlike their college counterparts, have an "inherently educational" function. For that reason, says Brown, the Federation opposes highly restrictive high school eligibility standards, like those in Texas, while supporting Proposition 48. . . .
>
> The Federation is not alone in what some might see as a contradictory stance. The National High School Coaches Association, accord-

ing to executive director Carey McDonald, supports Proposition 48, because it will encourage promising high school athletes to prepare themselves academically for college, rather than rely on their athletic prowess to carry them. . . .

Like the Federation, however, the Coaches Association opposes restrictive high school eligibility rules, with McDonald echoing Brines' philosophy that "you have to keep them in school to get them to improve academically, and sports has that kind of attraction." (*Athletic Business*, June 1986, pp. 22, 24)

This matter of more rigid standards for high school athletic eligibility is likely to continue to be a topic for debate. It is a legitimate issue. From one standpoint, one can hardly argue against the idea of improving the quality of education for all students, including athletes. The latter seem to be a special case for only two reasons: (1) the high visibility of athletic programs and (2) the contention that some students are only in school to play sports.

On the other hand, there is also considerable merit in the argument that athletics may be the motivating factor in keeping a student in school and that it is better for that student to be in school than to be a drop-out. At any rate, if there is to be a higher standard for eligibility, the passing grade in every course is certainly open to question. It seems that a "C" average in a core curriculum is a more reasonable approach.

MARKETING WITH SPORT

In the previous chapter, golf was used as an example of how marketing relates to sport programs both in terms of marketing of sport and marketing with sport. The latter primarily involves the corporate sponsorship of a sport event and/or advertising of a sport event or product. Some recent changes indicate that some adjustments will have to be made in assessing the potential for marketing with sport, particularly in the realm of television. The "Special Report" in the July 13, 1987 issue of *Advertising Age* indicates that it is a new ball game in terms of the television sports market.

"While we are enamored of sports programming because of its density of our target audience, it is clearly not a must buy for us," says Mark Reiss, director-corporate media, Adolph Coors Co., Golden, Colo. "It is a desired purchase for us, but it doesn't have elements that are so unique that it actually demands our participation."

To hear that kind of talk from any advertiser is bad news for the broadcast and cable sports networks. But Coors is not the only one. Advertisers of all kinds, including those that rely heavily on adult males, have re-written the rules of the TV sports market.

"For years and years, sports was an automatic buy if you were targeted to men," says Jim Bell, senior VP, group media director at Grey Advertising, New York.

"It no longer is, not even for cars and beer," he says.

Advertisers were willing to pay top dollar for sports because it was considered the most efficient way to reach adult males. Many advertisers didn't see another option. . . .

Then the networks' sports programming ratings dropped. The pivotal point came in 1984 when the College Football Association argued successfully for the right to cut its own rights deals, breaking up the networks monopoly. "So there was a ton of college football properties out there; fragmentation occurred," . . .

A proprietary network property suddenly diversified into syndication, regional packages and three network packages. It divided up the numbers...and advertisers said, "Wait a minute. I've got a tremendous amount of money devoted to sports. I've got a disproportionate number of dollars in individual sports or events and the numbers are eroding. I can't take that anymore." . . .

"The fundamental change in the sports media marketplace is there's a lot more places to go with your dollars," says Mr. Bell. (*Advertising Age*, July 13, 1987, pp. S-4, 5-6)

Essentially, two significant changes have taken place in terms of marketing with sport through television. The first is the fragmentation noted above. Even though network executives do not foresee major cutbacks, there is an overall softness in the sports market which can be attributed to the proliferation of sporting events on television. The combined Big 3 networks' sports weekend day rating dropped about 10 percent in 1987. This is largely a result of the sports available for viewing on the 13 regional cable networks. Consequently, the networks are increasingly showing more interest in only the "exclusive properties" such as the Super Bowl and the NCAA basketball playoffs. Overall, there is caution beyond the first tier of football, basketball, and baseball. Even NBC's Saturday baseball ratings were down about 15 percent in 1987.

The other major change is that involving the tie-in with corporate sponsorship. Aside from the premier events, the networks are now directing their interests to events that are "packaged" with advertiser sponsorship. The nature of the inventory is being changed. Much of the air time sold by networks in the past is now the responsibility of sporting event organizers who are able to obtain corporate sponsorship. Golf again provides a good example even though it is below the first tier of the three major sports on television. In 1987, NBC picked up the Tournament Players Championship sponsored by Mazda Motors of America. The network also plans to add the PGA Senior Tour' Skins Game on Super Bowl Sunday in January due to the probability of a tie-in with a well-known sponsor. Likewise, even though the ratings for tennis have been battered on the networks in recent years, ABC's "Wide World of Sports" picked up "The Challenge of the Champions" tennis match when Ocean Spray Cranberries signed as a sponsor. This enabled the network to make an initial advertising arrangement with Ocean Spray.

The increasing significance of the corporate sponsor in sport marketing is not limited to television. Whether or not it is tied in with a television contract, the event itself now attracts corporate sponsors in rapidly increasing numbers.

> More than 3,400 U.S. companies this year will spend $1.35 billion to sponsor sporting events, according to *Special Events Report*, an industry newsletter. That's a fourfold increase since 1983, and the numbers are still growing fast. . . .
>
> Advertisers are aiming to get more bang for their marketing bucks by sponsoring the event itself, rather than by just buying 30 seconds of air time during a sports show. At least 400 U.S. corporations now have event-marketing departments with separate budgets, up from 10 in 1982. . . .
>
> But it's the events themselves that now draw the most corporate spending. . . .
>
> To sponsor an event, a company typically gives money to a sports promoter or organizer, often for the prize fund. In exchange, the company associates its name with the sport. Big-spending companies may buy "title sponsorship," the right to name the event after themselves--the Coors International Bicycle Classic or the Sunkist Fiesta Bowl, for example. . . .
>
> Does sports marketing pay off in sales? Even active sports marketers aren't sure. Most acknowledge that they can't measure its effect on revenues, but many are content with image enhancement. . . . (*Business Week*, Aug. 31, 1987, pp. 48-49)

FINAL THOUGHTS

The purpose in this book was to explore various areas in which policies have been developed, should be developed, or could be developed in the sport enterprise. The idea of development is important due to the fact that it represents change in a continuous direction. Policies are not static. They are established to have standing decisions on important, recurring matters. Yet, they also must be continually evaluated, modified, and up-dated in light of experience and changing conditions.

In general, policies are developed to solve a problem and/or to establish a position with regard to an issue. The various issues and problems which we have considered are by no means all-inclusive. Personnel policies have been given priority, particularly those related to athletes and coaches at the collegiate level.

There are various reasons for establishing that kind of priority among these various policy areas. First of all, it is quite clear that the college sector is the area which is most in need of sound policy development. The major issues and problems in collegiate athletics are continually before us. Decisions at the college level are also pivotal in determining policy direction in the high schools and in professional sport.

The relative emphasis on policies affecting athletes also seems to be merited. Regardless of the level of competition, the athletes are central to any of the concerns in the sport enterprise. This, in turn, leads to the recognition that personnel policies affecting coaches should also be a prime consideration.

When one contemplates the significant issues and problems in the sport enterprise today, particularly in highly organized sport programs, there is no doubt about the need for sound policies. Some of the issues and problems have been in evidence for a long time. Perhaps the only real question revolves around the extent to which administrators and other management personal are willing to work toward the development of more innovative and effective policies.

REFERENCES

Bedell, D. "NCAA Speakers Parade Ideas, Emotions." *The Dallas Morning News*, June 30, 1987, Section B, pp. 1, 8.
"Drug-Testing Case To Be Heard in Federal Court." *The NCAA News*, Vol. 24, No. 29, August 19, 1987, p. 1.
Goodwin, M. "Survey: New N.C.A.A. Standards Sideline More Than 200." *The New York Times*, August 3, 1986, Section 5, pp. 1, 9.
Harwood, J. "No Pass, No Play." *St. Petersburg Times*, March 23, 1986, pp. 1, 15A.
Leaterman, C. "Female Athletes, Administrators Lobby for Bill to Counteract Effects of Grove City Ruling." *The Chronicle of Higher Education*, July 22, 1987, p. 24.
Lederman, D. "Civil Libertarians Forcing NCAA into Court to Defend Mandatory Drug Tests." *The Chronicle of Higher Education*, August 5, 1987, pp. 1, 24.
Lederman, D. "Presidents' Panel Increasingly Divided on Sports Issues." *The Chronicle of Higher Education*, April 29, 1987, pp. 1, 38.
Mallios, Harry. "Drug Testing of Student-Athletes: Storm Clouds on the Horizon." *Athletic Administration*, Vol. 22, No. 3, June 1987, pp. 12-16.
McGeehan, P. "There's More to Marketing Than Sports." *Advertising Age*, July 13, 1987, pp. S-4, 6, 7.
McGeehan, P. "Net Changes Move Sponsors Up in the Batting Order." *Advertising Age*, July 13, 1987, p. S-7.
Milverstedt, F. "Women on Par in the Pac-10." *Athletic Business*, Vol. 11, No. 8, August 1987, pp. 24-28.
Milverstedt, F. "A Federal Solution to Athlete Payoffs." *Athletic Business*, Vol. 11, No. 6, June 1987, pp. 24-28.
Moran, B. "Sponsors, Packages Key to Cautious Nets." *Advertising Age*, July 13, 1987, pp. S18, 20.
"NCAA to Examine Academic Records to Calculate Impact of New Standards." *The Chronicle of Higher Education*, April 23, 1986, pp. 35, 38.
Neff, C. "Bosworth Faces the Music." *Sports Illustrated*, Vol. 66, No. 1, Jan. 5, 1987, pp. 21-25.
"No Pass, No Play?" *Athletic Business*, Vol. 10, No. 6, June 1986, pp. 20-26.
"Nothing Sells Like Sports." *Business Week*, August 31, 1987, pp. 48-53.
"Scorecard." *Sports Illustrated*, Vol. 67, No. 2, July 13, 1987, p. 15.
"Scorecard." *Sports Illustrated*, Vol. 66, No. 3, January 19, 1987, p. 9.
"Scorecard." *Sports Illustrated*, Vol. 65, No. 5, August 4, 1986, p. 9.
Wieberg, S. "Colleges Go Searching for Answers." *USA Today*, June 29, 1987, Section C, pp. 1-2.
Wilson, T. A. "Delegates Act Swiftly to Ban Boosters, Cut Costs." *The NCAA News*, Vol. 24, No. 3, Jan. 14, 1987, pp. 1, 7
"21 Institutions Under NCAA Sanctions." *The Chronicle of Higher Education*, August 12, 1987, p. 42.
"650 Athletes Who Failed to Meet New Standards Are in College; Most Are Black." *The Chronicle of Higher Education*, May 13, 1987, p. 44.

Index

Osborne, Bruce, 305
Overby, Johnny, 186-187

PACE, (Professional Athletes' Career Enterprises, Inc.), 138, 139
Pacific 10 Conference, 55, 185, 186, 193, 322, 323
PACTI, (Professional Athletes' Career Transition Inventory), 126
Palmer, Arnold, 306
Palmisano, Mike, 274
Paterno, Joe, 66
Pell, Charlie, 37, 38
Pennsylvania State University, 40, 66, 272
Pepperdine University, 59
PGA Magazine, 309
Phil Esposito Foundation, The, 129-135, 139
Philadelphia Flyers, 138
Philadelphia 76ers, 113
Physical education, 231, 277, 280, 295, 296, 298, 299; majors in, 300; *See also*, coeducational sports, 294; instructional class usage, 253
Physiotherapy, 217
President's Council on Physical Fitness and Sport, 5
Promotion, collegiate, 265-270, 272-276; fund-raising, 265; marketing, 265, 275, 301-312; merchandising, 265; non-revenue, 5, 265-267, 270, 272; public relations, 268, 270
Propst, H. Dean, 96
Providence University, 40
Public relations, facility funding, 278; sports promotion, 268, 270
Pye, A. Kenneth, 319

Reagan, Ronald, 18
Recreational sport programs, 277-278, 280-281, 285-286, 287, 291, 293, 295, 296, 298, 299, 300; *See also*, leisure time sports, 301, 302, 306
Recruitment, collegiate athletic, 105, 244, 252-253, 267, 313, 317, 318, 319; NCAA violations of, 35-39, 41-44, 315-317
Regent Hospital, 113
Reiss, Mark, 325
Retirement: of professional athletes, 123-139
Rice University, 40
Rich Stadium, 201
Richardson, Michael Ray, 110-114
Richardson, Rene, 111
R.J. Reynolds Tobacco Company, 309-310
Roger L. Putnam Vocational Technical High School, 25, 27
Rogers, Don, 107
Rogers, Thomasina, 237
Ross, Kevin, 57-58
Ross, Michael L., 295
Roundball Enterprises, 111
Rozelle, Pete, 107, 108
Ryan, John W., 210

Sammy Davis Jr. Greater Hartford Open, 309
San Diego, University of, 36
San Diego Padres, 138
San Diego State University, 37, 316
San Francisco, University of, 137, 272
San Francisco 49ers, 218
Schembechler, "Bo", 315
Scholarships, athletic, 53, 84-85, 95, 237, 238, 241, 242-243, 253, 255, 270, 314, 315, 318, 319, 323

"School For Christian Workers, A", 295
SEC, (Southeastern Conference), 37, 39, 185
Service Corporation, 5
Seton Hall University, 137
Shirley, Joe, 207
Singletone, Harry M., 237
Skiing, downhill, 256-260
Slaughter, John, 314
Smith, Dean, 58
SMU, (Southern Methodist University), 36, 316, 319
Snead, Sam, 306
Soccer, 253, 257, 266-270; European Cup, 199; NEISL, 271; NSCAA, 271
Softball, 71, 239, 241, 251
Southern Mississippi, University of, 37
Southern University, 67
Southland Corporation, 214, 226, 227
Southwestern Athletic Conference, 71, 78, 185-186
Special Events Report, 327
Sporting News, The, 36
Sports Illusion, Sports Reality, 47-48, 228
Sports Illustrated, 1, 44, 52, 58, 59, 60, 95, 96, 113, 114, 136, 200, 201, 202, 203, 238, 313, 314, 320
Springfield College, 295, 298
St. John's University, 136
St. Louis University, 36, 269, 272
Stanford University, 40, 321
Steroids, anabolic, 108, 116, 320
Stickball, 298
Stolley, Mat, 205, 206, 208
Stone, Jesse Jr., 67
Sullivan, Patrick, 203
Sullivan Stadium, 202
Sunkist, 327
Swearer, Howard R., 45, 46, 47, 48
Swimming/diving, 24, 30, 71, 243, 247, 257, 298, 321
Syracuse University, 277

TAC, (The Athletics Congress), 215, 218, 219, 220, 221, 222, 224, 225, 226, 227, 228
Tapscott, Ed, 158
Tarkanian, Jerry, 158
Taub, Joe, 112
Tele-Media, 268
Television, network sports, 326; revenue from, 254, 304, 306; sports market, 325-327
Temple University, 137, 294
Tennessee State University, 37, 67
Tennis, 5, 71, 239, 241, 243, 247, 251, 256-259, 326, 327
Tenure, *see* Coaching, collegiate
Texas, University of, at Austin, 238
Texas, University of, at San Antonio, 22
Texas A&M University, 47
Texas Rangers, 204-209
Tiger Stadium, 199
Times-Picayune, The, 78, 85
Title IX, 142, 144, 171, 231-245, 247, 250, 322; *See also*, Women's athletics
Toner, John, 39, 116, 320
Toone vs. Adams, 202
Tow, Ted C., 76
Townsend, Nelson, 79
Townsley vs. Cincinnati Gardens, 202